Pilgrimage of a Presbyterian

Pilgrimage of a Presbyterian

Collected Shorter Writings

John H. Leith

Charles E. Raynal, editor

Geneva Press
Louisville, Kentucky

Book design by Sharon Adams
Cover design by Night & Day Design

First edition
Published by Geneva Press
Louisville, Kentucky

This book is printed on acid-free paper that meets the American National Standards Institute Z39.48 standard. ∞

PRINTED IN THE UNITED STATES OF AMERICA

01 02 03 04 05 06 07 08 09 10 — 10 9 8 7 6 5 4 3 2 1

Library of Congress Cataloging-in-Publication Data is on file at the Library of Congress, Washington, D.C.

ISBN 0-664-50151-6

Dedication

Dedicated with gratitude to the Presbyterian family that helped shape my life:

William Harnette Leith—Elder,
Superintendent of Sunday School

Lucy Haddon Leith—President of the Women of the Church, Synodical Officer, Sunday School Teacher

Mary Evelyn Leith Ellis—Elder, Teacher, author of five books in the Covenant Life Curriculum

William Harold Leith—Elder, friend to many

Ann White Leith—Elder and by actual count the cook of more than fifteen hundred meals for church members, students, and ministers

The works in this volume represent the writing of John H. Leith across his long career as preacher, teacher, and editor, and in reproducing Leith's works, we have wanted to honor both form and content. We have sought to allow each piece to reflect the time in which it was written. Because his sermons and most of his addresses and lectures were not intended for readers but for listeners, we chose not to load onto these pieces the weight of references. Most readers will recognize Leith's sources, and we ask that you accept this book as we offer it: as a full sampling of John Leith's work as a historical record, in the form in which it appeared over the course of his career.

Contents

Preface

The idea for this collection of sermons and shorter writings of John H. Leith developed in 1997 during his and Ann White Leith's move from their home in Richmond, Virginia, to Presbyterian Home in Easley, South Carolina. While I was visiting the Leiths and helping sort through his files, I asked his permission to edit a collection of his papers and seek a publisher. I felt that they provided the foundation of a chronicle of his pastorates and teaching, and that many people would be interested in having them as a record of remarkable ministry in the Presbyterian church. I was pleased when he gave his assent, and now I am happy to offer this book to John and Ann Leith's many friends and admirers, as well as to a larger group of readers.

John Haddon Leith was born in Hodges, South Carolina, on September 10, 1919. His parents were William H. Leith and Lucy Haddon. Because of his father's illness the family moved to Due West, South Carolina, in 1928. John Leith married Ann Caroline White of Chester, South Carolina, on September 2, 1943. Their children are Henry White Leith and Caroline Haddon Leith.

John Leith graduated from Erskine College (B.A.) in 1940, Columbia Theological Seminary (B.D.) in 1943, Vanderbilt University (M.A.) in 1946, and Yale University Graduate School in 1949 (Ph.D., dissertation published as *John Calvin's Doctrine of the Christian Life* (Louisville, Kentucky: Westminster/John Knox Press, 1989).

More than any other service, Leith wanted to be a pastor. He was ordained in the South Carolina Presbytery in April 1943 by the Presbyterian Church

in the United States. By the testimony of many parishioners and the statistical record of a number of churches, John Leith was a distinguished
pastor. He assembled a congregation in Mobile Presbytery, which became
Spring Hill Presbyterian Church in 1943. He served as pastor of Second
Presbyterian Church in Nashville, and while he was there, he pursued
graduate studies at Vanderbilt University. His longest pastorate was from
1948 to 1959 at First Presbyterian Church in Auburn, Alabama. Leith was
always thankful for the fellowship he enjoyed and for what he learned
about being a pastor as a student supply from April 1941 to June 1943 at
the Silver Creek Church, Lindale, Georgia, an unincorporated mill town.

Several notable achievements of his ministry demonstrate John Leith's
leadership. During his ministry, about one thousand new members were
received into the churches he served. As he built up the church in Auburn,
he was also active at Auburn University, developing facilities and leadership for campus ministry, and building a remarkable sanctuary and educational building. During the late 1940s and early 1950s he preached
sermons and provided community leadership for civil rights. The leadership of the Presbyterian denomination appealed to him and to Dr. Ralph
Draughan, president of Auburn University, to host the Quadrennial Youth
Conventions in 1951, 1953, and 1954, when no other school they
approached would host a racially integrated conference. Of the 2,200 people who attended in 1953 and 1954, about 150 were African-American
students. A decade before the Civil Rights movement of the 1960s, the
Presbyterian Church in Auburn stood openly for what the law and custom
of the land would come to adopt. Several sermons in this volume speak to
the race issue at this early date. In the 1940s and 1950s he vigorously
advocated freedom of theological inquiry (see "The Liberalism of the
Reformed Tradition" and "Presidential Address to Presbyterian Education
Association" in this volume) and spoke for church union and the ordination of women, which were both defeated in the 1950s.

Leith was active in the the organized life of the Presbyterian church,
serving as moderator of all the presbyteries where his churches were, and
as moderator of the Synod of North Carolina in 1978 (see his moderator's
sermon, "The Church as the People of God"). He served on four *ad
interim* committees of the Presbyterian General Assembly: on revision of
the *Book of Church Order*, 1955–1962; on "Brief Statement of Belief,"
1959–1962; on possible revision of Chapter III of *Confession of Faith*,
1959–1961; and to write a Brief Statement of Faith for Presbyterian
Church (U.S.A.), 1984–1991. Among other institutional leadership, he
was on the boards of Presbyterian School of Christian Education,

1957–1959; Erskine College, 1964–1968; *Presbyterian Outlook*, 1960–1999; *Presbyterian Survey*, 1961–1970 (chairman, 1970); the Peter Martyr Library; and Editorial Consultants for the *Bibliotheca Calviniana* (Meeter Center for Calvin Studies). In important and controversial issues before the church, he served ably and well, and he was forthright and direct, taking responsibility for his positions in the public forums of church debate.

John Leith has received many honors from the church and from secular organizations, but he is most grateful for the honorary degrees awarded by three Presbyterian church-related colleges: Erskine College, D.D. (Hon.), 1972; Davidson College, D.D. (Hon.), 1978; and Presbyterian College, D.Litt. (Hon.), 1990. The leadership of these colleges spoke for the many hundreds of church members who knew and appreciated John Leith's leadership in countless sermons, Sunday school classes, lectures, and pastoral conversations.

More people know John Leith worldwide through his theological scholarship than his congregational, denominational, and ecumenical ministry. He taught theology as a visiting professor at Columbia Theological Seminary, 1955–1957, and as Pemberton Professor of Theology at Union Theological Seminary in Virginia, 1959–1990. He has provided distinguished leadership in international circles of study of the theology of John Calvin. Although he never set out to be known as an author, the bibliography at the end of this volume records thirteen books and many pamphlets, articles, and reviews. Over three hundred thousand copies of his books are in print. *An Introduction to the Reformed Tradition* has been printed in Korean, Portuguese, and British editions. Across the world of church scholarship, many other scholars recognize and esteem his leadership in Calvin studies.

Anyone who reads his books will recognize that his purpose is to state theology in clear, simple sentences, in the language of ordinary discourse. In his theological classes he often quoted Reinhold Niebuhr's words from *Leaves from the Notebook of a Tamed Cynic* (New York: Richard R. Smith, Inc., 1930): "At any rate I swear that I will never aspire to be a preacher of pretty sermons" (p. 9). He understood John Calvin's preference for simplicity and succinctness of expression as a fruit of the morality of mind, which espouses directness of speech and honesty, and rejects pomp and artificiality. In his writings John Leith avoided the jargon, neologisms, and rhetorical flourish of many professional theologians. Behind his written words is a confidence in the power of the language of the Bible and the confessional heritage of the ecumenical church.

Heiko Oberman, the well-known scholar of late medieval and Reformation studies, wrote to John Leith about the style and meaning of the latter's *Basic Christian Doctrine*, saying,

> Last Friday I received from my bookseller a book I had ordered: *Basic Christian Doctrine*. Though initially I planned only to leaf through it and to take it with me to the Netherlands this coming Thursday—after the Princeton Calvin gathering—I found myself compelled to read it through from cover to cover.
>
> Hence, I want to thank you spontaneously in the name of all who are concerned about the precise documentation and contemporary interpretation of the reformed tradition. On certain points you are more conservative than me—in your treatment of abortion and homosexuality—and then on others I may seem to be more conservative in that I would be more explicit in dealing with the dark sides of the doctrine of predestination. But in both instances I found your presentation wise and lucidly communicated, obviously founded on the basis of a long teaching experience, the kind of teaching concerned with understanding the student rather than with a display of scholarship.

Albert C. Outler, who was John Leith's teacher and dissertation advisor at Yale University Graduate School, spoke for many of us at the Leith retirement celebration in Richmond, Virginia:

> This is a puzzlement and I hope you will puzzle with me about it—this fascination with the transient in theological education. In any case, the present plight of the older traditions of godly learning in our time and in the prospective future I can see is alarming and at risk. Classical Christian attitudes about norms of doctrine, about the spirit of God in the human soul, about our chief end and final hope, have turned into problems or . . . concerns that however urgent are plagued by a pervasive urge for contemporaneity, and contemporaneity turns out to be a synonym for anthropocentricity.
>
> Even in such times and still for however long his earthly span may be, John Leith has held his rudder steady and his course as constant as anyone I have known in his generation, learning himself and teaching teachers to learn, teaching preachers to preach, and preaching and teaching in his own right. He has been a diligent scholar. As a professor he has lived with the scriptures, the creeds, the confessions. He is building a lasting monument here at UTS and in the hearts and minds of a least a thousand students. He has been a pastor to many . . . in my case in these last years with telephone visits that have been more helpful than you could imagine, or than I can tell him. His vocation has been to the great cause of godly learning of which we have spoken, that cherishes erudition, but never for its own sake, that has honored reason in the service of faith, with no great care for fame nor self-aggrandizement that I know of. I am therefore proud to have had him as a student and as a friend.

For those of us who were John Leith's students, to hear these words from his revered teacher was a moving and fitting tribute. I am glad to join in the spirit expressed in these words of Albert Outler, and as a former student who is glad to count himself a friend of John Leith, I am glad to offer this collection of his sermons and other writings.

Acknowledgments

This book is possible only because other students and friends of John Leith believed it should have been compiled, and because they supported it generously with their financial gifts and personal encouragement. Among them, especially these deserve particular mention and special gratitude: Mark Achtemeier, Dubuque Theological Seminary; Wallace M. Alston, Center of Theological Inquiry, Princeton, N.J.; Robert Brearley, St. Simons Island Presbyterian Church, St. Simons Island, Ga.; John Debevoise, Palma Ceia Presbyterian Church, Tampa, Fla.; Ben Farley, Erskine College, Due West, S.C.; James Goodloe, Grace Covenant Presbyterian Church, Richmond, Va.; Vernon and Sallie Hunter, First Presbyterian Church, Greensboro, N.C.; John W. Kuykendall, Davidson College, Davison, N.C.; Arnold Lovell, Second Presbyterian Church, Knoxville, Tenn.; Allen C. McSween Jr., Fourth Presbyterian Church, Greenville, S.C.; John B. Rogers, Covenant Presbyterian Church, Charlotte, N.C.; Arthur Ross, White Memorial Presbyterian Church, Raleigh, N.C.; William T. Stuart, Richmond, Va.; George and Sally Telford, Charlottesville, Va.; Dr. and Mrs. James Wilson White, Knoxville, Tenn.; James W. White Jr., Fondren Presbyterian Church, Jackson, Miss.; Parker Williamson, Lenoir, N.C.; and William P. Wood, First Presbyterian Church, Charlotte, N.C. The Endowment Fund of Grace Covenant Presbyterian Church, Richmond, Va., was particularly generous in its support.

For data entry and technical assistance I want to thank Deborah Basie in the office of Davidson College Presbyterian Church, and Angela Basmajian of ABA Words and Design, Richmond, Va. Tom Long of Geneva Press provided welcome support. Martha Gilliss and Daniel Braden at Geneva Press worked tirelessly on this book, and I thank them. William Harris of Luce Library and Robert Johnson of General Assembly staff have helped find many references.

I wish to thank Rosemary, who is my partner in this and every other worthwhile undertaking in my life.

Charles E. Raynal
Columbia Theological Seminary
May 2, 2000

Author's Preface

The proposal to publish my "shorter writings" was very gracious. I am thankful for those who are responsible for this publication. My first critical reaction was that my books contain all that is in the shorter writings. With further thought and as the collection took shape, I felt that the writings presented here established their own reason for inclusion. They are all, including the sermons, specific responses to particular situations, controversies, or events. They remind me of my own history in my responses to events and challenges I encountered. These issues included the racial controversy of the 1940s, 1950s, and 1960s; the fundamentalist battles from 1940 to 1967 when fundamentalism became a dead issue in the Presbyterian Church U.S.; church union; the crises caused by evangelical liberalism's loss of a capacity for critical judgment; and a host of social, ecclesiastical, and theological dilemmas that have followed the breakdown of the old Presbyterian consensus during the last three to four decades. In retrospect I gladly stand on the record of what I said as the articles represent my commitments then and now.

The writings presented here for the most part are occasional pieces for a talk or as a basis for discussion. They were not written for publication. Some articles were written fifty years ago, and I cannot now recall the sources of some quotations or even poems. The usage of the more recent writings is more careful and perceptive in the use of gender, but the earlier writings have been left as they were written.

My debt to others is great. Teachers influenced every page: G. G. Parkinson at Erskine College; W. C. Robinson at Columbia Theological

Seminary; E. T. Ramsdell and Roy Bettenhouse at Vanderbilt; Albert C. Outler, Roland Bainton, and Robert Calhoun at Yale. I also owe a great debt to the theologians who shaped my theology: the theologians of Nicea and Chalcedon, Augustine, Martin Luther (especially the writings of 1520), Calvin, William Temple, Emil Brunner, Reinhold Niebuhr, and in recent years, Karl Barth. Reflected in these writings also is my rearing in a Presbyterian home and in Greenville Presbyterian Church—with their emphasis on the reading, study, and memorizing of scripture and the catechism—and Kingdom Highways (the Presbyterian youth program). These influences, too, are sources of my theology.

I owe much to the churches served: Silver Creek, Lindale, Georgia, as a student supply; the preaching mission that is now Spring Hill Presbyterian Church, Mobile, Alabama; Second Presbyterian Church, Nashville, Tennessee; and the First Presbyterian Church, Auburn, Alabama.

I am also grateful beyond words to staffs at Union Theological Seminary, Princeton's Luce Library, and the Center of Theological Inquiry. I owe much to the cheerful and able assistance of Martha Aycock Sugg at Union Theological Seminary and William Harris at the Luce Library, Princeton Theological Seminary, in finding references, articles, and books. Angela Basmajian has now typed three books, numerous articles, and countless letters. I also owe a great debt to friends and comrades and especially to students who took seriously what I tried to teach. I have had the support of a wonderful family. As historical life draws to a close, I am increasingly thankful.

My own theological position can best be described as critically ortho-dox (see *Reformed Imperative* 36–37). I have attempted to reaffirm the classic catholic and Reformed faith in the contemporary idiom of ordinary discourse while taking seriously the spirit and methods of the Enlightenment and the nineteenth century without their dogmas. Critical orthodoxy describes my theology, though I first heard the words from Albert Outler.

Editor Charles Raynal deserves special thanks. He is also my dear friend. I do not know at this writing the former students who have supported and assisted him in this project. I am very grateful to them, but I am most blessed as a teacher of theology by what they are doing as faithful preachers of the Word of God and as good pastors of congregations.

A word of gratitude must be expressed to Westminster John Knox Press and its editors through the years, Keith Crim, Richard Ray, and Davis Perkins, who have supported me even in critical writings that challenged the "orthodoxies" of movements and church leadership.

The community and staff of Foothills Retirement Community (Presbyterian Homes of South Carolina) along with friends and especially former students have been a great support to me. Without this support and the love of my children, Henry and Caroline, I could not have survived the crisis of old age and especially the death of Ann.

John H. Leith
June 20, 2000

PART ONE
SERMONS

"Life in the Shadow of Death"
December 30, 1942

Senior Sermon, Columbia Theological Seminary, Decatur,
Georgia; *Presbyterian of the South* (now *Presbyterian Outlook*),
December 20, 1942
Silver Creek Presbyterian Church, Lindale, Georgia,
January 17, 1943
Spring Hill Preaching Service (Now Spring Hill Presbyterian
Church) Mobile, Alabama, July 18, 1943

Scriptural basis: General tenor of Christ's teachings,
particularly Matthew 6:30–33, 1 John 2:15–17 (Moffatt's translation)

The peculiar function of the Christian community through the ages has
been to bear a double witness: a witness to death and a witness to life. The
varying fortune of the world—her periods of depression and her times of
prosperity, of war and of peace—have not changed this basic witness of
those who have been loyal to the Master. And now as the shadows of death
and destruction cast a mantle of gloom across the world, the followers of
the Nazarene still find and bear witness to life in the shadow of death.

The unbearable atrocities of an unscrupulous war, the tottering of economic systems, the drastic changes in ways of life, and the uncertainty of
the future have not caused the true church of Jesus Christ to despair. The
death of the things of this world has not dismayed her, for she has never
believed them to be ultimately real and permanent.

Amid the confusion and mad hurly-burly of this world, her faith has
been staked in another world, in the world of the spirit, in the kingdom
of God. With certainty of conviction, she has sought first this otherworldly Kingdom that she believes will stand when flesh and blood are
long since gone, when the Earth has disintegrated into space and the Sun
is as cold as the Moon.

This is simply the message of the church to our troubled world. Houses
and moneys, flesh and blood, stocks and bonds are not the really important things of life. Over these the sentence of death has been irrevocably

2

passed and to them God promises no resurrection. The really important things of life are beyond the power of the grave and the devil to destroy, and these belong to those who seek God's kingdom and his righteousness.

A consideration of this witness of the body of Christian believers to the teaching of their Master suggests this line of thought.

1. The world has rejected this witness and is a world of death.
2. In a similar world of death, Jesus found and imparted to mankind a way of life to the full.
3. From this way and philosophy of life flow certain practical conclusions.

A World of Death

We are living in a world of death. Our modern culture has believed that the material things of life—that which we can see, smell, and touch—were permanently and eternally real; and now this pagan, worldly civilization is dying its predetermined death.

Pitirim Sorokin, the internationally respected sociologist of Harvard University, has declared, in perhaps the most thought-provoking book of our day, that the crisis of our age is the crisis of sensate culture. For the past several centuries, our civilization has been becoming increasingly secular and man-centered. We have placed value only upon those things that affect in some way our five or six senses, though in some respects human senses are inferior to those of a dog.

Whatever the faults of the medieval ages may have been, they did not lie in the focal center of her culture, for God was the common denominator of life. Medieval architecture was but the Bible in stone. Music and art were primarily religious, and literature was theological in character. God was the center of life, and the whole of culture related to him.

About the thirteenth century, civilization began to drift from this God-centeredness, and now—let us not deceive ourselves—we live in a pagan, sensual culture. That which is nonmaterial—that which we cannot daily experience, see, hear, taste, touch, or smell—we have proclaimed to be unreal, nonexistent, and of no value.

Money is the supreme good of our day, and moneymakers are our aristocracy. We turn everything into money—everything from quintuplets to religious revivals. A poet wrote this parody as the national anthem of many Americans.

O beautiful for dividends
Of twenty-five percent
On oil and steel and real estate
On money freely lent,
America, America,
May riches be our fate.

Increase our wealth
And guard our health,
America the great.

Our art is no longer concerned with religion but with the police morgue, criminal hideouts, and base forms of love.

Statistical studies show that from 70 to 80 percent of all movie offerings concentrate on crime and sexual love.

An Atlanta daily newspaper in analyzing the popularity of the cheaper cultural fare that is flooding our country came to this conclusion from a story they observed. The appeal of the movies was apparently based upon the frequent repetition of the following words: *hell, damn,* and *darling.*

From a historical standpoint, every nation of any consequence today is now or has been within the past few generations imperialistic and gluttonous for the resources of mankind. The most elemental rights of man have been utterly disregarded in our mad rush of greed and covetousness.

And now this secular culture is turning to rend itself and to crush mankind in its death throes. Our present crisis is not a matter of good fellows Churchill and Roosevelt against wicked men Hitler and Mussolini. It is a godless and godforsaken civilization reaping that which it has sowed: death.

That we are living in the bloodiest century in the story of mankind is a fact as hard as a fact can be. Never before have destruction and death and uncertainty been so common to the lot of man. For centuries, men have ridiculed the otherworldly heaven of Christian faith and have busied themselves with the making of a this-worldly heaven. Now man sits amid the ruin of his erstwhile masterful edifice of material and social well-being, surrounded—both literally and figuratively—with a ghastly array of corpses. The one testimony that the tragedy of our secular culture bears is strangely similar to the words of the Christ. "If a man gains the whole world and loses his own soul, what shall it profit him?" What, but death? The judgment of scripture is confirmed by the analysis of a sociologist, Pitirim Sorokin.

The Way of Life

Jesus, too, lived in the shadow of death, yet in its very shadows he found life to the full. History and sociology tell us that then as now civilization was secular and greedy. Paganism was rampant through the known world and flourished in many forms. But Jesus was strangely unaware of the form and systems of heathen thought. He dealt then as now not with the outward form but with the essence. Paganism, he said, is preoccupation with things: food, clothing, and drink. These must be secondary to something more important. This paganism, Jesus warned his disciples, is the deadly and everlasting enemy of his gospel. Jesus never forgot that the things of this world must pass away with this world. His life was lived for another world that he called the kingdom of God. This otherworldly kingdom he found so real and valuable that when they offered him an earthly crown and glory he steadfastly refused—so real that we read he set his face like flint toward Jerusalem and never faltered as he climbed the rugged slopes of Calvary. Over against the essence of paganism, he set the essence of real life: "Seek ye first the kingdom of God and his righteousness and all these things shall be added unto you."

Jesus was not a sentimental pietist or absorbed in millennial speculations. He assuredly was not. He knew that faith and love and hope and righteousness are eternally real. He knew that in them and in them alone was life—life that the fire of hell cannot quench and over which the laws of decay exercise no control. Because Jesus knew these things, there was in his life an urgency and a decisiveness that cannot be gainsaid.

The centuries have vindicated this simple, almost naïve faith of the Christ. In this tragic hour we can but say, "Thou hast conquered, pale Galilean." We are forced to admit that he is the wholly rational fact that we know. No matter how deeply that which he said may cut into our ways of living, we cannot deny that he alone has seen life in its proper perspective—that he alone has played the game and won. Surely the wisdom of the world is but foolishness to God. For as we see the wisdom of a secular culture leading but to insecurity, war, unhappiness, and death, we can only conclude that Jesus was right. Several times before in the history of mankind the world has been forced to just this same conclusion.

Practical Conclusions

The church must seek God's kingdom and his righteousness first of all. In the past she has been too willing to come to terms with and even to flatter an essentially godless culture. Her task in the world today is to do more than merely lend a tone of respectability to a culture that is secularistic, man-centered, and man-devised. With utter abandon and disregard of worldly gain she must proclaim Christ and his kingdom.

Pierre Van Passen in *Days of Our Years* declares with truth that the church which identifies herself with this world will pass away with this world. And to make the condemnation complete the editors of *Fortune* write, "The voice of the church today, we find, is the echo of our own voice. When we consult the church we hear only what we ourselves have said. The way out is the sound of a voice coming from something not ourselves, in the existence of which we cannot disbelieve."

Yes, the church that shall survive this day of death will be the church that speaks not the language of this world but of the kingdom of God. It will be a church ready to die for her witness and that the world counts worthy of crucifixion. It is not enough to save a soul here and there, as important as that may be. The church that is to live must set herself over against a world whose foundations are pride, ambition, desire to dominate, and lust for worldly goods, for in these things are the seeds of death. To bear such a witness will be to go against the grain of the world, to come in conflict with the paganism of racial prejudice, of national pride, of greed and militarism. It may be that the world will crucify her, but in the language of another world her Master said, "He that shall lose his life for my sake shall find it."

Likewise we as individuals must learn to seek God's kingdom first. Tennyson well expressed the aspiration of man when he wrote of him:

> Thou madest him, he knows not why,
> He thinks he was not made to die.
> (Alfred Lord Tennyson, *In Memoriam*)

Yet for all his aspirations man has not learned to live. The pursuit of life, liberty, and happiness has not yielded much in return. For we have sought first the things of the world, yea even in religion and morality. Benjamin Franklin gave classic expression of our American attitude. "Honesty is useful because it insures credit, so are punctuality, industry and frugality and that is the reason they are virtues." Machiavelli, the great Italian thinker whose philosophy underlies the totalitarian movements in Europe, spoke of our entire secular civilization when he said it was advisable for a ruler to be religious because it was useful in controlling the people. Dr. John MacMurray speaks with foundation of men who have a religion but are not religious, religious in the whole of life. From such contorted views of religion, Jesus bids us to turn and with utter commitment seek God's kingdom first. It may be that some of the things of the world must go, for every aspect of life must be related to him. For it cannot be with a true follower of Jesus as someone said in caricature of the Puritan: "On Sundays he believes in God and eternity and on Mondays in the stock exchange. On Sundays the Bible is his ledger and on weekdays the ledger is his Bible."

Jesus offered life only to those who forsook all and followed him. No leader ever demanded so straight vows of his followers. But in this stringent commitment of life and in it alone is the victory that overcomes the world.

Finally those who follow in the train of the Christ cannot be pessimists. They must be optimists. However else we may define the spiritual, the kingdom of God, we must, as Dr. George Buttrick suggests, say it is that which endures. "Houses do not endure, they crumble. Flesh does not endure, it rots. The world does not endure, for science tells us it must end. Sin does not endure. It commits suicide. But love endures, speaking of an eternal love. Duty endures, speaking of an eternal compulsion. Conscience endures, speaking of an eternal right. Faith endures, speaking of eternal truth. The kingdom of God endures, speaking of him who spoke and that which was not come into being and before whom every knee shall bow and every tongue shall confess as Lord."[1]

Though the very gates of hell he loosed against it, the kingdom of God shall not be destroyed by the kingdoms of this world: the kingdoms of totalitarianism, of greed, of imperialism. God is still God, and he will be God tomorrow and next month and next year, yea, when the present struggle is remembered only in the dusty archives of history. Some day he will get tired of Hitler, as he did of Napoleon, and Hitler will be no more. Ah! Some day he will get tired of pagan Americans and they shall be no more. The prophets were never so supremely great as when they counseled Israel that to forsake the Lord was to invite destruction but to seek him was to live. For this reason a modern prophet of God's word, Karl Barth, could write to the Christians of Britain, "Our citizenship is today and always in heaven. For this very reason, we can and we shall today and always be of good cheer."[2]

Dostoyevsky, the Russian novelist, in *Brothers Karamazov*, paints a terrible, almost repulsive picture of the Grand Inquisitor. Amid the burning of heretics, Jesus returns to Seville, Spain, and the people recognized him. The Inquisitor has Jesus arrested and placed in a cell. That night he visits Jesus and explains to him that the church has been unable to follow his way and must get rid of him. He closes with these words: ". . . I shall burn

[1] George Buttrick, *The Parables of Jesus* (New York: Harper and Row, 1928).
[2] Barth, "A Letter to Great Britain from Switzerland," with an introduction by A. C. Vidler. London: The Sheldon Press, 1941, and in cooperation with Macmillan.

thee for coming to hinder us. For if anyone has ever deserved our fires, it is thou. Tomorrow I shall burn thee." And today the inquisition goes on. To a pagan and secular culture, Jesus is a rebuking, yea, repelling figure. He is the world's unquiet conscience. But though we crucify him over and over again, he ever arises. And in the depth of his atoning love he challenges us in the very shadow of death to seek the kingdom of God first and live. With outstretched arms he reaches down to the weariness of our world and says, "Come unto me, ye that are weary with it all and I will give thee rest."

"Our Protestant Heritage"
February 11, 1945

Second Presbyterian Church, Nashville, Tennessee

If someone were to ask the average man on the street why he professes the faith that he does, an honest answer would certainly include the fact that he was born in that faith. I was born in a Presbyterian home and nurtured in Presbyterian ways, and this fact in some real measure accounts for my being a Presbyterian now. Likewise, by birth and training I am a Protestant. Nevertheless, this is but part of the truth. I am also a Protestant by conscious choice and personal commitment. If I could not make this second affirmation about the origin of my belief, my inherited faith would be dead and worthless.

The epistle of Peter counsels that believers should always be able to give a reason for the faith that is in them (1 Peter 3:15). It is incumbent upon all people who take their faith seriously to be able to give a reason for that faith. Any man who claims Protestantism as his faith and who has neither understood that faith nor committed his life to it forfeits all claim to Protestantism. That faith is not living and effective but dead and worthless.

It is, therefore, a matter of vital concern that we rethink our Protestant heritage, gain fresh insight into its significance for our life and times, and unite all the forces of Protestantism in making its significance effective in our world today. This noble heritage is ours. Your forefathers and mine died martyr deaths and braved persecution to maintain this faith. Are you Dutch? Holland ran red with Protestant blood in a persecution whose brutality has never been surpassed. Are you French? The streets of Paris are made sacred with the blood of two thousand Huguenots who died in a massacre on St. Bartholomew's Day, 1572, for their Protestant faith. Did your ancestors come from Scotland? Patrick Hamilton and George Wishart

9

were burned, John Knox made to serve as a galley slave, and scores like them persecuted in their efforts to establish Protestantism in Scotland. Are you English? Many of your ancestors, like Cranmer, Ridley, and Latimer who were burned in Oxford Market Place, were persecuted for their faith. And so the story goes. Whatever else Protestantism may be, it is made sacred by martyr blood. I submit to you that faith for which people have died, which even the Inquisition could not conquer, is worthy of our deepest consideration.

The origin of the Reformation is usually given as October 31, 1517, when Dr. Martin Luther nailed his Ninety-five Theses on the church door at Wittenberg. Of course the Reformation did not begin in one day. As Carl Ullman has pointed out, the Reformation is a great historical result, the issue of a spiritual process extending through the centuries. Luther's Theses kindled a fire that had been long in the making and that led to an open break with Rome. The occasion of the Theses was the selling of indulgences by John Tetzel, the income from which was partly used in the building of St. Peter's Church at Rome. Whatever indulgences were in theory, in practice those who bought them regarded them as pardons for sin. Tetzel is said to have boasted that he saved more souls by indulgences than the Apostle Peter by his preaching. Luther protested against this selling of grace for gold, as he described it, because of its devastating effects upon the lives of men. "He took the position that repentance means turning from sin to God; and that when a man does turn from sin and places his trust in God, his sins are immediately and entirely forgiven without the absolution of a priest or the indulgence of a pope."[1]

The logic of events immediately widened the breach between Luther and the Roman Church. In attacking the sale of indulgences, Luther had really attacked the power of the Pope, which now became one of the crucial issues. Luther came out with clear statements that popes are not infallible and that "councils are not the ultimate authority over the souls of men." In 1520 the Pope issued a bull excommunicating Luther in sixty days if he did not recant. Instead of recanting, Luther burned the bull.

The German people flocked to Luther's support, and the papal bull had little effect. In 1521, however, Charles V summoned Luther to the Imperial Diet at Worms where the papal representatives hoped to have Luther further condemned by civil authorities. When asked to recant, Luther made his famous reply: "My conscience is bound to the word of God. Unless convinced by clear arguments of reason based upon the Scriptures,

---

[1]Carl Ullman, *Reformers before the Reformation* (Edinburgh: T & T Clark, 1855).

I will not and cannot recant, since it is unsafe and dangerous to do anything against conscience. . . . Here I stand. God help me. Amen." Protected by German princes and people, Luther escaped the martyrdom that otherwise would have befallen him. The old triumvirate—pope, emperor, and council—was broken; its complete power over people's lives belonged to the ages. A new triumvirate—scripture, reason, and conscience—had taken its place.

When the followers of Luther protested against the action of the Diet of Spires, which sought to destroy the freedom to worship that they had won, these protesters became known as Protestants. While the word is somewhat negative in its historical origin, Protestantism denotes not merely a protest against an old church but a positive and creative movement—a *deliberate* return to primitive, biblical Christianity.

Consider now the principles for which the Reformation stood, principles for which men and women in our spiritual tradition have given their lives.

Protestantism holds that the Bible is the ultimate and final spiritual authority. It believes in no infallible man and in no infallible institution. Protestantism believes all men err and all institutions, even the church, have at times made grave mistakes. As the final court of authority, Protestantism sends every individual back to the scriptures. The Scots Confession of 1560, written largely by John Knox, was genuinely Protestant when the preface stated in substance that the Confession was binding only so far as it was true to scripture.

In many ways Protestants have always honored the scriptures. Protestant biblical scholarship has contributed much to our understanding of the Bible. We may be proud of the activities of Bible societies that have placed scriptures in the hands of the most distant tribes and have maintained the Bible as the best-seller after all these years. We present-day Protestants, unfortunately, have done almost everything with the Bible except to read it: that which is most important of all. The Reformers did this first of all. Is it not time that we lay claim to our Protestant heritage in the scriptures by reading them?

Another principle of Protestantism is justification by faith alone. People are not saved by works, nor by ceremony and rites. They are saved by the relationship of their hearts, their very beings, to God; from that relationship flow good works. Good fruits are produced by a good tree, not a good tree by good fruits. As Luther said in "The Freedom of a Christian," "Good works do not make a good man, but a good man does good works." Religion, therefore, as Protestantism understands it, is an inward thing. Faith does not mean merely intellectual assent to certain doctrines but the commitment of all of life—body, mind, and soul—to God as revealed in Christ and to his purposes for life. People who so commit their lives will find God merciful and forgiving. "By grace are ye saved through faith; and that not of yourselves: it is a gift of God."

This emphasis upon religion as an inward matter means that man's relationship to God is not through a priest, not through an institution, but is personal and immediate. Every believer is a priest who must answer before God. Ministry is a function, not a status.

Protestantism likewise teaches the sanctity of the common life. Protestant faith sees all of life as sacred and religious, and therefore knows of no special religious acts or life. The Protestant who is truly Protestant regards daily tasks as a divine calling and performs them for the glory of God. Luther and Calvin insisted that the humblest calling is a sacred task. My work as a minister is not more religious than your work as a business man or a teacher. Your work and mine are both sacred, and we both must perform our work, as best we can, for the glory of God.

Protestantism also stands for the independence of church and state. Generally speaking, there are three theories on the relationship of church and state. One holds that the state is superior to the church, and the church must, therefore, be controlled by the state. This view is illustrated in Nazi Germany. The second is the theory that the church is superior to the state, and the state, therefore, must be subservient to the church. This is the view of medieval Catholicism of the thirteenth century. The third theory is that the church and state are independent entities. Neither is subservient or superior to the other. Protestantism accepts this theory, believing that both church and state are ordained of God and that both must be governed by his will. The church has no right to assume the affairs of the state, and the state must not infringe upon the liberty of the church.

Protestantism stands for another principle: religious liberty. Of course Protestants have at times been intolerant. For this we should be ashamed and repentant. No person or group of people can claim a monopoly on truth. Ours should be the humility of seekers after truth. Nevertheless, religious liberty as we know it in Western civilization is largely the result of the Protestant spirit. Make no mistake about that. Dr. William Warren Sweet, professor at the University of Chicago and an authority on American church history, is responsible for the idea that *religious liberty in the United States is a Protestant accomplishment. If religious liberty is to be maintained in this country, it must be maintained by the united efforts of Protes-*

tants.[2] Protestant minorities in other countries of the world are today being persecuted by the Roman Catholics, who in this country as a minority group enjoy religious liberty freely. (Read John Mackay in the preface of *Religious Liberty in Latin America.*) "Protestantism resists coercion whether by political or ecclesiastical authorities in matters of faith and practice." That is our heritage. Let us claim that heritage today; as Dr. John Mackay reminds us, the battle for religious liberty is not won. We must be alert to the forces that are working against that liberty in our own country and throughout the world.

Protestantism's emphasis upon religious liberty and the right of private judgment makes it especially congenial with democracy. The United States, Canada, Scotland, England, the Scandinavian countries, Holland, the Union of South Africa, and Australia are predominately Protestant in their religious belief. The roll call of those nations is just about the complete roll call of the democratic nations. That is more than striking coincidence.

"The hour has struck," said Samuel McCrea Cavert, executive secretary of the Federal Council of Churches of Christ in America, "for a strong reaffirmation of faith in the basic principles of Protestantism." I submit to you he sounds a timely warning.

[2]See William Warren Sweet, *The Story of Religion in America* (New York: Harper & Brothers Publishers, 1939), 274–80.

"On Mistaking the Clean for the Unclean"
Race Relations Sunday, February 13, 1949

First Presbyterian Church, Auburn, Alabama

The Apostle Peter has a perennial charm for people who see their own strength and weakness reflected in that rugged fisherman. Only recently Lloyd Douglas's *Big Fisherman* has become a best-seller in spite of the fact that it takes Douglas 581 pages to tell a story that the New Testament writers relate in a much better manner in about 25 pages. Douglas's story of Peter is the product of the author's imagination and has little to do with the real fisherman of the New Testament. Somewhere between the bottom of pages 566 and the top of page 567 Peter does his work as an apostle. As one reviewer has said, a more accurate title for the book would be *Little Peter and Less Church.*

The Peter of the New Testament, however, was no imaginary man. We understand Peter, for we can see ourselves playing his part sometimes as a hero and then again as a coward. Like Peter we say impulsively to our Master, "Lord, I shall follow thee whithersoever thou shalt lead me," and then our Lord leads us through some Garden of Gethsemane and we fail. Some of the disciples like John seemed to be prepared for any emergency, but not Peter. The call of discipleship was continually confronting him with surprises and demands about which he never dreamed. One day the Lord commanded him in a dream to arise and eat the flesh of a four-footed beast that was set before him in a vision. For all of his life Peter had been taught that that kind of meat was unclean. He had lived in the midst of a society where civilized people just did not eat that kind of meat. Any child would know better than to obey that command. Surely this was a temptation of the devil who was appearing as an angel of light. We can imagine Peter answering with gusto, "Not so, Lord; for nothing common or unclean hath entered into my mouth" (Acts 11:8). But this was no temptation of the devil. Society had been wrong. The Master spoke to Peter in tones whose authenticity he could not doubt. "What God hath cleansed, that call not thou common" (Acts 10:15).

Of course the vision had far deeper implication than the matter of eating meat that in itself was nothing more than a bagatelle. Whether or not to eat pork is an aesthetic question, I suppose. At least it stands on the periphery of life. Peter had been calling some people unclean, which was no trifling matter. Such an act was and is of crucial significance. Peter had been raised in a society that had taught him from the early days of childhood that he as a Jew was better than others. Many of Peter's contemporaries refused to travel through Samaria even though the best roads were there. They did not want to contaminate themselves or their children by contact with the Samaritans. And now Peter was confronted with the exacting demands of Christian discipleship. "What God hath cleansed, that call not thou unclean." God had made all men clean.

This problem has perennially tormented men. For some strange reason men like to call their brothers unclean. That is a sin of which I am guilty, and I strongly suspect that some of you share this guilt with me. Today as of old, our Lord confronts us with the demands of discipleship. "What God hath cleansed, that call not thou unclean."

I

In order to consider this demand of Christian discipleship in its proper perspective, let us remind ourselves of two tenets of our faith that must serve as a background for everything else we may say. The first affirmation concerns the Christian church. Its constitution is not the customs and mores of society, but the Lordship of Jesus Christ as revealed in the New Testament. My personal opinion about any demand of discipleship is, from the Christian point of view, wholly irrelevant except insofar as it is in accord with the New Testament.

The starting point for every Christian is the Lordship of Jesus Christ. Paul identified himself first of all not as a Jew or a university graduate or as a rich or poor man as the case may have been. He was first of all a bond slave of Jesus Christ.

The primary fact in the life of every Christian is not whether he is white or black, educated or uneducated, but whether he belongs to Jesus Christ. The Christian does not begin with the customs of society or the opinions of neighbors in the solution of any problem. The starting point is the New Testament. In these latter years we have confused Christianity with being respectable, and to discover that loyalty to Jesus Christ may sometimes cost us our respectability comes as a rude shock. Our Lord truly said the way is narrow and few there be that find it.

The second affirmation of faith declares that God has made every man in his own image. It is sometimes said that according to the Bible, God put a curse on the Negro, but that is sheer nonsense. The Bible teaches us that God loves everyone as his children. He knows them by name. In the New Testament we read that he had made of one blood all nations for to dwell on the face of the earth. "There is neither Greek nor Jew, circumcision nor uncircumcision, Barbarian, Scythian, bond nor free: but Christ is all, and in all" (Col. 3:11). Certainly the Bible knows nothing about the special prerogatives of any race. Before the cross of Christ the ground is level and in Christ all men are brothers. Christ died equally for black people, white people, yellow people, red people. As far as we can tell, everyone shall sit together in the Father's home, for everyone is of equal worth before God.

II

Come a step further now and observe the relevance of our faith to our relationship with the Negro. Surely in no area of life do the words of our Lord have greater meaning: "To whom much is given of him shall much be expected" (Luke 12:48). "This is my commandment that ye love one another, as I have loved you" (John 15:12). "Whatsoever ye would that men should do to you, do ye even so to them" (Matthew 7:12). What now is the meaning of these words for our daily relationship with our brothers in black?

In the first place, we can be patient with the Negro. He deserves our patience. Our grandfathers brought Negroes to this country in the reeking hole of some ship and kept them in slavery until eighty-six years ago. Some Negroes who were born in slavery are still alive. Since freedom came, their opportunities have still been restricted. Thus we need to be patient with his ignorance.

Heaven above knows that his white neighbors have not given him much of an example of humility. Let us remember the many provocations that must continually needle the Negroes' pride and ask ourselves if we would be as humble in case the tables were reversed and we were the Negroes. After all, we are white people, not by any virtue of our own, but solely by the grace of God. Let us therefore be humble and patient with those who by the grace of God have a little more of a certain kind of pigmentation in their skins. Our Negro neighbors need kindliness and understanding on the part of every Christian. As the New Testament says, "Bear ye one another's burdens" (Gal. 6:2).

In the second place, we can be careful about the words we speak. Untold harm is done to the spirit of brotherliness by calling Negroes unkind names. No good cause is served by jokes told at their expense. But Christ is honored when some brave soul has the courage to speak a word in defense of an abused Negro's honor and dignity. Furthermore, we can address Negroes with common courtesy when we meet them upon the street or deal with them in private. Above all, we can stop gossiping about Negroes and every effort to better their condition. Whispering campaigns have ruined many attempts to better relations. If words do not contribute to the establishment of constructive goodwill, they should never be spoken. Gossip can be terribly malicious. Our Lord knew that when he said that men shall be brought into the judgment for every idle word they speak.

In the third place, we can work by word and deed for justice for the Negro. There is the old saying, "Justice may be blind, but she ain't colorblind." Only recently, it was front-page news when white men were given a prison sentence for raping a Negro woman, whereas if the situation had been reversed, the Negro would have almost certainly been given a more severe sentence. Law enforcement officials and juries have a notoriously poor record in bringing to court and punishing those who are guilty of mob violence and terrorism against Negro people. It is common knowledge that the Negro citizen is not granted the privileges of citizenship on an equal basis with white people.

The Negro also needs justice in the matter of an equal opportunity for an education. The per capita expenditures for public education were weighted on the side of the white child. The state of Alabama in 1946 spent $67.09 for the education of every white child and $29.19 for the education of every Negro child. In 1948 the proportion was $95.74 to $59.07, which indicates that progress is being made. In Lee County, so far as I have been able to learn, still greater progress has been achieved. There is no discrimination in teachers' pay. While the pupil load for each Negro teacher is greater than for white teachers, very great progress has been made in lessening the teacher load in the Negro schools during the past ten years. There are, however, thirty-two school buses transporting white children in this county, but none transport Negroes. The fact that progress has been made should encourage us in the days that lie ahead. Much still needs to be done before the Negro shall have equal opportunity with whites to develop those talents and gifts that God has given. The conscience of no Christian can be complacent until this goal is attained.

In the fourth place, the Negro needs the gospel of God's love made manifest in Jesus Christ just as white people need it. Our church, which is located in the southern states, does not have a good record in the evangelization of the Negro. During all the years since the Civil War we have been preaching the love of Christ, and today we have a Negro membership of exactly 3,349. At the same time 5,530,488 Negroes in the South belong to no church at all. We have sponsored a junior college for Negroes, but the record indicates that exceedingly little money has been contributed to its support.

Today we have to face the fact that someone is going to win the allegiance of the Negro. Significantly some of the leading Communists in America are Negroes. I once heard the secretary of the national committee of the Communist Party in America say that communism is the one hope for the Negro. A young Negro student in the Yale Law School auditorium declared that communism offered nothing to him as a Negro, if he were not Communist. His only hope as a Negro, as a human being, he said, was for the people of both races to be truly Christian. There was spontaneous applause for that declaration of faith. The Communist said he was naïve. Christ is the answer wherever people accept the demand of discipleship. This, however, must be clear to us all. The Negro shall never accept the gospel from our hand if we do not offer with the other hand deeds of love and service that authenticate the faith we profess.

III

We have been dealing with a subject this morning that is admittedly hard and difficult. On the one hand it involves technical problems that no amount of goodwill can fully solve. On the other hand, none of us finds it easy to conquer our own sins in this matter. I remember an experience that I had as a college sophomore on a debating trip. We were eating in the cafeteria of Rutgers University in New Brunswick, New Jersey, when a Rutgers student sat down beside me. He was as clean as I was. He was better dressed than I was. If I had been in his classes I might have had the embarrassing but extremely wholesome experience of watching him make better grades than I would have made. But he had a black face. I remember still how uncomfortable I felt. I had to struggle against eighteen years of indoctrination. It has been a long struggle for me, and no one knows better than I how far I still miss the mark of the prize of the high calling of God in Jesus Christ.

It is hard to be a Christian. But after all, it is about time that we should get into our thinking that this business of being Christian is and always will be an arduous and dangerous business. It is not made for cowards and the weak. In the past, people died martyrs' deaths for their faith. Today, none of us is in any danger of a martyr's death, but we shall have to face up to the scorn of friends and the displeasure of a vast segment of our society if we are to be really Christian. Yet this is the joy of being a Christian—the thrill of standing with God in the midst of the darkness of some monstrous evil and watching for the light to come.

As we gather in God's sanctuary for worship, we have to take seriously the words of the Lord. "If thou bring thy gift to the altar, and there rememberest that thy brother hath aught against thee; Leave there thy gift before the altar, and go thy way; first be reconciled to thy brother, and then come and offer thy gift" (Matt. 5:23–24). Do our Negro neighbors have ought against us?

"Christ and Human Differences"
Race Relations Sunday, February 12, 1951

First Presbyterian Church, Auburn, Alabama

This Sunday has been designated in America as Race Relations Sunday. It is a reminder that people are different, as if we needed a reminder. Some are tall; others short. Some rich; others poor. Some are highly educated; others lack formal education. Some are mechanics; others teachers. Some are lawyers; others businessmen. Some are British; others Americans. Some are southerners; others northerners. Some are black; others white. Some are men; others women. This great variety in the human family enriches our common life and delivers us from the dreary monotony and poverty of experience that would exist if we were all alike.

But our differences are also the occasions for misunderstanding, suspicion, hate, brutality, and violence. We are suspicious of people who are different. We try to exploit them. We do violence to them, sometimes to protect ourselves, sometimes with no reason at all.

One of the pressing tasks of our time is to eliminate the rancor that exists between people who are different in color, race, nationality, and culture. Only when we succeed in this endeavor can our differences serve to enrich our common life.

This problem is stated very clearly in our text, which also provides us with the answer. "There is neither Jew nor Greek, there is neither slave nor free, there is neither male nor female; for you are all one in Christ Jesus" (Gal. 3:28).

I

Let us begin the application of our text to life today with the frank recognition that people are different. A certain type of equalitarianism has glossed over the differences that exist. Our own Declaration of Independence declared that men are born free and equal. But if we push this point too far, it becomes plainly untrue. For it is a self-evident fact that men are not equal. There are significant differences.

Within the Christian community men continue to be men and women remain women. In the last century many things have been done to equalize the rights of women, as it should be. The denial to woman of the right to vote, the control of man over her life even to the point of tyranny, a double standard of morality for men and women—these and many similar discriminations should have fallen away much sooner before the aroused Christian conscience.

Yet it remains a fact that men and women, who are one in Christ and in human dignity, are still different. And as long as women give birth to babies, their function in society will be significantly different from that of men. Any interpretation of life that ignores this basic difference between man and woman is doomed ultimately to failure. In the Christian community these differences between man and woman may be seen in a new light, but they are not ignored or forgotten.

A second difference that Paul mentions is between bond and free, between the capitalist and the wage earner. This difference also continues to exist in the Christian community. Someone here may contend that this difference ought not exist. But so far as I know every society distinguishes between the bond and free, and in every society people belong to each of these groups. A society such as the communist may annihilate the capitalists—or to use Paul's word, the free—but under another guise the same function is still performed by party bureaucrats. Even in labor unions there are labor leaders. And in the primitive Christian church in Jerusalem where everything was held in common, still certain individuals were called apostles and were accorded unique honor.

Now many people who today are the free, the capitalists, the administrators, the politicians, have the place they do because of business dealings that were shrewd rather than just, or because of political campaigns that indulged in lies to win votes and capitalized on hate to stay in office. Certainly no Christian supports this kind of power. But every society has a hierarchy of competence. Some people are equipped to be administrators and others ditchdiggers. Some are prepared to carry heavy responsibility; others are prepared to do a routine job that calls for few decisions.

People differ in their capacities to perform the various functions of society. This fact is plain and inescapable. As long as this fact continues to be true, some will be bond and others free. Within the Christian community this difference may be seen in a new light, but it cannot be ignored and to pretend that it does not exist is foolishness.

Paul refers to a third distinction: the difference between the Jew and the Greek. Here was a difference of culture. The Greek had been reared in a university atmosphere with the heritage of Socrates, Plato, and Aristotle; of Homer, Hesiod, Euripides, and Herodotus; of Pericles, of Phidias. For centuries the Greek had been trained to ask and to attempt to answer important questions about the universe, about truth, about right and wrong.

The Hebrew had been trained in the rigors of the desert and the country with the heritage of great saints who were convinced that they knew God: Moses, David, Amos, Isaiah. The great aim of a Jew's life was not to be clever, but to be obedient to the will of God.

From the beginning of recorded history there have been cultural differences between people. Even in the United States where people have been amazingly mixed up, there are still significant differences in outlook and in manner of life between groups of people.

In the Christian community the Greek continued to be a Greek and the Jew a Jew. The person with a first-rate university education remains what he is and the person with little formal education remains what he is. These differences may be seen in a new light by those who follow Christ, but they are not blotted out.

This difference between Greek and Jew, however, was deeper than culture. It was rooted in a racial distinction. One of the very first problems that confronted the early church was how two different races could live together in the same church. Peter the Jew did not want to eat with Cornelius the Gentile. You can read about this great struggle in the tenth and eleventh chapters of Acts.

Yet even in the church it remained a fact that one man was a Greek and the other a Jew. It is not easy to say precisely what the differences between races are. So far as I know, there is no scientific evidence to support the notion that any one race is innately superior to another. Certainly nothing in the Bible justifies the idea that one race is to serve another, and much scripture warns against this viewpoint.

But the fact remains that races are different. One difference may be seen in physical characteristics. Even if there are no other differences, this physical difference is usually embedded in important cultural distinctions. None of this is to suggest that one race is superior to another, but some differences between races are significant. Within the Christian community these differences may be—indeed must be—seen in a different light, but they cannot be ignored.

These distinctions between sexes, between classes, between cultures, between races, certainly do not exhaust the list of human differences, but they do include those significant differences that are not wrong in themselves, that may contribute to richness of human life, but that frequently serve as occasions for suspicion, hate, brutality, and violence. If we are to redeem these differences from becoming occasions of misunderstanding and make them occasions for a symphony of mankind, we must begin with a plain and honest recognition of the fact that they exist.

II

But Christian faith has another word to say. "There is neither Jew nor Greek, there is neither slave nor free, there is neither male nor female; *for you are all one in Christ.*" The ultimate fact in the Christian community is not our differences but our oneness, more specifically our oneness in Christ. Here is a community where a great loyalty, a great devotion, a great faith transcends and goes beyond the differences. Here is a faith great enough to take people who are different and make them members of one body.

As John Oxenham's hymn puts it:

> In Christ there is no East nor West,
> In Him no South or North;
> But one great fellowship of love
> Thro'-out the whole wide earth.

The important fact in the Christian community is not whether a person is male or female, bond or free, Greek or Jew, but whether that person is a Christian, of Christ. So when a person comes to enter the membership of this church we don't ask about sex, class status, culture, or race. We ask simply about faith, devotion to God, and love for his fellow man. Nothing else matters when a person comes to the house of God. The doors of the church, of any true church, are as wide as the words of him who is the only Lord of the Church: "Come unto me all ye that labor and are heavy laden, and I will give you rest" (Matt. 11:28).

On the one hand Christian faith acknowledges the fact of human differences. On the other it declares that faith in God and love for one's fellow man are more important than human differences.

III

This aspect of Christian faith carries us a step further. We have to admit that we are inclined to underscore the differences and to ignore the faith that is more important, which transcends the differences.

This Sunday, which has been set aside by most churches as Race Relations Sunday, is a solemn reminder that underscoring our differences and ignoring our faith is particularly true in race relations. Evading this problem is no longer possible. Nor can we keep conditions as they are. Racial patterns in the South and in our world are rapidly changing. The only thing that we can do is to seek to approach the problem in the spirit of Christ and to attempt to shape according to his will the events that are now developing.

The communists know that an old pattern of life is breaking up and that they have an opportunity to shape a new pattern. Today they are exploiting racial hatred everywhere in the world. In our own South the pattern of life is changing, and the Roman Catholic Church is seeking to have a hand in the shaping of the pattern that is to take its place. This is a legitimate aspiration on the part of the Roman Church. The question that remains is, What will Protestant Christians who have had an unparalleled opportunity in the South have to say about the shaping of this new pattern of life? Shall we vainly cling to a pattern of life that is falling to pieces before our eyes? Shall we retire from the field and leave it to communists and other secular forces, to Roman Christianity? I do not believe that Protestants who are sincere in their faith will do either. I am convinced that people of faith will measure up to the demands that these days of opportunity and judgment place upon all those who bear the name of Christ.

It is not possible to give a detailed program that every Christian must follow in this matter. This problem is complex with room for differences of opinion. But all of us as Christians can agree on two things.

The first is the necessity of goodwill. Many of the problems arising out of the racial situation in the South are technical. Even if all of us, both White and Negro, were Christian, there would still be problems of terrible complexity. We cannot define with preciseness what action we should always take. But clearly in all of our actions we must be people of goodwill. We must have the intention of helping every child of God be what God means for that person to be. We must value persons not in terms of what they can do for us, but in terms of God's love for them. Goodwill may not give us the intellectual answer to all of our problems, but without respect for persons as children of God, no answer will ever be possible.

In the second place we can let the church be the church. We do not always do that. We sometimes take the church and make it another country club, luncheon club, sewing club, or business organization. Can we say that the average church is any different from our state universities, our social groups, from organizations that never acknowledge the fact of God? Let us stop trying to make another club out of the church. Let us let the church be the church, where people live together in the family of God. Let us acknowledge here the sole lordship of Jesus Christ.

These two things we can do. We can have goodwill. We can let the church be the church.

IV

The conclusion of this matter is that the biggest and most important difference is not that of sex, race, class, or culture. It is the difference of faith. Faith does not mean verbal assent to some proposition but the deep-seated and genuine attitude of a person toward God, the world, and man. Our faith is revealed in the assumption that habitually determines how we act.

The only real difference in the human family is drawn between those who believe and those who do not believe, between those who love and those who hate. Only this difference ultimately matters.

In the end God himself will divide between those who have believed and disbelieved, between those who have loved and those who have hated. He will say to those at the right hand,

> Come, O blessed of my Father, inherit the kingdom prepared for you from the foundation of the world; for I was hungry and you gave me food, I was thirsty and you gave me drink, I was a stranger and you welcomed me, I was naked and you clothed me, I was sick and you visited me, I was in prison and you came to me. . . . As you did it to one of the least of these my brethren, you did it to me. (Matt. 25:34–37, 40)

"Christian Faith and Political Decisions"
November 2, 1952

First Presbyterian Church, Auburn, Alabama

A man stepped out of the multitude one day and said to Jesus, "Teacher, bid my brother divide the inheritance with me." This was a very natural request. Religious leaders were frequently called on to decide questions in those days that are now settled in the courts. The answer of Jesus was unexpected: "Man, who made me a judge or divider over you?" (Luke 12:13–15).

Now certainly Jesus must have recognized that this was a legitimate request. Presumably the man had a real grievance against his brother. Yet Jesus would have nothing to do with the details of this case. He refused to decide between this man and his brother.

Actually Jesus did something for this man that was more important than settling the particular grievance. He said to the man and to people who were standing by, "Take heed, and beware of all covetousness; for a man's life does not consist in the abundance of his possessions." And then Jesus proceeded to explain what he meant by telling the story of the rich fool (Luke 12:15).

I

This incident from the life of Jesus has a real meaning for us as we prepare for the election on Tuesday. We are all faced with a concrete and specific decision. We shall cast our ballot for a man who we think ought to be president of the United States. We shall also have to vote for or against measures to provide more adequate care for those who are sick. In short, we shall have to translate our Christian faith into specific deeds on Tuesday.

None of us is likely to find this a very simple responsibility. It would be very simple if one candidate appeared wholly corrupt and the record of his party wholly evil, if we had adequate and accurate information, and if the issues involved were not complex. Perhaps someone here this morning sees the issues in the coming election in just these simple terms, but I imagine not. Thus, we too are faced with a decision like that of the man who wanted Jesus to divide his inheritance for him.

It is easy to understand why some people are glad enough for their church to tell them how to vote. It relieves them of the responsibility of decision. But we are proud that the Presbyterian church does not tell anyone how to vote. In fact the one safe prediction about this election is that a Presbyterian will be elected. And it is certain that equally conscientious Presbyterians are going to vote as Democrats and Republicans. The church does not tell us how to vote any more than Jesus settled the question of the inheritance.

But as Jesus told the man to take heed and beware of covetousness, so he says to us on Tuesday, "Take heed and beware." The church does not tell us how to vote, but it does tell us to take heed and beware of the motives that lie behind our votes.

If Jesus were speaking to us concerning the election, he might very well say the same words to us that he gave to the man who was disputing the inheritance with his brother. Take heed and beware of covetousness. We do not need a historian such as Charles Beard to remind us that economic forces have exerted a tremendous influence upon American politics and history. It is obvious enough. One major question that some may ask as they mark their ballots is, "What is in it for me?" Our vote is determined too frequently by covetousness for some personal advantage.

I do not suppose that anyone is wholly free from this motivation, Christians as well as non-Christians.

The Christian, however, has the advantage of being aware of this temptation. A Christian can at least take heed. A Christian can at least criticize a ballot in the light of what Jesus Christ has said. A Christian at least knows that the vote ought to be determined by something more important than personal gain. This is true not only of our decision about the presidency but also in providing hospital facilities for those sick with tuberculosis and with mental illness. Reinhold Niebuhr has reminded us that Christians are distinguished in political decisions by contrition and a capacity for critical self-criticism, not by any infallibility.

Material prosperity will damn us in the long run if it is bought at the price of human blood and suffering. An abundance of money in our pockets will curse us if gotten by the oppression or neglect of our fellow man. Special privilege will reek vengeance upon us if it is based upon injustice.

Jesus might have said, "Take heed. Beware of a political partisanship that goes deeper than Christian faith." The real question is not so much how we vote but whether our political loyalties go deeper than our loyalty to Christ. No Christian can ever be a *reverent* member of a political party or of any human organization, for reverence belongs only to God. Every Christian must be somewhat irreverent toward political parties and toward every human organization. Christians must not take such claims too seriously and must criticize a party by a deeper loyalty to Christ.

So Jesus says to us today, Beware lest your political partisanship goes deeper than your Christian faith.

II

The reverse side of this warning against a political partisanship that goes deeper than Christian faith is the positive task of criticizing our political action by our faith.

Christian faith has something more important to say to us than "Vote, get the facts." We ought to be able to take it for granted that Christians will get the facts, that they will vote. Our special task is to apply the teaching of Jesus to our decisions in politics and to the issues of the day. Our first allegiance is to Christ, and in the light of that allegiance we must act in the realm of politics.

The church does not tell us how to vote. It does insist that we vote in such a way that we can feel satisfied with ourselves when we read the Sermon on the Mount or the story of the Good Samaritan or the account of the last judgment.

There is no one Christian candidate for president. One of the best signs of the current campaign is the indication that Mr. Eisenhower and Mr. Stevenson are seriously religious. That they are both Presbyterians is a source of pride. At least in regard to the presidency there is no one Christian way to vote.

And let us take an issue like the H-bomb. This may be the most serious issue of the campaign, but who can claim infallibility?

Certainly foreign policy is an issue. But who is without doubts?

Some of the serious issues of our day involve not only moral considerations but technical problems that go beyond our knowledge and understanding.

Is there no difference in the way a Christian and a non-Christian vote?

Outwardly, Christians and non-Christians alike will vote Republican and Democrat.

This very important fact distinguishes a Christian vote: The Christian decides how to vote in the light of Christian faith, in the light of a loyalty that is deeper than politics.

Certainly one of the most potent forces in American politics today is covetousness for money. The reason you have corruption in government is that people love money more than truth. Yet it is not only people in government office or in the inner councils of politics who love money. It is also the person on the street—the sharp critic of corruption in government—who sometimes loves money more than truth.

But surely Jesus meant more than money when he spoke of covetousness. There is covetousness of office and power and privilege. Can we doubt that the righteous indignation of many campaign speeches is anything more than a put-on act to win votes?

In the casting of votes, we too can be covetous for things that do not rightly belong to us—for political patronage jobs, for unholy privileges for our group, class, or race.

"Take heed, and beware of all covetousness; for a man's life does not consist in the abundance of his possessions." Jesus might also say, "Take heed, and beware of political revivalism." We like to think of ourselves as rational people, but few if any of our decisions are made on the basis of reason alone. Politicians have taken advantage of this fact during the past few months. They have been lambasting the multitudes with threats of hell-fire and damnation.

So far as the records show, Jesus never engaged in this kind of revivalism. He did not, so far as we know, make as many converts as either the political or the religious revivalists of our time. Once when enthusiastic men came to him asking to be his disciples, he warned, "Have you counted the cost?" So today he would say to all of us, "Have you counted the cost of the political oratory?" "Have you assessed its real meaning and content?"

Political revivalism is more dangerous and deadly than religious revivalism. The religious revivalists appeal to fear of hell, which doesn't hurt the average person too much and in most cases may be definitely salutary. But political revivalism appeals to hate—to hate of other races, to hate of other classes, to hate of other nations. It creates suspicion and thrives upon it. Its method is one of reckless disregard for truth and of personal vilification.

Beware of political revivalism. Jesus would also say to us, "Take heed and beware of arrogance." In George Bernard Shaw's play *Joan of Arc*, the dauphin of France appears as a banal sort of fellow. On one occasion, however, he shows a flash of brilliance as he says to Joan, "The trouble with you, Joan, is that you think you have got God in your pocket." A great many people in politics as elsewhere think they have God in their pocket. Oliver Cromwell once advised some of his political opponents to consider, by the mercy of Christ, the possibility that they might be wrong. It is difficult for people who give their whole devotion to a cause that they believe is right to cherish the possibility that they might be wrong, but Christ's is the only possible way for mortals who lack both the goodness and omniscience of God.

We need to beware lest we lose respect for honest and intelligent people who differ with us politically. For this respect is one of the bases of democracy and it is an expression of Christian humility. This respect is an article both of our Christian and of our democratic faith that no single person is either good enough or wise enough to have all the answers. The honest and intelligent person who differs with us may possibly be right.

True humility means that we shall do what we can to learn the facts about the candidates for whom we vote and the issues at stake. It would be interesting to know how many members of this congregation have read the platform of either party or the major speeches of either candidate. Very frequently our emotional intensity on many issues exists in inverse proportion to our knowledge of the facts involved.

III

True humility also means that we are repentant for our involvement in the sins of our nation and world. None of us has clean hands when it comes to corruption in government, to character assassination, to hate of fellow man, to war. These things would not exist if we, the people, were different. The notion that we are innocent in these matters is at best a pious fiction and at worst a pious fraud. Abraham Lincoln never took it for granted that God was on the side of his party or nation. W. H. Auden puts it this way: "All true democracy begins with free confession of our sins."

Political, social, and economic activities, are—as Reinhold Niebuhr has taught—always morally ambiguous. We do not have simple choices between good and evil. All political and economic activity involves us in evil as well as good. Hence the Christian must always pray for forgiveness. For this reason groups of Christians have said again and again in church history that they would have nothing to do with the government, that they would leave this to the non-Christians.

There have also been people in every age, as John Mackay has warned, who have wanted to live on the balcony while life passed on the road beneath.

Now it is true enough that Jesus refused to involve himself in the details of political life in his day. Many were disappointed that he did not lead a campaign against Rome. His vocation was not the ordering of society. Ours is not the vocation of Jesus but the vocation of his followers who— as best as we can in the complicated and ambiguous issues of American life—seek to do what is possible for a more just, humane, and productive society.

The church does not dictate our vote. It does call us down from the balcony. The church does tell us that our vote must be cast as an expression of our faith. The vote must point in the direction of brotherhood, justice, peace, and a productive society. The vote must be against hate, injustice, any needless shedding of blood, and parasitical patterns of life.

So long as we choose freedom to slavery, so long as we are children of God, we cannot escape from this responsibility. No infallible authority can tell us how to vote. The decision on Tuesday is ours to make. There is less likelihood that we shall vote wrongly if, before we vote, we say a prayer, not upon the street where we can be seen, but in our closet where only God can hear and see us. If we pray that God may remove from us all malice, all placing of self before the common good, then we may rightly ask that his blessing may rest upon our vote that it may be for the good of our nation and of people of goodwill everywhere.

> God of our fathers, known of old,
> Lord of our far-flung battle line,
> Beneath whose awful hand we hold
> Dominion over palm and pine:
> Lord God of hosts, be with us yet,
> Lest we forget—lest we forget.
> (Rudyard Kipling, "Recessional")

"The Pilgrim Church"
January 10, 1954

Sermon for Dedication of New Church Building,
First Presbyterian Church, Auburn, Alabama

Today we are met together as a Christian community to dedicate this church building. To dedicate means to set apart for a special purpose, but originally it meant to proclaim. For the past several years we have been busy with financial campaigns, blueprints, and brick and mortar. Now we are ready to proclaim to this community and to ourselves why we have been so engaged.

We are met to make this declaration as the people of God, as people who stand in an unbroken succession of believing men and women with Abraham, to whom the call of God came in the words of our text: "Go from your country and your kindred and your father's house to the land that I will show you" (Gen. 12:1). It is our faith that this call of God to Abraham is also the call of God to us—indeed, that this call brings us together as the church.

I

Thus at the very outset we are confronted with the apparent contradiction between our call and what we have done here. Has the work of the past few years been a denial of our faith? Have we taken seriously the call of God to go into a far country? Are we the spiritual descendants of those who said, "For we are strangers before thee, and sojourners, as were our fathers: our days on the earth are as a shadow, and there is nothing abiding" (1 Chron. 29:15)? Apparently we have not taken our call seriously.

For this church is no transient abode. We pride ourselves that it is well built and of enduring construction. This church is no mean building. We pride ourselves that without extravagance it does please aesthetic sensibilities.

This church does not bespeak the pioneer spirit nor the call into a far country. It invites us to put our roots down. Here we shall be content to worship all our days. Here we shall baptize our babies. Here we shall marry our sons and daughters. Here we shall bury our dead and be buried ourselves.

How then shall we square what we do today with the call of God that brings us together as Christians? The fact is we cannot—if the call of God to Abraham was simply to cross geographical boundaries. Abraham, to be sure, did leave Ur of the Chaldees. He never had a permanent home. Like him many another man has left his native home and gone to a far country. Paul walked across the Mediterranean world. Carey went to Africa. Yet we do not honor Abraham and those who followed after him because they covered so many miles of the earth's surface—an achievement we can far exceed with airplanes and automobiles. We remember Abraham because he dared to pioneer in more important realms than geography. As the New Testament says, "He looked for a city which hath foundations, whose builder and maker is God" (Heb. 11:10).

Today our faith is that this church does invite us on a pilgrimage toward the city which hath foundations. Our faith is that this church is a symbol of our discontent with what we now are, of a hunger that no earthly bread can ever satisfy. To be sure, we are proud, perhaps inordinately proud, of the beauty of this church. To be sure, we are tempted to point to the work of our hands. But underneath our shallow vanity and sinful pride there has been a deeper faith—the faith of Abraham who left his country, his kindred, and his father's home to follow the leading of God.

Thus we dedicate this church with the proclamation that it is the pilgrim church. We dedicate it with the hope that this steeple pointing to heaven and the simple beauty of these walls, this pulpit, and this communion table with the open Bible will keep us discontent with every city of Earth.

We have not come to proclaim the end of a journey but the beginning. In the words of Paul, we do not believe that in building this church we have obtained the perfection of our calling; but forgetting what lies behind and straining forward to what lies ahead, we press on toward the goal for the prize of the upward call of God in Christ Jesus. We have not come today to point to our achievement but to declare what we hope this building will do for us.

II

We dedicate this church in a day when the judgment of God, so far as we can tell, is forcing us to be pilgrims. We do not like to be pilgrims. We are continually tempted to identify God's will with the place where we and our ancestors have stood, with the old established patterns of life, especially those patterns that treat us generously. We imprison God in a creed or an order of society, even in a building. We find it easier to worship an idol than the living God.

But God destroys our idolatry. Ever and again in history, the judgment of God has broken down the old familiar landmarks that were too easily declared to be the will of God. Certainly in our time the familiar landmarks are falling, and it may well be that this is God's judgment upon those of us who have refused to be pilgrims.

In the nineteenth century the discoveries of Darwin, the rise of modern science, and the development of a critical historical methodology shattered many of the neatly written creeds that people thought contained the whole truth of God. Some in dismay were convinced that modern science had destroyed God. But now it is clear that the creeds were not great enough to hold the full truth of God.

The impact of modern knowledge upon our creeds was just the beginning. More recently, communism has challenged our established patterns of society. The revolt of colonial people has shifted the center of world power. We do not know how society will be organized twenty-five or fifty years hence.

In our own South we are confronted with inevitable changes. It matters little that some are determined to accept no change, for we are powerless to prevent a shattering of the old patterns of our life. We cannot stop the changes, but we can listen to the voice of God in the midst of change and thus influence the resulting patterns of life. From the beginning of our nation, Protestantism has shaped the religious life of the South. The great question now is whether Protestantism will remain the dominant spiritual force in the new South. Will it match with equal vigor and creativity the industrialization of this region, the dynamic and rapidly changing social structure of our society? A Protestantism which simply repeats clichés that are effective now because of their emotional overtones, which can only preach some word memorized from the past, is not only unworthy of the name but is irrelevant to the South in which we now live.

We do not know why mighty forces have rocked our civilization. Perhaps it is because we have been too content with the way we are. Perhaps we have too easily declared that the way we live and the way we think are the will of God. Perhaps the shattering forces of our time are a reminder that we have on Earth no continuing city.

The last advice that John Robinson, the Puritan pastor at Leyden, gave to the Pilgrims before they sailed for the New World was to keep their hearts and minds open to the promptings of the spirit of God. He was sure that there was more truth and light yet to break forth out of God's holy Word. This conviction is the Protestant spirit at its best. For Protestantism demands that we continually bring all of life under the judgment of God in Jesus Christ and learn the will of God for our life in our own time.

We dedicate this church with the hope that it will keep us ever mindful that we do not know the full counsel of God—which we have not fully obeyed—that it will keep us pilgrims toward the city which hath foundations, whose builder and maker is God.

III

What is this city that hath foundations? We cannot say precisely, for surely it is beyond our imagining. Yet certain qualities are clear enough.

It is a city of faith. Too long we have thought of faith as propositions that our forefathers codified and that we memorize and repeat. Obviously such faith is not very important. True faith is more than that. It is a profound awareness of the presence of God in Jesus Christ. It is the power to see all of life—the birth of a child, the marriage of youth, the choice of vocation, the routine of daily existence, the frustrating disappointment, and finally death—in the light of God. A person cannot memorize a few phrases, however orthodox, and come to understand life in the light of the God and Father of our Lord Jesus Christ. Faith that transforms life develops only as people walk with God.

We need this faith today. We covet peace of soul, peace among nations, security in the presence of the precariousness of life. Even those who do not go to church, who do not consider themselves religious, talk about freedom, democracy, beauty, goodness. All of these words presuppose a great faith—a faith about the origin and the destiny of our world, about the source and end of human life. We must ask if people who use these great words have a faith great enough to support them.

The city that hath foundations is a city of faith and of conscience. Herbert Butterfield, the distinguished Cambridge historian, has said that the spirit of Christ has given a humane quality to our civilization that is to be found nowhere else. Certainly this church is a reminder that our Saviour is also our Lord, that we follow him who talked with the woman of Samaria, who declared that a cup of cold water given to a thirsty man is given to him, who despised all cant and hypocrisy. Following this Christ is not easy. Sometimes it means a lonely pilgrimage that even our family and dearest friends will not understand. Sometimes it means breaking with the established practices of the community. Sometimes it means risking job and even life. This church is a reminder that we are pilgrims of the Way.

It is a city of faith and conscience and fellowship. The paradox of the Christian life is that while every man must believe for himself, no man can believe alone. We believe within the Christian community. We have come to understand the meaning of the Christian fellowship in building this sanctuary. We have shared our money, our time, and ideas of individuals. This church is the sum total of money, time, and ideas of individuals. It is the expression of a shared fellowship. But our Christian fellowship goes deeper. It is a shared faith, a shared purpose, a shared commitment. Those who share this faith, this purpose, this commitment rise above personalities and pettiness. They share a common attitude toward life that triumphs over the differences that set people asunder.

We dedicate this church by proclaiming that we have built it to call us to a deeper faith, a more Christlike conscience, a profound fellowship.

* * *

We are tempted today to say that in these walls is enshrined our faith, that this brick and mortar is the guarantee of our salvation, that this church building is the perfection of our calling. But the true embodiment of Christian faith cannot be a building, however symbolic. It cannot be any work of our hand. The Christian faith can be embodied only in the life of the Christian community. Not brick and mortar, said Chrysostom, but faith and life make a church. This church building is worth the effort that has gone into it only if it is a means of deepening our faith, quickening our consciences, and enriching our fellowship.

May this church building call us out of the Ur of Chaldees, out of the stodginess of established patterns, out of the peril of complacency, out of the blight of mediocrity, out of the hardness of insensitivity, out of the shallowness and insecurity of no faith to the city that hath foundations, whose builder and maker is God!

"Who Is This Man?"
March 27, 1955

First Presbyterian Church, Auburn, Alabama

Let us suppose that a man from Mars suddenly plummeted into our midst. And let us suppose further that he had sufficient command of our language to converse with us, but that he was without sufficient knowledge of our tradition, our outlook on life, to understand fully the meaning of our words. And let us suppose he should ask us what we are doing.

The answers would be varied, but sooner or later any answer would make mention of Jesus Christ. We are here because of some relationship to him. He has an importance for us that requires us to lay aside our usual tasks and gather here in his name. But who is Jesus Christ?

What would you say to the man from Mars or to anyone who should ask you, "Who is this man, Jesus of Nazareth?"

It is a great pivotal question. On it hinges the destiny of individuals and of great societies. Who is this man who lived at a particular time and place on this planet that men and women should find in him the clue to the mystery of their own existence and of the world in which they live?

To be sure, many never ask the question. Some simply do not bother. Others assume that it has been answered. Yet the question remains. Every time we gaze into the heavens at night, or search the depths of the human heart, or look into the face of death, questions are raised that people claim to find answered in him.

I

Who is he?

Let us begin where the first followers of Jesus began—with the man, Jesus of Nazareth. There can be no serious doubt that upon this Earth a man named Jesus lived in an eastern province of the Roman Empire and was put to death by Pontius Pilate. To be sure, if one wishes to be a thoroughgoing skeptic, no absolute proof beyond living memory exists for any historical event. Yet it is little short of ridiculous to suppose that Julius Caesar or Napoleon or George Washington never lived. Only a man on the lunatic fringe of society would seriously deny that once almost two thousand years ago there lived a man named Jesus.

The only history that we have of his life makes very clear that he was, as the creeds say, truly man. He was born of a woman. He grew in knowledge and in body. In common with other men he ate and slept. He grew weary and rested by the side of the road. He prayed. He wept when his friend died. He knew the meaning of joy. He experienced tensions and suffered great anguish. Finally he was crucified and buried. There is no doubt that he was truly man. None of his contemporaries ever questioned his humanity.

We can begin by saying that Jesus was a man like us, living in a particular time and place, subject to the limitations of humanity. All of this any competent historian can certify.

II

But once we have said that he was a man like any of us, we have to go a step further and say the very opposite. He was a man unlike us in at least three ways.

First of all, he differed from us in the quality of his life. According to the New Testament, he was tempted in all points as we are, yet without sin. Certainly he was tempted. The temptation stories are too vivid to leave any doubt. The tension and the anguish that he experienced during his ministry reveal the struggle of faith. Yet nowhere in the record of his life do we find any intimation that he regretted any of his words or deeds, any vain wishing that he had acted some other way. A spiritually callous man is expected to have few regrets, but Jesus was not calloused. Moreover, his disciples found that his words were confirmed by his life, else they would not have followed him.

We say that he was sinless, but the word is beyond our experience. We do not really know what it means. Only a sinless man could know its meaning. If we are to know, it must be revealed to us from beyond. What standard do we have that is adequate for a final judgment on this man? Yet Jesus confronts us with a manner of life that compels us to say with Peter, "Depart from me, for I am a sinful man, O Lord" (Luke 5:8). Christlike is the highest adjective we know. Sinless is the tribute we pay to a life that overwhelms us with its sheer goodness.

Yet sinless is an anemic, negative word. Jesus' life was not simply without sin. His life was possessed by a positive goodness that sets him apart from other men. As Emil Brunner puts it,

> His life flows on harmoniously in an unbroken series of acts, in which, in Holy Love, in free obedience to God, He does and says what only a man could do and say whose will is wholly surrendered to the will of God. . . . We know of no other man in whose life sin plays no part, whose life is pure and unstained, reflecting the holy love of God; who therefore, without hypocrisy or self-assertion could come forth to meet man as One coming from God.[1]

He was a man like us—and yet so unlike us in the sheer goodness of his life.

This man, Jesus of Nazareth, was unlike us in a second way: his mighty works. The miracles have been a stumbling block to many modern persons whose outlook on life has no place for the miraculous, to whom the world is a closed system of cause and effect. Miracles simply do not happen. Yet the fact remains that the story of the mighty works is inextricably mixed up with the record of Jesus' life. Fully 31 percent of Mark, the earliest Gospel, is devoted to them. These mighty works were reported by people who knew nothing of modern science. We might have reported them differently. Yet the fact remains that those who were Jesus' contemporaries, both friend and foe, marveled at his mighty works.

What we do with the mighty works depends finally upon our view of the universe and on our estimate of Jesus. If we insist on believing that the universe is just iron and concrete, we shall go on insisting that mighty works are only illusions. But if we believe that Personality finally rules this universe, then miracles become possible; and if that Personality is love, then miracles become probable. In any case the mighty works cannot be removed from the record of Jesus' life. Those who seek to remove them from the record have no record left. As the record stands, they set him apart from other men.

Jesus is also set apart from other men by the authority that he claimed for himself. He spoke of himself as no ordinary man can. Yet we search in vain for some title that is adequate for him. He was given many titles:

---

[1]Emil Brunner, *The Christian Doctrine of Creation and Redemption* (Philadelphia: Westminster Press, 1952), 324–25.

master, teacher, prophet, messiah. Yet none is adequate. He was master, but more. He was prophet, but more. He was teacher, but more. He was messiah. Yet he was not the messiah, for he was not the messiah the people expected. His authority was greater than any king's or prophet's to lead the people of God. His words astonish us, for he speaks not as any man.

"My son, your sins are forgiven" (Mark 2:5).

"So everyone who acknowledges me before men, I will also acknowledge before my Father who is in heaven" (Matt. 10:32).

"Come to me, all who labor and are heavy laden, and I will give you rest" (Matt. 11:28).

"You have heard that it was said . . . but I say to you . . ." (Matt. 5:38, 39).

"I have come not to abolish them but to fulfil them" (Matt. 5:17).

"I came not to call the righteous, but sinners" (Mark 2:17).

"I came to cast fire upon the earth" (Luke 12:49).

At the beginning of his ministry Jesus read a great passage of scripture from Isaiah and announced that this scripture had now been fulfilled. He ended his ministry with the remarkable words of the Last Supper: "This is my body. . . . this is my blood of the covenant, which is poured out for many for the forgiveness of sins" (Matt. 26:26–28).

We began by saying that Jesus was a man like any of us. Then we said the very opposite. He is unlike any of us in three ways: in the goodness of his life, in his mighty works, and in the authority that he claimed for himself. Competent historians will certify that there once lived a man like us named Jesus. And the competent historian will also certify that he lived a most remarkable life, that many of his contemporaries knew him as a good man who did mighty works and who made unusual claims for himself.

III

We still face the question, *Who is this man?* The old Scottish professor, "Rabbi" Duncan, stated the options very clearly I think: "Christ either deceived mankind by conscious fraud, or he was himself deluded, or he was divine. There is no getting out of this trilemma."

None of Jesus' contemporaries ever accused him of conscious fraud. His disciples believed him to be genuine. It is simply incredible that one who loved as he did and who was crucified for his convictions perpetrated a gigantic hoax on mankind.

Some did say that he was beside himself. Even his friends doubted his sanity once. And people have said it of his followers ever since. Festus said it of Paul. And others said it of Francis Assisi, of William Carey, and of Albert Schweitzer. But the lives of these men belie the verdict, as did the life of Jesus. Sinclair Lewis once wrote of a man who had as his project the organizing of a "Society for the Promotion of Madness Among the Respectable Classes." Perhaps it would not be a bad idea.

There is another answer to the question, Who is this man? It is the answer of Peter, "Thou are the Christ" (Mark 8:29). It is the answer of Thomas, "My Lord and my God" (John 20:28). He who *speaks* through the words and *acts* through the deeds and *makes himself* known in the suffering and death of Jesus is none other than the eternal God. This man is God spelled out in a human life and the destiny that is its end.

These answers of Peter and Thomas were more than mental assent to a proposition about Jesus. It was the decision to stake life and death upon what this man said and did. It was "soul-trust for time and eternity."

But someone asks, Why did Peter and Thomas do this? Why were they willing to risk their lives on this man? The answer is simply that he came to them as one from God. And they accepted him. It was very simple, yet very profound. What authority could be compelling save the sheer fact of his life? As no rational argument, no human tribunal compels human friendship and love, so this faith is no conclusion to an argument. It is the venture of life.

Yet it was no irrational venture. It was undergirded by two facts. The first was the experience of the resurrection. If the cross had been the end of Jesus, then his life would have been an enigma. There would have been no guarantee that God spoke and acted through him. Indeed there would have been compelling evidence that no matter how wonderful his life may have been, he was just a man like us and, more than that, he was a badly mistaken man. This was the disciples' conclusion when in discouragement they went back to their fishing nets. Then Jesus appeared to them. God had raised him from the dead. In the light of the resurrection his life became intelligible.

A second fact that supported the disciples' faith was their own experience. This venture of faith that staked life and death upon Jesus Christ authenticated itself in daily life. It gave meaning and illumination to life. It made sense of what had been a mystery. It gave comfort in place of despair, and purpose in place of aimlessness. As Abert Schweitzer put it,

"To those who obey Him, whether they be wise or simple, He will reveal Himself in the toils, the conflicts, the sufferings which they pass through in His fellowship, and, as an ineffable mystery, they shall learn in their own experience Who He Is."

* * *

So in answer to the man from Mars, we would tell him of the good news that has come into the world of concrete and steel, of great galaxies and millions of light years, of birth and death, of joy and sorrow. The God who made it all and who sustains it by his power has spoken a message of love and redemption in the life and death and resurrection of Jesus Christ.

If the man from Mars had not heard this message of good news about his universe and ours, we would invite him, as we invite all of our neighbors, to share it with us.

"Who Am I?"
April 17, 1955

First Presbyterian Church, Auburn, Alabama

If a stranger were to stop you on Toomer's Corner tomorrow and ask you who you are, what would you say? Presumably you would tell him your name, if you thought he had any right to know. But let us suppose that this stranger is a persistent man who reminds you that a name is just a cipher, a tag to identify you. So he asks again, Who are you? If you were not in a hurry, you might say that you are a professor, a student, a business man, a white man, an American, or any number of other things, as the case might be.

But let us suppose that the stranger still persists with his question, Who is man, any man? What would you say?

I

Someone may object, Why bother with the question anyway? You can go on being a man without knowing who a man is. This is what most people do.

So let us note that the question is important. In the first place it has a significant influence on the way we act. If we think we are just animals, however complicated, we shall sooner or later act as though appetite and force alone matter. But if we think there is some nobility in us, we shall act nobly, at least some of the time. G. K. Chesterton is said to have remarked that you do not slap a crocodile on the back after he has eaten a man and say, "Be a crocodile." But you do slap a man on the back when he has had too much to drink and say, "Be a man."

Furthermore, the answer that we give to this question influences the way we treat our neighbors. If our neighbor is simply dust, then we shall not likely think that he is worth very much unless he serves our own purposes. Who is man that I should bother about him, or who am I that I should expect men to treat me the way I do?

The importance of this question becomes clearer when we realize that the ideas and movements that have shaped our modern world have all been answers to it. Who is man? Darwin, Freud, Marx, and Nietzsche replied to this question. Communism, fascism, capitalism, and democracy are based upon beliefs about human nature.

II

Let us note that a variety of answers is being given to this question in any American community today.

Some say that a person is just a child of nature. Human life is a product of natural forces. Bertrand Russell wrote that a person is simply an "accidental collocation of atoms," a product of forces "with no prevision of the end." As far as can be seen, there is no purpose, no plan, no intelligence, certainly no love motivating those forces that brought him into being. Russell, who has an eminent place among modern philosophers, declares, "No one can adduce any good evidence that cosmic processes have any purpose whatever." So he concludes, "The earth is a minor star which is one of many millions of stars in a galaxy which is one of many million galaxies. Even within the life of our own planet man is only a brief interlude. . . . Man, even if he does not commit scientific suicide, will perish ultimately through failure of water or air or warmth. It is difficult to believe that Omnipotence needed so vast a setting for so small a result."[1] So according to one view current in our time, human beings are children of nature with no purpose behind them and no goal in front of them.

Others think of a person primarily as an economic animal. Karl Marx spelled out the theory. But you hear it very plainly and crudely stated when it is said that a man has his price.

Some define man in terms of sex. This definition is associated, somewhat inaccurately, with Freud, whose studies emphasized the role of sex in life. The popular version, as seen in advertisements on billboards and in slick paper magazines, as portrayed in many a Hollywood movie and in countless cheap novels, declares that man is primarily a sexual animal.

Others say that man is best understood in terms of the will to power.

[1]Bertrand Russell, "The Faith of a Moralist," in *On God and Religion*, ed. Scekel (Buffalo: Prometheus Books, 1989), 89.

Nietzsche incorporated this in his answer to the question. But again a common version expresses itself in the ordinary shuffle of life when men act as if might makes right.

Another popular belief about man is that he is a machine. He is like a jukebox. Instead of inserting a nickel, a stimulus of some kind raises a question and the machine plays its piece (See Fitch, *Preface to Ethical Living*). Most people would insist that this theory greatly oversimplifies the facts of experience, but no one can deny the influence of this doctrine.

Amid the medley of modern opinions, who do you say that man is? Who do you say that you are?

III

What does Christian faith say? It does not deny that the current definitions of human nature contain significant truth, but it does insist that none of them does justice to the complexity and uniqueness of his nature. Any Christian interpretation would include at least six affirmations.

First, man is a *child of God*. The most frequent name that Jesus used for God was Father. He interpreted the kingdom of God in terms of the family. No other symbol in our language conveys the meaning so well. We are children of our heavenly Father. In his life are embodied the purposes of the eternal God.

In this view, a purpose in the cosmic forces supports human life—the will of a heavenly Father. In this day of anonymity, when people are known by numbers, the church insists that the child's name be given in baptism. Rightly so, for God knows the child by name. He gives to each person an inalienable identity.

To be sure, we are a part of nature. The body is subject to the laws of chemistry. Medicines can put us to sleep or cure our pneumonia. We grow weary. We get hungry. Finally we die. Yet we are not simply nature. Our life has been willed by God.

When we say that a human being is a child of God, justice is done to his *uniqueness*. Those who insist that a person is just a product of natural forces have to admit that we are a most remarkable product. We fashion tools, invent languages, and create cultures as no other animal does. We distinguish between the ugly and the beautiful, between the true and false, between good and evil. As a product of nature, a human being is a most remarkable product.

Man's uniqueness has been defined by some in terms of reason. The mind of man is surely the most remarkable thing in all the earth, except a life motivated by love. Somehow in the history of the universe there emerged the human mind with the power of memory, with the capacity for conceptual thinking, with the power of analysis. Moreover, the mind has a remarkable ability to read the facts of the universe. The laws that govern its operation so correspond with the structure of the world that a man can calculate and predict within limits the behavior of the universe. The most significant recent advances in science, we are told, have not been the result of observation of data but of theoretical study.

The more you identify mind with nature, the more nature calls for explanation. Is it credible that the mind should have just happened? (Cf. William Temple: *Nature, Man and God.*) Is it not far more simple and more believable to say that mind appeared because God called it forth?

Man's uniqueness has also been defined, as Reinhold Niebuhr does (*The Self and the Dramas of History*), in terms of the power of dialogue. Man carries on a dialogue with himself, his neighbor, and God. So far as we know, man alone of the creatures can talk with himself. He can step out of his life, so to speak, and bring his whole existence under scrutiny. He can praise or blame. He can defend or excuse himself. This dialogue that man carries on within himself is the most meaningful of all his speaking. The novelist, when wishing to reveal the depths of a man's life, pretends to be privy to what he says to himself.

Man also has the capacity for meaningful community life. He can talk with his neighbor. He can establish intimate friendships and give himself in love. He can live a shared life, participating in the faith, the commitments, and the fellowship of a community. No animal, so far as we know, has this capacity to live a shared life.

Man likewise has the capacity for dialogue with God. Some thoroughgoing naturalist may protest that man only thinks he talks with God. Still it is a most remarkable fact that men have thought they talked with God from the very beginning. And certainly it is a unique fact that man has a yearning for God that no earthly thing can ever satisfy.

Man's uniqueness may also be defined in terms of a felt sense of responsibility. Man knows that he is under obligation. "He is haunted by norms to which, often in contradiction of present desire, he tries to measure up. His animality is shot through with felt responsibility. . . . His being is haunted by what seems a perpetual summons from beyond every present moment" (Reinhold Nieburh, *The Self and the Dramas of History*). Someone may protest that his sense of obligation is simply the pressure of the community, but what of the obligation that summons in defiance of the social pressure?

Man is unique in the power of his mind; in his capacity for dialogue with himself, with his neighbor, and with God; and in his sense of obligation and responsibility. All of this uniqueness, so difficult to account for on any other basis, becomes wholly credible when we say that man is a child of his Father in heaven.

Christian faith declares in the second place that every man is of *exceptional worth*. We have talked very casually in our democratic culture about the sacredness of personality, as though it were a self-evident truth. The brutality of our time should cause us to ask why man's personality is sacred. Plainly in many situations when a man no longer serves the interests of the dominant individual or group, he is discriminated against or liquidated. If man is simply the product of impersonal and blind forces, what value does he have as a man?

But if man is a child of God, he has rights that no man has the authority to violate. They are inalienable because they have been given to him by his Creator. Jesus declared that man is more important than institutions: "The sabbath was made for man, not man for the sabbath" (Mark 2:27). He is more important than animals: "You are of more value than many sparrows" (Matt. 10:31). He is more important than all the wealth of the world. Jesus saw unrealized possibilities of greatness even in the woman taken in adultery.

A third Christian affirmation about man is that he is a *brother* to all other men. Martin Buber, the distinguished Jewish philosopher of this day, has said that real life is meeting. This definition of life, as J. H. Oldham has pointed out, can be trivialized to mean no more than a tea party or a card game. But in its rightful context it is profoundly true. Real life is meeting. Only in community with other persons can a man develop those unique capacities such as language that establish his individuality and his personality. The deepest and most significant of all human experiences is love. Nothing else—intelligence, accumulation of wealth, or status in the social or professional hierarchy—so reveals man's true nature. According to the Christian understanding, "Man is as he loves."

The New Testament makes very clear that the test of sonship is brotherliness. No man can have God as his father unless he is a brother to his fellow man. In his description of the judgment, Jesus pictures sin as unbrotherliness—the rich man who daily ignored Lazarus; the indifferent who fail to recognize Christ in the disguise of the prisoner, the hungry, the thirsty, and the naked. God made man to be a brother.

The fourth affirmation of Christian faith is that man is a *sinner*. Something has gone wrong. Men refuse to live according to the destiny for which they were made. There has been a rebellion and the consequences are far-reaching. Men do not trust God as a father but frantically attempt to build some security of their own as protection against life's precariousness. They do not live in community as brothers but as anarchic centers of self-interest and egotism. Everywhere they now find that being good is like going uphill and following evil impulses is like going downhill. Moreover, the problem is not simply an individual concern. For men are involved in a sinful society that confronts them with choices, not between good and evil, but between the more or less evil.

The fifth affirmation that Christian faith makes is that man who is broken by sin *can be made whole again in Christ*. There are divine resources that can redeem. Despair of man must not become despair of God. Thomas Hobbes once said that without state control, the life of man would be solitary, poor, nasty, brutish, short. It is not strange, says John Whale, that Hobbes was accused of atheism.

The sixth affirmation of Christian faith is that man's life finds *completion beyond death*. Man's end is not dust and ashes. The God who gave man life has power over death—a power that he has demonstrated in raising Jesus Christ from the dead. We do not know what the resurrection of the body may mean. But surely it does mean that life which is lived in trust and hope shall be brought to fulfillment beyond the grave.

The Bible speaks of the blotting out of one's name: the complete extinction of identity as the final tragedy. The great promise is, "I will not blot his name out of the book of life" (Rev. 3:5). God guarantees the permanence of man's identity.

* * *

Who is man? The question is unavoidable. And today it stands behind the conflict of ideologies, the struggle between nations, and the cleavages in society. It also intrudes itself into such personal concerns as the choice of a vocation, the decision to marry, the way money is spent, and the manner in which treatment is meted out to neighbors.

The options are not many. Some say that man is just an animal, albeit a skillful animal. Some say that he is the product of forces with no prevision of their end, an accident in the history of the universe. But others say that he is a child of God and that it does not yet appear what he shall be. It is our conviction as Christian people that this faith does more justice to the facts of experience and makes more sense out of our life than any other.

"When Silence Is Treason"
October 13, 1957

First Presbyterian Church, Auburn, Alabama

Once when Jesus was under attack, he confronted his friends and his enemies with a demand for a clear-cut decision: "He that is not with me is against me, and he that gathereth not with me scattereth abroad" (Matt. 12:30). Thus Jesus declared that the lines are drawn. But on another occasion in his ministry, Jesus seemed to modify this demand for decision. When his disciples were disturbed by a stranger who claimed their master's name, he cautioned them, "He that is not against us is for us" (Luke 9:50).

How are we to put together these seemingly contradictory statements? "He that is not with me is against me." "He that is not against us is for us." They appear irreconcilable, and yet they are both true. For they were spoken in different situations, and each statement is true in its particular context. In one situation, Jesus was a popular leader. In the other, he was under attack and criticism.

I

Let us look for a moment at the statement "He that is *not* against me is *for* me." The occasion for this pronouncement was the protest of the disciples that they had seen a stranger casting out devils in the name of Christ. And they forbade him to do so. Jesus rebuked them and refused to join with them in their demand that the man stop. He took it for granted that the stranger was for him.

These words of Jesus are a warning against a bitter sort of pessimism that destroys a person's usefulness to society and takes all joy out of life. I suppose everyone here is familiar with the type of person who is against

49

everything before knowing what it is and who is suspicious of everybody even before knowing who they are. Such people build walls around themselves and shut other people out.

This narrow, exclusive spirit that seems to enjoy pessimism has no justification in the words of Jesus. Jesus was open to goodness wherever he found it. He looked under or beyond labels to the realities of the human heart and life. He judged a man by his actions, his attitude, and his spirit. Jesus rejoiced wherever he found true goodness.

There are situations in which we ought to take for granted the goodness of our fellow man. We simply assume, under normal circumstances, that a man loves his wife and that a father cherishes his son. If a man finds it necessary to make public declarations of his love for his wife, then we rightly suspect that he does not love her very much. There are occasions when it is only vulgar immodesty to parade one's loyalties and reveal one's deepest faith.

In every area of life there are situations when silence means loyalty and professions simply raise doubts. Preoccupation with loyalty oaths is always a symptom of a sick society. There are, to be sure, occasions where loyalty oaths are necessary; but when small-minded men, under guise of protecting society or in search of political gain, try to cut everybody down to their own size, they only aggravate the illness. The newspapers of the past week have indicated that irresponsible suspicion of scientists may have done incalculable harm to our own nation.

"He that is not against me is for me." This word of Jesus, which was spoken in an hour of popularity, is true. It is a reminder that there are situations in which silence can mean loyalty, and it is a warning against a narrow, mean, and pessimistic spirit that looks for a devil behind every bush.

II

Let us come a step further now and note that there are situations in which silence is treason. "He that is *not for* me is *against me.*" When Jesus said this, he was no longer the popular hero. His opposition was sullen and mean. He could not take for granted that those who were silent were for him. A crisis had arisen which demanded that every man show his colors. So Jesus put the issue very bluntly and very simply: "If you are not for me, you are against me."

There is abundant evidence that the common practice in our day is the very opposite of these commands of Jesus. The newspaper headlines make it clear that a popular cause or leader does not lack for followers who are eager to make their support a matter of public record. They also make it clear that few people in public life have the courage to give their support to a cause simply because it is right. Recent studies of American life such as the *Organization Man* and *The Lonely Crowd* indicate that individual integrity is being destroyed by the terrific pressures in our society toward mass conformity. The face of the individual is lost in the face of the crowd. Increasingly in America, we speak when it is unnecessary and we are silent when we ought to speak.

III

Let us apply this more specifically to life in our times by noting that some of the values that formerly we took for granted are today in question. We live in an age when it is becoming increasingly necessary for Christian people to take a stand for certain elemental virtues that are part of our Christian and cultural heritage.

I suppose every age believes that its own day is unique, but surely this is true of ours. More changes have taken place in our world since 1914 than in any comparable period in universal history. And the end is not yet in sight. None of us dares to predict what life is going to be like even ten years from now. In such a day we are called upon to live and bear witness.

There was a time when we could assume that people believed in freedom of speech and freedom of religion. But this is no longer the case. There is a sullen and mean spirit abroad today that seeks by threats, intimidation, and violence to coerce men and women into conformity with the party line. It would be a tragic affair if we who have criticized the brainwashing of the communists should in the practical affair of everyday life deny to men and women the right to think according to their best conscience, to speak what they think, and to worship God according to the convictions of their hearts.

We have created in America an atmosphere in which the life of the mind is suspect. Walter Lippmann wrote last week that our safety as a nation is menaced by "popular disrespect for, and even suspicion of, brains and originality of thought." In other countries, in Germany and in most of Europe and Russia, it is an honor, universally recognized, to be a professor. Here the person who cherishes the life of the mind is put on the defensive, requiring him to show that he is not a highbrow and that he is not subversive. . . . The damage that has been done is very great.

There is a prudential reason that men of goodwill should speak out for freedom of religion in this day. According to an old adage, when you fight a monster, beware lest you become like him. In opposing a tyranny such as communism, there is the danger that we ourselves shall become the victims of its spirit. There is for us, however, more than prudential warrant for our support of freedom of speech, freedom of thought, and freedom of worship. As Christians, we speak for these freedoms in obedience to a divine command. It is the conviction of our faith that this freedom belongs to the inalienable dignity of a child of God.

There was a time when we could safely assume that people believed in the dignity of the human person, in the sanctity of a man as a child of God. This is no longer true. Communism tells us that a man has worth only if he is a communist. Hitler told us that a man was of worth only if he was of the Aryan race. Can we say that we believe that a man who does not belong to our group has an inalienable dignity that must not be violated by slanderous word or violent deed? In our best moments we know the dignity of the human person. But must we not confess that we are tempted in these days to deny the real dignity of a child of God to a man who does not belong to our group?

We live in a difficult time, when little-minded politicians, whether they are running for governor of Alabama or for Congress in Harlem, have sought to distort facts and to confront us with false alternatives. According to the politicians, you have to be either for the White man or against him, either for the Negro or against him. For the Christian this is not the issue. As Christians we are primarily concerned neither with integration nor with segregation, but with the reconciliation of men to God and to one another as members of the family of God. This is the real issue, the issue upon which hangs the destiny of our souls.

The real issue in our world today is between those who respect a man as a child of God and those who do not, between those who are humane and those who are brutal. It is not to be found between men who are for or against this cause or that cause; this group or that group; this or that sectional, national, or even international interest; but between those whose highest loyalty belongs to God, as best they know his will, and those whose highest loyalty belongs to some earthly concern.

As Christian people, we all believe that our highest loyalty belongs to God and that there belongs to everyone the inalienable dignity of a child of God. In this we all believe. The time has now come for us to stand up and say so when we drink cups of coffee or when we talk upon the street corners, to say so when we hear our friends and neighbors say things upon which we know the blessings of Christ cannot rest.

* * *

There comes a time when as Jesus said, "He who is not with me is against me." That time is now. The real hope that the world of tomorrow will be the kind of world we want our children to live in is not to be found among the selfish and irresponsible politicians who use man's inhumanity to man as a means of personal gain. The hope that there will be a decent world for our children rests with ordinary people who fear God, read their Bibles, say their prayers, and who gather on Sunday morning to acknowledge that their highest loyalty belongs to God, and that in obedience to him they must love their neighbors as themselves.

"The Salt of the Earth and the Light of the World"
September 2, 1962

Christian Action Conference, Montreat, North Carolina

From earliest childhood we remember the words "For God so loved the world, that he gave his only begotten son" (John 3:16). God loves the world. Even when he quarrels with it, it is, as Robert Frost would say, a lover's quarrel. And this is the reason we are here today in this Christian Action Conference. We too love the world because it is God's world— because God loves it. When we quarrel with it, with its falsehood, its brutality, its selfishness, we love it. We quarrel with it because we love it; for we remember the world as God made it, and we hope for the world that which by God's grace it may become again. We are responsible for the world because it is God's world, because he loves it, and because we are the servants of God.

I

The responsibility that we have for the world has its warrant in the words of Jesus to his disciples, which are our text: "Ye are the salt of the earth." "Ye are the light of the world." These words make clear that the followers of Jesus have a ministry to the world, a mission to fulfill, work to do. Nowhere does Jesus or the New Testament provide a blueprint for this ministry. Indeed, any such blueprint is impossible, for the Christian witness is radically historical. Jesus does not call men in general to be his disciples. He calls particular men living in a particular time and in a particular space. The obedience that he demands is a particular obedience. He does not ask of us the obedience of men who lived under Roman domination in the first century, but the obedience of Americans living in the twentieth century with freedom to influence significantly the social, economic, and political affairs of the communities in which they live. Jesus calls us to be the salt of the earth and the light of the world in a way that is appropriate to the situation in which we have been placed by the providence of God.

Nevertheless, the words "salt" and "light" suggest something of the ministry that we have as Christian people. Salt very obviously has a twofold function. On the one hand, it gives taste to food, and on the other, it preserves food. To be the salt of the earth is to give tone to life. For many people life, like salt, has lost its savor and has become insipid. As one modern man put it, "Life must go on, I forget just why." Or as A. E. Housman wrote,

> Yonder see the morning blink
> The sun is up, and up must I
> To wash and dress and eat and drink
> And look at things and talk and think
> And God knows why.

But the tonic of Christian faith is the conviction that God wants us to be here and he put us here and gave us work to do.

Life today is also threatened by corrosion and decay. We do not know whether there will be anything left of us personally or of society collectively when the petty hates and prejudices and bitternesses of life have wreaked their toll and the final word in man's knowledge in atomic matters has been spoken. But Christians know that whereas evil is always in the end self-destructive, love endures. They know that God is able to keep that which has been committed unto him against that day. For this reason an early Christian wrote, "Christians are folk who hold the world together" (*Epistle to Diognetus*).

Light attracts attention and dispels darkness. A city set on a hill cannot be hid. Moreover, the purpose of light is to attract attention. We do not light candles and put them under a bushel. The disciples are to be the light of the world that men seeing their good works may glorify their father who is in heaven. Now certainly there is no guarantee that when the light of faith shines before men, they will glorify God. They may try to put the light out. Nevertheless, one of the facts of history is that the life of the Christian community has frequently transformed the larger community and has won from it a grudging respect. Even when Julian was trying to restore paganism in the fourth-century Roman empire, he had to explain, "These godless Galileans feed not only their own poor but ours; our poor lack care."

II

Historically we stand in the tradition that has taken very seriously the command to be the salt of the earth and the light of the world. Calvinists have never been satisfied simply to go to church, to read the Bible, to say their prayers, as important as these things may be. They have always believed that they were the soldiers of the Lord in conquest of the world, the flesh, and the devil, and that it was their high calling to take the world captive to Christ. The doctrine of predestination, as Eustace Percy has pointed out, gave men a new energy and sense of purpose and mission. For they had been elected not simply to the ultimate destiny of heaven, but to the service of God in this particular time and space. The elect had been called to a work. They were to be the means for the working out of the eternal purposes of the sovereign God in history and space. For this reason the Roman Catholic historian Christopher Dawson has observed that Calvinists are unique in their power to shape culture and to influence the direction of human history.

John Calvin was concerned not simply that individuals in Geneva should be saved but that Geneva should be a Christian community. Likewise his followers sought to make Scotland a Christian nation and to build the new Jerusalem in England's green and pleasant land. The Puritans who settled in Massachusetts had gone, as they put it in their sermons, on an errand into the wilderness to establish the model Christian community. John Winthrop, their first governor, thus warned them that their undertaking was no individual matter: "For we must consider that we shall be as a city set on a hill; the eyes of all people are upon us." So Perry Miller, a historian of Puritanism, concludes that the Puritans who came to Massachusetts were an organized task force, executing a flank attack on the corruptions of Christendom.

It is not so clear that we today in the South in the middle of the twentieth century are moved by this passionate faith that the sovereign God has called us to be his servants for the working out of divine purposes. It is not clear that many local congregations consider themselves task forces, amid the economic, political, and social conflicts of our times, for the embodiment of the realities of Christian faith. Historically the vision of Holy Community was replaced by an all-too-exclusive emphasis on personal evangelism, the snatching of a brand from the burning. The understanding of the Christian life as involvement in the working out of the divine purpose in the drama of universal history was replaced by the picture of a Christian on a lonely and solitary pilgrimage through a strange and sinful world. The definition of the Christian as a soldier of God in conquest of the world was replaced by the pietistic definition of a Christian as a person who prays, who goes to church, who does not drink or swear, and who is faithful to one's spouse. Now Christians ought to be concerned to save an individual soul, and they ought to be pious; but no Calvinist can ever be happy when he gives up responsibility to take the world captive to Christ, when life becomes nothing more than a pious and lonely pilgrimage through this world that God made and that God loves and that by God's grace can be restored.

Now, admittedly, our situation is different. We live in what some call a post-Protestant world. Some even speak of a post-Christian civilization, by which they mean in part that specifically Christian demands are no longer acceptable to the total community. Moreover, the local congregation is no longer defined as a geographical parish in which that congregation has responsibility for a particular community, but as a congregation of believers gathered from here, there, and yonder. Admittedly we are a gathered and voluntary church in a free and pluralistic society. But we ought to remember that the only real power that Calvin ever had in Geneva was the power of a Christian personality and the power of the preached word to create a godly public opinion. We too have the power of the word when it is honestly, authentically, and forthrightly preached. Is it too much to hope that the church should be something more than another amiable society? That it should be the people of God whose life and witness must be taken seriously by the politicians at the courthouse or city hall, or by the White Citizens' Councils and Ku Klux Klan? Is it too much to hope that there are and will be some communities in the South in which some things happen and some things do not happen in race relations or in the city hall simply because there is a Presbyterian church in the community? One of the most authentic tests of the integrity of a local congregation is the seriousness with which it is taken by corrupt politicians—by brutal men who prey like vultures upon all those who cannot defend themselves. Is it too much to hope that some Presbyterian churches in our South will be the salt of the earth to save it from corruption and destruction and the light of the world to guide a confused people?

III

And now to bring this matter of being salt and light to more specific focus, let us note four areas of our common life that desperately need the salt and light of Christian faith. The first has to do with the disintegration of marriage. There was a time when, under the influence of Christian faith, monogamous marriage was the accepted community standard. Today serial polygamy is increasingly the accepted standard of our life, even among church people. Not infrequently when young people marry they regard divorce as a live option from the beginning. We need today within the church a recovery of the conviction that Christians should marry in the Lord and that marriage is between one man and one woman for life.

The second area is the disintegration of personal life as it comes to expression in the use of alcoholic beverages. At least ten million people are in serious trouble because of their drinking. In addition, drinking takes its toll in murder on the highways, in the breakup of home life, and in the loss of efficiency in daily work. Surely Christian people have an obligation to think through anew the meaning of the command to love one's neighbor as it relates to social drinking. In view of the fact that the only cure for the alcoholic is total abstinence and in view of the fact that a certain percentage of social drinkers always become alcoholics, we need to emphasize the fact that no Christian can in obedience to God be a party to a situation that places a person under social pressure to drink alcoholic beverages.

A third area in which we witness disintegration is international relations and the threat of nuclear war. Here we face economic, political, and social issues of overwhelming complexity. Yet the complexity of the situation must not be allowed to silence the church. The possibility of nuclear war raises ethical and spiritual issues as no other problem in our time.

A fourth illustration of the disintegration of life is found in the separation of man from man, the brutal inhumanity of man to man, as it comes to expression in the racial conflicts of our day. Whenever racial conflicts enter the church, the ethical issue is always complicated by issues of heresy and apostasy. We have always said that the church exists where the Word is rightly preached and the sacraments rightly administered. A serious question is raised as to the right preaching of the Word and the right administration of the sacraments whenever any man presumes to make race a requirement for hearing the Word preached and receiving the bread and wine.

In divorce, in the use of alcoholic beverages, in the threat of nuclear war, in racial conflicts, we see four vivid illustrations of the disintegration of life in our time. And in these areas that threaten our common life, we have to confess that the salt of the Christian community's proclamation and practice is in danger of becoming insipid and the light of the Christian community's life sometimes burns very dimly.

IV

What shall we do? Certainly none of us can guarantee that we shall be the salt of the earth and the light of the world. Surely the presumption that we are the salt of the earth and the light of the world is replete with dangers of spiritual death. But we can do some things; and if we do them, there is more likelihood that we shall be the salt of the earth and the light of the world.

1. The first is the acquisition of technical knowledge. We ought to be informed about the facts. We are under a moral and Christian obligation to know the South in which our church is set. Christian action calls for sound and knowledgeable minds as well as good hearts. As life becomes increasingly complicated, knowledge of facts becomes indispensable to Christian strategy and decision. As yet, no agency in our church is adequately equipped to provide Christian people with the technical facts that they need to live as Christians amid the social, economic, political, and racial affairs of the South. We have not yet employed professionally trained experts in such fields as rural sociology, industrial society, and the problems of the inner city and urban life. Yet the day has arrived when without this kind of knowledge we shall be severely crippled in the making of responsible Christian decisions.

2. We can become theologians, that is, Christian theologians. Every person is a theologian. We decide every day whether we are going to tell the truth or how we are going to treat our neighbors in the light of some theology. The Christian is the person who has learned to make the public and private decisions of life in the light of the life, death, resurrection, and ascension of Jesus Christ. Recently someone observed that in a meeting where representatives of various traditions commented on a particular issue, each person identified himself by the perspective. The Anglican referred to the early creeds. The Roman Catholic referred to the church. The Protestant was likely to begin, "Well, I think. . . ." This is the peril. We have fallen into the notion that theology is just what somebody thinks. But the fact is that some things in theology are as definite as two plus two equals four. Until we acquire theological knowledge and the ability to theologize, we are not likely to be able to think as Christians—to make our decisions and to read headlines of the

newspaper in the light of the fact that God has spoken his mind to us in the life, death, and resurrection of Jesus Christ.

3. We can be what we say we are, the church of Jesus Christ. W. A. Visser t'Hooft, the executive secretary of the World Council of Churches, once said that the purpose of the church in our day as in every day is to manifest to the world that the church exists. Nothing is more important for the integrity of the church than the authenticity of its ministry. The calling to be the church demands that we be willing to support such a ministry. To be sure, we would not crucify or behead anyone. We would not even stone a minister. But there is ample evidence that we would explain him away. We would say that his personality was defective, that he lacked tact and skill in personal relations, that he no longer had an effective pastoral ministry. In any case we would reason that the institution must be saved, though such reasoning scarcely has a New Testament basis. We would talk about love when we ought to talk about justice. There is, in sum, sufficient ground for fearing that if an Amos were to appear in our denomination today, he would be explained away by "successful" ministers and "respectable" church members. The Confession of Faith puts this matter very quaintly. It says the church is sometimes more visible, sometimes less visible. As a building, as an organization, the church is always visible. But as the body of Jesus Christ, as the people of God, we have to confess that the church is sometimes more, sometimes less, and sometimes hardly visible at all. Our calling is to be what we say we are, the church of Jesus Christ; and when the church is visible in the midst of us, we shall be in truth the salt of the earth and the light of the world.

"Predestination: What Is It?"
January 24, 1950   July 3, 1966

East Alabama Presbytery   Montreat, North Carolina

Presbyterians are either famous or notorious for their doctrine of predestination. There is some basis for the notoriety and the fame. The Westminster Confession has some very explicit paragraphs on the subject. John Calvin not only devoted lengthy chapters in the *Institutes* to "Predestination," but he also gave many hours of a very busy life to the exposition and defense of the doctrine. Some Calvinists have not hesitated to entertain the possibility that little children were among the damned. It may well be that predestination has come to mean very little for many Presbyterians of this day, but the fact remains that the doctrine is inextricably interwoven in our heritage and in our creeds.

Presbyterianism and predestination rightly belong together. And yet it is worth remembering that we share this doctrine with all Christians. In some form it is a universal Christian doctrine. As Presbyterians, we differ from other Christians only in the fact that we have stated the doctrine more rigorously and placed more emphasis upon it than they. Presbyterians are people who have found special meaning in the doctrine of predestination. Our task tonight is to discover what this meaning is and the practical, everyday implications of the doctrine. Predestination raises a host of theoretical questions, but we shall never be able to deal with the theoretical issues until we know the practical implications. What does predestination mean for everyday life?

I

First of all predestination means that our lives have roots in eternity. As Paul writes in his letter to the Ephesians, God chose us before the

61

foundation of the world and destined us to be his sons. In other words, God thought of us before we were born and elected us to a high and holy destiny. We are here because God willed for us to be (Eph. 1:1–6).

This truth is well illustrated in the sacrament of baptism. I suppose that when I finished seminary, the sacrament of infant baptism had as little practical meaning to me as any in the life of our church. Yet as I shared in the baptism of little children, and as a boy and then a little girl came into our own home, it came to be meaningful indeed. In the sacrament of baptism the child's name is called, indicating that God gives the child a name, that God knows the child by name, that God wills for the child to be. This child did not just happen. Behind his life is the purpose of God. God, not man, guarantees the child's identity and gives to him a dignity that no man dares abuse or take from him.

Almost the worst thing that the Bible can say about any man is that God shall blot out his name, destroy his identity, take from him the dignity of a life that is undergirded by the love and power of God. And, on the other hand, surely one of the greatest declarations that can be made about any man is the assurance that God chose him before the foundation of the world and elected him to be his son.

Now the real significance of these concepts becomes clear when we place over against it the opposite faith that man just happened—an accident, as it were, in the history of the universe. As Bertrand Russell has put it, man is but the accidental collocation of atoms, the product of forces with no prevision of their end, and his destiny is the debris of a universe in ruins. Now someone here tonight may have to believe that his life is just an accident in the history of the universe. But no one can be happy to believe this. As someone has put it, atheism leads not to badness but to an incurable loneliness and despair.

A prominent South American artist, born on a seaport dock of parents whom he never knew, described his origin in this way: a man and a woman came together and an artist came forth. Apart from this faith that God chose us before the foundation of the world there is little more that any of us can say about our origin. Our existence, humanly speaking, is dependent upon biological forces and the accidents of history, some of them casual and some of them trivial.

Arthur Koestler, who was once a communist, has carried on a very brilliant polemic against his former faith through his writing. In his perceptive novel *Darkness at Noon*, a communist defines an individual as a multitude of a million divided by a million. A number and nothing more.

When men are moved by this faith, it is not surprising that there is no respect for the dignity of a man, that liquidations are not murder but political strategy. Nicholas Berdyaev, the Russian philosopher who died in exile in Paris, exclaimed, "Where there is no God, there is no man!"[1] When God is left out of the picture, then a man has value only as he belongs to the right nation or the right party or the right race.

Over against these faiths that are current in our world stands the Christian affirmation, God chose me before the foundation of the world and elected me to a high and holy destiny.

II

Predestination means, in the second place, that God chooses us before we choose him and does for us what we could not do for ourselves. According to the popular idea of religion, man chooses God first. Through moral achievement and spiritual striving man knocks on the door of heaven and asks for admission very much as a man might present himself to an exclusive club, offering as his credentials his bank account and his social status. The Bible insists that God chooses us and does for us what we could not do for ourselves.

The most significant experiences in human life are beyond the power of the human will. To be sure, the human will has a remarkable capacity. It can organize the energies and vitalities of human existence in the pursuit of a freely chosen goal. Man is not at the mercy of impulse and instinct and momentary need as animals are, so far as we know. Man has a will. We ought to use our wills more than we do. But certain depths in human life are beyond the will.

We cannot forget ourselves by trying hard. The more we try to forget ourselves, the more we think about ourselves.

We are not grateful by trying hard. By discipline of will, we can write thank-you notes according to Emily Post. But gratitude is not a product of discipline.

We cannot be humble by trying hard. If a proud man should become humble by trying hard, he would be proud of his humility.

We cannot love by trying hard. To say we *ought* to love comes very near to being a contradiction, for there is a spontaneity about love that is beyond the power of the will.

[1] Nicholas Berdyaev, *The End of Our Time* (New York: Sheed and Ward, 1933), 54.

Now the human predicament, according to Christian faith, is self-centeredness. Man, who ought to be God-centered, is ego-centered. He judges everything by the way it affects the ego—myself, my race, my family, my church, my country. There is no way for a self-centered man to become God-centered by his own efforts. There is no way for a man who loves himself to force himself to love God. This is the basic human predicament.

T. S. Eliot's great play *Murder in the Cathedral*, is a splendid illustration of what I am trying to say. Thomas à Becket had served his king well as chancellor. So when the king wanted control of the church, he appointed Thomas Archbishop of Canterbury. But Thomas became a great archbishop, defending the independence of the church. The controversy that followed between king and archbishop ended with the archbishop's martyrdom. While Thomas waits his execution, Eliot pictures the tempters coming to him.

The first reminded him of the good old days when he and the king were friends, and of the good times that they had on the Thames. But Thomas easily dismissed the tempter. Some sins are effectively cured simply by old age.

Other tempters came to offer the prospect of chancellor's power again or an alignment with barons against the king. But Thomas had expected these tempters, and he rejected their pleas.

The fourth tempter comes unexpectedly. First, he offers the glories of martyrdom, of the pilgrimages to the grave, of the miracles that would there be done.

> Think of the miracles, by God's grace,
> And think of your enemies in another place.

But Thomas had thought of these things too, and he knew that history has a way of exposing martyrs and discarding them. Now the tempter comes with the final thrust:

> Yes, Thomas, you have thought of that too.
> What can compare with the glory of Saints
> Dwelling forever in the presence of God?
> What earthly glory, of king or emperor,
> What earthly pride, that is not poverty
> Compared with richness of heavenly grandeur?
> Seek the way of martyrdom, make yourself the lowest
> On earth, to be high in heaven.

Finally Thomas cries out,

> Is there no way, in my soul sickness,
> Does not lead to damnation in pride?

> Can sinful pride be driven out
> Only by more sinful?

This is the ultimate predicament and the ultimate temptation.

> The last temptation is the greatest treason:
> To do the right deed for the wrong reason.

This is the predicament for which predestination is the answer. Men cease being self-centered and the saints cease making themselves lowest on earth in order to be first in heaven only when something happens to them that draws their attention from themselves, that moves the center of life from self to God.

Our faith is that this is what God has done through the life, death, and resurrection of Jesus Christ. God was in Christ reconciling the world to himself and doing for us what we could not do for ourselves.

The question now arises, how are we to understand this experience in which God in Jesus Christ lays hold of us and changes the center of life from self to God?

We have to think of it in terms of some human analogy, and these analogies are very limited. We have mechanical analogies. A man, for example, drives a nail into a wall. Some people think of predestination in this way, as though man were a thing, a nail to be driven into a wall.

But there are also personal analogies. Since man is a person—and since our faith is that whatever else God may be, he is at least personal—we are most likely to understand predestination rightly when we think of it in terms of personal analogies. John Calvin declared that in this matter of predestination God does not deal with us as sticks or stones but as persons. Augustine once said that a man who never had a friend could never understand faith. Friendship is more like faith than anything else in human experience.

If there is any clue in human experience as to the nature of predestination, it is to be found in the deepest of those experiences—friendship and love. Whenever a person falls in love—that is, if he loves very deeply—there is always something in the life of the person loved that reaches out and elicits love. You simply do not fall in love by making up your mind that you are going to fall in love. There is always something about the person loved that calls forth love. And yet love is called forth in such a way as to do no violence to our own will. We love freely. In fact, we are never so free as when we do the will of the person whom we love. But love can never be explained in terms of our own will. We are elected into love.

In Christopher Fry's play *The Dark Is Light Enough*, the Countess explains why she never fell in love:

> I mean, simply
> It never came about.
> There we have no free will.
> At the one place of experience
> Where we are most at mercy, and where
> The decision will alter us to the end of our days,
> Our destination is fixed.
> We are elected into love.

Predestination means that the love of God in the life, death, and resurrection of Jesus Christ reaches forth and lays hold on us perhaps in the nurture of youth, perhaps in some moment of great joy, or in the face of a decision that lays bare our soul, or in the crisis of death, and calls for a love of God that is not selfishness but true salvation.

III

Predestination also means that we are elected for service. God's elect are not God's favorites but God's servants. John Calvin did not relegate God's sovereignty to the ultimate destinies of heaven and hell. He believed that God's election gives a man something to do here and now in time and space. God's purposes are being worked out in history, and to be elected is to become an instrument of the divine purpose. Whatever else a Calvinist may be, he is convinced that God is using his life to accomplish God's divine purpose in history.

Predestination means that

> God knew us before we were born and chose us for a high and holy destiny.

> God chooses us before we choose him and does for us what we could not do for ourselves.

> We have been called to be the servants of God, the instruments of the divine purpose in history.

Now the mystery of those who reject the love of God is still not solved. Some of our Calvinist forefathers eliminated the mystery by saying quite frankly that God passed over them and left them to their just fate. This solves the mystery, but it is difficult to reconcile with the clear assertion of the New Testament that God desires the salvation of all men and with the revelation of the love of God in Jesus Christ. For this reason many of us prefer to leave as a mystery the problem of those who reject God. We do not know how or why it is that the love of God can be rejected. We do know that when we reject God the cause is within us, and when we turn to God we do so because he first laid hold of us.

Predestination is a doctrine that belongs at the end, not at the beginning, of the Christian life. In writing his systematic theology, Calvin experimented with the location of the doctrine of predestination. In the final edition of the *Institutes* he located it after the doctrine of salvation and just prior to the doctrine of resurrection. This location of the doctrine seems to suggest that the doctrine stands not at the beginning of the Christian life but at the end when the Christian looks back over his Christian experience and exclaims, "This is what God has done in and through my life!" This is the testimony of all the great saints. They have regarded their own lives, insofar as they were good, not as their own achievements, but as the work of God's grace.

As Calvin put it, knowledge of predestination is nothing more than the testimony that we are children of God, that is, of the grace and mercy of God. And in the presence of that grace we can but exclaim, "O the depth of the riches and wisdom and knowledge of God! How unsearchable are his judgments and how inscrutable his ways! 'For who has known the mind of the Lord, or who has been his counselor?' . . . For from him and through him and to him are all things. To him be glory for ever. Amen" (Rom. 11:33–36).

"The Perseverance of the Saints: What Is It?"
October 1965

First Presbyterian Church, Auburn, Alabama

Christians used to argue whether a man who was once saved was always saved. They disputed about the possibility of falling from grace. Today such questions are remote from human experience, and we dismiss them as a peculiarity of a religious age.

The remoteness of these questions underscores our twofold problem. On the one hand, there is the disparity between human experience in the twentieth century and what we have known as Christian faith. When we argue about the death of God, other questions are trivial. Is faith in God after all a possibility? On the other hand, our problem is the meaning of faith itself. What does the faith mean for those who stand within the circle of faith? This morning we shall concern ourselves with this internal problem of faith, in particular with the doctrine that Christians of a previous generation called the perseverance of the saints and with the question about which they debated: If a person is once saved, is he always saved?

The name of the doctrine is unfortunate. *The perseverance of the saints*—the words seem to suggest that the doctrine is saying something about saints and their perseverance. Saints ought to persevere, but the doctrine is about the perseverance of God. This whole matter is stated for us in the words of Paul to the Philippians: "Work out your own salvation with fear and trembling; for God is at work in you, both to will and to work for his good pleasure" (Phil. 2:12–13). Historically and psychologically, salvation is 100 percent a human act. It is something man does himself. But it is also the work of God. This morning our concern is with salvation as God's work. "For God is at work in you, both to will and to work for his good pleasure."

Let us now note three areas of life in which this affirmation from Paul is of fundamental importance for everyday living and experience.

The first is the light that it throws upon the inequities of life. During the dark days of the Depression a widowed mother left hanging by the fireplace a calendar with this inscription:

> Behold, we know not anything;
> I can but trust that good shall fall
> At last—far off—at last, to all,
> As every winter changes to spring.
> (Tennyson, *In Memoriam*)

Now some, especially those who have never known such dark days as the Depression, may dismiss this verse as the romanticism of the nineteenth century. But in my judgment it was more in this home of faith and devotion. It was the expression of the hope and of the conviction that God some day and in some way would overcome the inequities of existence— the hope that this lack of correlation between faith, goodness, trust, and the actualities of life was not the final and permanent state of things.

The inequity of life is a very troublesome problem for those of us who believe in God. *After Auschwitz* is part of the death-of-God literature. The grim brutality of the concentration camp is a reality that must be taken seriously in trying to understand our world. If there is a God, why was he silent while millions of Jews were liquidated? Much of contemporary atheism is rooted in the inequities and the absurdities that we continually discover in human existence.

What did the psalmist mean when he exclaimed,

> A thousand may fall at your side,
>   ten thousand at your right hand;
>   but it will not come near you.
>
> For he will give his angels charge of you
>   to guard you in all your ways.
> On their hands they will bear you up,
>   lest you dash your foot against a stone.
>   (Ps. 91:7, 11–12)

Well, that is in any literal sense not true in Vietnam. It is not true in Alabama. There is no easy correlation between goodness and one's fate in this world. Anyone who has not learned this already from actual experience will learn it some day.

Therefore, we have to set beside the words of the psalmist the words of Jesus: "Do you think that these Galileans were worse sinners than all the other Galileans because they suffered thus? I tell you, No" (Luke 13:2–3). There is no simple correlation between goodness and one's fate in this world.

Of course, in a relative way there is a correlation between goodness and happiness, between faith and one's fate in this world. A person who leads a dissolute life usually suffers the consequence, and goodness has its earthly rewards. But there is no final equalization. There was none for six million victims of Nazi concentration camps, nor for the dead in Vietnam. But the psalmist was unwilling to acquiesce before the rugged facts of existence. He sought to express his conviction that nothing can separate us from the love of God.

Therefore, over against the inequities of life, we put the words of Paul, "For God is at work in you, both to will and to work for his good pleasure." Here is expressed the faith that this lack of correlation between faith and goodness and the actualities of life is not the final state of things, that God is working to fulfill his purposes. We are united by the conviction that the ultimate reality is the God and father of our Lord Jesus Christ who is working his purposes out.

This doctrine is also important in the realm of personal salvation. It has, of course, been the basis of silly arguments about whether a person who is once saved is always saved. But this doctrine is not so much a boast or an argument as it is a confession, a prayer, a hope that once we have known God's grace, we shall never finally lose it.

We can at least say that it is a fact of experience that once a person has stood in the circle of faith, he is always the person who has stood in the circle. The experience is indelible. No matter what he does, one is always the person who has known at one point God's presence and God's grace. Now no one can argue in a abstract way that this experience is a simple and easy guarantee of the particular outcome of a person's life. Nevertheless, the significance of the indelibility of this experience cannot be overestimated. Ortega y Gasset, the social critic, has testified to it: "When I was a child, I was a Christian; now I am no longer. Does this mean strictly speaking, that I do not go on being a Christian? The Christian I was—is he dead, annihilated? Of course not; of course I am still a Christian, but in the form of having been a Christian."[1] In Dostoyevsky's *The Brothers*

---

[1] José Ortega y Gasset, *History as a System and Other Essays* (New York: W. W. Norton & Company, 1941), 208.

Karamazov, Ivan exclaims, "One good memory is perhaps the best education."

This becomes clear in those dark nights of the soul when faith fades, when God is absent. In these moments, we know that faith is no simple human achievement. But we know also that the experience of having believed is indelible, and we have the hope that the God who has worked with us will finish his work.

This truth has application in Christian nurture. No one can guarantee the consequence of baptism or Christian nurture in home and church. But again baptism and Christian nurture are indelible experiences. No matter how violently a teenager or a young adult may rebel against and seek to deny the fact, he or she is always the person who has known life in the Christian community. Two-thirds of the university students today are in rebellion, according to a recent study. But in the end that against which they rebel is likely to be more significant in shaping their future than the rebellion itself. Having known God's presence, we dare in dark and difficult moments to utter the prayer and express the hope that God will complete what he has begun.

This word from Paul has its application also to world history. What after all is the significance and the fate of this human history of which we are a part? This universe in the present episode of its existence has a history of about fifteen billion years. The earth has existed for perhaps four and a half billion years. Human beings have been around perhaps one hundred thousand years or more. Is human existence in the history of the universe simply an accident? Shall human beings some day disappear from this planet, leaving no living memory that they ever were? This is one possible faith, but it is a faith that is too frightful to contemplate and that does violence to our experience of the meaningfulness of life.

There is another faith. It is the vision of Teilhard de Chardin, the French scientist and priest whose works were forbidden publications by his church until after his death. Teilhard saw in a great vision that God has been at work from the primeval sludge to the appearance of human beings who can think and—more than this—who know what they think, and who therefore work with God in moving toward the Omega point when God's purposes will be fulfilled.

Teilhard did not know what the final purposes of God were; he did not know how everything fits this purpose. He himself suffered bitterly while writing this faith during the Japanese invasion of China. The important points are that he had a great vision of God at work in the world fulfilling his purposes and that deChardin lived in the confidence that God's purposes would be fulfilled.

This is the important point for us: a vision of God fulfilling his purposes in the world. And we ought not overestimate our ignorance of those purposes. We know that every deed done or word spoken for truth, for humanity, for the dignity of human existence is a part of those purposes. And we have more than a vision; we live by the conviction that these purposes will be accomplished. "For God is at work in you, both to will and to work for his good pleasure" (Phil. 2:13).

Two protests can be made to what I have said. One is that we live in a desperate day when life is short. Will not this trust that God is going to work his purposes out undercut our efforts? Have not critics from Karl Marx to John Dewey said that men are encouraged to endure injustice for the sake of heaven, or a pie in the sky? If this is a danger, then we have to remember the first half of the text: Work out your salvation. What we do need to be delivered from in personal life and in public affairs is a sort of frenzy, a sort of fanaticism that hurries too much, that destroys our patience. The Bible speaks of the long-suffering, the patience of God. It tells of the God who put a sign on Cain to protect him when men wanted to kill him. God gave Cain space and time that he did not deserve. God's patience is manifest in his willingness to provide us space and time that we do not deserve for the working out of his purposes.

One quality of the Christian life now must surely be patience: patience with the working out of the divine purpose in our very revolutionary history, and patience in the working out of the divine purpose in individual life. The old doctrine of the perseverance of the saints gave a basis for patience, for a poise that we very much need today.

A second protest is the question, Is this faith possible? Can we believe that God will work out his purposes in individual lives and in our history? Every act of belief involves a decision about what in human experience is to be taken as the criterion of the real and true. This conviction that God is at work both to will and to do his good pleasure is based upon our experience of God's presence, and on the basis of this experience, perhaps a fleeting experience, we dare affirm that he shall complete what he has begun.

This faith distinguishes a Christian from the humanist and from the good person. The humanist, the good person, and the Christian act very much alike. Christians are distinguished by the conviction that the good and the true and the beautiful are supported by the ultimate power in the universe, God.

The conclusion of the whole matter is that the perseverance of the saints is far from being a boast about what man is going to do. It is the conviction that the purposes to which we have committed our lives are undergirded by the ultimate power in the universe. This is our hope of salvation. Reinhold Neibuhr put very well in his comments on the abiding quality of faith, hope, and love our dependence in salvation on forces outside ourselves:

> Nothing that is worth doing can be achieved in our lifetime; therefore, we must be saved by hope. Nothing which is true or beautiful or good makes complete sense in any immediate context of history; therefore, we must be saved by faith. Nothing we do, however virtuous, can be accomplished alone; therefore, we are saved by love.[2]

In the end there is no faith, no hope, and no enduring love apart from God.

> Did we in our own strength confide,
> Our striving would be losing;
> Let goods and kindred go,
> This mortal life also;
> The body they may kill:
> God's truth abideth still;
> His Kingdom is forever.
> (Martin Luther, "A Mighty Fortress is Our God")

---

[2]Reinhold Niebuhr, *The Irony of American History* (New York: Charles Scribner's Sons, 1952), 63.

"Christian Faith and the Common Pleasures of Life"
September 29, 1991

Peachtree Presbyterian Church, Atlanta

Human existence is distinguished by its capacity for pleasure, fun, and even frivolity, by its capacity for sorrow and repentance, and by the power of the human spirit to organize the energies and the vitalities of life in the pursuit of a freely chosen goal. Human beings have the capacity to work when they want to play and to play when they need to work.

These capacities may enhance human life, but amid the conditions of contemporary society they may destroy life. In any case, they confront us with the responsibilities of freedom. The traumatic events of life and the constant requirements of food, shelter, and clothing accentuate the gravity of life. The problems of productivity in our economy remind us that some have dispensed with the Protestant work ethic prematurely. We are aware, as we were not a few years ago, of the fragility of life and its institutions.

But more than any people in human history we have the leisure and physical supports that make possible life's common pleasures. A century ago it took almost all of life's energies to provide food and shelter. Today more than any other society in history, ours is geared to provide life's common pleasures: gourmet eating establishments, resorts at the beach and mountains, spectator sports without parallel. Our society is so affluent that celebrities and entertainers have replaced the heroic in our affections and are paid more than those who provide the material and social necessities of life. Hence we rightly ask how we are to understand life's common pleasures in the light of our faith.

The biblical warrant for this consideration is found first of all in the example of Jesus, who enjoyed a pleasant meal with his friends and who found time in a busy life to attend a wedding feast. It is also grounded in a text from Genesis: "God saw everything that he had made, and behold, it was very good" (Gen. 1:31a). And in a text from Paul: "For freedom Christ has set us free; stand fast therefore, and do not submit again to a yoke of slavery" (Gal. 5:1).

I

Let us begin our consideration of life's common pleasures with the observation that they have been regarded with suspicion throughout much of Christian history. The notion has been very common that fun either must be avoided or kept under surveillance lest it corrupt the Christian life. This is less true of those who are here this morning than it has been for most Christians—than it was for our parents. Certainly it is less true of our hedonistic, pleasure-loving culture. But the fact remains that even in the 1990s Christians are uneasy if they have a good time or engage in frivolity. And there may be some who still count it a virtue not to have a good time at all in this business of living.

Examples of Christians who have been uneasy with life's common pleasures are easy to find. Tertullian, a churchman of the third century, believed that athletic contests were incompatible with Christian faith. He once said that wrestling was the business of the devil, and he regarded the theater as off-limits for Christian people. Tertullian declared that by merely being in the world we fall from faith. Going to the circus or to the theater is no different from sacrificing in the Temple of Serapis. All efforts to enhance human appearance violated the work of the Creator. Women who try to make themselves attractive tempt other men, if only in thought, and thus lead them into sin. Cosmetics and jewelry are sources of temptations to sin, if not sin themselves. Tertullian was also critical of men who dyed their hair, believing that the more one tries to conceal old age, the more evident one's old age becomes. Tertullian was more extreme than most, but he gave expression to a persistent Christian perspective.

Other Christians have been suspicious of pleasant food and drink. They vied with each other to live the more strenuous life, to eat the coarser food, to wear the rougher hair shirt. They left the cities and went to the deserts in pursuit of their Christian vocation.

Still other Christians have always been nervous about the joy of sex and even marriage. Jerome, who translated the Bible into Latin, put up with marriage only because he could think of no other way for virgins to come into the world. "I praise marriage, praise wedlock," Jerome declared, "but I do so because they produce virgins."

In our own immediate Protestant background, sin was sometimes defined as card playing, dancing, theatergoing, and horse racing. General Assemblies passed resolutions concerning such sins with the same confidence and self-righteousness that General Assemblies today pass resolutions about Nicaragua and South Africa. The General Assembly of 1818 condemned dancing as a fascinating and infatuating practice that dissipates religious impressions and hardens the heart. The West Tennessee Presbytery was more direct. The dancer was guilty of criminal conduct and should be banned from the church.

Macaulay, the British historian, once declared that the Puritans opposed bear-baiting, not because of the pain it gave to the bears, but because of the pleasure it gave to the spectators. This was a false judgment about the Puritans, but there is ample grounds for believing that Macaulay accurately assessed the attitude of some Christians toward the common pleasures of life then as well as now.

II

Now let us ask, Why have Christians regarded the common pleasures of life with suspicion?

One reason is an ancient heresy—the notion that the created world is evil. This is one of the most persistent ideas in the history of ideas. The intellectual, the spiritual, the ethereal are valued to the exclusion of the sensuous and the material. Salvation is escape from the world of flesh and blood, which we can see, taste, touch, and handle. Deprecation of the body, of food and drink, of physical comforts and pleasures is regarded as a superior virtue. Earth is rejected for heaven, this world for another world, the sensuous for the spiritual. One early Christian heretic, Marcion, rejected the creator God because he was offended by alligators, snakes, and the way babies come into the world. Dorothy Sayers once said that for many people, sin is anything you enjoy doing and original sin is anything you enjoy doing very much.

The second reason Christians have regarded the common pleasures of life with suspicion is the loss of faith in God. A philosopher once said that atheism does not necessarily lead to badness. The atheist may be a very good person, but atheism always leads to an incurable loneliness and despair. We lose the capacity for joy, not only when we give up on the world but also when we give up on God. In fact, we give up on the world because we at first have given up on God. A profound faith in God leads to joy in created existence.

Many common pleasures have been corrupted by evil. Card playing has been associated with gambling; the theater with immorality; boxing with brutality; horse racing with a parasitic style of life; car racing with irresponsible risks to human life; and college sports have led to the corruption of the academic integrity of great universities.

Some popular sports or recreational activities appear to be inherently evil. Some sports are brutal and violate the conviction that human life is precious. Some pleasures are inherently selfish and are engaged in at the expense of other people. Some lifestyles are parasitic and productive of nothing for the common good.

The pleasures of life have been condemned because they may trivialize life. Augustine liked to say that sin is the inordinate love of ordinate goods. Some activities, useful when properly integrated into the order of life, become demonic when their practice becomes inordinate. Card playing may be a relaxation of the human spirit but when it becomes an all-consuming passion of life, it becomes destructive of the human spirit.

On one level the question how many home runs Dale Murphy may hit is interesting and a diversion from weightier matters. The hitting of home runs is important as an expression of the wonder of the human body and as an achievement of personal discipline. But in the ongoing of the human race it is not very important at all. Some simple and unknown act of justice, some unnoticed achievement in a laboratory performed by an unknown person may be far more important and significant in shaping human life on this planet. Whenever the pleasures that are a real diversion and a relaxation of the human spirit become the all-consuming passion of life, they destroy life.

The most brilliant handling of a trifle, someone has said, is always trifling. The trivilization of human existence in our time is a very real danger. As T. S. Eliot put it in "Choruses from the Rock," "Here were decent godless people: Their only monument the asphalt road/And a thousand lost golf balls."

A fourth reason the common pleasures of life have been regarded as evil is the temptation to oversimplify Christian faith and reduce it to manageable prescriptions. The New Testament command to love your neighbor is very complex and very difficult. What does it mean to love your neighbor when you face a Middle East crisis, or a city school crisis, or when you are making out a payroll, or are called upon to do a day's work? Life is greatly simplified if morality can be identified with some simple prohibition: "Do not play cards," or "Do not dance." And the older one gets the simpler this kind of prohibition becomes. Some sins are cured by old age. The prohibition of some common pleasures, even a justifiable prohibition, may become a substitute for the more serious demands of the law.

III

Now let us come a step further and ask, How can we as Christians understand the common pleasures of life as part of our Christian vocation?

First of all, we can understand the pleasures of life in terms of the freedom that Jesus exemplified and that Paul proclaimed. Once when Jesus was attending a wedding, the wine gave out. He did not admonish the guests to go home, to think about the more serious things of life, or even to consider the poor who had little to eat or drink. Rather, he provided wine for the reception. When his enemies sought to destroy him, they said he was a glutton and a wine drinker. This was an exaggeration, but it was unlikely that they would have made the charge if he had been an ascetic. Jesus made a place for fun and pleasure in his life and there ought to be a place for it in the lives of most people. Fun ought not to be crowded out of life by work or work by fun.

God alone is our Lord, and no person should be mastered by work no matter how noble, or by fun however enjoyable, or by any human enterprise. The Christian person has one Lord, the creator of heaven and earth, and this allegiance delivers the Christian from every lesser lordship. Jesus was apparently free to give up his work to go to a wedding feast or to eat a dinner with a friend. Those of us who follow him ought to share his freedom.

But a person ought to be free to give up the common pleasures also. In any case, they must be integrated into a properly ordered life. Ordinate goods ought to be loved ordinately. Moreover, there are some goals and achievements for which persons may be commanded by God to "scorn delights and live laborious days." The obligation to put food on the table, or to find a cure for cancer, or to relieve some acute social problem may properly in some circumstances require a person's total energies. The same freedom that makes it possible to give up our work also ought to make it possible to give up our pleasures in certain times and places. This, too, has warrant in the life of Jesus. He set his face like flint toward Jerusalem.

Jesus' example of freedom in giving up his work or in giving up pleasure has special importance in our time. On the one hand we see persons, slaves of their work and slaves of a money economy, who have no time for the common pleasures of life and who are in the end broken by the system and by their slavery to the work. On the other hand, we see persons partly in rebellion against slavery to work, in rebellion against discipline, rejecting what has been called a Protestant work ethic for the sake of being oneself, of being natural, or doing one's own thing. Yet the options of life are exhausted neither by slavery nor by the license that allows one to do one's own thing at the expense of a productive life.

The freedom that Jesus exemplified and that Paul proclaimed is not autonomy, license, exemption from discipline. It is rather a quality of spirit that is rooted in a profound awareness that life is a gift and that the giver can be trusted. Gratitude for the gift qualifies the freedom for which Christ has set us free. In this gratitude and thanksgiving for the sheer wonder of being alive and for the experience of grace, the acceptance of discipline becomes a joy, not a grievous burden and a means to a greater freedom. The freedom for which Christ has set us free may include a work ethic and a discipline that scorns delights for some worthy goal. Both work and pleasure must be set in the deeper context of life's source and security in the love of God.

Life's common pleasures must also be set in the context of the doctrine of creation. "God saw everything that he had made, and behold, it was very good." The refusal to accept the goodness of creation and to rejoice in the day that God has made or the life that he has given is to rebel against the creator. There is an incongruity between the confession that the God and Father of our Lord Jesus Christ is the creator of heaven and earth and the suspicion that the world is evil and that life is a grievous burden.

Thomas Jefferson and John Adams, who in their younger days had been fierce political antagonists, in their older days as the last survivors of 1776 became warm friends. In their correspondence Adams asked Jefferson about his view on Christian faith. Jefferson defined the faith chiefly in terms of duty. John Adams replied,

> The love of God and his creation—delight, joy, triumph, exultation in my own existence—though but an atom, a molecule organique in the universe—are my religion.[1]

Life's common pleasures must be understood in terms of the worthwhileness of human existence in its own right. Human life is a precious gift from God, and on this basic level it needs no further justification, either by work or play. It is justified simply by being. We rightly say to people, Be good for something. Yet we sometimes say it so much and so

---

[1]Lester J. Cappon, ed., *The Adams–Jefferson Letters: The Complete Correspondence* (Chapel Hill: University of North Carolina Press, 1988).

exclusively that we leave the impression that unless people are good for something, they are good for nothing, that their worthwhileness is measured by what they produce. This becomes most pathetic when an older person who is no longer capable of useful work says in despair, I am good for nothing. Yet it is a basic tenet of our faith that we are saved not by being good for something or by what we produce, but by the love of God who has given us life. A person's worth is guaranteed not by his or her function but by God's gift of life itself.

Human existence is not exhausted by work. Neither is it exhausted by play. Work and the common pleasures of life must be understood and appropriated in terms of the freedom that Jesus exemplified and that Paul proclaimed, the Christian doctrine of creation, and in terms of the Christian doctrine of human existence. God alone is a person's master, and every person ought to be free to work and free to play, free to give up work and free to give up play. "For freedom Christ has set us free; stand fast therefore, and do not submit again to a yoke of slavery" (Gal. 5:1). Life is a gracious gift and those who live it fully must receive it graciously.

"The Church as the People of God"
June 6, 1978

Sermon as Moderator, Synod of North Carolina—Myers Park
Presbyterian Church, Charlotte, North Carolina

In a day when many Jews as well as Gentiles were homeless, with no sense
of personal identity, the writer of 1 Peter boldly declared the identity of
the Christian community: "You are a chosen race, a royal priesthood, a
holy nation, God's own people. . . . Once you were no people but now you
are God's people; once you had not received mercy but now you have
received mercy" (1 Peter 2:9–10).

In our pluralistic, secular, mobile, mass-media-dominated society in
which young and old alike feel alone, homeless in the vast immensity of
culture as well as space, without community and with no compelling sense
of identity, it is appropriate at this meeting of Synod to listen again to this
declaration of our identity as the church. "Once you were no people but
now you are God's people; once you had not received mercy but now you
have received mercy."

So let us fasten our attention upon three statements taken from these
verses from 1 Peter, particularly as they have been interpreted in our
Protestant tradition.

I

Let us begin with the declaration "Once you were no people but now you
are God's people." No other New Testament metaphor for the church
speaks so directly to the needs of the church in our time. The church is
not an institution, an organization, a polity, or a theology. The church is
not even an aggregation of individuals seeking replenishment for their
individual needs. The church is a people, a community that lives a shared
life. Our Puritan forefathers refused to call the building the church. They

said it was a meeting house, the place where the church gathers. Martin Luther wanted to change the words of the Apostles' Creed from "I believe in the holy catholic church," which had too institutional a sound, to "I believe there is a holy Christian group or congregation" ("Sermons on the Catechism").

The need for this shared life is today everywhere apparent in the futile attempts of vast numbers of people to achieve it in the common sharing of the human interests of sex and food and status, as well as the various human neuroses and psychoses. But the church is more than a human community. It is, as Paul puts it, a colony of heaven. The sharing of human interests in the church is always in the context of a faith in a transcendent God and in the context of a worldview and of a commitment of life based on that faith. The church is not just another community for the sharing of human interests, for it knows that human existence is completed and fulfilled by no human achievement and by no purely human community.

The church as the people of God also differs from every human organization in that it is the creation of God, called into being by the word and spirit of God. Those who were the church in the New Testament days did not plan to be the church. They suddenly discovered they were the church, and they had to improvise continually to meet needs they did not anticipate. They were people who had experienced the impact of the life, death, and resurrection of Jesus Christ, and this experience had made them a community. Today we celebrate this truth about the church in the doctrine of election and in the practice of the baptism of infants.

When we say that the church is the people of God, we are saying that the reality and unity of the church is in the hearing of the word of God. It ought not to be said, as Emil Brunner and others have come close to saying, that the procedures, orders, and bureaucratic organization of the church are unimportant. But they are never, as Karl Barth makes so clear, the reality of the church. The reality and unity of the church is in the proclaiming and hearing of the word of God. This reality is most visible in the worshipping, believing community that gathers to hear and receive the word of God in preaching and sacraments. Martin Luther in his day was compelled to declare that the council is not the church. So we in our time may have to say with emphasis that the church is not the bureaucracy, the staff, the organization, the committee, not the institution, not even the seminary. The church is not a religious society, not a therapy group, not a study group, not a community for social change. The church is a community of faith that lives in the world by the hearing of the word of God.

The church as the people of God cannot be programmed, cannot be planned or prioritized, cannot be commanded. Its existence is finally a mystery. The church is called into being by the grace and mercy of God. It is a gift. It exists where the word of God in preaching, teaching, and sacraments is proclaimed under the power of the divine Spirit and where it is heard by the same power. We cannot create the church by any human planning. Yet if we do what we can in preaching and teaching, if we administer the sacraments, if we exercise pastoral care that is the incorporating and sustaining of people in the Christian fellowship, then it is likely that the church as the people of God, which is beyond our power to create, will exist in our midst.

II

The church is also a people who live by the mercy of God. Such metaphors of the church as the people of God, the body of Christ, the bride of Christ are likely to give us too exalted a notion of ourselves and of our moral superiority to the world unless they are balanced by an awareness that the church as a community of forgiven sinners always lives by the mercy of God. In the church we ought never to underestimate the residual powers of goodness in evil people nor should we ever underestimate the powers of evil in good people. In the church we must neither be cynics despairing of human goodness nor sentimental optimists living with utopian dreams. The church lives by a Christian realism that holds in balance the facts of human nature and the power of God's grace. "Once you had not received mercy, but now you have received mercy."

Augustine's controversy with Pelagius was, next to the Arian debate, the most serious doctrinal dispute in the history of the church; and it had to do with the nature of the church.[1]

Pelagius was a great hulk of a man, a native of Britain, who came to Rome at the end of the fourth century when Roman society was in a state of collapse. Pelagius had a great vision of human dignity and of the power of the human self to determine its own life, and he had a great vision of what it means to be a Christian individually and socially. Many of the homeless, confused people of the time, who had sensed that life should be better than it was, were attracted to Pelagius, and under his influence many lives were transformed.

---

[1]In this sermon I have been influenced by R. A. Markus's *Saeculum: History and Society in the Theology of Augustine,* Peter Brown's *Augustine of Hippo,* and Charles Cochrane's *Christianity and Classical Culture.*

The Christian life, as Pelagius understood it, was simple. There are the good people and the bad people. The bad people sin out of perversity, out of contempt for God and his will. They sin out of set purpose and willfulness. Pelagius knew the power of habit and example. Yet he did not believe that the power of habit reached very deep into one's life, and he believed that its hold could be broken by the human will and discipline. Pelagius knew the need for grace, but the grace that was needed was enlightenment. Americans, it has been observed, are Pelagians by birth. This is true of morally sensitive people in and out of the church who see the moral life in very simple terms, who easily divide people into the good people and the bad people. For Pelagius, as for many middle-class Presbyterians today, the Christian life was relatively simple and the options were clear. Interestingly enough today, the orthodox on the right and the social actionists on the left are alike inclined to be Pelagians.

Pelagius also wanted a church without spot or wrinkle. The church was a morally elite people who had achieved a clear understanding of who they were in contrast to the mediocrity of pagan life in general.

Pelagius, furthermore, wanted a reformed society. The church stood in judgment on society and was the means of its reformation. Under Pelagius's influence remarkable changes did occur. Rich nobility, for example, gave up their wealth and renounced self-seeking. Perhaps nowhere is the heart of Pelagianism more clearly revealed, especially its optimism about human nature, than in the conviction of some Pelagians that accumulated wealth was "just another bad habit that could be shrugged off by the Christian on baptism."

This vision of human life and human society transformed by the human will and by the enlightenment of grace is very compelling. Here is the triumph of the human spirit over passion, weakness, temptation—over every obstacle. Here is the victory of the human will over the heritage of the past, over fate, over the corruptions of the social order. The Pelagians were determined to maintain a different quality of life from the conventional, mediocre lives of their neighbors. The importance of this Pelagian vision and intention ought never be underestimated. Whenever this vision of the possibilities of human existence is lost and whenever zeal to be perfect as the Father in heaven is perfect dies, the Christian community will be the loser.

But Pelagius's position challenged a North African theologian's basic understanding of the Christian life and of the church. Augustine thought that Pelagius had a zeal for righteousness but not according to knowledge. Augustine understood the church to be an inn for convalescence, for healing, not a morally aristocratic elite. Augustine knew the significance of the human will. Indeed he defined a person in terms of the will.

A person is as he or she wills, as he or she loves. But Augustine knew there are forces in the human existence beyond the power of the human will. Augustine also knew that grace must be more than enlightenment. It must be a power of deep healing. He rejoiced in making a case for grace: "No subject gives me greater pleasure. For what ought to be more attractive to us sick men than grace, grace by which we are healed; for us lazy men than grace, grace by which we are stirred up; for us men longing to act than grace, grace by which we are helped."

Augustine's case was difficult to make. The ordinary Christian saw in Pelagius only a sincere believer who wanted Christians to take the faith seriously. But Augustine knew that the moral life, to say nothing of the Christian life, is not so simple. First of all he knew about original sin. Our problem is not simply that we sin but that we are born into a situation where sin is already present and has become part of the structure of the social order in which we live. Sin penetrates our lives before our first conscious decision. Augustine knew that the only options we have are frequently choices of the more or less evil.

Augustine knew second that evil is not simply a matter of perversity or contempt for God. It penetrates deeply into the human person. In a very remarkable sentence he wrote to the Pelagians, "Many sins are committed through pride, but not all happen proudly. . . . they happen so often by ignorance, by human weakness; many are committed by men weeping and groaning in their distress" (*On Nature and Grace* XXIX). Augustine knew in the third place that we frequently conquer one sin only to fall victim to another. He once wrote a rich widow who was attracted to the Pelagians, "I have, however, often observed this fact of human behavior that, with certain people, when sexuality is repressed, avarice seems to grow in its place." Peter Brown, Augustine's biographer, comments that the Pelagians in their shrill denunciation of the way of the world never said anything as shrewd as that.

In sum, Augustine knew that the Christian life is never simple. The good are never as good as they think they are and the bad are never as bad as they are thought to be. Augustine knew that we sin in our best deeds as well as our worst. As Reinhold Niebuhr puts it for contemporary Pelagians, our causes are never as righteous and our participation in them is never as devoid of self-interest as we think they are. T. S. Eliot was truly Augustinian when he wrote,

> Let me disclose the gifts reserved for age
> To set a crown upon your lifetime's effort.

First, the cold friction of expiring sense
Without enchantment, offering no promise
But bitter tastelessness of shadow fruit
As body and soul begin to fall asunder.
Second, the conscious impotence of rage
At human folly, and the laceration
Of laughter at what ceases to amuse.
And last, the rending pain of re-enactment
Of all that you have done, and been; the shame
Of motives late revealed, and the awareness
Of things ill done and done to other's harm
Which once you took for exercise of virtue.

(*Little Gidding*)

Augustine knew that the Pelagian controversy had to do with the nature of the church. For Pelagius the church is an elite company of moral and spiritual heroes. For Augustine it was an inn of convalescence, a community of healing for those who know that their only hope is in God. Pelagius thought sinners needed enlightenment. Augustine thought they needed healing. The church always needs Pelagiuses, for all of us do less than we can. But Augustine was more profound in his understanding of the human situation. And the church decided that Pelagius, for all of his greatness, was a heretic and that Augustine in spite of faults was a doctor of grace.

III

The church is the people of God. The church is the community that lives by the mercy of God. It is also a royal priesthood, or as Martin Luther and the Reformers put it, the church is the priesthood of believers.

The priesthood of believers, as Luther understood it, is twofold responsibility. The believer as a priest is accountable before God. No person, no institution can answer before God for any other person. Every person must answer for himself or herself. Everyone must believe for himself, Luther said, because sooner or later everyone must die by himself. Luther went on to say that to be a priest is not only to give an account for oneself, but also for one's neighbor. A Christian is a Christ to his neighbor. By this Luther not only meant that as God in Christ loves us, so we must love our neighbor. He also meant that as Christ bore our sins so we must bear our neighbor's sins. A Christian is never a spectator to any moral or human loss or tragedy.

The church is, in our Protestant understanding, a community in which we are each responsible for ourselves before God and also responsible for our neighbors. The task of holding together these twin responsibilities is not easy. And yet the well-being of the church depends on our holding together these two dimensions of our responsibility as Christians and as the church. Paul once wrote, "Bear one another's burdens, and so fulfil the law of Christ" (Gal. 6:2). But in the same paragraph Paul goes on to say, "Each man will have to bear his own load" (Gal. 6:5). The same New Testament that tells us to feed the hungry also declares that if one does not work, let him not eat (Matt. 25 and 2 Thess. 3:10). This is more than a prudential warning that if one does not work, there will be nothing to eat. It is ethical. If one does not work, he or she has no right to eat.

The Presbyterian Church in the United States is an affluent church. And, therefore, we have said and we must continue to say much about our responsibility to bear our neighbor's burdens. All of us without exception ought to be more sacrificial. But there are dangers in rhetoric about self-sacrifice. Self-sacrifice, as Reinhold Niebuhr said so well, can never be made a public policy. For then it becomes the sacrifice of other people's money, time, or even children. It is all too easy to talk about sacrifice in general or about the sacrifice of other people, of South Africans, of anonymous stockholders. We must beware lest the command to bear our neighbor's burdens becomes a means by which we achieve victory for our own plans and ideologies. Therefore, we must always say to ourselves and to other people, "Bear your own burdens." We must say this in society. Joseph Califano in the current issue of *Time* (June 12, 1978) speaks of the new attitude toward work and toward the receiving of welfare assistance. The old Protestant ethic insisted that every person who could should work conscientiously and diligently, but it has likely been a long time since many sermons were preached on this theme.

We must also say in the church that we bear each other's burdens and that we also bear our own burdens. In recent years too many special-interest groups talk too exclusively of what the church owes them, especially in terms of appointments and election. We must again put the emphasis on what we owe the church. The first question is not what can the church do for me but what can I do for the church. We must learn again that office in the church is not first of all an honor but a responsibility, a responsibility to gather congregations, to build church buildings, to support people in Christian existence. We have got to learn again that we are obligated to contribute not only to the church but also to the world at least as much as we take out. John Calvin in a very remarkable chapter on Christian Liberty (*Institutes* III, 19) makes a distinction between the offense given and the offense taken. Part of the Christian life is in not giving offense unnecessarily. But part of the Christian life is in not taking offense too easily. As Paul puts it, we have got to bear our neighbor's burdens and we have got to bear our own burden.

Henrik Ibsen, a shrewd observer of human existence, has a play entitled "The Doll's House." It is the story of people who in eight years of married life never had a serious conversation. They never asked, What does life really mean? What is its purpose and destiny? They lived on the surface, but there came a day when the doll's house collapsed.

A doll's house is not only a good symbol of much of modern life, but also of much that goes on in the church. When the church becomes a doll's house, it always collapses. The church is the people of God, and the really critical fact in the church, the reality and unity of the church, is our relationship to God. No one ought to underestimate the importance of such questions as the Panama Canal treaty or homosexuality or South Africa, and certainly we dare not underestimate the danger of nuclear war. Neither ought we underestimate the importance of church organization or many activities of the church. But in a real sense these are all secondary questions.

This was put very dramatically by Emil Brunner in a lecture at Yale University in 1947. The United States, he said, is the finest achievement of the human spirit in the history of the human race, but there will come a day when the United States will no longer exist. When that day comes, he added, each one of you will still be. So in a real sense what happens in the history of the human soul, a human self, has a significance beyond what happens in a great society.

We hear very much about the breakdown of the church's witness in the moral and social realm, and this is proper. But let us not forget that the church's primary witness is a firm faith in God, a faith that wrests a measure of serenity, poise, dignity, and true humanness from the raw stuff of life, from the vicissitudes of history, and from the ultimate test of death.

The heart of the matter was put remarkably well in that psalm Presbyterians have sung for four centuries:

> Know that the Lord is God indeed;
> Without our aid he did us make;
> We are his folk, he doth us feed,
> And for his sheep he doth us take.

> The Lord our God is good,
> His mercy is forever sure;
> His truth at all times firmly stood,
> And shall from age to age endure.
> (Psalm 100)

"The City of God and the Nations of Earth"
October 21, 1967

Symposium on The Confession of 1967,
Princeton, New Jersey

Grace Covenant Presbyterian Church,
Richmond, Virginia, July 4, 1982

Isaiah 40:6–17; Romans 8:28–39, 13:1–7

We have gathered today as a Christian community to worship God. We also have gathered as citizens of the United States, a citizenship that gives us unprecedented privileges and likewise enormous responsibilities for ourselves and the whole human community. And thus, we have to face the question of the relation of the two communities to one another.

No Simple Answer

When we turn to the Bible, we find no simple answer to our problem. In the scripture that was read, Isaiah declares that the nations are like a drop from a bucket. They are as nothing before God. The prophets of Israel made the kings of earth the particular objects of their indictment. Yet the Old Testament also designates the king as the Lord's anointed, and David was a type of the coming deliverance of the Lord.

The New Testament declares that all authority is ordained of God, that paying taxes is a Christian duty. "Honor the emperor" is a Christian exhortation. Yet the book of Revelation refers to the emperor as a satanic beast and Rome as the great harlot.

The ambiguity of the human situation is nowhere more clearly expressed than in Paul's declaration that our "commonwealth is in heaven, and from it we await a Savior . . . who will change our lowly body to be like his glorious body" (Phil. 3:20–21). The New Testament is everywhere moved by the conviction that this world of flesh and blood is not the only world there is. Furthermore, this world is not the most important world.

There is an order of existence at work in this world of flesh and blood, yet not enclosed by nor bound to nature and history, which moves by the

89

power of God to its fulfillment as his eternal kingdom. At few points is the dominant ethos of our time, even in the church, so at variance with the New Testament and also with most of Christian history.

There are, to be sure, good grounds in the Bible for affirming this world. The Bible begins with the assertion that God created the world and found it to be very good. From beginning to end it asserts the significance of historical existence. It teaches that ordinary household and social duties are important. It bestows praise upon those who establish justice and do deeds of mercy.

Yet it nowhere promises that human existence is fulfilled by any human achievement or by any human community. Human survival, to say nothing of human comfort, can be bought at too high a price. "Do not fear those who kill the body but cannot kill the soul; rather fear him who can destroy both soul and body in hell" (Matt. 10:28). And so in every age Christians have been willing not only to give up creature comforts but to choose martyrdom, the refusal to maintain life at the expense of life's meaning—a faith that can be justified only beyond history.

This whole dimension of the Christian life is put bluntly in the question of Jesus, "What will it profit a man, if he gains the whole world and forfeits his life?" (Matt. 16:26). The world here is surely inclusive not only of economic but also of social, political, and cultural achievements. Human life does not finally consist in the abundance of what a person possesses.

The limited character of all human achievements is partly due to the sin that flaws our best as well as our worst deeds. In retrospect, what once we thought was virtue is always seen to have been less than virtue. As Reinhold Niebuhr taught us, our causes are never as righteous as we think they are and our participation in them is never as free of self-interest as we claim.

A more basic problem is the finite and partial character of all human achievements and communities. The human spirit is free to transcend our highest achievements. No matter what we achieve in any realm of life, there is always something beyond to elude our grasp. Long ago Augustine declared, "Thou hast made us for thyself and restless is our heart until it comes to rest in thee" (*Confessions* I,1).

No one in our time has so profoundly understood the "twilight of the gods" better and stated more clearly the plight of human existence without God than Richard Niebuhr: "The causes for which we live all die. The great social movements pass and are supplanted by others. The ideals we fashion are revealed by time to be relative. The empires and cities to which we are devoted all decay. At the end nothing is left to defend us against the void of meaninglessness."[1] The New Testament never minimizes the goodness of the created order or the significance of history, but it always affirms them in terms of a kingdom that is not bound by nor enclosed within either nature or history.

The Two Cities

From the beginning the church had to decide concretely how it would understand and relate to the kingdoms and achievements of the secular order. This experience, when some of the ablest theologians in our history concentrated on the problem, gives both perspective and illumination to our engagement with the question today. One early churchman, Tertullian of Carthage, living about 200, thought that the church and empire were wholly antagonistic. You could be Christian or emperor, but you could not be the two at the same time.

A century later, when Constantine, the emperor, became Christian, another theologian and churchman, Eusebius, saw in the Christianity of the emperor the fulfillment of human history. Even the young Augustine was tempted to rejoice that in the "Christian empire" of Theodosius "the whole world has become a choir praising Christ."[2]

The fall of Rome put the question in sharper focus. For three days in August 410 the Goths overran the city, an event of tremendous psychological impact. The pagans were angry and the Christians were dismayed. The old Romans said that Christianity had undermined the Roman Empire, that Christianity was subversive of social order.

How can you have a stable social order when Christians advocated forgiveness of enemies and the policy of turning the other cheek; when Christians declared that a person's highest loyalty belongs not to the state, but to God; when over against the kingdoms of earth, Christians affirmed a commonwealth in heaven?

All persons, whether pagan or Christian, who had found their personal security and the meaning of their lives in the stable, rationally ordered society of Rome, were distraught. Rome itself had promised—through its

---

[1]Richard Niebuhr, *Radical Monotheism and Western Culture* (Louisville, Ky.: Westminster/John Knox Press, 1970), 122.

[2]In the treatment of Augustine's theology, insight and help have been received from R. A. Markus's *Saeculum: History and Society in the Theology of Augustine,* Peter Brown's *Augustine of Hippo,* and Charles Cochrane's *Christianity and Classical Culture.*

great emperors, such as Caesar Augustus, and its great poets, such as Virgil—to give meaning and security to life.

In fact, the poetry of Virgil was so messianic that some Christians believed it to be predictions of Jesus. As Christians looked for the fulfillment of life in Jesus Christ, the Romans looked for the fulfillment of life in the rationally ordered society of Rome. Now Rome had collapsed under the onslaught of the barbarians from the north.

In answer to the anger of the pagans, Augustine argued that Rome had been done in not by Christians but by the failure of the old gods and, more particularly, by its love of self and its greed, which flawed every achievement.

Augustine himself was a Roman who was proud of the achievements of Rome. He believed that these achievements were undergirded by the providence of God. Yet Augustine knew that the Roman achievements were limited by time and space, that they were transient, that they were flawed.

Hence, Augustine's basic point was that the meaning of life can be fulfilled by no human achievement, however remarkable—not even by Rome. Rome may have been the greatest empire that history had known, but Rome, too, would fail and pass away. Ultimate security can be found in God alone. Hence, the fall of Rome, Augustine argued, should be taken seriously, but not too seriously.

Augustine, as an old man, had increasingly come to this conclusion even before the fall of Rome. He had become aware of the limited character of all human achievements. He knew that finally the human community, like the human self, is more a mystery than a problem. Problems are unraveled by human intelligence, but mysteries must be illuminated by grace.

The fall of Rome was the occasion for writing what he already had concluded. Apart from this catastrophe, Augustine had looked forward to the time when death is swallowed up in victory, when there should be peace, the peace of ordered wills.

Hence, Augustine could exult in the achievements of Rome, yet he also knew that those achievements were limited, transient, and flawed.

Augustine thought of Christians as resident aliens. As a resident alien, the Christian affirmed the achievements of Rome, indeed, worked for the best possible social, economic, and political order. The city of God, Augustine said, has to do with "our business within this common mortal life."

The Christian would strive for perfection, for the perfect society, but would not "denigrate the second best" as do so many secular critics of contemporary society. Augustine did not expect the impossible from human society, and he rejoiced in the actual achievements of that society.

Human history from the beginning, Augustine believed, had been the story of two cities, the city of God and the city of Earth. These cities were constituted by two loves: "the earthly is formed by love of self to contempt of God; the heavenly by love of God to contempt of self. The one glories in herself, the other in the Lord. . . . In the one, lust for power prevails. . . . in the other, all serve each other in charity."

In human history, the city of God and the city of Earth are mixed together in culture, in empire, even in the church. The interaction of the two cities and their lines of demarcation are much too subtle for human wisdom to decipher. Hence, we have to be content with relative judgments and leave the final summation of all things to God.

Task and Destiny

Let us come a step further now and ask what we can learn about Christian discipleship today in the light of this scripture and this reading of scripture by those who have gone before us in the faith. Three conclusions follow from the scripture and the reading of it by Augustine.

First, we should learn, as Augustine did, that the United States of America—our economic, social, cultural, and political achievements—are part of God's good creation and gifts of divine providence. For them we should be thankful and in their presence we should be humble.

To most, if not to all of us, there has been bequeathed a tradition of freedom and justice, unprecedented for a great society. In the providence of God we live in the most affluent and probably the most peaceful great nation in history. On the front page of almost every paper we are reminded that hundreds of millions of people covet what has been bequeathed to us.

In a conference celebrating a reformed creed, it is appropriate to mention the heritage of the Protestant Reformation, the Puritan movement, and the evangelical awakenings. Without these movements, life in the United States would be significantly different from what it is. As the power of these events dissipates in a secular society, life in our culture will change. There is no convincing evidence that it will change for the better.

The influences that shape a culture are subtle and hard to define, yet history would likely have been different if James Madison had gone to William and Mary rather than to Princeton, for in Princeton, he learned—under the tutelage of John Witherspoon, in the house next door to where this sermon is being preached—to understand politics from the Reformed rather than the Enlightenment perspective.

Yet gratitude and humility are not characteristics of our society. Narcissistic delight in our own achievements seems to preclude humility and gratitude alike. Even in the church we have been scornful of the labors into which we have entered.

The protest movements likewise have given little evidence of humility or gratitude, yet without gratitude, the blessing of our heritage gives to us not joy but a pathological sense of guilt. Without gratitude we find it difficult to interpret our own personal privilege in terms of responsibility. Furthermore, without gratitude, contrition and constructive protest are no longer possible, for without gratitude they become self-righteousness, contempt, and even hate. Hence, we can learn first from Paul and Augustine humility and gratitude.

Second, we can learn from the example of Jesus—from the teaching of Paul and the reflection of Augustine—to do deeds of love and mercy; to seek to resolve problems; to plan for the future; to struggle for economic, social, and political achievements that will enhance human life; and to put as much into society as we take out in salaries, privileges, and expense accounts.

Calvin, more than Augustine, understood that the Christian calling is to embody the purposes of God in the achievements of human history. He thought of God first of all as activity, energy, moral purpose, and intentionality. Calvin believed that God had called him not simply to the ultimate destinies of heaven or hell, but to work out the divine purposes in Geneva, in Western Europe, in the world.

Wherever the Calvinists went, they carried with them the vision of the holy commonwealth, the Christian community, a sense of being predestined by God. They found the meaning and deepest joy of their lives in the conviction that at least in a broken and fragmentary way they embodied the purposes of God—in their homes, in their work, in their society.

There are other ways of being Christian, but this way has validated itself in Reformed history. True Calvinists have never been content in being Christian, as some in our time must, in very personal ways. Christopher Dawson, the Catholic cultural historian, has observed that the Calvinists, more than any other people, shaped history and formed culture.

What Calvinists called a saint, a later generation, Michael Walzer would say, called a politician. If Augustine and Calvin did not expect too much of society, neither did they expect too little. Today, as aware as we must be of the limitation of our finiteness as well as our sin, we must not expect too little.

Third, let us remember that we are resident aliens whose citizenship is in heaven. Augustine did not have unrealistic expectations of Rome. Thus, he could rejoice in its greatness without despairing over its failures. He did not ask that it give what was beyond its power. Rome the eternal was the eternal arrogance and pretension of man. Augustine knew that Rome was finite, limited by space and time, transient, and flawed by human self-seeking.

We have to face the fact that there is no assurance that the problems of our time will be solved or even can be solved. In the course of history many problems have passed before they were resolved. Nothing in the New Testament assures us that love will ever triumph in history, or that nuclear war, for example, will be avoided. Our tasks are to contribute as much as we can to the establishment of liberty and justice on this planet, and to accommodate the vision of the city of God to an imperfect society without losing the vision and without deceiving ourselves that we are the "righteous"; but our destiny may be to live in the midst of only partially resolved problems, trusting God and seeking to do his will, sustained by the serenity that such faith and commitment distill from the stuff of life.

Eustace Percy once wrote of John Knox that the best servants of the state are those who have as their first loyalty not the state but God. It may well be that the best solutions of the great problems will come from those whose first concern is not the solution of those problems but fidelity to God and his cause in all the earth. The vivid awareness of God, of his cause, of the self in the presence of God are themselves historical events that shape history in ways not deliberately intended.

Herbert Butterfield, one of the most distinguished of twentieth-century historians, has observed that the convictions (the spiritual character of personality, for example) that illustrate the importance of Christianity in our mundane history spring from the nature of the gospel itself and "show that the Church has best served civilization not on occasions when it had civilization as its conscious object, but when it was most intent on the salvation of souls and most content to leave the rest to Providence."

Emil Brunner, in an address at Yale University in 1947, summarized this whole matter very well. He said that the United States was perhaps the greatest achievement of the human spirit, but he went on to say that the time would come when the United States no longer would exist. Yet when that day comes, every human self still will be. In this sense, what happens in the history of a human soul (self) is more important than what happens in a great society. This truth about life was confirmed for Augustine when Rome fell.

Our task is to do the best we can, committing our work to the providence of God, knowing that all that is good and faithful will be preserved in the city of God, which endures eternally. Human security is to be found in no human enterprise. The only permanence is in God.

The great hymn of our tradition, which Presbyterians may have sung more than any other, confesses this confidence in God.

> The Lord is God indeed;
>   Without our aid he did us make
> We are his folk, he doth us feed,
>   And for his sheep, he doth us take.
> The Lord our God is good,
>   His mercy is forever sure;
> His truth at all times firmly stood,
>   And shall from age to age endure.
>   (Psalm 100, *Psalter*, 1561)

"Remembering the Protestant Reformation"

November 5, 1990   October 26, 1990

Nassau Presbyterian Church,   *Presbyterian Outlook*
Princeton, New Jersey

Martin Luther nailed (or, as some say, mailed to the archbishop) the Ninety-five Theses to the church door at Wittenberg on October 31, 1517. This is a convenient date for remembering the origin of the Protestant Reformation.

The Reformation was one of the great revivals of the Christian church, if not the greatest. Roland Bainton has said that the Reformation postponed the secularization of Europe for a century and a half and made Christian faith, once again, the concern of political leaders, of business people, and even of the person behind the plough.

Reformation Sunday occurs this year during a period when the church desperately needs to understand the significance of the Reformation. The Reformation was not, first of all, a protest against corruption in the church; it was not preoccupied with the organization of the church or with the relevance of its message to the political, social, and economic concerns of the day. The emphasis of Reformation was not on what people do, but on what God has done. It was supremely a message about God's intentions for his creation and what God has done for the salvation of human beings.

The slogans of the Reformation—*Scripture alone, Grace alone, Faith alone*—all point to this emphasis upon what God does for us and for our salvation.

Martin Luther experienced God's action preeminently in the awareness that God's favor cannot be earned but is freely given and that out of the forgiveness of God the Christian life flows. For Zwingli and for Calvin, there was an added emphasis upon the word that God has spoken out of the mystery that encompasses human existence about the meaning and significance of human life.

The Primacy of Theology

The Reformation took theology with supreme seriousness. The primary qualifications of the minister were the capacity to interpret scripture and to explicate it theologically and apply it to life. Luther expressly declared that Protestants may be no better than papists. The significance of Protestantism was not in the Protestants' moral virtue, but in the fact that they proclaimed the message that was for the salvation of all people.

Stephen Ozment has written that the Reformation for the first time in human history declared that ideas are critically important in the shaping of life. What a person believes determines in considerable measure who that person is and how that person shapes society in community with others. The church lives by the hearing of the word of God, not by organizational skills, not by political, economic, and social nostrums. Only the word of God is necessary for the church's existence, especially the proclamation of the word with integrity under the power of the Holy Spirit.

Thus the Reformation emphasis stands in contrast to the prevailing ethos of our society. In contemporary life, civility takes priority over faith, in part because faith is not considered as important as the various political, economic, and social agendas of our society. Those who are the most tolerant about faith are not infrequently the most intolerant about their various social, cultural, political, and economic programs.

On several occasions in my life, I have been a member of civic clubs. A few years ago, I became a member of a downtown club in the city of Richmond. I was impressed originally by the fervency with which members of the club prayed before we ate our meal and with the conviction in which they made their prayers in the name of Jesus Christ. All of this changed in the past several years, and only infrequently now does a member of this civic club mention the name of Jesus Christ.

Even church publications substitute the letters C.E. (common era) for A.D., *anno Domini* (in the year of our Lord). Increasingly, global missions minimize preaching the gospel to make converts and to establish churches, though one-third of the world has never heard of Jesus Christ and some six hundred cities with populations in excess of one hundred thousand have little or no Christian witness. We are increasingly reluctant to say clearly that Jesus Christ is incomparably the most important event in human history and that the commitment of life to Jesus Christ as Lord and Savior is the most important human decision any person ever makes.

Pluralism and diversity are good words in our society. Yet the fact is that neither pluralism nor diversity is an unqualified good. While diversity undoubtedly contributes to human creativity, there always comes a point where diversity and pluralism become destructive—not only of political and economic good, but also of human life. The Bible emphasizes that the human race is one; but from the patriarchs' concern about their sons marrying Canaanite women to the powerful imagery of the book of Revelation, a continual stream of biblical teaching emphasizes the separation of the community of faith from social, political, and economic life that denies that faith. In the Bible, God has enemies: "Come out from among them and be ye separate" is a persistent admonition.

The Reality of Faith

Fifty years ago, the Christian faith could be taken for granted. Christians may not have been *au courant*. They may not have read the Sunday *New York Times* or gone to the theatre or been open to every new economic and political nostrum. Then the great battle in the church was against conservative Christianity. (I do not use the word *fundamentalism* here, because *fundamentalism* has become jargon for any views we do not like.) The issue was being with the times.

The plight of the church today is that many people in the church, even in the leadership of the church, are not aware that the issues have changed. Today, modernity is not at risk, but the Protestant faith and, more basically, the catholic faith of the Apostles' Creed, the Nicene Creed, the Chalcedonian Definition, and the Doctrine of the Trinity are at risk.

The doctrines at risk in our society and even in the church can be stated more specifically:

1. God's personal activity in the created order
2. Jesus Christ as the Word made flesh, fully God, fully human
3. The doctrine of justification by grace through faith—that is, God's work for our salvation bearing our sins upon the cross
4. God's raising of Jesus Christ, crucified, from the dead
5. God as Triune in being
6. The experience of the Bible as the word of God written
7. Eternal life as a continuance of personal existence beyond death

All of these doctrines were firmly affirmed in the church until quite recently. Historically, the churches that have grown, that have made converts and built new congregations, have been passionately convinced of this faith. There is no evidence that those who refuse to affirm these doctrines have ever built many churches or brought many people into the life of the church. There is increasing evidence that the decline of mainline churches is closely related to the loss of passionate Christian conviction and the tendency of theological seminaries to become institutes for the study of religion rather than the training of pastors to preach the word of God, to teach the word of God, and to exercise pastoral care in the light of the faith.

The church has more to learn from those memorable lines from W. B. Yeats's "The Second Coming" than it does from most sociological and psychological studies of the churches' decline that are now so popular but that seldom touch upon preaching, teaching, and pastoral care:

> The blood-dimmed tide is loosed, and everywhere
> The ceremony of innocence is drowned;
> The best lack all conviction, while the worst
> Are full of passionate intensity.

The Central Issue

The central issue for the churches today is the question Jesus put to his disciples, "Who do you say that I am?" (Matt. 16:15) Those who have built churches and established congregations have answered with passionate conviction in the words of Peter, "You are the Christ, the Son of the living God" (Matt. 16:16).

The changing events of our day are likely to confront us in the church with the crisis of faith. For the past century, the chief alternative to Christian faith has been communism. The communist movement was beguiling. It took words that had received meaning from Christian faith, such as justice, peace, and community, and used them to advertise and sell its own program. The current criticisms of communism are not new. Most of them were available in Milovan Djilas's *The New Class,* which was published in the 1950s.

Yet the church did not hear. Many in its leadership were much kinder to the communists than they were to any right-wing rulers, forgetting that the transcendence of God must be acknowledged over all political orders, communism or democracy, and over the left wing of the Democratic party quite as much as the right wing of the Republican party. The transcendence of God over all human activity and the moral and theological ambiguity of all theological problems was forgotten. Some in the church even wanted to make socialism a fundamental article of Christian faith.

Events in our time have made painfully clear what many in the church refused to acknowledge in the past century. Now communism and Marxism have been exposed and have been demonstrated by history to be flawed ways of organizing society, as well as false faiths.

The Challenge of Islam

The chief option to Christian faith in the decades that lie ahead is likely to be Islam. The challenge of Islam will radically change the way in which human life can be lived. The rise of Islam, no less than the demise of Marxism, exposes the inadequacy of the ideologies of the left in Western society.

This was amply demonstrated in the Salman Rushdie affair when the liberal establishment, in Britain as well as in America, was paralyzed. The Rushdie affair called into question all the axioms and presuppositions of diversity and pluralism. When pluralism and diversity are contrasted with Islamic societies, the virtues of pluralism become apparent. Yet the confrontation of Islamic society also exposes the limits of pluralistic interpretations of human life in society.

In Islam, we are confronted with people who are not only passionate about their economic and political convictions, but are also passionate about their religious faith. The Muslims have the motivation of those who are convinced that Allah wills it. (Max Weber once pointed out how the doctrine of predestination invigorated Western societies of Northern Europe and of the United States.)

We ought to recognize the profound truth in Weber's observation today in the reality of the Islamic community. The recent "London manifesto" of the Islamic community made very clear that the Muslims in England have no intention of being assimilated into English society, as the liberal ethos has modified all other communities of faith.

The communist movement and Marxist philosophy can be understood theologically as the judgment of God upon the social lethargy of Christian communities. By the same token, Christians may—and indeed ought to—understand the confrontation with Islam as God's judgment upon the theological ambiguity and the anemic faith of many Christian communities.

Islam may force Christian churches and theological institutions to place as high a value upon the theological message and upon the theological competence of pastors to explicate the word of God found in scripture as Islam does upon the passionate faith of its own communities.

Reformation Day is once again highly relevant. The Reformation made clear that the church exists not upon human activity but upon what God has done. The church lives by the passionate proclamation of the message of God's gracious acts for our salvation.

The only thing essential for the church is the word of God. Pastors are important for the life of the church not because they are community goodwill activists, therapists, or civic club leaders, but because at 11 A.M. on Sunday, they interpret the scriptures with passionate integrity.

"The Crucifixion and the Mystery of Freedom"
March 1972   March 27, 1972

Union Theological Seminary   *Presbyterian Outlook*

Many dimensions of human existence come to focus in the crucifixion of Jesus, but none comes more sharply to focus than the mystery of freedom: the freedom of Jesus who set his face like flint toward Jerusalem and who from the cross prayed for his crucifiers; the freedom of the crucifiers and scoffers who nailed him to the cross and who taunted him; the freedom of the people standing by watching; the freedom of the criminals crucified with Jesus, the one joining the scoffers and the other asking for help. And then there is the freedom of God, who in sovereignty over nature and history raised Jesus from the dead.

The very possibility of a crucifixion tells us something significant about the nature of human existence. Animals do not have crucifixions. Crucifixion is a human phenomenon that we have to take seriously if we are to understand who we are. And the sheer wonder of a resurrection tells us about a freedom that is beyond us and that is our hope.

I

Let us begin with the mystery and the wonder of human freedom. Some three billion years ago, life appeared upon this planet. Some two million years ago, perhaps, an extraordinary species called man emerged. The evolution that produced him was a succession of unique and unrepeatable events, events in which no cause was ever an adequate explanation of its consequence. In his book *So Human an Animal,* Theodore Dobzhansky of Rockefeller University has put it like this: "It is most unlikely that anything remotely resembling man has ever emerged in the evolution of extraterrestrial life, even if intelligible beings exist elsewhere. It is just as

103

unlikely that if mankind were destroyed or should destroy itself, a new mankind would evolve. The possibility of an exact repetition of man has a probability close to zero."

Man's uniqueness can be described in many ways. His remarkable achievements in no small measure depend on so seemingly an insignificant fact as opposing thumb and forefinger. Man is unique as a toolmaker.

Man's uniqueness can better be described in terms of his brain capacity and the powers of the human mind. The appearance of the human mind with its powers of analysis, memory, speech, and concepts is a most remarkable fact in the history of the universe. The mind has the power to read off the facts of the universe, indeed to think the universe in some measure. A scientist sitting in his study can by thought conclude there ought to be an unseen planet; then when he checks his thoughts by observation, he finds that his thoughts were true to the facts. Next to a life of love, the human mind is the most remarkable thing in all the universe. (William Temple, *Nature, Man and God*)

Man's uniqueness can be described in terms of language and symbol-making, or in terms of a cultural memory that enables one generation to pass on its achievements to the next.

In all of these ways man is unique, but man's uniqueness comes most sharply to expression in his freedom. Man not only thinks; he also knows that he thinks. Man is not only conscious of the world; he is self-conscious. He has the remarkable capacity to make the world the object of his thought and, beyond this, to make his own existence the object of critical reflection. Man can, as it were, stand outside of himself and look at himself, evaluate himself, talk to himself, and praise or blame himself. In this way man gains a freedom over nature, over history, and over his own life.

Man can objectify his own existence and be aware of the fact that he is a creature of instincts, impulses, and momentary desires. Animals, so far as we know, cannot. They are slaves of their instincts, impulses, and momentary desires. If you put food in the presence of a hungry dog, he eats. But if you put food in the presence of a hungry man, he may not eat. He may simply want to lose weight, or he may want to give up a meal to feed hungry people in Asia.

Man can also objectify his cultural existence and gain some freedom over the history of which he is a part. Some of us are native Americans and Southerners. Every word we speak betrays this fact. Of greater significance than our cultural origin is the fact that we know that we are Americans and Southerners, and we can imagine ourselves as being British or Vietnamese. The fact that we know that we are Southerners is the occasion for the freedom to break with our cultural origins.

Man can also objectify his own personal existence. He can critically reflect upon his petty envies and his silly jealousies, and he can resolve to eliminate them. He can also objectify his loyalties and his commitments, and resolve to deepen and enlarge them.

The most significant fact about man is his freedom to break the chain of nature and instinct, to stand in judgment of his own culture, to evaluate his own life, and in some measure to change its direction. Because men have this freedom, we have crucifixions.

II

But the crucifixion of Jesus was not simply a matter of freedom. As Peter put it in his sermon after Pentecost, "When he had been given up to you, by the deliberate will and plan of God, you used heathen men to crucify and kill him" (Acts 2:23). Heathen men willed to crucify him, but they were caught up in a destiny that obscured their freedom. On the level of all human activities, we are very much aware of a destiny that shapes our future quite as much as we are aware of our freedom. The ineluctable forces of environment, biochemical inheritance, and historical situation move us relentlessly toward our destiny. When we think back to the significant moments in our own lives, we are very much aware that we were in those crucial situations not simply as a result of our free acts but also of a destiny that was thrust upon us.

This has been illustrated very well for us in the case of Lt. William Calley. In part, the protest against his conviction grew out of an awareness that his acts at My Lai were not simply acts of free will. Ineluctable forces of history had placed Lt. Calley at My Lai. And moreover, as Robert J. Lifton has commented, Calley did not invent the "body count," which in the retrospect of history may be the greatest atrocity of Vietnam; nor did he invent the "free fire zone." By the ineluctable forces of history, Lt. Calley was in an atrocity-producing situation. And yet there is the haunting awareness that, whatever our judgment of Lt. Calley may be, My Lai cannot be simply a matter of destiny. It was also a matter of freedom. In a sense, we all willed and did not will My Lai.

This matter of destiny and freedom is again illustrated in the generation gap. Certainly this gap is more a matter of destiny than it is the result of free choice. It is the destiny of those of us who are fifty, for example, to have lived through the Depression: a reality, a symbol, that is surely unintelligible to those under thirty. Following his monumental study of Hiroshima, Robert J. Lifton concluded that the most significant consciousness of those born after August 6, 1945, is the awareness that they may be the last generation in the experiment of living, which again is a consciousness that those of us who are fifty and older cannot fully grasp.

The crucifiers of Jesus did not simply put him to death in their freedom. Many forces relentlessly moved them to this act. In relation to most people in our society, readers of *The Outlook* are likely to have a maximum amount of freedom as a result of genetic endowments, education, and place in society. We must therefore never forget that many people have very little freedom at all. They are caught by the inexorable demands of their biochemical inheritance and of their histories. But for all of us human life is in varying mixtures a compound of destiny and freedom. The crucifiers of Jesus chose but did not choose to crucify him. Today we choose but do not choose Vietnam.

III

The role of destiny in human life should lead us to judgments of charity concerning our neighbors. But let us come a step further and note that for us the emphasis must be on freedom. A consideration of the crucifixion leads straight to the question, What am I doing with my freedom that is my radical uniqueness as a human being?

Limited as man's freedom is, he has a residual dignity that makes him responsible for the time and energy that have come to him as gifts from God.

Limited as man's freedom is, he has a residual dignity that makes him accountable for the Vietnams, for the crises in the city and in the schools.

Victor Frankl has borne this testimony: "We who lived in concentration camps can remember the men who walked through the huts comforting others, giving away their last piece of bread. They may have been few in number, but they offer sufficient proof that everything can be taken from a man but one thing: the last of the human freedoms—to choose one's attitude in any given set of circumstances, to choose one's own way."[1]

Ortega y Gasset has well written, "There is no doubt that the most radical division that is possible to make of humanity is that which splits it

---

[1]Victor Frankl, *Man's Search for Meaning* (Boston: Beacon Press, 1962), 65.

into two classes of creatures: those who make great demands on themselves, piling up difficulties and duties; and those who demand nothing special of themselves, but for whom to live is to be every moment what they already are, without imposing on themselves any effort towards perfection, mere buoys on the wave."[2]

Today we stand in judgment on the abuse of human freedom in the crucifixion of Jesus. But Christians through the centuries have always heard in the crucifixion the judgment of God upon their own abuse of the dignity and possibilities of human existence. We who are the critics of the crucifiers of Jesus must ask, What are we doing with the gift of freedom in the time and place where God has put us?

IV

The freedom of man in the crucifixion of Jesus is not, however, the last word. The last word is the freedom of God. This freedom is the source of our freedom. How else can we explain the miracle of freedom in the history of the universe? This freedom is also the answer to man's misuse of freedom. In the resurrection there was manifested a Divine Freedom that undid what men had done in the crucifixion, and a freedom that broke the power of nature to destroy man in death.

Man's freedom is man's misery as well as his grandeur. Freedom as well as destiny has led to Vietnam, to narcotics addiction, to sexual debauchery and irresponsibility, to human tragedy and misery. Even our highest achievements contain hidden flaws that are finally their undoing. Man's freedom is the uniqueness and the possibility of human existence, but it is not a gospel that heals the hurts or puts together the broken pieces. The gospel is not the freedom of man, but the freedom of God, who forgives the sinner and who raises the dead.

[2]Ortega y Gasset, *Revolt of the Masses* (New York: W. W. Norton, 1932), 69.

"If a Man Die, Shall He Live Again?"

First Presbyterian Church, Charlotte, North Carolina
March 21, 1993
Nassau Presbyterian Church, Princeton, New Jersey
March 28, 1993

(Job 14:14)

Job's question "If a man die, shall he live again?" is the human question. Job knew that life is short, that our days are numbered and that we cannot add to them. And sooner or later each of us knows this too, even in an affluent, scientifically and technologically advanced society. Life is an uphill battle, and in spite of illusions along the way, we all in the end lose. We all die.

Job's question is no longer asked so frequently in our society, in part because of the illusion that we can somehow avoid it and in part because of the idea that death is simply a natural biological fact that is not too serious. A secular society cannot bring itself to take death seriously. We debate endlessly in our schools about the origin of the world, but we say little or nothing about the end of the world, though that should be the more pressing question for us. A secular society cannot take either death or the end of the world seriously because it has no plausible answer to the questions they raise.

Job's question also is no longer asked in the New Testament, but for a very different reason. Here everything is seen in the light of the greatest event in human history: God raised Jesus Christ from the dead, changing, as Clement of Alexandria, a second-century theologian, said, all of our sunsets into sunrises. Thus John writes, "Let not your hearts be troubled" (John 14:1), and Paul declares that we sorrow not as those who have no hope (1 Thess. 4:13). In the light of the resurrection, we shall reflect on Job's question this morning.

I

Let us begin with the fact of death, as sooner or later every culture, every society, and every person must. Ambassador George Kennan, in a personal

108

letter to me, once declared on the basis of his experience in Moscow that nothing in all of the world is quite so dreary as a communist funeral in which the meaninglessness of life is expounded by the meaninglessness of death. Ambassador Kennan also reported that Ambassador Bohlen who had preceded him had believed that communism was doomed because it had no adequate answer for the fact of death. A secular culture has very little to say in the presence of death, and it repudiates the ancient wisdom that human life should be a meditation upon death. In a secular culture death is at best a natural fact, a biological event.

Death may be simply a natural fact for animals. But for human beings death is never simply a natural, biological fact. Death is complicated by the power of the human spirit to imagine something beyond this present life, to contemplate a life not enclosed by death, and to above all grasp something of the meaning and significance of life itself. Augustine, the great North African theologian, spoke of the basic difference between dying and having to die. Animals simply die. But human beings have to die. They know that death is unavoidable. Yet they can imagine something greater than death. The New Testament declares that death is the last enemy to be destroyed. Writers of the New Testament knew full well that death is part of the created order and as such belongs to the goodness of God's world, but they also knew that sin complicates the fact of death and makes death itself the occasion of great sin. They knew, apart from their faith that God raised Jesus from the dead, that death calls into question the meaning of human life and history.

Death is not simply a natural fact for human beings. Yet neither should Christians conceive of it as a fate or a power that overwhelms life. Karl Rahner, the most influential Catholic theologian of the twentieth century, insists that death should be understood as an event in which the dying person participates. Death should be the occasion when we bring to an end this particular episode of our human existence. Indeed Rahner concludes that death is the occasion of the greatest human freedom when we make the final commitment of who we are and of our life's work.

Death is not simply a personal and individual problem. It is also a social, public, and community problem. Individuals die but so do institutions, cultures, societies, great nations. In recent years many have found the meaning of life, not so much in their own personal existence, but in the causes with which they are identified. Yet the fact is our causes all die. Hence death is the pivotal question not simply for the individual but also for public social existence.

Reinhold Niebuhr in his great study of the limits and possibilities of history concluded with a chapter on the end of history. Everything depends on whether the end is finish or fulfillment. Without the doctrine embodied in the Christian affirmations of the resurrection of the body, the judgment, and the second coming of Jesus Christ, it is impossible for a Christian who trusts the living God to make any sense out of history.

II

Over against death, we hope. This hope arises first of all in human experience. The hope of individual existence beyond death is one of the few universal ideas, not that everyone has affirmed it but in every human society going back to Neanderthal people the idea has been affirmed in the care of the dead, in burial rites, and in literature.

Human beings in every time and in every place have known the reality of meaning and of love, and on the basis of this deep human knowledge they have challenged the sovereignty of death. As Tennyson put it:

> Thou madest man, he knows not why,
> He thinks he was not made to die;
> And thou hast made him: Thou art just.

Our awareness of that in human life that ought not to die may be more apparent in others than in our own lives. It may be more apparent in the life of a friend whose friendship has blessed us along life's way, in persons whose lives remarkably embody intelligence, judgment, courage, and generosity. A world that does not care for the wonder, dignity, beauty, and generosity of human lives is unjust and irrational.

The injustices of life must be noted. The expectancy of life after death has been declared a reason for injustice. Feuerbach insisted that immortality and God alike were projections of human desires. Eternal life is an articulation of our desire for ourselves, simply wish fulfillment. Karl Marx and Freud followed in Feuerbach's train. Admittedly there is some truth in the contention that hope of heaven may be only the projection of human desires. Yet even if it is, the fact that we wish for heaven does not invalidate the idea, however much the wish may corrupt it.

In some societies religion perhaps has been the opiate of the people, and persons have been persuaded to put up with injustice now for glory later. But this is surely not true of the secular society in which we live. Our society may be uncertain about whether or not there is a heaven beyond death, but many groups in the society certainly intend to establish heaven here on Earth. When God is forgotten, everything depends upon the human act. Hence in many social activities, and not least in the communist world, a fanaticism frequently has developed in bringing in a heaven on Earth that would not exist apart from human effort. Belief in heaven and in a God that raises the dead has given Christians through the centuries a certain equanimity in the face of martyrdom as well as the tragedies of society. At its best it has led to responsibility without fanaticism.

Christian hope does have relevance to the needs for justice today. It is reported that in the 1950s Karl Menninger lectured at a prominent school in the Deep South. During the discussion period a student asked him to emphasize to the audience how injustice had been perpetuated particularly in the South by the promise of heaven and that, by and by, religion really was the opiate of the people. Dr. Menninger replied that as a Presbyterian elder he believed in eternal life and that he would like to make just one comment. If there is no pie in the sky, by and by, he said, then a great many people in our society are never going to get any pie at all.

Furthermore the doctrine of eternal life has added a certain dignity to every human life. It declares in the clearest way that just as God is the origin of life, so God is the end of life. The meaning of human existence cannot be written on earth between birth and death. It has its origin in God's grace and its fulfillment in God's heaven.

Our real hope in the presence of death is not based upon human experience or on the need for justice. Our understanding of the Christian hope is determined by our belief about God.

When we say, "I believe in God, the Father Almighty," we declare that the world and human life are not the products of impersonal forces but are the expression of purpose and intentionality. And when we affirm that the God and father of our Lord, Jesus Christ, is the creator, we declare that the world and human life are the expression of grace and of love.

The foundation of our Christian hope rests finally not on our human experience and not even upon our general belief in God but upon the New Testament witness that God raised Jesus Christ from the dead. As God raised Jesus from the dead, we affirm that God will raise us. Paul declared, "If Christ has not been raised, your faith is futile" (1 Cor. 15:17). The resurrection is the unique event in human history on which everything else depends.

III

Let us come a step further and ask, What is this personal destiny or identity for which we hope? The traditional language both of the New Testament and of Christian theology has been the resurrection of the body. By this the church has meant not the resuscitation of a dead body or the reconstruction of the biochemical elements of the human body but rather that the life lived in history and expressed through the body is fulfilled beyond history. The resurrection of the body means that a person's life in history, work done in history, human relationships that grew in this history, and the character shaped in this history are brought to their completion in the consummation of all things. Existence beyond death does not annul but fulfills life in history.

The soul in popular language stands in contrast to the body. Yet it must be understood in distinction not in contrast from the body. The soul may be, as John Eccles speculates, a higher form of energy than the body. In Christian theology the soul is the person, the deciding, acting, speaking, living I. The soul uses the body and in history acts through the body.

A secular society has a strong bias in affirming that the self is simply the function of the brain. The New Testament always assumes that the self is more than simply a bodily function, though it expresses itself through the body. This conviction of the New Testament is also intimated in our own personal knowledge of self. We know in the depth of human experience that the I is more than the body. Wilder Penfield of McGill University, a distinguished Presbyterian elder and a leader in the field of medicine, made an interesting observation in an autobiographical summary of his work as a neurosurgeon. He said he began his work with a conviction that the self or the mind is simply the function of the body, but after a life of work on the human brain, he came to the opposite conclusion. He declared that by the manipulation of the cerebral cortex he had compelled people to do many things: to raise their arms, to utter words, to recall things that they had forgotten more vividly than they had understood them before. Yet he said in all of his experience, he had never caused a person by manipulation of the brain to act personally. The person always said, "You did this to me. You made me do this." Penfield concluded that it would be impossible simply through manipulation of the brain to bring the person to a personal act.

John Eccles, a Nobel Prize winner in neurology, likewise was so impressed with the human self that he affirmed the possibility of the old medieval doctrine of creation or ensoulment when at a particular time God creates the soul in the fetus. And he also concluded as did Penfield that the self uses the brain as a computer and as a source of power.[1]

----

[1] See John C. Eccles, *The Human Mystery* (New York: Springer Verlag, 1979) and Wilder Penfield, *The Mystery of the Mind: A Critical Study of Consciousness and the Human Brain* (Princeton: Princeton University Press, 1975).

The New Testament speaks of the soul going immediately into the presence of God. Paul tells the Philippians he does not know whether it would be better to work with them or to go to be with Christ. Later in the Philippian letter he looks forward to the consummation of all things when every knee shall bow and every tongue shall confess Jesus is Lord. It is impossible to bring into complete harmony all the New Testament statements about the end of human life and the consummation of all things. These statements point to that which is beyond our experience and about which we must speak very modestly. Yet the New Testament speaks with great finality about a final judgment and resurrection on the last day.

The soul going to be with Christ at death and the final judgment are not necessarily in conflict. The simple fact is there can be no final judgment until the end of all things. We do not know the significance of historical events in our time until many years have passed. We do not know the meaning of an individual human life until we see its full ramifications in society and in subsequent history. The significance of events in our own history are not fully known until long after they have occurred. The last judgment also means there is no individual destiny apart from the destiny of the entire human race. We are not simply individuals; we are a community, and the significance of human life has to be seen in both dimensions. We are individuals and we are the human community.

The New Testament affirms but never puts together what happens at the moment of death and what happens in the consummation of all things. Neither is complete without the other.

The New Testament speaks of individual destiny in terms of heaven and hell, and so has Christian literature and Christian piety.

No one can be glad there is a hell, and no one ought to foreclose on what God's grace can do. Particularly, none should desire a hell in order to seek revenge or punishment for other people.

Nickolas Berdyaev once said the only legitimate argument for hell is that if people want to go to hell there ought to be a hell for them to go to. Hell can be understood as God's final ratification of the decisions that human beings have persistently and tenaciously made over a long period of time concerning their own lives.

The best indication we have as to the nature of heaven is the experience we now have of life with God—that is, a life of trust, gratitude, humility, openness to the neighbor, generosity of spirit. John Baillie, a Scottish theologian writing in 1934, quotes a novelist as saying that the "banality of human amusements is the most cogent argument against the immortality of the soul."[2] This statement written before World War II is even more true today. Who would care for an eternity watching soap operas or listening to much of the music on radio and TV, or even watching sports? Heaven is life with Christ in the presence of God. The joys of heaven are the joys of a life of grace.

Eternal life has a depth and a breadth that goes beyond anything we know in human experience, but those moments when we experience the breadth and depth and greatness of what it is to be a human being made in the image of God are our best indications of what heaven is like.

IV

The ancient question of Job, the truly human question, confronts us with the ultimate option of faith. On the one hand is the option of a radical pessimism that finds human life without ground, without meaning, and without purpose. On the other hand is the hope of everlasting life with God. John Baillie concludes his book on eternal life with the observation that none of us can sneer at those who in the dark night of the soul conclude that human life has no meaning. Yet those who have passed into or at least have had a glimpse of the marvelous brightness of Christian expectation can only exclaim, "Now to him who by the power at work within us is able to do far more abundantly than all that we ask or think, to him be glory in the church and in Christ Jesus to all generations, for ever and ever. Amen" (Eph. 3:20–21).

[2]John Baillie, *And the Life Everlasting* (London: Oxford University Press, 1934), 198.

"The Holy Spirit and the Christian Life"

First Presbyterian Church, Auburn, Alabama,
(and many other churches)

Acts 2:1–13

Today is Pentecost. It was originally a Jewish festival, but in the Christian church we observe this day because it commemorates the coming of the Holy Spirit upon the disciples. It has been called, with good reason, the birthday of the Christian church. Our task today is to ask, What does Pentecost mean concretely for the life of the church today?

The account of Pentecost was read as scripture this morning. For most of us this record is something of a bewilderment. We are not sure what to make of it. We are not sure we can approve what we can make of it. The setting was a Jewish festival, which possibly was better attended than any other. For this reason, a large number of Jews were in Jerusalem, representing many countries. The disciples of Jesus were also there gathered in one place. "And suddenly a sound came from heaven like the rush of a mighty wind, and it filled all the house where they were sitting. And there appeared to them tongues as of fire. . . . And they were all filled with the Holy Spirit and began to speak in other tongues, as the Spirit gave them utterance" (Acts 2:2–4). The reaction of the visitors to Jerusalem was diverse. Some thought the disciples were drunk. Others heard them speaking in their own language, the word of God. Now what are we to make of this? What does it mean for us who live in the twentieth century?

Let us seek to answer this question by asking three questions. What is the Spirit? What does the Spirit do? How does the Spirit come alive in a person's life?

I

Spirit is not an easy word for a modern person to understand. We cannot see a spirit, and that which is not somehow material reality—affecting in

115

some way our senses—seems to us to be unreal. And yet we cannot get along without the word. We refer to the spirit of a person. Again it is somewhat difficult to define precisely the spirit of a person, but we know that a person's spirit is more important than the physical reality. The spirit of a person is the power of one's personhood. The spirit is a power by which a person is recognized to be himself. The spirit enables us to be truly present to one another.

We also refer to the spirit of a group. Again, the spirit of a group is a most important fact that we can know about the group. So while the word *spirit* is difficult for us, it is also an indispensable word.

It should not surprise us that the word *spirit*, which is so important in human affairs, should also be important in religion. From the earliest times people have been aware—or at any rate they felt they were aware—of the presence of God. God's presence could not be seen. The presence of God was an experience that only images could convey, such as the fierce wind of the desert, or the breath of a living creature. It is significant that the same word has been used for *wind* and *breath* and *spirit*. We can see the effects of the wind, and yet we cannot see the wind. We know that there is such a thing as life which we call breath, and yet we cannot see life. People in all ages have taken these words for breath and wind and used them to indicate the spirit of God. When the Old Testament speaks of the spirit of God, it means God in action. The spirit of God is the power of God's personhood, the power by which God is present to us. The Bible begins by ascribing the creation of the world to the spirit of God. The history of the universe is the spirit of God in action. The spirit of God is ever at work in nature, in history, in human life and wherever there is a flagging of energy or corruption of life or self-destruction, the spirit has been present to renew, energize, and create again. The spirit is the inspiration of the prophets and the creator of civilizations. The spirit of God is the power of God's personhood at work in the world.

Now someone may protest that the spirit of God is a very vague and diffused term. How can we know that the spirit that moves us, that we see moving other people, is the spirit of God? The Hebrew prophets answered that the spirit of God is the Holy Spirit. Holy means separated. But the emphasis in the Hebrew religion was so strongly upon the ethical that the word *holy* came to mean righteous. The Holy Spirit is the spirit of righteousness. The spirit is distinguished from all other spirits by ethical consequences.

For Christians there is a further distinguishing mark of the spirit. The spirit of God is the spirit of Christ. So the New Testament uses the spirit of Christ as a synonym of the spirit of God. If there is need to test the spirit to see if it is of God, the New Testament had a clear answer: see if the spirit is the spirit of Christ. As Karl Barth has put it, the Holy Spirit is the spirit of Christ at work in the world.

The doctrinal issue that contributed to the secular separation of Western Christendom from Eastern Christendom seems on the face of it to be rather trivial. The Western version of the Nicene Creed declared that the Holy Spirit proceeds from the Father and the Son, while the Eastern version simply declares that the Spirit proceeds from the Father. This difference in phrases seems to a modern person to be a theological quibble, and yet it involves something that is very important. The spirit of God is not a vague, diffused spirit, but it is the spirit that is projected through the life, death, and resurrection of Jesus Christ.

The spirit of God in general may be compared to a ray of light that is projected upon a screen. We can see the light, but it has no content, no meaning. If this light is projected through a color slide, then it has content and meaning. So Christian theology is saying, in what appears to be a theological quibble, that the spirit of God has been thrown on the screen, as it were, through the life and death and resurrection of Jesus Christ. Now the spirit of God is no longer a vague spirit, but a spirit whose personality we know: the spirit of Christ.

II

Now let us come a step further and ask, What is the work of the spirit of God? The description of the coming of the spirit of Pentecost is somewhat disconcerting. The spirit came as a rushing wind or as a tongue of fire. Taken literally, this phrase means little or nothing to us, but symbolically it is as adequate a description as any modern person could give for the coming of the spirit into a group. Quite evidently the spirit produced excitement. Some thought that those who were excited by the spirit were drunk. Others believed that they heard them speak the things of God in their own language. We know this power of the spirit in many areas of life.

Let us take by analogy the excitement of a crowd at a football game. A person who did not understand what was happening would think that some ordinarily sober persons were drunk. Others, who understood, could appreciate the excitement and also find intelligible many quite nonsensical exclamations. Any real spiritual excitement produces these results. Many find the second chapter of Acts unintelligible simply because they have never been as excited by the spirit of God as they have by a football game.

Yet the real test of any spirit is not the excitement that is produced. All spirits produce excitement. The spirit is judged by the lasting consequences in human life. The disciples who were excited by the spirit of God at Pentecost were transformed. Prior to this excitement they had been a bewildered group held together by the memory of Jesus. Henceforth, they were steadfast disciples. The only explanation that the New Testament ever gives for this remarkable change that came into the lives of these disciples is the simple statement: the Holy Spirit came upon them.

The spirit of God makes us open to and present to God, the world, and each other. The spirit makes us alive. The Holy Spirit is the power that causes us to see and to recognize another person or an ordinary experience of life in a way that we had not recognized or seen before. The Holy Spirit opens our eyes that had been closed, our hearts that had been unaware, and our minds that did not discern reality.

Let us also note that the chapter which begins with the account of Pentecost ends with the economics of an experiment in communal living. This makes very clear that the spirit does not deal with vague, indefinite religious notions, but with the concrete decisions of everyday life. The truest test of the spirit is ethical. Paul put it this way: "the fruit of the Spirit is love, joy, peace, patience, kindness, goodness, faithfulness, gentleness, self-control; against such there is no law" (Gal. 5:22–23).

III

Let us come a step further now and ask, How does this spirit work? How does the spirit enter a person's life? Here we encounter the mystery. And yet we do know that human life is porous. For example, we have all seen persons whose lives reflected the spirit of another person. We say sometimes, "There goes So-and-so all over again." The spirit of one person can enter another person so that it affects the physical movement, the manner of expression, the outlook upon life of the other person. So Paul could exclaim, "I live, yet not I, but Christ who lives in me."

Let us also take the illustration of a group that has a strong and dynamic leader. The leader is not the group yet the group is porous to the leader's influence, so that the life of the group reflects the spirit of the leader.

We do not know exactly how the spirit of the leader can penetrate the group, but we know that this happens. Something very similar happens when the spirit of Christ penetrates the congregation of a Christian church. Now the question remains, How can this happen to me? To my church? The answer is not simple. The spirit cannot be coerced. We cannot simply will for the spirit to possess us as we can take a dose of medicine. Nothing on the personal level is ever so simple. And yet we can do some things. We can control the influences to which we shall deliberately expose our lives. William Temple has well said that the most important choice a person ever makes is a choice of the influences to which this person deliberately submits his or her life.

Anyone who wants to be molded by the spirit of Christ can determine that he or she will stand under the means by which the spirit makes itself known. God's presence is always mediated. No one has seen God face-to-face and lived. God's presence to us is mediated to us through images, through words, through objects: the bread and the wine and the water of the sacraments, or the burning bush in the desert.

The New Testament quite clearly points to means by which the Holy Spirit most frequently makes itself present: the preaching of the word of God, prayer, the singing of praise to God, the fellowship of Christian believers in worship and as they worked and ate together, the reading of scripture, the giving of money in Christian stewardship.

None of us can coerce the spirit's presence, yet if we wish the Holy Spirit to be present to us and to move our lives, we can place ourselves in the context that the Holy Spirit has appointed to be the usual means of grace.

Those who want to know the spirit are most likely to know the spirit if they hear the word of God preached and read the scripture for themselves. If they lift their voices to God in prayer and in praise, if they participate in the fellowship of Christian people, if they are good stewards in offering to God the fruits of their labors, if they go about doing God's will in the world.

Those who want to be molded by the spirit of Christ can seek out the movements of the spirit in the world about them and take their stand in them. There is no difficulty in finding such movements. Wherever you find love for other human beings, and love for God and trust in God increasing, there you can be sure is the movement of the spirit of Christ.

Pentecost has been called the birthday of the church. And rightly so for the church is simply that community of men and women in ages past and in this day and in ages to come who have been and shall be moved by the spirit of God.

Charles Williams has called this history of the church the descent of the dove, or the history of the Holy Spirit in the life of the church. Where the spirit of God is, there is the church as the ancient dictum. The question that confronts us this Pentecost is, Are we ready deliberately to submit our lives to the influence of the Holy Spirit? This is one of the most important choices we shall ever make.

"The Presence of Christ in the Sacrament"

Auburn, Alabama
(No date on record)

An awareness of the divine presence is characteristic of all great religions. Without an awareness of the divine presence, religion in any deep sense simply does not exist. And more than this, without this sense of the divine presence, human life is exceedingly shallow. Men who live deeply, even while repudiating the term *religion*, give evidence of an awareness of the sacred in beauty, truth, and goodness. Until a man knows what it is to stand in the presence of that to which he is unconditionally obligated, he has not known either the meaning of great religion or of human existence.

This awareness of the divine presence comes to a focus for the Christian in the celebration of the sacrament of the Lord's Supper. All Christians have been convinced that the spirit of God is uniquely present in this celebration. For this reason Paul admonished the Corinthians to examine themselves when they came to this table lest they should eat and drink judgment to themselves. And for this reason the ancestors of some of us, the Highland Scots, hesitated to come to this table at all. They had so high an awareness of the divine presence at this table that some of them, though devout, refused to take the elements at all.

In our day talking about the divine presence is not easy, in part due to the lost sense of mystery. Ours is a secular culture. But in part it is due to a well-founded suspicion of those who talk too easily about God and his presence. If there is a God, creator of heaven and earth, no man is going to be on too familiar terms with him or have him at his beck and call. And more than this, we have found much talk about the divine presence to be, in the end, fraudulent. So we rightly hesitate to talk too easily about the divine presence even in the sacrament. In any case we come with questions.

I

Let us begin with the question of magic. How does the spirit of God make this sacrament different from magic? Magic, by definition, is an act that when correctly performed produces its desired consequence automatically, and such an act may be directed toward God and toward other men. Religion, and in particular sacramental religion, is always in danger of becoming magic by attempting to gain control of God through some technique or by attempting to influence people without their knowing what is happening to them or by evading personal, responsible, critical decisions on the part of human beings.

The church has been tempted to fasten God to these elements of bread and wine so that, when this sacrament is celebrated, those who do not consciously put some block in the way automatically received the divine grace. So churchmen on a very crude level once debated what happened to a mouse who ate a consecrated wafer to which the divine presence had been fastened and on a more sophisticated level what to do with the bread and wine that remained after the celebration. If God can be fastened to some finite, limited object that is within our control, then we can dispense divine grace as a commodity and manipulate God to serve our purposes. But the living God can never be fastened to the finite, limited objects that we control. He speaks when and where he chooses. We cannot control his speaking or program his presence. We come to this table in confidence because of the promised presence of God, and in humility because we know that he may speak sometimes in places far removed from this table, even in places where we least expect to know the divine presence.

The church has also been tempted to manipulate people by bypassing conscious, personal decision. A solemn occasion such as the Lord's Supper inevitably alters the subconscious as well as the conscious self. Many children have been more deeply moved and shaped by the participation of their parents in this sacrament, which they did not understand at all, than by many church activities that they understood very well. No one ought to deny those dimensions of human existence that are beyond our self-consciousness. Public speakers, Madison Avenue advertisers, and mass communications experts are all very much aware of the possibilities of influencing people without engaging their self-conscious selves. But we in the church must beware of any attempt to influence the human consciousness in which the self-consciousness does not participate. For this reason, our Protestant forefathers said there is no receiving of the sacrament apart from faith—a personal, responsible decision of the human person.

So we come to this sacrament rejecting magic, any attempt to fasten the living God to the limited finite object we control, and any attempt to influence people without the participation of their self-conscious awareness. The decisive moment in this sacrament is the moment when we hear the words of institution and believe them.

II

Now let us come to a second question. How is Christ present in this celebration? How are we to understand his presence?

Donald Baillie, a Scottish theologian, has suggested that we can best understand the presence of Christ at this sacrament if we begin by asking how he is present elsewhere. Our faith is that God is everywhere present. We believe that God is present in our homes, in the streets of our cities, in the countryside. In fact, God is present everywhere.

And yet we are aware of the fact that God is present with us more in certain places than in others. We are more aware of God's presence usually in the church than on the street.

And more than this we are aware of God's presence in certain special experiences in life and not at other times. In the presence of death, in the face of some great decision, in the moments of joy, we may be aware of God in a way that we are not at any other time.

The simple fact is that God's presence is not so much a spatial thing as a spiritual relationship. We describe this spiritual relationship in spatial terms as though we could localize God and objectify him. By these spatial symbols we mean we are spiritually aware of God at certain times and places as we are not at others. We speak of God as being here and there when what we mean is that we have been spiritually related to God in a unique way at this time or place.

Donald Baillie, in his exposition of the presence of Christ, was influenced by the French philosopher Marcel's analysis of the preposition "with." *With*, he says, points to a spiritual relationship between persons, not simply to juxtaposition in space. A chair may be alongside a table and beside a table but not really *with* a table in the true sense. There may even be two persons in the same room without their being *with* each other except in some minimal sense. "We can have a strong feeling that somebody who is sitting in the same room as ourselves, sitting quite near us, someone whom we can look at and listen to and whom we could touch if we wanted to make a final test of reality, is nevertheless more distant from us than some loved one who is perhaps thousands of miles away or perhaps, even, no longer living. We could say that the man sitting beside us was in the same room with us, but he was not really present there, that his presence did not make itself felt."[1] In some such fashion Christians have conceived the real nature of the presence of Christ in the celebration of the Lord's Supper. God makes use of these elements of bread and wine to awaken in our consciousness an awareness of Christ. In this sacrament Christ is as truly present to faith as these outward symbols of bread and wine are to our senses.

III

This leads us to a third question: What is the content of the divine presence in this sacrament? *Divine presence* or even *spirit of God* are indefinite terms, and we have filled them with amazingly different content. But in this sacrament the spirit is named. The spirit present here is the spirit of Jesus Christ. The content of the presence is his life, what he said and what he did. The breaking of the bread and the pouring of the wine represent to us what he said and what he did. For this reason, the sacraments must always be united with the Word. There is no better preparation for receiving the sacraments than the rereading of one of the Gospels, and there is no faithful participation in the sacrament apart from the recollection of what he said and did. The church has never been willing to say that this sacrament is simply a memorial, a recollecting and remembering, but neither has it been willing to say that it is simply a divine presence, for *presence* alone is undefined. For Christians, God is defined by what Jesus said and did, and so are these elements of bread and wine.

IV

Now all of this brings us to a better understanding of what Paul meant when he said that some who partake of this sacrament eat and drink damnation unto themselves. I can still remember the terror that I experienced as a boy in church when the minister read these words from Paul. And it is surely not pure gain that I no longer experience that terror in the same way.

For this terror is not simply the outcropping of some magical notion of the sacrament. It is the terror of betraying that which is unconditionally

---

[1]Donald M. Baillie, *The Theology of the Sacrament and Other Essays* (New York: Charles Scribner's Sons, 1957), 98–99.

worthy of our loyalty, of treating casually that which demands awe and reverence.

No one in our time has been more aware of this terror than William Temple. Whenever we treat casually that which calls for awe, whenever we lose the sense of reverence for that which demands reverence, we eat and drink damnation unto ourselves.

We catch glimpses of the meaning of this in every realm of life. Let a boy treat lightly the devotion of his mother, let anyone treat casually the claims of truth, let someone trample on beauty, let a person take advantage of loyalty and friendship, and the results begin to show in life.

Let a man come to this table unworthy and he will inevitably eat and drink damnation to himself, for he has sinned against the real presence of the holy.

William Temple once wrote these words, which deserve our most serious consideration:

> If you come there giving nothing, with no intention that your life should be used by God and for him, then you will receive nothing. . . . When we come with those things about us which are the opposite of God, because they are the opposite of love—envy, contempt, resentment, spite—they make a block in the channel through which the life of Christ might reach us. . . . The reality of our communion with Christ and in Him with one another is the increase of love in our hearts. If a man goes out from His communion to love and serve man better, he has received the real presence. If he feels every thrill and tremor of devotion, but goes selfish as before, he has not received it. It was offered but he did not receive it. . . ."[2]

The presence of Christ is always a gift that we cannot program. Yet God's promise is that if we come to the sacrament with faith and repentance, we shall experience the reality of the Christ whose life, death, and resurrection we remember.

[2]William Temple, *Christian Faith and Practice* (London: Student Christian Movement Press, 1931).

An Awareness of Destiny
March 13, 1977

The *Protestant Radio Hour* Sermon

Ephesians 1:3–6

The Christian community lives by tradition. Tradition is the authoritative delivery of a faith, a style of life from one person to another, from one generation to the next, enabling each generation to live out of the accumulated wisdom of the past.

In Joseph Stein's play, the fiddler on the roof had a hard time trying to scratch out a pleasant, simple tune without breaking his neck. His predicament was a parable of life for us all. You may ask, "Why do we stay here if it is so dangerous? We stay because Anatevka is our home. And how do we keep our balance? That I tell you in a word—'tradition' . . . because of our tradition, we have kept our balance for many, many years."

The great tradition by which the Christian community lives is God's revelation and work for human salvation in Jesus Christ. The gospel of God's presence in Jesus Christ has been traditioned in many ways. In this series of *Protestant Hour* services, the contribution of the Reformed tradition to the total Christian community is being emphasized. The Reformed tradition had its origin in the Reformation of the sixteenth century, particularly in Zurich under the leadership of Huldrich Zwingli and in Geneva under Calvin. It has greatly influenced American life, particularly through the achievements of the Puritans. Today it is represented in Presbyterian, Reformed, and Congregational churches. Many Baptist churches also are Reformed in theology. For 450 years the Reformed tradition has been one of the ways the Christian community has maintained itself. From this tradition, men and women, boys and girls have learned how to be the Christian community, and it has impressed upon them a distinctive piety and way of understanding the Christian life.

The central thrust of the Reformed tradition that shapes everything else has been a vivid apprehension of God as energy, activity, intention, and purpose. The great fact is the God "who sits above the circle of the earth, who stretches out the heavens like a curtain, who brings princes to nought, and makes the rulers of the earth as nothing" (Isa. 40:22). The final fact in the universe is not impersonal power, is not even beauty and truth, but the personal will of the creator. This perception of God has given to Reformed piety its special character. The final end of every human person is not so much the vision of God as it is the embodiment of the purposes of God in human life. The meaning of life is not to be found in personal happiness but in the glory of God and loyalty to God's cause in all the earth. More than any people in Christian history, Reformed Christians have understood their lives in terms of a destiny given to them by God, and more than any people they have interpreted human history in terms of the fulfillment of the divine purpose. They have been vividly aware of the majesty and lordship of God, the creator of heaven and earth. They have believed with all their hearts that God was working his purpose out in individual lives and in human society. The awareness of a destiny, given by God, instilled in Reformed believers a sense of purpose and of direction that made them strong people personally and the shapers of history in their public lives. This awareness of the glory of the Lord God—this awareness of a destiny given to each human person by God—is the heart of the Reformed tradition.

Calvin found the scriptural basis for this vivid awareness of human destiny in his two favorite books, the Epistle of Paul to the Romans and the Psalms, especially those Psalms that celebrate God's activity in all the earth. The writer of the letter to the Ephesians has also given classic statement to our theme: "Blessed be the God and Father of our Lord Jesus Christ . . . [who] chose us in him before the foundation of the world, that we should be holy and blameless before him. He destined us in love to be his sons through Jesus Christ" (1:3–5).

Let us note first of all that the Reformed awareness of destiny is established by the conviction that every human life is rooted in the will and intention of God, the creator of heaven and earth. "Blessed be the God and Father of our Lord Jesus Christ . . . (who) chose us in him before the foundation of the world." This conviction is celebrated in the baptism of little children. In baptism the child's name is called because our faith is that God thought of this child before this child was, that God gave to this child an identity, an individuality, a name, and a dignity that no one should dare abuse. Human existence has its origin not in the accidents of history and biology but in the will and the intention of the Lord God, creator of heaven and earth. Human life is not lived on the surface of history and nature but has its roots in the purposes of God.

This faith has found classic cultural embodiment in the portraits of Rembrandt, the Dutch painter of the seventeenth century, whose portraits convey the deep mystery of the human person whose life is not lived on the surface of history but has roots in eternity. Rembrandt was at best an irregular churchman, but he lived in a culture that had been informed by the debates about predestination and God's sovereignty. This faith is the opposite of the definition of an individual given in Arthur Koestler's novel *Darkness at Noon*, in which the communist declares that an individual is a multitude of a million divided by a million—that is, a cipher.

This awareness that human existence has its origin in the purposes of God is no easy faith. The impersonal character of the forces of nature, the absurdities and brutalities of historical existence, all seem to belie the faith. It is easier to believe, or so it seems at times, that human beings are the product of forces with no prevision of their end and their destiny the debris of a universe in ruins. Human beings simply happened in the history of the universe. Some day they will disappear, leaving no memory that they ever were. Bertolt Brecht has expressed this chilling faith in these dreary words:

> Praise ye from your hearts the unmindfulness of heaven
> Since it knoweth not
> Either your name or your face,
> No one knoweth if you are still there.[1]

The ultimate choice in the matter of faith is between the option that believes that human life is at best an accident and at worst a mistake in the history of the universe, and the option that believes that human life is the expression of purpose, of love of God. The Calvinists have had the intense conviction that they existed because God willed for them to be. This faith, because of its very intensity, gave the Reformed tradition its special quality.

Let us come a step further and note that the Reformed community has not only believed that God called his people into being; it has also believed that God gave to his people a task to accomplish, a purpose to fulfill. As the author of the letter to the Ephesians put it, "He destined us in love to be his sons through Jesus Christ." Paul Scherer once said that the joy of

---

[1]Bertolt Brecht, "Grand Chorale of Thanksgiving," in *Selected Poems*, trans. H. R. Hays (New York: Harcourt, Brace & Co., 1947).

religion was not in being good—people get tired of being good—but standing with God against some darkness and waiting for the light to break. No Calvinist could have said it better. Predestination has reference not simply to the ultimate destinies of heaven and hell but also to human life here and now in time and space. Whatever else an elect person may have been in Calvin's Geneva, this person was called to serve God's purposes in Geneva. The elect are the fulfillers of the purposes of God in human history.

The Calvinist conceived the Christian life in terms of the working out of the purposes of God in the great dramas of human history. Calvin was concerned not simply that individuals should be Christian but that Geneva should be a Christian community. The Puritans sought to build a New Jerusalem in England's green and pleasant land and to demonstrate in New England the possibility of a Christian society. Michael Walzer has written that "what Calvinists said of the saint, other men would later say of the citizen. The saints saw themselves as divine instruments, and theirs was the politics of wreckers, architects, and builders—hard at work upon the political world. They treated every obstacle as another example of the devil's resourcefulness, and they summoned all their energy, imagination, and craft to overcome it."

This leads us to a final point. The meaning of human life is to be found not in personal comfort or even in personal happiness. The gospel promises neither. The end of life is the embodiment of the divine purpose in the life of the individual, the family, the church, the state. The Calvinists did not expect life to be easy, but they did expect it to have a glory. They did not, writes Roland Bainton, a distinguished church historian, eat their hearts out or consume their energies in concern for their own salvation. They believed that there is something not only more important than personal pleasure and happiness but also more important than the salvation of a human soul: namely, the glory of God and God's cause in all the Earth. This led the Calvinists to question the kind of revivalism that placed an inordinate concern on the salvation of the soul: "I have got a soul and I am going to save it no matter what the cost." Nicholas Berdyaev, a Russian philosopher and theologian, paints a horrible word picture of the righteous trampling over each other trying to crowd through the narrow gates of heaven. The Calvinists have always insisted that there is something more important than the salvation of one's own soul: the glory of God and his cause in all the world. And only those who know this shall know the blessedness that is real happiness.

Today not too many people are inordinately concerned with the salvation of their souls, but the secularized version of this ancient concern is everywhere apparent. Self-realization, realizing one's personhood or human potential, is a prevalent concern. The counterpart of the revivalist's concern is the secular concern: I've got a personhood, and I shall fulfill it no matter what the cost to human society and to others. The Calvinists understood that personal happiness was not the primary end of life, and they did not count life as failure when personal happiness was not achieved. The Calvinists and the Puritans alike knew the joy of creation. The old calumny that the Puritans opposed bear-baiting not for the pain it caused the bears but because of pleasure it gave human beings was false. But they knew that happiness, pleasure, and physical comfort are in the end rewarding only if they have an appropriate place in the ordering of life, and they knew that when they are made at the end of life they are self-destructive. For this reason they were ready to deny themselves pleasure and to reject the desires of the moment for the sake of a later good. They knew that the important question is not, Does this make me happy? Does this give me pleasure? But rather, does this fulfill the purposes of God? They knew that the blessedness that comes from having fulfilled the purposes of God in a human life, even a very ordinary human life, is a deeper and more enduring fulfillment of life than happiness, pleasure, or worldly success. They could pray with Unamuno, "May God deny you peace, but give you glory."[2] And they became strong people who shaped the ongoing of history as few people ever have.

The Reformed tradition is only one way of being the Christian community. Yet it has special meaning for life in our time. Its vivid awareness of God as energy, as activity, as power, as moral will and purpose; its understanding of human life as destined by God, the creator of heaven and earth, to fulfill his purposes, are the good news of the gospel for people who have lost a sense of human dignity and significance and who have given up not only on the meaningfulness of their own lives but also on the meaningfulness of the history of which they are a part.

> O the depth of the riches and wisdom and knowledge of God!
> How unsearchable are his judgments and how inscrutable his ways! . . .
> For from him and through him and to him are all things. To him be glory for
> ever. Amen.
>
> (Rom. 11:33, 36)

---

[2]Miguel de Unamuno y Jugo, *Tragic Sense of Life*, trans. J. E. Crawford Flitch (New York: Dover Press, 1954).

PART TWO
CHAPEL MEDITATIONS
UNION THEOLOGICAL SEMINARY

"The Gospel of God"

Our text and topic, the gospel of God, is justified on two grounds. The first justification is that the purpose of the sacrament is the proclamation of the gospel. The second is that as we stand at the beginning of a school year, it is appropriate to ask, What is the faith that brings us together on this campus as an academic community and at this table as the church?

So we ask, What is the gospel that this sacrament proclaims to us? The use of the word *gospel* has many ramifications in the New Testament. In different times and places it has been expressed in different ways. But the church through the centuries has understood the gospel to have two meanings for everyday life.

I

Gospel means first of all that the ultimate reality, the creative and sustaining power in the universe, is love. Jesus taught men to call God "Father" in a more intimate way than they had called him Father before, and to believe that this universe is our Father's home. God is the heavenly Father who numbers the hairs on our head, whose eye is on the sparrow, who cares for the birds of the air and the lilies of the field, who knows us by name.

The stupendous quality of this gospel becomes apparent when we set against it the bleak prospect that a modern poet has put so clearly:

> Praise ye from your hearts and unmindfulness of heaven

> Since it knoweth not
> Either your name or your face,
> No one knoweth if you are still there.

Praise ye the cold, the darkness and corruption!
Look beyond.
It heedeth you not one jot,
Unmoved, you may do your dying.
(Bertolt Brecht, "Grand Chorale of Thanksgiving")

But the gospel is more than the loving Father who creates; it is also the God who redeems. Jesus healed, forgave sins, and restored hope. He lived in such a way that those who knew him best came to see in his death the redemptive love of God when they might have seen the very opposite.

In some brief moments in life, especially when we are young, we feel no need for this God who redeems life from destruction. Our health is good; our personal endowments enable us to exult in the freedom of the "secular city"; our physical defenses are such that we easily convince ourselves of our own righteousness. But these moments are brief. For health breaks; hopes are unfulfilled; the limits of our willpower become painfully clear. Sooner or later we discover that life is an uphill battle, which in the end every man loses. Finally, every man must be saved by grace, if he is to be saved at all. If life is to be redeemed from destruction, it must be redeemed by God.

The gospel means that there are resources of divine mercy and power that can give meaning, that can forgive, that can assure us even in our failures that each of us is the object of divine love. This is the gospel that enables a man in Bonhoeffer's words to take life in one's stride with its duties and problems, its successes and failures, its experiences and helplessness.

II

The gospel means in the second place that the love of God who creates us and redeems us is at work in the world to fulfill his purposes and is also at work in us to change the quality of our lives.

Now, it can be said that the New Testament says very little about this gospel in its historical and social consequences. The historical character of the New Testament precludes any such reference. But I do not see how Paul's letter to the Romans can make sense unless it can be related to what men of goodwill attempt to do in Miami or in Chicago, or to what they do about Vietnam. There ought, it seems to me, to be an optimism of grace about what happens in public as well as private life that is rooted in the gospel.

But the fact is clear that the New Testament does not guarantee the success of any life or of any public enterprise. Love may always be suffering love in history. It may be, as John Gardner has predicted, that we are in for a century and a half or two centuries of disintegration before there is recovery.

There is not much in human experience to tempt one to universalism or utopianism. For there is always waste, loss, and defeat in our human experience.

Therefore, if there is to be any gospel, there has to be some kind of permanence, something more than the assurance that God works in my life to change its quality and that he works in history to fulfill his purposes. If there is to be any gospel there has to be some hope that what is accomplished and what is achieved will not be lost. We take the gospel most seriously precisely in that moment when we trust the fate of conscious personality, our own and of those we love, to the love of God. Hope demands a treasury where moths do not corrupt and where thieves do not break through and steal.

So the gospel means in the second place that God works to change the quality of our lives and to fulfill his purposes in history; that he guarantees the permanence, in ways perhaps beyond our imagining, of that which is committed unto him.

III

Now let us come a step further and note that the gospel of God is the gospel of Jesus Christ, as Paul makes clear in the scripture that has been read. If we want to know the gospel, we must turn to him who is himself the gospel. We have always spoken of this sacrament as one of the ordinary means of grace, allowing for extraordinary means apart from it. Now the decline of Christian community in the West and surging populations of non-Christian peoples may reveal this designation to be a bit of Western parochialism. The sacrament may in our lifetimes become an extraordinary means of grace in relation to the population of mankind.

Certainly today we cannot put any limits on the grace of God. If there is a God who created the world, there ought to be intimations of his gospel and grace everywhere. What we do say is that God has made known his gospel in the life, death, and resurrection of Jesus Christ; and if his gospel is known anywhere else, it is this gospel that is known, even if men do not know that it is the gospel of Jesus Christ or even the gospel of God.

In conclusion, let us note that the gospel is God's gift. Its final validity rests upon nothing we do but upon the presence and work of the divine

Spirit. We cannot command the gospel, or force it, or coerce it. We can only pray that this gospel shall be ours: The good and glad news that the creator is our father whose mercy can redeem our lives from destruction. It is the good and glad news that the God who is at work to change the quality of our lives and to fulfill his purposes in history, and who guarantees permanence to what is committed to him, meets us in the sacrament.

"The Joy of Christmas"

Everyone agrees that joy is a Christmas virtue. The angels announce the birth and good news of great joy. But no one seems quite sure as to the nature of this joy. The joy ranges from the clanging of cash registers to eggnog parties, to The Lord's Supper of the church. But obviously, the joy of the cash register and the joy of Eucharist are not the same. Obviously they are not equally the tiding of a great joy that the angels announced. Christmas is a time when the elemental as well as the sophisticated joys of human existence abound, often in contrast to the dreariness of much of modern life. Yet for people in the church as well as out, the joy of Christmas raises questions as to both the source and ground of joy. Why should we experience this joy? We also know the incongruity between any real joy and many of the brute facts of our lives.

Everyone in the church is rightly concerned about the ambiguity of Christmas joy and also about the abuse of Christmas. The vitalities of nature have a persistence and fascination for us and tempt us to find life's meaning and fulfillment in them rather than in the moral and personal achievements of history. Yet it is doubtful that we shall recover an authentic faith by any asceticism that denies the joy of creation and of human friendships and looks askance at every human pleasure, especially those that have some physical or sensual basis.

The plain fact is that some people who never think of friends do send greetings at Christmas. Some people who are never generous are generous at least momentarily at Christmas. Some people who never enjoy living do have a good time for a while at Christmas. Certainly at Christmas there are more spontaneous acts of kindness than at any other time.

At Christmas time there is the joy of the created world, and it shall do neither theology nor the church a service to deny this joy with rhetorical asceticism. Yet it is also a plain fact that Christmas can never become simply a festival of nature. Christmas can quite clearly be taken away from the church, divorced from the faith. Nature can be celebrated not as God's gift but as God itself. Perhaps for this reason the early church was cautious in establishing the festival of Christmas and Christians are concerned about the abuse of Christmas today.

Christians in Rome in the first half of the fourth century began celebrating the birth of Jesus on December 25 when the pagan world celebrated the sun. Augustine declared that Christians worshipped not the sun, but the Son of Righteousness who created the sun. The final reality is not the world of nature but the creator who called nature into being.

Christmas began as the protest of Christian faith over against the worship of nature. Yet as Christians celebrated the birth of Jesus, the elemental responses of the human spirit to the world of nature attached themselves to the celebration of Christmas. In this day of electric lights and central heating, it is very difficult for us to imagine the darkness and the cold of the world at the winter solstice. In response to that darkness human beings began to celebrate with the evergreens, the cedar and the holly, with candles and lights, with the Yule log and with the myths of someone, who in the darkness of the winter solstice, brought gifts to children.

As a boy I grew up believing in Santa Claus and with Christmas trees, lights, and stockings hung by the fire. I do not wish to do away with any of these. I rejoice in the traditional Christmas cards. Now it is estimated that over four billion are sent each year. I also grew up rejoicing in the family dinners and in the Christmas parties.

Our Calvinist and Puritan ancestors were always uneasy about Christmas. Calvin was happy enough to eliminate the festival from life in Geneva, though he did not think it was worth fighting when some brought it back. The Puritans were more adamant in rejecting Christmas, in some cases exacting fines on those who celebrated Christmas. In the Presbyterian Church U.S., some presbyteries protested the mentioning of Christmas in our church school literature as late as the year 1908.

Christmas is now back as the major festival of our society. While much of it is pagan and some of it an expression of human greed and selfishness, there are still signs of a far deeper meaning. As a matter of fact, many young people in some churches are more likely to learn the Christmas carols in the mall than they are in churches.

The human spirit still yearns for meaning and joy at the winter solstice, a yearning that cannot finally be satisfied by electric lights, by eggnog parties, or by the achievements of an affluent, secular society, or by the vitalities and energies of nature.

How then shall we in the church regard the secularization of Christmas in our society? The obvious excesses of a secular culture must be opposed. But on the other hand we should be careful not to destroy what has its roots in Christian faith.

The church must make clear at Christmas that if the joy of creation is the only joy we know, in the end there will be no joy at all. For over the joy of creation there stand the marks of sin and death.

The tidings of great joy of which the angels sang were the announcement of a savior. Christmas joy is not simply joy in creation—sin and selfishness have jeopardized this joy and death annihilates it. The joy of Christmas is first of all the joy of the kingdom that is near, the joy over the sinner who repents, joy at the outpouring of the Holy Spirit, joy that faith rests from affliction. We rejoice in the created world because the Word that became flesh is also the Word by which all things came into being and without whom nothing was made that was made. At Christmas time the church must focus its attention on proclaiming that the Word, the mind of God, God in God's self-expression, became flesh, was embodied in a human life, and dwelt among us full of grace and truth. This is the great joy of Christmas and the joy that makes possible all other joys.

"The Wonder of Christmas"

Our first knowledge that the Word became flesh, at least for many of us, came through the singing of the Christmas carols or acting out the Christmas drama in church/school plays. Singing the Christmas carols still has something of the nostalgia for the innocence of childhood. But we are no longer innocent. For some this means the stories can no longer be read nor the carols sung as an adult commitment. Our eyes have been opened.

It is also true that in the Gospels, the shepherds and the wise men quickly fade away. They have no part in the ministry or the passion of Jesus. They are attached as an appendage to the Gospels, but the account of the life and work of Jesus could have begun without them. Even Mary, likewise, has little place in the Gospels or in the Epistles of Paul. Her role and that of her family become secondary to the family of faith constituted by believing and obeying.

For us, as for the first disciples, the decisions of faith have to be made not in the context of the Christmas stories, not in the innocence of childhood, but in the context of life in which shepherds praising God, wise men bringing gifts, angels singing glory to God are certainly not visible. Our world is sometimes harsh, frequently frustrating, and God seems far away. In such a world God speaks to us through his Word by the power of his spirit and in the context of the blood, the sweat, and the grime of life.

All this seems to suggest that carols are for children who in their innocence can imagine the kind of world in which angels sing and shepherds praise the living God.

There is, however, another possibility. The carols may belong not simply to children but also to adults—to those who are no longer innocent but who in the midst of life believe that the Word did become flesh (John

1:14), that in him all things were created, that in him all things hold together (Col. 1:16–17).

Carols are for children, but they are also for persons of mature faith, for whom the Christmas narratives are one of the most effective ways we have of saying what we believe and what we have discovered to be the true nature of things. For those who believe, the carols are profoundly true. They are an unsurpassed way of expressing our faith about what is reality. They save us from the shallowness and the banality of a secular culture.

The Roman Catholic sociologist Andrew M. Greeley has written this indictment of our culture, which should be a warning to all of us who confess our Christian faith.

> When angels in the marvel-filled scriptures go out the front door, alien beings and science fiction come in the back door along with astrology, witchcraft, tarot cards, God's enflaming chariots and a lot of other pre-biblical superstitions. It is no accident. You can demythologize wonder out of your sacred books, but you can't demythologize the hunger for the wonderful out of human personality, or at least those who have tried it have not yet succeeded. . . . The churches don't even try because they have yet to perceive that someone else is stealing their stock and trade. This Christmas we need to recover the capacity for wonder which is an expression of our faith.[1]

William F. Hocking of Harvard University was surely one of the great philosophers of the twentieth century. His son, Richard Hocking, once told me how his father broke into tears when he read the Lukan narrative to his family at Christmas because he was so overwhelmed with the beauty and the wonder of the Christian message. For many whose earliest memories include these stories, nothing can replace the account—of the birth in the manger, the shepherds in their field, the wise men coming from the East—in proclaiming the meaning of Christian faith.

[1]Andrew Greeley, "Christmas," *New York Times Magazine*, 23 December, 1973.

"In Earthen Vessels"

Let us give our attention to the words "But we have this treasure in earthen vessels" (2 Cor. 4:7). These words speak to the needs of every Christian but they have an especial relevance for those of us who are ministers. When we are hard-pressed, they encourage us because the gospel we preach is the power of God. When we are satisfied with ourselves, they warn us that without God we are nothing. "But we have this treasure in earthen vessels."

I

Let us note that these words speak to our needs precisely because we are Presbyterians. We belong to a tradition that has exalted the ministry and, in particular, the preaching of the word. Calvin himself speaks of the preached word as the word of God and the minister as the mouth of God. The people must listen to the minister as to the voice of God. This lofty conception of the preacher has produced greatness, greatness that so far as we can tell has been a means of God's grace. We ought not to forget that the only power that Calvin ever had in Geneva was the power of the preached word to create a godly public opinion. And yet it is a greatness that is fraught with peril. For Calvin and his successors in every generation have confused their own words with the word of God. The Christian ministry is life on a precipice simply because we must combine the enthusiasm, the confidence, and the vigor of men who speak and do the will of God with the humility of men who know that they may be mistaken about that will. Over against the greatness of our vocation there must be set this word of Paul, "But we have this treasure in earthen vessels."

141

II

Let us note also that this word has special meaning for us because of the culture of our times. Preachers along with medical doctors are the pampered group of our society. We hear a great deal about the hardships of the ministry. There are hardships. Many pastors in humble situations, especially in the Deep South today, are performing a ministry at great personal costs. Nothing that I say should forget the cost that many ministers, indeed most ministers, are paying. But this truth should not obscure the complementary fact that we in the ministry are pampered. Theological education is not as expensive as professional education in other fields and frequently less exacting intellectually. Ministers' salaries in Presbyterian circles are not as bad as sometimes advertised. They compare very favorably indeed with those of university professors who hold Ph.D. degrees.

As ministers we go into communities with a social status that we could not earn for many years and sometimes not at all. And, in addition, there are the personal kindnesses that are heaped upon us by good people, partly because of what we do but also in part because of that which we represent.

We must not forget that the ministry is a privileged and pampered group in our society. But we must likewise not forget that from those to whom society gives much it will in the end exact much. We enjoy now the popularity of religion. But unless we answer our privileges with responsibility and professional competence, there shall in the end be visited upon us not only the wrath of God but also the wrath of man. For this reason we need to remember that we have this treasure in earthen vessels.

III

We need to note this word from Paul because the fact that we are earthen vessels does not mean that most of us need to be as earthen as we are.

Do we need to be as earthen as we are in our concept of the successful minister? Here again the dialectic of the Christian life is not simple. Faith is concern about success: about the success that can be recorded in the statistics of the minutes of the General Assembly or in the brick and mortar of a church building. But faith also is ready to give up these symbols of success because they are not the ultimate expression of God's will.

Several weeks ago a "successful" minister pronounced this judgment upon a Presbyterian minister who has stood courageously for the integrity of the church in our time. This minister, he declared, no longer had an effective pastoral ministry. These words were spoken with the finality of an executioner's ax. To such a judgment there is only one suitable reply. The New Testament nowhere demands an effective pastoral ministry as the final criteria of a ministry. For the sake of the gospel, Jesus gave up a successful pastoral ministry to many people, and so did Paul.

We are earthen vessels, but we do not have to be as earthy as we are. We do not have to be as earthy as we are in the professional incompetence that is indifferent to the success which is recorded in statistics, or as earthy as we are in failing to see that this is a kind of success that we must be prepared to surrender for the sake of the gospel. We are called to be fools for Christ, but we are not called to be what the world calls blank fools.

But we have this treasure in earthen vessels. The recollection of this truth ought to remind us that most of us need not be in this and many other ways as earthy as we are.

"On Being Faithful"

We are gathered here on Commencement Day. Our attention is directed to future ministries for which the past years have been in preparation. But our common human predicament is our inability to guarantee the future. No amount of training, no amount of discipline, no offering of prayer can control or coerce the future. At best they can offer promise and hope.

Our anticipation of the future is subject to the vagaries of nature and of history. The Lisbon earthquakes and Buchenwalds of history have their counterparts in the pastorate and in the intimate and personal experiences of life. The perils of nature and the perils of man's inhumanity, even of our own inhumanity, expose the Achilles heel of our existence.

There is a certain appropriateness of our gathering for the sacrament of the Lord's Supper in a moment when we are aware of the fragile and uncertain character of our future. For the church in its reflection upon the broken bread and poured wine has always seen them as symbols of a body that was broken and of blood that was shed. We ought at this table to be under no illusions about our ability to guarantee our future.

The biblical text that we shall set over against the future that cannot be guaranteed comes from Paul's letter to the Corinthians: "It is required in stewards, that a man be found faithful" (1 Cor. 4:2). Seen from one point of view, this is a warning to us in our ministry. John Calvin in commenting on this passage rated hirelings, those who make a good thing out of preaching the gospel, as little better than wolves. Moreover, as the parable of the steward teaches us, a steward is accountable for prudence and wisdom.

But we can look at this text from another point of view and see in it not so much a command or a warning but a very gracious word. Paul does not say that it is required of stewards that they guarantee the future or that

144

they be successful. Rather, this text declares, it is required of stewards that they be found faithful. None of us is in a position to guarantee the future or to give any assurance of success. The commitment that we shall be faithful is a much more realistic possibility, even though here too we have to pray, "Lord, I believe; help thou mine unbelief" (Mark 9:24). Finally, fidelity as well as success is a gift of grace, but we can be more realistic in pledging to be faithful.

Faithfulness is a more realistic possibility because it knows the imperative to be perfect is set beside the declaration that none is good save God alone, because it knows of the very intimate relationship between forgiveness and the command to be perfect even as our Father in heaven is perfect. God can act successfully through human acts that are not successful.

It is very interesting to ponder the fate of faithful men in our own church who twenty years ago, forty years ago, made possible the witness of the church today. They did not always succeed. Today men who are successful sometimes get credit for what they did. But God acted successfully through human acts that were unsuccessful. God in his grace allows sinful men to work for him in their sinfulness.

Faithfulness is a more realistic possibility because, as Emil Brunner puts it, the reformation of society as a principle is always subordinate to the personal meaning of life. The decisive question, for me, is not whether I succeed in changing the structure of society, or in revolutionizing the form of the church, but whether I have been faithful. It is much more realistic for me to pledge that I shall be faithful, than that I shall revolutionize society, especially in the first three years of my ministry. Brunner speaks of the man to whom no place in the world is good enough until he has put something right. His whole life is spent in this unceasing endeavor to alter conditions, until the personal meaning of his life is lost, a nervous haste takes possession of him, and he falls into a state of mind either of cynical resignation or irritated hostility to everything and everyone.

Faithfulness is a more realistic possibility because it leaves responsibility for results in the hands of God. Our responsibility is not so much for the results as for fidelity in the place where God in his providence has placed us. Whatever we do, we commit to God's keeping, as in death we shall finally commit the fate of conscious personality.

But God is concerned with success. The Christian life not only seeks to demonstrate love but to accomplish loving deeds for real people. Therefore, we always have to keep striving after perfection, as Reinhold Niebuhr put it, without the illusion of having attained it. We shall always have to keep poverty of spirit in union with hunger and thirst after righteousness.

We shall have to accommodate the vision of perfection to an imperfect world without losing that vision. Faithfulness knows the importance of success, but it likewise knows that God does not ask us to guarantee it.

Faithfulness is a more modest and realistic possibility. We cannot guarantee the future, but we can here and now pledge that come what may, we shall be faithful. But faithfulness too is a gift of God. Like the disciple who asked, "Lord, is it I?" we do not know that we shall be faithful. Here we know that if we are to live with any degree of serenity, we must live by some assurance of grace. Beyond our pledge of faithfulness as we take the bread and cup, there is the pledge of God's faithful, steadfast, and boundless love. Here we are fully known and fully loved. This is the grace by which we live and work and in which we face the future.

"A Sober Life"

The writer of the letter to Titus was concerned about the quality of life in the Christian community and in particular about the quality of the church leadership. He repeatedly lists soberness as a Christian virtue and a style of life appropriate to the gospel. Yet there is nothing particularly Christian about soberness—self-control, self-mastery, sensibleness, responsibility. The Greek philosophers speak of this virtue too. But the writer to Titus apparently is convinced that it represents a style of life appropriate to the gospel, and that its secular meaning has been enriched and enlarged by the grace of God that has been manifested for the salvation of all men.

So this morning for our meditation, as we seek to hear this letter to Titus as the word of God to our lives, let us ask, "What does it mean to live soberly as Christians today?"

Forty years ago soberness would have been related immediately to the use of alcoholic beverages. More recently Protestants have been embarrassed by prohibition. Church and society reports have been more concerned to justify social drinking than to point out the problems connected with the practice. But our newspapers have reminded us that the use of alcoholic beverages is the most critical drug problem in our society. So once again one of the most serious ethical decisions any minister makes has to do with his relation to the use of alcoholic beverages, which are the occasion for such devastating destruction of life and happiness in our society.

But soberness in the context of this text certainly does not have primary reference to the use of alcoholic beverages. So we have to ask the question in other contexts. What does it mean to live circumspectly, soberly in an affluent society enflamed by advertising techniques that create artificial wants and desires? There is no easy answer to this question. It is certainly not enough to reject the affluent society, though rejection may be better than acquiescence in it. We have therefore to struggle honestly with the question "What is a sober, circumspect style of life for a Christian in any affluent society where color television is a necessity?"

We have to ask this question also of our work as theologians. For we are living in a theological era that has been characterized by a lust for novelty and narcissistic delight in being different, when theological dilettantes, as well as some who should have known better, have found a certain thrill in playing Russian roulette with the basic doctrines of Christian faith. What does it mean to be sober as a theologian?

Soberness is a universal virtue. But the soberness of which the writer to Titus speaks is grounded not simply in reason but in the revelation of God in Jesus Christ. A sober life is a life moderated by a Christian understanding of human existence. So the question is not simply what is it to live soberly, but what is it to live soberly as people who worship the God and father of our Lord Jesus Christ?

John Calvin and our Reformed tradition thought of soberness in terms of moderation and simplicity. Calvin rejoiced in the goodness of creation. The enjoyment of creation is a Christian virtue. Yet our use of creation should be moderate so that use of this world's goods does not corrupt human responsibility or undermine Christian faith and vocation. It must be simple so that we do not try to cover up the poverty of our lives with ostentation and extravagance.

This morning we have to ask, What does soberness mean in buying a car or a house, in the clothing we wear, in the food we eat, in the vacations we take, in our work as ministers? These are questions each of us must answer as we seek to live as Christians in contemporary society.

PART THREE
PHOTOS

John H. Leith and Ann White Leith at Second Presbyterian Church, Nashville, Tennessee, 1945

John Leith relaxes with Albert Outler at Keble College, Oxford University, Quadrennial Conference on Wesleyan Theology, 1982.

John Leith presenting a portrait of Professor E. T. Thompson to Union Theological Seminary at the Outlook Dinner at the General Assembly of the Presbyterian Church U.S., 1975. E. T. Thompson is seated on the left. Lawrence Bottoms is seated on the right.

John Leith and Roland Bainton

Kent Fellows, assembled in Meadville, Pennsylvania, 1950. Includes "Older Theologians" Amos Wilder, Edgar S. Brightman, Nels Ferre and John Bennett; "Emerging Theologians" Waldo Beach and Paul Ramsey. "Younger Theologians" Hans Frei, Niels Nielsen, Herndon Wagers, John Dillenberger, Roger Shinn, and Claude Welch. John and Ann Leith are seated in the third row from the top, left-hand corner.

John and Ann Leith speak with President Jimmy Carter at the Jefferson–Jackson Dinner, Richmond, Virginia, 1978.

John and Ann Leith with their children, John and Ann Leith, 1999.
Henry White Leith and Caroline Haddon
Leith at the 10th anniversary celebration
of his pastorate, First Presbyterian Church,
Auburn, Alabama, 1958.

First Presbyterian Church, Auburn, Alabama, where
Leith served from 1948 to 1959. Built 1953. (Photo-
graph by Allen Patterson)

PART FOUR
THEOLOGY, FAITH, AND LEARNING

"Faith and Liberal Learning"
May 20, 1984

Commencement Address, Erskine College, Due West, South Carolina

The rising generation, according to the President's Commission on Education, is the first in the history of our country to be less well-educated than the previous generation. This judgment is subject to debate, but there can be little doubt as to its accuracy in the areas of human and liberal learning that have traditionally been associated with church colleges.

The quantitative evidence is to be found on the one hand in biblical and literary illiteracy and on the other hand in the inability of so many college graduates to express clear ideas in coherent English sentences.

Hence, today, let us ask what a college graduate should take from a church college on the occasion of graduation. One reason for asking this question is found in the very nature of education itself. Four years in college can only be the beginning of liberal and humane learning. Some rare persons become educated in the humane and liberal tradition without going to college at all. In a real sense, a liberal education is a human vocation in which colleges can assist but can neither guarantee nor complete.

The tradition of humane and liberal learning in the church has always emphasized three dimensions of human life.

I

First, liberal learning in the church has always had a profound respect for the life of the mind in the service of God. William Temple, the great archbishop of Canterbury and surely one of the leading churchmen of the twentieth century, once said that the human mind, next to a life of love, is the most wonderful thing in all the world—the human mind with its powers of conceptual thought, of analysis, of memory, and of language; the human mind with its power to read the facts of the universe; indeed

156

the human mind with its power to read the facts of the universe; indeed the human mind with its capacity to at least in some measure think the universe. The emergence in the history of the universe of the human mind is a most remarkable fact. The more the human mind is identified with nature, the more nature itself becomes inexplicable. How is it that the human mind emerged with all its unique capacities unless there is behind all things Mind, spelled with a capital M?

Liberal learning has always had as its goal the enhancement of the powers of the human mind on the one hand, and on the other the liberation of the human mind from all oppressive forces that would restrict its freedom.

Liberal learning has encouraged the asking of the really great questions. Who am I? What am I here for? What is the meaning of our earthly pilgrimage? What is the true, the good, the beautiful? What faith controls and shapes my life? Liberal learning has always subordinated the "how" questions. Certainly, none of us today should depreciate the "how" questions. How to manipulate the world? How to engage in agriculture? How to do engineering? How to run a business? The land-grant colleges in the last one hundred years have changed the shape of American life more significantly than the liberal institutions. They account for the fact that we have more food than we can eat and for an industrial capacity that is the envy of the world. But the fact still remains that when you have fed a hungry person, all the fundamental problems of human existence remain. Learning how to do things is critically important, but we ought not to confuse learning how to do things with being educated in the liberal tradition.

Liberal training has also given perspective to life, which frees it from the tyranny of the moment. Liberal training introduces one to the best that has been written or painted, to the great achievements of the human spirit in ancient Rome or in the great cathedrals of Europe. It enables us to bring the wisdom of the ages, the best that has been thought and done, to bear on the demands and pressures of the moment.

The liberal tradition has endeavored to enhance the powers of the human mind, to teach us how to read the words on a printed page, grasping the meaning and distinguishing between that which is primary and that which is subordinate. Its purpose has been to teach us "to think effectively, to communicate thought, to make relevant judgments, to discriminate among values."

Susanne Langer, the philosopher, has an essay, "The Growing Center of Knowledge." Trees, she said, seem to grow on the edges. The human self grows from the center, even biologically. The central nervous system does not increase by multiplying its cells; it has no growing edge. From infancy to old age we have essentially the same cells we start with at birth. Miss Langer's point is that the human self grows not so much at the edges but at the center.[1]

The modern world seems to know so much with its television, its computers, its prodigious material resources. But is it not knowledge at the edges? This knowledge is not likely to be productive of human good unless there is growth at the center—in the capacity to think effectively, to read serious books, to express thought in coherent English sentences, to make relevant judgments in the light of the wisdom of the race, and to discriminate among values.

Forces seek to limit the human mind in our time to reading instructions and directions. The various communist nations often boast of the high level of literacy that they have been able to achieve in their societies. One ought, I suppose, to be happy when anyone learns to read, but one has to ask what literacy in a communist nation really means. It does not mean reading great books. The writing of great books is severely circumscribed in those lands, and great writers and philosophers have notoriously become refugees from places such as Cuba and the Soviet Union. Yet even in our own society, subtle temptations limit the power of the human mind to deciphering instructions and directions. This is even true in all the professions including the ministry. A liberal education ought to leave us with an awareness that the instructions and the directions that we decipher, even when these instructions and directions can save life and put food on the table, are secondary to the more fundamental questions: Who is a human being? What is the significance of this world in which we live?

This freedom and power of the human mind is essential not only to the enhancement of the human self, but also to the freedom of the community. Only in those societies in which there is freedom for the human mind to pursue truth, to reflect upon the practices of society, and to suggest alternatives has that society been freed from slavery to the momentary fads and passions on the one hand and protected from arbitrary tyranny on the other. We hear much about free enterprise in economics. Today we need most of all the free enterprise of a disciplined human mind in the service of God.

There is no better way for a person to celebrate his or her graduation than by resolving to read at least one great book a year, to read one magazine more critically reflective than *Time* or *Newsweek,* to pursue the vocation of becoming a truly educated person.

[1]Suzanne Langer, *Philosophical Sketches* (Baltimore: Johns Hopkins Press, 1962), 143–82.

II

A liberal education should give to us a profound respect not only for the human mind, but also for the human spirit. The Greeks defined the uniqueness of the human person as reason, but Christians have defined the image of God in terms of the power of the human spirit.

Animals, sofar as we know, are conscious of the world. But human beings are conscious not only of the world but also of themselves. This capacity of the human self to transcend the self, to reflect upon the self, to objectify the self is the source of our most unique capacities and gifts.

Self-consciousness is the source of our freedom. Animals are the slaves of instinct and impulse. Place food in the presence of a hungry dog, and the dog eats. Place food in the presence of a hungry person, and the person may likely eat, but he or she may also give up food even when hungry in order to lose weight or to feed hungry people whom one knows only through the capacity to imagine their existence tens of thousands of miles away. The power of the human spirit to reflect upon our instincts and impulses both complicates and enhances the human imagination, e.g., influencing every physical vitality from hunger to sex for good or evil. Human beings do nothing as simply a natural fact. But this power of the spirit also gives us a measure of freedom over instinct and impulse and the power to use instincts and impulses for the purposes of the self.

This power of the human spirit to objectify one's existence also gives us a freedom over our culture. All of us are shaped by the social matrix in which we were born. Some of us will always reflect our origins in our speech and in our ways of thinking. But more significant than the fact that we were born in a particular place and time is our knowledge of our origin and the power to imagine our having been born somewhere else. This power of the human spirit gives us some measure of freedom over culture.

This capacity of the human spirit for freedom and self-direction can be enhanced or almost totally lost. One of the great purposes of a liberal education is to provide persons with the categories, the cultural and literary memory, the insights, the vision of what human life ought to be that enhances and enlarges this power of the human spirit.

Again we talk a great deal in our society about free enterprise in economics. The most important free enterprise in our society is not in economics but in the life of the mind and in particular in the life of the human spirit.

The human spirit not only enables us to reflect upon our own lives, therefore giving us a certain freedom, but it also goes beyond every human achievement and knows there is something more. Every human achievement always opens up new possibilities of achievement that finally elude us. Every act of love always opens up new possibilities of love that are beyond us. There is no way for us ever to exhaust the possibilities of human life. No matter how much we achieve, we always know there is something more. Read the biography of any successful person. It becomes very clear that the most successful are in the end most aware of the unfulfilled possibilities of their lives.

One of the great heresies in our time is the notion that human life can complete itself—that we can fulfill the meaning of human existence by our own efforts, by our own work. Hence, we have very unrealistic expectations of what careers can do for us, what the accumulation of money or power can do for us, even what marriage can do for us.

God has made us so that the highest human achievements leave us incomplete, unsatisfied. As Augustine put it, "Thou hast made us for thyself and restless is our heart until it comes to rest in thee."

III

This leads us to the question of faith. Medieval culture distinguished human beings according to faith, believing that faith was far more fundamental than race, sex, or nationality. Our culture pretends that faith is unimportant. It practices a tolerance not of respect for human freedom and dignity, but of indifference.

Yet the fact is we all live by faith. To be human is to live by faith. We have no other alternative. Before we have been up three hours on almost any day, we are compelled to make decisions that involve some faith commitment about the meaning of the universe and the significance of human life. The most important thing you can know about any person is what that person really believes about God and the meaning of human life.

The really important questions we have to answer in life are not very many. The first is the question of God. The second is the question of marriage and of personal relationships. The third is the question of vocation (what shall I do with my life), and the fourth is the question of our relationship to things. The most important question has to do with God and with our relationship to the ground and source of our existence. What we really think about God determines everything else in our lives.

Each of us has some faith about God. Life compels us to. The only question is whether or not the faith we have corresponds to the reality of God and whether it is adequate for the lives that we live.

The Christian faith rests upon the simple claim that it does more justice to the facts, makes more sense out of life, illuminates human experience as does no other faith. The God to whom Christian faith points is our only and final security.

The really important question is not the question of El Salvador, or the deficit, or even nuclear war. The really important question is our awareness of the reality of the living God and our knowledge of his purposes.

In 1947, Emil Brunner, the distinguished Swiss theologian, speaking at Yale University, declared that the United States is the most remarkable achievement of the human spirit in the history of the human race, but there will come a time when the United States will no longer exist. When that day comes each one of you will still be. Hence, what happens in the history of the human soul is in some ways more significant than what happens in the history of a great society.

Phyllis McGinley once wrote birthday poems for *The New Yorker* magazine. On her forty-third birthday, she wrote "The Vanity of Human Wishes," a poem that was brought to my attention by Kenneth Orr, the president of Presbyterian College, in response to an assignment twenty-five years ago to find sermon illustration in *The New Yorker* magazine. It goes like this:

> Age six, she learned ambition. Her desire
> Was to perform upon a circus wire.
> Riper at nine, she longed (in Indian dress)
> To lead explorers through a wilderness.
> At ten to yodel; burned as time went by
> To be in turn nurse, ballet dancer, spy,
> Film star, a famous playwright, something clever
> In, say, design. So greedy hearts forever
> Outdistance reason. Now, at forty-three,
> She ponders sainthood's possibilities.

A French philosopher, Simone Weil, summed it up by saying that there always comes a time in life when the only sorrow is not to be a saint. She did not mean a caricature of a saint, in some petty legalistic fashion, but a saint in the sense of having been called by the living God and having embodied at least in a broken and fragmentary way the purposes of the living God in one's life.[2] Kierkegaard, the Danish psychologist, warned that there always comes the midnight hour when most of the things we spend life's time and energy into getting turn to dust and ashes in our hands and a bitterness in our mouths.

Commencement day is a splendid time to begin to live for those things that will give meaning to life at its end and that shall survive in God's eternal kingdom.

[2]Simone Weil, *Waiting for God* (New York: Harper, 1951), 99–100.

Presidential Address to
Presbyterian Education Association of the South
1956

Montreat, North Carolina

The presentation of the accomplishments of our church in the field of higher education is a thrilling reminder that we as Presbyterians believe in education—or at least we think we do—and that we are ready to do something about it. We do not really need a reminder that we believe in education. In fact, we have been at times inordinately proud of the fact.

There is some basis for our pride. John Calvin was an educated man, able to hold his own with the best minds of his day. He believed that education is a part of the essential ministry of the church. In fact, he said far more about education than he did about what we nowadays call evangelism and missions. There are reasons that Calvin did not say much about these subjects, as they are popularly understood. The important point for us tonight is Calvin's belief that education is indispensable to what we call the church's evangelistic and missionary task.

From the beginning of his ministry in Geneva, Calvin insisted that provision be made for the education of the people. He so convinced the people of the need for a college that one contemporary reports that the enthusiasm of the people rose above their poverty in the establishment of the college. It is important for us to remember that they did not build this college to enable them to qualify for better jobs or even to teach them how to do things. There was a deeper reason. The liberal arts, they said, are props and aids to the full knowledge of the word and are not to be despised. The *Ordonnances* of the church declared that a man cannot really profit in the study of scripture unless he has been first instructed in languages and humanities.

John Knox insisted that the revenues of the church should be shared in the support of the ministry and an educational system. The first *Book of*

Discipline contains an elaborate educational program for Scotland, since God, he said, does not instruct his church by angels.

The followers of Calvin came to America and built schools alongside churches. When confronted by the demands of the frontier, they declared that the educational standards of the ministry and the intellectual integrity of the faith could not be compromised for momentary advantage. When an overture was made to the Synod of 1785 to relax the educational requirement for the ministry, the members not only voted it down, but some also proposed that they be increased by one full year of study.

Today we are rediscovering the meaning of this ancient heritage.

We are rediscovering it in a day when the church no longer provides the intellectual leadership of society.

We are rediscovering it in a day when the church no longer has a monopoly on education.

We are rediscovering it in a day when the Presbyterian minister is not always the best-trained person in the community.

We are rediscovering it in a day when people have lost their sense of security in an incredibly big and complex universe, when they have lost any sense of direction, meaning, and purpose, and are overwhelmed by the apparent futility of life.

In this world in which we live in 1956, what does the recovery of our heritage mean?

I have no knowledge to speak of its meaning in terms of buildings, endowments, and the like, but I want to suggest three things that the recovery of our heritage does mean and without which our buildings and endowments have no real significance.

I

First, the recovery of our heritage means that we are seriously concerned to understand the meaning of human existence in the light of the life, death, and resurrection of Jesus Christ. This is our concern whether we are college presidents or preachers or teachers. This is our task as Christians and Calvinists.

The confession that Jesus is the Christ is no dull theological formula that when once repeated certifies a man as safe from hell. It is no magical gimmick. What happened in Jesus Christ is an event that caused and has never ceased to cause excitement. No wonder those who first heard it called it news—and good news at that. God, the God who made the world, has come to us and made himself known. This is something incredibly tremendous. When the early Christians had to spell out in precise terms what they believed happened in Jesus Christ, they said that he was the same being as the Father. This is "it." There is nothing more to be said. When we have seen Christ, we have seen God. Now we know who we are. We know where we came from, what we are here for, and where we are going. We know the meaning and purpose of human existence. Now we know who our fellow man is and the meaning of the human community. Now we know what this thing we call history is and how it is going to end.

All of this is no casual information. This thing which has happened in Jesus Christ concerns me. It has my name and address on it. It confronts me with decision. In Christ, God claims me in love.

Suffice it here to say that this faith enables me to understand human existence and the world in which I live. There is a popular notion, which is heresy as far as we are concerned, that reason can take you so far and when it gives out faith takes up. But Augustine was nearer to the truth when he said that we believe in order that we may understand. Unless we believe, we cannot understand.

Our problem today is not so much that we lack knowledge but that we understand and organize our information in the light of a false or inadequate faith.

The Christian claim is simply that this faith makes more sense out of life, illuminates more clearly our experience, and does more justice to the facts of human existence than any other faith whatsoever. It is our conviction that if a man is truly to understand human existence and this universe, he must interpret it in the light of God's mighty act in the life, death, and resurrection of Jesus Christ. This is the faith that unifies knowledge and turns it into wisdom.

II

The recovery of our intellectual heritage means that we have set before us the ideal of intellectual competence.

It is a strange fact that while we have bragged about our heritage, we have at times condoned a cult of anti-intellectualism. It has been possible to find in our ranks some who seemed to thank God that they were ignorant and to believe that someday it would be accounted unto them for righteousness.

When we read "The Order of the College of Geneva," two facts become clear. The first is Calvin's intention that his students should be trained, in the words of the Harvard report, to think effectively, to communicate thought, to discriminate among values, and to make relevant judgments.

The second clear fact is Calvin's intention that his students should be trained in the best thought of the day. Calvin himself was trained as a humanist, and he was not afraid of humanism. Some have said that he was deficient in scientific interest, but this is to judge him by issues that were more alive after his death than during his lifetime. One statement that he made concerning science indicates his willingness to come to terms with the best scientific learning of his day. "Moses," he said, "makes two great luminaries, but astronomers prove, by conclusive reasons, that the star of Saturn, which, on account of its great distance, appears least of all, is greater than the moon. Here lies difference; Moses wrote in a popular style things which, without instruction, all ordinary persons, endued with common sense, are able to understand; but astronomers investigate with great labor whatever the sagacity of the human mind can comprehend. Nevertheless, this study is not to be reprobated, nor this science to be condemned, because *some fanatic persons are wont boldly to reject whatever is unknown to them.* For astronomy is not only pleasant, but also very useful to be known; it cannot be denied that this art unfolds the admirable wisdom of God" (*Commentary on Genesis*).

Do we today have this ideal of intellectual competence?

Can we boast about the level of the sermon tastes of our congregations?

Can we boast about the intellectual competence of our preaching?

Can we boast about the intellectual leadership of our church in society?

We have talked about Calvin, but until a few years ago we did not own in our church a complete set of Calvin's published works. The Methodists, however, would loan them to us.

Are we, as Presbyterians, genuinely concerned to be able to talk intelligently about our faith and its meaning for life?

Are we interested in knowing why the art of Rembrandt is more expressive of Reformed theology than the art of Leonardo de Vinci?

Do we have any desire to know the significance for the Christian community of Christopher Fry or T. S. Eliot or W. H. Auden or even Arthur Koestler or Picasso?

Are we really interested in understanding the live decisions of economics and politics in the light of God's mighty act in the life, death, and resurrection of Jesus Christ?

The question I am raising is this: Do we really share Calvin's ideal of intellectual competence?

III

The third element in the recovery of our Calvinistic heritage is intellectual integrity.

The command of Christ is that we love God with our minds as well as our hearts. The ninth commandment is part of the orthodox doctrine of Christendom: "Thou shalt not bear false witness against thy neighbor." And this includes your neighbor's theology! False dealing in the realm of ideas is more serious than dishonesty in matters of money only, for ideas are more important than money.

Now, intellectual dishonesty is never a matter of sheer perversity. We Calvinists would know better than others how subtly human reason is corrupted by human evil. Hence we should be more careful than others about the perils of intellectual dishonesty.

In this connection we can learn a lot from the evolution controversy in Tennessee. (The following account is dependent on Norman F. Furniss, *The Fundamentalist Controversy, 1918–1931.* New Haven, Conn.: Yale University Press, 1954.) In the years 1923–25, a frenzied, hysterical anti-evolution movement swept the South. In quick succession, Oklahoma, Florida, North Carolina, and Texas passed laws to enforce orthodox teaching in the schools.

The victory of the fundamentalists was complete in Tennessee. George Washington Butler, a farmer, part-time school teacher, and clerk of a Primitive Baptist Association, put himself up for election to the legislature on the sole platform that he would outlaw the teaching of evolution. And in the legislature he accomplished his goal. The House passed his bill by a vote of 71–5 and the Senate by a vote of 24–6. The result was the Scopes trial.

The important point for us is not the rightness or wrongness of certain science instruction, but rather the irrational hysteria and the desire to legislate thought control.

The legislature was stampeded.

The newspapers with few exceptions were silent.

The ministers had little to say. The *Christian Century* reported that of fifty ministers with "liberal" points of view, perhaps ten had the courage to speak openly.

Leaders in the field of education, with few exceptions, did not fight for academic freedom.

In the meantime, the teaching of evolution was identified with a communist conspiracy and appeal was made to sectional prejudice against the North.

A Georgia legislator declared that the only books a man needed were the Bible, the hymnbook, and the almanac. Therefore, he concluded that he was against libraries.

Why did intelligent people fall victim to this hysteria? Why were they cowed by it?

One reason is ignorance. They understood neither Christian faith nor science. Hence they were afraid.

A second reason was social pressure. They feared men more than God and valued diplomacy above truth.

A third reason was lack of courageous leadership. There was no Luther to say, "Here I stand."

A fourth reason was self-interest. When a Chattanooga newspaper, seeing the publicity advantage of the Scopes trial, sought to take advantage of a lull in the trial to get one started in Chattanooga, the Dayton merchants threatened to boycott the wholesale merchants in Chattanooga. Intellectual dishonesty may be the tool of economic and ecclesiastical imperialism.

The recovery of our Calvinistic heritage means that we must stand for intellectual integrity amid the emotional pressures and the hysteria of our own day.

In conclusion let us note that the intellectual task of the church is close to the center of the Christian life and community. The intellectual worship of God is an integral part of the life of the soul.

Intellectual worship of God calls for *repentance*. As Augustine said long ago, we must first love the truth if we are to know it. We have failed in maintaining our ideals of intellectual competence and integrity, not because we have not been smart enough, but because we have not been good enough.

Intellectual worship of God calls for true *evangelism*. Evangelism is more than the repetition of theological phrases. It is commitment to God, who confronts us in the life, death, and resurrection of Jesus Christ and all that this commitment means for human existence. We have too often been content with theological formulas, and we have not bothered to communicate the gospel in its full meaning. Will Herberg tells this revealing incident. When Ignazio Silone, the Italian socialist and writer, was asked to name the most important date in universal history, he replied without a moment's hesitation, "December 25th in the year Zero." When one hundred American educators, scientists, newspapermen, and leaders in other fields were asked to name the hundred most important events, they gave first place to the discovery of America by Columbus. The birth and death of Jesus was tied for fourteenth place with the discovery of X-ray and the Wright brothers' first plane flight.[1] Quite obviously Silone, who is not an orthodox Christian, takes his faith seriously in a way that the one hundred Americans do not. Or, in any case, he understands the implications of the birth and death of Jesus more profoundly.

The intellectual worship of God calls also for *commitment.* Calvin's interest in theology was practical. All true doctrine edifies. The real test of religious conviction is life. Christian education must be translated into the life of the Christian community.

The time seems to be ripe for the recovery of our Calvinistic heritage. On a college campus a speech therapist reads the theology of Tillich because it helps him understand his work as a therapist. A young mathematician reads with avid interest the best theology of our day, because he has found that Christian faith gives meaning to his life. Suddenly the faith that he learned as a boy becomes alive. These examples can be repeated many times on every university campus. This is a time not simply for revivalists who "revive" the faith, but for evangelists who can proclaim the faith in the depth of its meaning to men and women who do not know the language of theology or of piety. Perhaps the very thing that cost us our opportunity on the frontier will be in the providence of God the ministry by which multitudes will come to know Jesus Christ as Lord and Savior in this day.

---

[1]Will Herberg, *Protestant-Catholic-Jew: An Essay in American Religious Sociology* (Chicago: University of Chicago Press, 1983).

"Calvin's Awareness of the Holy and the Enigma of His Theology: What Is Reformed Calvinist Theology?"
1986

Symposium in Honor of John Calvin (1509–1564), McGill University, Montreal, Canada

Calvin's theology appears to be simple, logical, consistent, and in the language of ordinary discourse. Some have found it such, but for others it is a puzzlement that they have sought to unravel by uncovering some central dogma from which it is deduced or the precise method by which Calvin did his theological work.

The diverse conclusions reached by Calvin research raise the question whether Calvin can be understood in terms of the methods most familiar to theologians of the last two centuries. Calvin himself regarded theology as a practical science designed for the edification of the church. He explicated the intensely personal relationship of God and man in the light of the scripture, and he did this "before God" and under a powerful awareness of the holy. Calvin's *Institutes* is more a practical achievement than a theoretical work. The recognition of Calvin's intense sense of the holy and the practical determination of his theological work opens up new possibilities for understanding his theology.

I

In 1909 William Adams Brown, one of the most competent of American theologians, undertook to speak on Calvin's influence upon theology and was embarrassed for lack of anything original to say. He found it impossible to approach Calvin's theology in the spirit of an explorer, for the latter's teaching was already commonplace knowledge. Further study of the reformer's theology, he felt, offered no chance of a new discovery.[1]

---

[1]William Adams Brown, "Calvin's Influence upon Theology," *Three Addresses Delivered by Professors in Union Theological Seminary* (New York: 1909), 20: "It is difficult to say anything original about Calvin. . . . There are certain great thinkers whose systems it is possible to approach in the spirit of the explorer, conscious as one turns each page, of the chance of some new discovery, but with Calvin it is not so. What he believed and what he taught has long been a matter of common knowledge."

The persistence and number of Calvin studies in the seventy-seven years since Brown's assessment indicate that his judgment was not correct. The search for the key to Calvin's thought continues, and there are those who believe that once that key is found vast new insights into his theology will be uncovered. The intensity of Calvin studies in the last decade—and in particular studies that are focused on the clue to or the nature of his theology—indicates that this search continues to be a lively theme.

Three comments concerning Brown's judgment may be made in a preliminary way. First, Brown was right in a fundamental sense. Calvin wrote his theology for ordinary Christian believers. In every generation since Calvin, Christians have been persuaded that they understood his theology. As disconcerting as it may be for scholars who are always searching for something new, the simple fact is that responsible interpretations of Calvin today and in the future are not likely to vary very much from those in the past.

Second, continuing studies of Calvin do uncover aspects of his theology or traits of his character that have been obscured in particular times and places. In our reading of Calvin we are continually covering up as well as uncovering what he actually said and did. Hence, the study of Calvin must go on to uncover what is still hidden and also what we have in our time forgotten or distorted. Yet the search for something new in Calvin's thought may be counterproductive if it becomes a passion. A certain modesty in Calvin research is appropriate. Greater emphasis upon the explication of Calvin's theology for the life of the church in our time and less stress upon highly sophisticated efforts to make new discoveries or to uncover what no one else has known may be more useful and also more in accord with Calvin's own way of doing theology.

A third observation is also appropriate. Contemporary theologians are far more concerned with method than was Calvin. The observation of Joseph Sittler on theological method can be applied to Calvin:

> My own disinclination to state a theological method is grounded in the strong conviction that one does not devise a method and then dig into the data; one lives with the data, lets their force, variety, and authenticity generate a sense for what Jean Daniélou calls a "way of knowing" appropriate to the nature of the data. An enduring memory is an evening spent with a group of graduate students who had invited Professor Paul Tillich, then in his seventy-third year, for a round of discussion. To the aggressive demand of several students that he state forthwith his theological method, Professor Tillich replied that the student was asking that something be supplied at the beginning of the sentence that could only come at the end! He added that

he himself had not even raised the methodological question until he was two-thirds of the way towards the completion of his *Systematic Theology*!

Every theologian, Professor Sittler argues, has a theological method, but the clarity and the permeative force of it is likely to be disclosed even to himself only in the course of his most mature work. When that method does become clear it may be seen to have been a function of a disposition toward the evaluation of data in their living historical force and not an imposition of abstract norms for 'truth,' or 'authenticity' arrived at early and exercised consistently.[2]

Calvin was deliberately concerned with language and with the careful expression of human thought, with the power of the spoken and written word to persuade. Nevertheless, the dominating force in his theology was his own convictions, the expression of his own understanding of the faith that had grown in his experience of the living God. To put it another way, the mastery of method never creates the theologian. The personal apprehension of the Christian message in one's life and experience comes first, and method is very much subordinate to that. The final word about method or about the nature of a theology is finally hidden in the mystery of the self of the theologian.

II

The persistence of Calvin scholars in searching out the precise nature of Calvin's theology for at least 150 years must, however, be taken seriously. From these studies, we can learn a great deal about Calvin the theologian. We also learn that no one clue or insight unlocks Calvin's theology.

Modern Calvin research received its initial impetus from the efforts to unite the Reformed and Lutheran churches in Germany in the first part of the nineteenth century. This effort toward church union naturally raised the question of Calvin's place in the history of Christian doctrine and especially of his relation to Martin Luther. The first study attempted to point out the importance of the personalities and cultural background of the first Reformers in accounting for the differences that arose in the various theologies of the Reformation.[3]

A more fruitful type of research approached the problem of Calvin's theology from the viewpoint of a system and asked what is the fundamental

[2]Joseph Sittler, *Essays on Nature and Grace* (Philadelphia: Fortress Press, 1972), 20.
[3]E. G. Ullmann, "Zur Charakteristik der reformierten Kirsche, Mit Beziehung auf neuere litterarische Erscheinungen," *Theologie Studien und Kritiken* XVI (1843): 749ff.

dogma from which the system is deduced. Alexander Schweizer made a well-known effort in this direction. He found that the feeling (*Bewusstsein*) of the absolute dependence of all creatures upon God is a peculiar material principle of Reformed theology. This principle is reflected in the strong protest of the Reformed church against all paganism in the medieval church, whereas the Lutheran church protested primarily against Judaistic relapses into Pelagian work-righteousness.[4]

F. C. Baur, who defended the superiority of the Lutheran church against Schweizer, saw value in Schweizer's designation of the material principle of Reformed theology. According to Baur, the distinguishing feature of the Reformed theology is the idea of the absolute causality of God.[5] Schneckenberger took issue with Baur as well as with Schweizer and vigorously maintained that Calvin did not deduce his theology from any objective idea of God.[6] The distinction between Lutheran and Reformed theology, according to Schneckenberger, lies in the difference of religious and ethical psychology. For the Lutheran, the decisive point is faith, the experience of justification. For Reformed theology, the decisive point is the origin of faith itself.[7]

F. W. Kampschulte, who made a real contribution to Calvin scholarship by his biography of the reformer, also regarded Calvin's theology as a system that was deduced from predestination.[8] Martin Schulze made another notable attempt to interpret Calvin in terms of one doctrine. Schulze found that eschatology of an otherworldly sort is a central doctrine and the basis for the interpretation of the whole of Calvinism.[9]

Studies on Calvin and his theology received a tremendous impetus from the publication of the *Opera Calvini* in the *Corpus Reformatorum* from 1863 to 1897. And they reached a climax in 1909 when the 400th anniversary of Calvin's birth was celebrated.[10] By no means do all these

[4]*Die Glaubenslehre der Evangelisch Reformierten Kirche dargestellt und aus den Quellen belefi* (Zurich: Orell, Füssli und Co., 1844), I, 45.

[5]F. C. Baur, "Über princip und Charakter des lehrbegriffs der reformierten Kirche in seinem Unterschied von dem der lutherischen, mit Rücksicht auf A. Schweizer's Darstellung der reformierten Glaubenslehre," *Theologische Jahrbücher* VI (1847): 333.

[6]————, "Die neueren Verhandlungen, betreffend das Princip des reformierten Lehrbegriffs," *Theologische Jahrbücher* VII (1848): 74.

[7]"Recensionen: Schweizer, *Die Glaubenslehre der evangelisch reformierten Kirche*," Theologische Studien und Kritiken XX (1847): 960–61.

[8]F. W. Kampschulte, *Johann Calvin, Seine Kirche und sein Staat in Genf,* (Leipzig: Duncker & Humblot, 1969), 263.

[9]Martin Schulze, *Meditatio futurae vitae; ihr Begriff und ihre beherrschende Stellung im System Calvins* (Leipzig: T. Weicher, 1901).

[10]Among the more important works were the following: Ellis Gauteron, *L'autorité de la Bible d'après Calvin* (Montaubon, 1902); Williston Walker, *John Calvin* (New York: G.P. Putnam's Sons, 1906); *Calvinreden aus dem Jubiläumsjahr 1909* (Tübingen: J.D.B. Mohr [P. Siebeck], 1909); *Calvin-*

studies follow the pattern of the central dogma research. In a study published as early as 1868, Köstlin maintained that Calvin's theology can be regarded as a system only if the word is duly qualified. While the *Institutes* reveals a tendency toward systematization, there is an increasing hesitancy in the various editions to draw the conclusions that a systematic approach demands.[11]

The most exhaustive work on Calvin was done by Emile Doumergue, when he incorporated a lifetime of research in his *Jean Calvin, Les Hommes, et Les Choses de Son Temps.* This collection of material is monumental, though it is marred by the hagiographic tendency of the author. In the study of Calvin's theology, Doumergue underscores the importance of the honor of God, but at the same time he rejects the thesis that Calvin's theology is a system that is deduced from material principles. Doumergue describes Calvin's procedure as a *méthode des contrariétés.*[12]

Another landmark in Calvin studies occurred in 1922 when Hermann Bauke published an important analysis of Calvin's theology.[13] The Calvin research of the previous century had produced a confusing medley of contradictory interpretations and evaluations. Bauke asked the question, "What is the peculiar character of the theology which makes all these contradictory opinions possible?" He was convinced that the experience of the preceding century had proved the inadequacy of every attempt to solve these problems by the study of any one doctrine or even the content of the whole theology. The solution of the problem, he felt, may be found in a study of the *Formgestaltung* and not of the content of the theology. Three characteristics of the *Formgestaltung* provide an explanation of the contradictory conclusions of Calvin research and offer a key for a true consideration of his theology.

The first is a formal, dialectical rationalism. This does not mean that Calvin's theology is rationalistic in the Stoic or eighteenth-century sense. It is not a rationalism of material, but of form in which the dogmatic

---

studien, ed. J. Bohatec (Leipzig: Rudolf Haupt, 1909); Schulze, *op. cit.*; Willy Lüttge, *Die Rechtfertigungslehre Calvins und ihre Bedeutung für seine Frömmigkeit* (Berlin: Reuther & Reichard, 1909); A. Lang, *Johannes Calvin* (Leipzig: Verein für Reformationsgeschichte, 1909); Abel Lefranc, *La Jeuness de Calvin* (Paris: Librairie Fischbacher, 1888); Hermann Strathmann, *Calvins Lehre von der Busse in ihrer späteren Gestalt* (Gotha, 1909); Max Scheibe, *Calvins Prädestinationslehre* (Halle: M. Niemeyer, 1897); Gisbert Beyerhaus, *Studien zur Staatsanschauung Calvins, mit besonderer Berücksichtigung seines Souveränitärsbegriffs* (Berlin: Trowitzsch & Sohn, 1910).

[11]D. J. Köstlin, "Calvins Institutio nach Form und Inhalt," *Theologische Studien und Kritiken* XLI (1868): 475.

[12]Emile Doumergue, *Jean Calvin, Les Hommes, et Les Choses de Son Temps.* 7 vols. (Lausanne: 1899–1927).

[13]Hermann Bauke, *Die Probleme der Theologie Calvins* (Leipzig: J. C. Hinrichs, 1922).

materials appear, by which they are bound together and in which they are expressed and systematized. This fact accounts for the difference between theologies of Calvin and Luther, which, in regard to content, are very much the same. It also accounts for the fact that the German who thinks in terms of content rather than form has difficulty understanding Calvin's theology.

The second characteristic of the form of Calvin's theology, according to Bauke, is the *complexio oppositorum*. Calvin's theological method is not the deduction of a system from one or two central doctrines. He does not seek to find some *diagonal* or *Stammlehre* or central doctrine or material principle from which individual dogmatic teachings can be deduced and developed. On the contrary, he seeks to bind existing individual dogmatic teachings that were in logical and metaphysical contradiction into a systematic coherence. This characteristic in turn explains the existence of many contradictory interpretations, for interpreters have concentrated on one doctrine and neglected others that are equally important.

The third characteristic is biblicism, by which Bauke meant a law that governed the pattern of Calvin's thought. The reformer sought not merely to take the materials of his theology out of the Bible, but also to make his theology a complete and consistent representation of the Bible.

Bauke's study contains many useful insights, for it made plain that every attempt to interpret the *Institutes* must consider the form as well as the content. He dealt a devastating blow to the notion that Calvin was a speculative systematizer who deduced the system of theology from one or two principles. Subsequent Calvin scholars agree with Bauke's conclusion in this regard, or at least they take his work seriously. However, Bauke's study did not put an end to contradictory interpretations.

The development of the New Reformation theology following Karl Holl's essay on Luther's understanding of religion in 1917 stimulated a new body of Calvin research, particularly under the influence of the theologies of Karl Barth and Emil Brunner.[14] This new theological development raised interesting questions as well as conflict between students of Brunner and Barth and conflict between the traditional interpretation of Calvin and the interpretation that was informed by the New Reformation theology. Even the controversy over whether Calvin knew about Copernicus became the occasion for this type of conflict between Pierre Marcel and Richard Stauffer.[15]

[14]John T. McNeill, "Fifty Years of Calvin Study," in Williston Walker, *John Calvin* (New York: Schoeken Books, 1969), XVII–LXXVII.

[15]Pierre Marcel, *La Prédication de Calvin*, à propos du livre de M. Richard Stauffer, *La Revue Reformée* 117 (1979); Richard Stauffer, "Calvin et Copernic," *Revue de l'Histoire des Religions* 179 (1971): 37ff.

The most comprehensive treatment of Calvin's theology that the crisis theology produced was Wilhelm Niesel, *The Theology of Calvin*.[16] Niesel rejects Bauke's thesis that the problem of Calvin's theology can be solved by the study of its form. The true genius of this theology is found in the recognition of its Christocentric character. Calvin has but one subject in all of his teaching, which is God made flesh: "Jesus Christ rules not only the content but also the form of Calvin's thought." In regard to form, Niesel points out two predominant characteristics. The first is Calvin's use of the Chalcedonian formula as a guide for his thought on many important doctrines. The second characteristic is that the activities of God in all their diversity must be considered as a unit in regard to their execution. While very suggestive, Niesel's study completely ignores those aspects of Calvin's thought that are not Christocentric, so a good amount of material in Calvin's writing cannot be accounted for on the basis of Niesel's thesis.

The problem of Calvin's theology continues to be the theme of studies published since 1950. Edward Dowey argued for the importance of the distinction between knowledge of God as creator and knowledge of God as redeemer.[17] Benjamin C. Milner Jr. has argued "that it is not the *duplex cognitio Domini* which underlies the final organization of the *Institutes*," but Calvin's conception of order that appears "when the work of the Spirit is correlated with those manifestations of the Word."[18] Alexandre Ganoczy noted the dialectical structure of Calvin's thought,[19] but Raymond K. Anderson found support for a living and organic unity, not for "an eclectic or dialectic, combination of diverse principles."[20] For David Willis and Heiko Obermann, the "extra Calvinisticum" becomes a key to understanding Calvin.[21] Ford Lewis Battles, after a life of Calvin studies, argued that Calvin's theology is a *via media* "between the Scylla of aberrant Romanism and the Charybdis of the radical tendencies of his time, whatever name he might give to them." Calvin's work is done in a field of tension in which the true-false principle is at work. Yet for Calvin the expression of truth never exhausts in this life the possibility of falsehood.

[16]Wilhelm Niesel, *Die Theologie Calvins* (1938) E.T. 1956.

[17]Edward A. Dowey, *The Knowledge of God in Calvin's Theology* (New York: Columbia University Press, 1952). Edward A. Dowey, "The Structure of Calvin's Thought as Influenced by the Twofold Knowledge of God," ed. Wilhelm Neuser, *Calvinus Ecclesiae Genevensis Custos*, 1984.

[18]Benjamin C. Milner, *Calvin's Doctrine of the Church* (Leiden: E.J. Brill, 1970), 4.

[19]Alexandre Ganoczy, *Calvin Theologien de l'eglise et du ministere* (1964), 59.

[20]Raymond K. Anderson, *Love and Order: The Life Structuring Dynamics of Grace and Virtue in Calvin's Ethical Thought* (1973), 395.

[21]E. David Willis, *Calvin's Catholic Christology* (Leiden: E. J. Brill, 1966); Heiko Obermann, "The 'Extra' Dimension in the Theology of Calvin." *The Journal of Ecclesiastical History*, January (1972).

Unfaith is always present in faith. Theology is the work of "fractioning off" the false from the true, and it works under limits in which the fractioning is never complete.[22] Carlos M. N. Eire in a study of Calvin's position on idolatry emphasizes as Battles did the tension between true and false in Calvin's writings and work.[23] Charles Partee has recently argued that union with Christ is the central dogma, a conclusion that is related to the proposal made in this paper.[24]

Two recent studies relate the secret of Calvin's theology to his personality and to his relation to Renaissance humanism. These studies are relevant for the analysis of Calvin's theology that follows, with its emphasis on the role of the believing self in theology.

Suzanne Selinger, in a very comprehensive discussion of Calvin's theology in terms of its psychological origins, relates Calvin's love of polarities and contrarities as well as his doctrine of predestination to peculiarities in his personality. Many conclusions seem somewhat tenuous to one who is not learned in psychological studies, but the net impact of her investigation is simply to indicate that theology, Calvin's in particular, is deeply rooted in human personality.[25]

William Bouwsma finds many indications in Calvin's writing that he was afflicted with the general anxiety of the age, and that in particular he had to struggle with serious doubt. These factors help to shape his theology.

Bouwsma, in an essay entitled "Calvinism as Renaissance Artifact," writes,

> He saw himself as a biblical theologian, working with and following texts, not coercing them with logic. He contrasted what he described as "the most beautiful economy of the Scriptures" with the philosophical discourse favored by the Schoolmen, noting with some irony that the Holy Spirit "did not adhere so exactly or continuously to a methodical plan." On the other hand, his repudiation of system had its positive corollary in his recognition of the "paradoxes" at the heart of the gospel, which he noted, "are contemptuously rejected by the common understanding of men," and which he listed with something like defiance: "That God became a mortal man, that

---

[22]Ford Lewis Battles, "Calculus Fidei," in *Calvinus Ecclesiae Doctor*, ed. W. H. Neuser (Kampen: J.H. Kols B.V., 1979).

[23]Carlos M. N. Eire: *War Against Idols, The Reformation of Worship from Erasmus To Calvin* (Cambridge: Cambridge University Press, 1986).

[24]Charles Partee, "Calvin's Theological Method: The Question of a Central Doctrine." A paper delivered at III Colloquium on Calvin Studies, Davidson College, 1986.

[25]Suzanne Selinger, *Calvin Against Himself, An Inquiry in Intellectual History* (Hamden, Conn.: Archon Press, 1984).

life is submissive to death, that righteousness has been concealed under the likeness of sin," etc.[26]

Calvin, Bouwsma emphasizes, took over the rhetorical style of humanism with its strong intent to transform human life and society, and this intention shaped his theology.

A survey, however cursory, of the studies during the past 150 years that have sought to uncover the secret of Calvin's theology raises important questions, some of which Bauke asked in 1921. The very diversity of the conclusions about Calvin's theology indicates that these studies may have asked a question for which there is no adequate data or a question that cannot be answered because of the final mystery of the self who theologizes.

Theology is not a mechanical process, but a personal activity, and the real nature of theology must remain hidden, as every human personality is finally a mystery to every other person.

No great theology is ever simply the product of a method. Every living theology has its origin in the experience and vision of a self. Theologians themselves frequently cannot describe how they came to an insight or a conclusion. All theology has its origin in the self, and its judgments are intuitive and tacit as well as disciplined and critical.

III

The purpose of this paper is to suggest another way of understanding Calvin that, on the one hand, throws light on Calvin's theology and, on the other, enables us to make abundant use of the many studies of the past century. No claim is made that this is the only way to understand Calvin's theology. Instead, this way of looking at his theology is descriptive and thus helps us to understand Calvin as well as his work.

This approach to Calvin's theology is based upon the opening words of the *Institutes:* "Nearly all the wisdom we possess, that is to say, true and sound wisdom, consists of two parts: the knowledge of God and of ourselves. But while joined by many bonds, which precedes and brings forth the other is not easy to discern" (I, i, 1). Calvin then goes on to say that "it is certain that man never achieves a clear knowledge of himself unless

---

[26]William Bouwsma, "Calvinism as Renaissance Artifact," in *Calvin Studies*, II. Papers presented at a colloquium on Calvin Studies at Davidson College Presbyterian Church and Davidson College, 1985. See Professor Bouwsma's studies, "Calvin and the Renaissance Crisis of Knowing," in *Calvin Theological Journal*, November (1982) and "The Quest for the Historical Calvin," in *Archiv für Reformationgeschichte*, 1986. "John Calvin's Anxiety," *Proceedings of the American Philosophical Society*, 128, no. 4 (1984).

he has first looked upon God's face" (I, iii, 2). Here Calvin's words suggest that the theme which holds together his theology is the relationship of God and man—God's relationship to man and man's relationship to God. In theology everything has to do with God and with God's relationship to man. This theological rubric appearing in every edition of the *Institutes* sets the limits and the conditions for understanding what Calvin will write. The particular formula that true wisdom consists of knowledge of God and knowledge of man and their interrelationship had been used by other theologians, but Calvin gives it a decisive place at the very beginning of his theological work.

This same theme also runs through Calvin's understanding of Christian existence and of the Christian life.

> . . . Now the greatest thing is this; we are consecrated and dedicated to God in order that we may hereafter think, speak, meditate and do nothing except to his glory.
>
> We are not our own: let not our reason nor our will therefore sway our plans and deeds. We are not our own: let us therefore not set it as our goal to seek what is expedient for us according to the flesh. We are not our own: insofar as we can, let us therefore forget ourselves and all that is ours.
>
> Conversely, we are God's: let us therefore live for him and die for him. We are God's: let his wisdom and will therefore rule all our actions. We are God's: let all the parts of our life accordingly strive toward him as our only lawful goal. (III, 7, 1)

For Calvin the presupposition of the Christian life is the vivid awareness that the chief end of life has to do with the living God.

His theology can best be understood as the explication of this intensely personal—or, as many would say today, existential—relationship between God and man and between man and God.[27]

Calvin's theology may be compared to a wagon wheel without the rim. The center hub of the wheel holds it together and spokes extend from the hub, but no outer rim brings the spokes into a self-contained order.[28] As the explication of the intensely personal relationship of God and man, the hub of the wheel is the personal relationship, or to put it more theologi-

---

[27]This position was argued by the writer in his dissertation, "A Study of John Calvin's Doctrine of the Christian Life" (New Haven, Conn.: Yale University, 1949). In this study the centrality of the existential and gracious relationship between God and man is abundantly documented as well as Calvin's inability to maintain the freedom and the graciousness of this relationship, sometimes substituting the signs of God's gracious presence for that presence.

[28]I first heard the model of the wheel with spokes but no rim used by John Dillenberger. This model has been very useful in my thinking about Calvin.

cally, faith. The spokes represent the various attempts to explicate this relationship according to particular themes, which are developed as far as Calvin can take them but which are never fully related to other particular truths. Hence, you have the unity of Calvin's theology in the relationship of God and man, which is explicated in numerous ways.

The unity consists in the fact that theology explicates the relationship of man and God as God has revealed himself in Jesus Christ. The various explications are not systematized. For example, Calvin says all he can on human responsibility and on God's lordship in the world. But he does not put them together in systematic unity.

Calvin's explication of the personal, existential relationship of God and man must also be interpreted in the light of Calvin's intense and vivid awareness of the holy or the presence of the living God. The church is a community of faith that stands in the presence of the wholly other, creator of heaven and earth. In the church and in all of its activities there is a sense of the numinous, of the *mysterium tremendum,* at once frightening and fascinating but in whose presence we stand in awe and devotion. The writing and teaching of theology in the church begins with this awareness and with this sensitivity.

One difficulty all modern interpreters have in understanding Calvin arises at this point. Everything Calvin wrote presupposes the presence and activity of the living God in immediacy and power. This awareness now has grown dim for those who are heirs of the Enlightenment. We are all children of the Enlightenment. The dogmas of a post-Enlightenment culture, though not the spirit of the Enlightenment, may hinder our understanding of Calvin more than the complexities of his theology. Calvin's awareness of the immediacy of the divine presence and activity cannot be translated without remainder into the language and experience of our time. Yet a recovery of an awareness of the holy God, who works personally in the created order, without doing violence to facts or the mind's integrity is the precondition for understanding Calvin.

Recent studies have emphasized that theology bears the mark of those who write it. Preachers and bishops, monks, university professors in Christendom, and university professors in secular universities and societies all leave the marks of their vocation on their theology. Calvin was very much the preacher whose pastoral responsibilities included a geographically widespread Christian community. Sermons and letters comprise more than half his writings. Roman Catholic theologians have always been dismayed at Calvin's failure to define his theological terms with precision, a failure in part due no doubt to his busyness as a pastor, to the perspective of a pastor, and in part to his endeavor to put theology in the language of ordinary human discourse.[29]

The audience for whom theology is written also influences its form and content. Theology may be written for university professors or for intelligent readers, for "despisers" of the faith or for the church. Calvin did not write theology for university professors. He did not even write it for other preachers or at least not for them exclusively. He wrote theology, as Reinhold Niebuhr in our time wrote theology, for intelligent readers, and he wrote theology for persons who were authentically involved in the life of the Christian community. He did not have the agenda that most historians and theologians have today.

Calvin's theological work is not consistently an exposition of the personal relationship between God and man. He continually allows the Bible, the law, the ecclesiastical structure or theological speculation—as, for example, about predestination—to become substitutes for the divine presence. This inconsistency in Calvin's work runs throughout his theological endeavors and the practice of the faith, yet it does not seem to be intentional. It derives in part at least from Calvin's intense concern to maintain the glory of God in Geneva and the temptation that every churchman has known to use the force of structures, of morals, or of theological orthodoxy to achieve what can only come as a gift of the Holy Spirit.

Calvin does not indicate much concern about what would today be regarded as theological method. The method grew out of his work, though there is his own testimony that he struggled with the arrangement of the *Institutes* a concern that is more pedagogical and practical than systematic, as William Bouwsma points out. His theology was a commentary on scripture, directed to Christian experience and living, in the light of the theological reflection of the Christian community. Calvin wrote his theology to persuade and to transform human life, and to this end he endeavored to write with transparent clarity. He also wrote out of the intensity of his own personal experience and theological commitment. For this reason, the method of his theology is finally hidden from us in the mystery of his own Christian experience.

IV

The central unity in Calvin's theology is in the explication of the personal relation between God and man. Yet, within this explication there are ways

---

[29]Kilian McDonnell, *John Calvin, The Church, The Eucharist* (Princeton, N.J.: Princeton University Press, 1967).

of doing theology and theological perspectives that give a coherence to all of Calvin's writings and that frequently have deceived people into finding in the *Institutes* a logical unity it does not have.

Calvin's theology is unified by certain ways of theologizing.

First, all of Calvin's conscious theological activity was subordinate to the authority of the Bible as the revelation of God. Theology is the coherent explication of scripture in the language of ordinary discourse. This involved bringing the disparate texts and themes of scripture into some coherent whole. Calvin never elaborated the point, but he clearly had a ground plan of the Bible in the light of which he organized his theology. (Calvin never wrote a chapter on the interpretation of scripture as Bullinger did in the *Decades*.)

Calvin read scripture at least in part as the church had read it before him. He considered it theologically wise to take seriously the judgment of great theologians and more particularly the great church councils, however subordinate they were to the authority of scripture.

The most important perspective that governs Calvin's theology is the authority of scripture as the norm of all theological thinking and speaking.[30]

A second concern that governs Calvin's theological work is the role of experience and the concreteness of the situation in which he wrote. Over and over again Calvin subjects what he has written theologically to the common-sense wisdom of experience. Revelation may go beyond human experience, but it cannot and does not contradict the clear facts of human experience or common sense. Calvin's theology is not an explication of Christian experience, but it never takes place apart from it and from the demands of the concrete situation. Calvin intends to explicate the relationship of God and man in light of the word of God, always with reference to experience and to the concrete situation.

Third, for Calvin, theology is a practical, not a theoretical, science. When Thomas Aquinas raised the question of whether theology was practical or theoretical, he answered that it was both but he gave the greater weight to theory. For Calvin, theology was overwhelmingly a practical science, and he showed little interest or concern for theoretical questions. The purpose of theology is to glorify God, to save human souls, to transform human life and society. Questions and issues that do not directly bear upon these practical concerns receive very scant attention from Calvin. One significant test of the authenticity of any doctrine is the power of that doctrine to edify.

[30] *Institutes:* I, 13, 3.

William Bouwsma speaks of Calvin's "rhetorical theology" directed to practical results rather than a systematic theology intended for the ages.[31] Calvin understood the Reformation as a great effort, mediated by language, to transfuse the power of the spirit into human beings. Bouwsma finds the most succinct statement of the principle that governs Calvin's theology in his commentary on Matthew 3:7: "It would be really a frigid way of teaching if the teachers did not determine carefully the needs of the times and sense the people concerned, for in this regard nothing is more unbalanced than absolute balance." In other words, in a particular situation theology must be expressed in an unbalanced way to be balanced.

In a very remarkable passage, Calvin expressed his desire for an ecumenical council. However, he believed that an ecumenical council was an impossibility, and therefore he dismissed it from his mind. "In regard to the whole body of the church, we commend it to the care of its Lord! Meanwhile, let us not be either slothful or secure. Let each do his best. Let us contribute whatever is in us of counsel, learning and abilities, to build up the ruins of the church."[32] Theoretical interests or ideal possibilities must not be allowed to undermine what is possible and close at hand.

Fourth, Calvin's theological work is also unified by style of expression. He attempted to write and to express theology simply—without ostentation, with transparent clarity, and in the language of ordinary discourse. He despised the pompous, the artificial, the contrived.

Other themes that are more directly theological unify Calvin's theological work; that is, they are basic theological decisions that govern Calvin's thinking:

1. One theological perspective is Calvin's way of relating the transcendence and immanence of God. His profound awareness of the sharp distinction between creator and creature reflects itself in his doctrine of the person of Christ, which is Antiochene rather than Alexandrian; in his doctrine of the presence of Christ in the sacrament, however concerned he was to emphasize the genuineness of our participation in the reality of Christ; and in his doctrine of the church, which he never confused with an extension of the incarnation. Calvin radically desacralized created existence as the contemporary idiom puts it. He emphasized the immediacy of God's presence and activity in the world, but he always jealously guarded

[31]William Bouwsma, "Calvinism as Renaissance Artifact."

[32]Final paragraph of "Canons and Decrees of the Council of Trent with the Antidote," *Calvin's Tracts* (Edinburgh: 1851), 3:188.

the integrity of the creator and the creature, allowing for no confusion or mixture.

2. A second unifying theme in Calvin's theology is his understanding of God primarily in terms of energy, activity, power, moral purpose, intentionality. God is the sovereign Lord of heaven and earth. Every doctrine in the *Institutes* reflects Calvin's insistence on the immediacy of the divine presence and upon the activity of God in his creation. David Wiley has persuasively argued in a Duke University dissertation on Calvin's doctrine of predestination that while predestination is not the central dogma in Calvin, it impinges upon everything Calvin wrote, emphasizing the immediacy of God's activity and the initiative of divine grace.

3. A third unifying theological perspective is Calvin's way of putting together nature and grace or the way knowledge of God the creator and God the redeemer are related to each other. Creation and redemption cannot be opposed to each other. Yet they cannot be identified, for redemption is more than creation, not simply as its completion but in the light of sin as its transformer. The practical priority is on redemption. Calvin refused to discuss the possibility whether the Word would have become flesh if man had not sinned (II, 12, 4).

4. A fourth unifying theological perspective is Calvin's way of relating gospel and law, justification and sanctification. Gospel and law cannot be separated, for the gospel is in the law and the law is in the gospel. Yet they are different and must not be confused. Likewise, salvation as God's mercy—justification by grace through faith—and salvation as God's power—sanctification—must never be separated or confused. Calvin knew that justification is the principal hinge on which religion depends, but he also knew that the presupposition of sanctification is the end toward which salvation moves on the human level.

5. Calvin's theology is also unified by a vision of the human community under the authority of God. Calvin wished to maintain the independence of church and state. He was not (at least intentionally) a theocrat in the sense that he gave divine authority to any human personage. Yet he had a profound awareness that the world is God's creation, and he saw it as the theater in which God's glory is revealed and where God's people received the divine blessing and lived together as the Christian community. In his preaching Calvin

sought, as he said in a sermon on 2 Timothy 2:16–19, "to draw the world to God and to build a Kingdom of our Lord Jesus Christ that he may rule among us." He never defined the Christian life simply in terms of personal piety.

This paper wished to argue that Calvin's theology can best be understood as the explication of the very personal, existential relationship of God to man and man to God; that this theology finds its unity in this relationship and that the various facets of the relationship are explicated to the best of Calvin's ability without a final attempt to bring them in a unity on the circumference; and that while Calvin's explication does not issue in a theology that is fully unified as to details, a unity and a distinctive character are provided by certain ways of doing theology and certain theological perspectives. These ways of doing theology and these theological perspectives give an easily recognizable identity to Calvin's theological writings in sermons, letters, church polity, and theological tracts as well as the *Institutes*.

PART FIVE
THEOLOGICAL
EDUCATION

"On Teaching Theology
at Union Theological Seminary in Virginia"
1976

(The following article was not written for printing but as a basis for discussion in the theological department at Union Theological Seminary in Virginia and with visiting theologians. It is printed here because it still represents in rough draft my convictions about the teaching of theology to future pastors of Presbyterian congregations. J.H.L.)

The following reflections indicate how I perceive my responsibility for teaching theology at Union Theological Seminary.

I

The first assumption is that Union Theological Seminary is an institution of the church whose primary purpose is training persons to be ministers of the word in the local congregation. The final goal is not the theologian but the minister as preacher, teacher, and pastor. Theology taught in the context of the graduate school as such differs significantly from theology taught in a seminary as an institution of the church. Theology may be taught as the fulfillment of ordination vows; theology may also be taught under the claims of the critical inquiry of the university. Seminary and university need each other and are not mutually exclusive—ideally the university for the sake of honesty, the seminary for the sake of life.

More important than the particular responsibilities of seminary or university are the actual communities of faith in which theologians truly live, communities or perspectives of faith that in reality exist in great diversity on both seminary and university campuses. This assumption means that theological procedure is subordinate to and determined by the substance of theology. Also the question of the possibility of theology is secondary to the practice and substance of theology. An intense preoccupation with procedure and possibility over against substance is a telltale clue that theology is taking place outside the organized life of the church.

II

Theology in the service of the preaching, teaching, and pastoral work of the minister presupposes basic competence. The following prerequisites are in practice ideal but are in reality minimal and indispensable:

1. Life within the organized church. I doubt if persons who do not worship faithfully and who do not participate in church activities can be taught to be theologians of the church.
2. College courses in philosophy and logic as well as in history, English, et al., as a requirement for admission.
3. A two-year college course in Bible or its equivalent, as a requirement for admission. (We are currently giving a D.Min. for work that is on the bachelor's level.)

   Reformed theology presupposes a *biblical* message or perspective that is consistent, coherent, and comprehensive, even if this perspective cannot be defined with precision. Apart from this comprehensive grasp of a coherent biblical content, Reformed theology is not possible. Ability to exegete an individual pericope cannot substitute for synoptic vision and understanding. The old rubric that scripture must be interpreted by scripture meant that individual passages must be interpreted not by other individual passages but by the "general sense" of scripture. The same is true of the rubric, the analogy of faith. The "general sense" of scripture can be construed in terms of a framework (Otto Weber: ground plan) such as creation-fall-redemption-consummation, or in terms of pervasive themes such as covenant and election, or in terms of metaphors, images, symbols, and narratives.

   A good basic requirement for admission to the study of theology would be having read the Bible through at "one sitting."
4. Basic to the constructive work of Reformed theology is the mastery of texts.
   a. A survey course in the history of doctrine
   b. Ability to write a theological commentary on the Apostles' Creed, Nicene Creed, Chalcedonian Definition

c. Knowledge of the development of the doctrine of the Trinity, culminating in the works of the Cappadocians and Augustine
d. The reading of the following documents:
  1. Letters of Ignatius
  2. Justin's Apology
  3. Athanasius on the *Incarnation of the Word*
  4. Augustine: *City of God; Confessions*
  5. Anselm: *Proslogium*
  6. Thomas: *Summa Contra Gentiles,* Ch. 1–25 or *Summa Theologiae,* Q. 1–4
  7. Luther's Writings of 1520: *Christian Liberty; The Babylonian Captivity of the Church;* Address to the German Nobility; Sermon on Good Works
  8. John Calvin: *Institutes of the Christian Religion*
  9. Reformed Confessions
  10. Schleiermacher: *Christian Faith,* pp. 1–31
  11. Jonathan Edwards: *Treatise Concerning Religious Affections*
  12. One of the following: Turretin: *Institutes;* Charles Hodge: *Systematic Theology;* A. A. Hodge: *Outlines of Theology;* Heppe: *Reformed Dogmatics;* Strong, Mullins, et al.
  13. One of the following: Karl Barth, Emil Brunner, Otto Weber
  14. Ability to explicate the following rubrics:
    (a) We believe in order to understand
    (b) Faith seeks intelligibility
    (c) *Lex orandi, lex credendi*

III

Theology is not a mechanical exercise that can be programmed or established by a precise and fixed method. It is the imaginative work of the human spirit as well as the more pedestrian command of techniques and procedures. In this sense theology is like poetry or any creative achievement of the human spirit; it is beyond teaching and learning.

Yet some factors in the task of constructive theology can be identified, including particular Reformed emphases:

  1. Constructive theology is done in the light of the conviction that there is a coherent, consistent, rational understanding of the Christian faith.

2. Reformed theology has generally understood its task as the interpretation of scripture and tradition in contemporary idiom. Creativity in theology is more likely to issue from the more modest endeavor to interpret the faith than it is out of the intention to be a creative or speculative theologian, as one of my best teachers, Albert Outler, always insisted. The desire to be "the great theologian" or to impress professionals with one's learning is self-destructive.

3. Systematic theology in the Reformed tradition has been more historical than philosophical. Its unity has inhered not in its deduction from one principle but rather in the existential relationship between God and man that it seeks to explicate. The explication of any doctrine or of Christian faith in its unity always gives attention to (1) its basis in the biblical witness, (2) the church's reflection upon it, and (3) its intelligibility in terms of contemporary experience, especially experience in the church. The claims of intelligibility lead to a fourth element in responsible theological work: empathy with culture, skill in language usage, and an awareness of the demands of coherent, logical, sustained discourse.

4. Theological reflection may be prompted by the study of scripture; by life in the church; by the challenge of a personal, social, or cultural crisis; or by the study of theology itself. Hence, no one method can be applied to all theological reflection. No particular "starting point" is normative. Method and procedure grow out of the data and the situation.

5. In mastering the basic texts of theology the theologian participates in theology as it has been done by theologians whose work has been confirmed in the life of the church. As the theology of the church is assimilated into one's own thinking, indeed into one's own personal existence, the theologian acquires the sensitivity as well as the skills and knowledge to engage in theological thinking today.

IV. On Being a Reformed Theologian

Being a Reformed theologian can be defined as follows:

John Calvin and the Reformed theologians generally intended to write theology, not for their particular churches and communities, but for the one holy catholic church. They were writing Christian theology, not "reformed" theology.

Yet, within the theologies of the one holy catholic church, Reformed theology is distinguished by nuances, perspectives, and stances, by a particular way of doing theology, by characteristic emphases.

1. Reformed theology is practical rather than theoretical or speculative in its primary thrust. A test of any theology is its usefulness in edification.

2. Reformed theology has the characteristics of simplicity, rational clarity, and precision. It is spoken in the language of ordinary human discourse to convince and to persuade by uncovering the truth.

    The "rhetorical" style of the "preacher-theologians" of the sixteenth century was succeeded by scholasticism. The two styles have their peculiar strengths and weaknesses. Calvin was quite as careful and precise in contending for what is important in a "doxological" theology in the context of the church as a worshipping and believing community as Turretin represents what is important for the demands of rational reflection and for the church as "school." The theology that has shaped the Reformed community has had strong rhetorical qualities even in its most scholastic periods, that is, simplicity in style using the language of ordinary human discourse to persuade. (Cf. Westminster Assembly Directory on rhetorical style in preaching.)

3. Reformed theology is based on revelation as attested in scripture.

4. Calvin's particular understanding of the transcendence and the immanence of God in personal categories, of the distinction between creator and creature, gives a unity to his doctrines of the person of Jesus Christ, of the presence of Jesus Christ in the sacraments, of justification and sanctification, of the church as a human work and divine work. (While Calvin is only one among many Reformed theologians, his theology gave a precise, clear, seminal statement of Reformed theology generally. Hence Reformed and Calvinist theology are here used interchangeably. The reader should be aware that Reformed theology is broader than Calvin's theology.) (William Temple, in *Nature, Man and God*, provides a twentieth-century exposition of transcendence and immanence that illuminates Calvin's exposition.)

5. A fifth unifying stance is classically expressed in the doctrine of predestination with its emphasis upon the immediate activity of God and the initiative of divine grace.

6. Another unifying perspective is Calvin's understanding of the relationship of revelation in Jesus Christ and general revelation, of

grace and nature, of gospel and law, of church and society.

7. A seventh characteristic perspective is Reformed theology's understanding of the relation of justification and sanctification, emphasizing sanctification while maintaining integrity of justification.

   Richard Niebuhr, in his classic typology, *Christ and Culture,* found that Calvin belonged among the transformers and converters of culture, not among those who separate themselves from culture or who identify Christian faith with culture.

8. An eighth unifying factor in Calvin's theology and churchmanship is his doctrine of the Holy Spirit, especially his emphasis upon the unity of the word and spirit. The objective and the subjective are united in one personal experience. The dichotomy between the mystical and the scientific is overcome. Truth is experienced in the doing. "Knowing involves being saved." Piety is wisdom, a *sancta eruditio.*

Reformed theology is not identified by a signboard with a clear and indubitable designation. It is recognizable sometimes more clearly, sometimes less clearly, in the light of certain emphases and nuances. Reformed theology will always be characterized by an emphasis upon the immediacy of God's action and the initiative of his grace, by a clear distinction between and insistence upon the integrity of divine activity and human activity which, even while they cannot be separated or divided, nevertheless cannot be confused or changed. In other words, Reformed theology will always emphasize the distinction between creator and creature and the integrity of the creature and the creator in their activities. Reformed theology, likewise, will always place an emphasis upon sanctification, upon the fulfillment of the purposes of God here and now in time and space. Finally, Calvinist theology will always reflect the conversionist or transformationist motif rather than withdrawal or identification with society and culture. This transformation or conversion is the work of the spirit of Christ, not of the spirit or ideology of the age. Reformed theology is characterized by a particular way of holding together spirit and word, Holy Spirit and human spirit, knowing and doing.

Reformed theology shares almost every doctrine, certainly all the major doctrines, with all Christians everywhere. The distinctiveness of the Reformed community is not the originality of the doctrines or its possession of something that others do not have but rather "the nuance, perspective, and stance" in the light of which the doctrines are expressed and in terms of which they are united in one coherent whole that give

Reformed theology its distinctive character.

Reformed theology is not a system that has been deduced from any one doctrine. Reformed theology is an explication of the relationship of God, the creator and redeemer, and man the creature, the sinner and the redeemed. Its unity inheres in this relationship. A basic rubric is the conviction that any knowledge of God involves knowledge of man and that any knowledge of man involves knowledge of God. The varied aspects of this relationship are explicated without being brought together in a closed system and without affirming everything that the demands of logic and reason seem to require.

This way of doing theology must be known not simply by rote but must be assimilated into one's personal existence. This assimilation comes from living, reading, and studying in the Reformed tradition.

V. The Everyday Task of Theology

In a seminary or graduate school environment it is easy to expect too much or too little of congregational ministers.

The partial mastery of the above-mentioned data is not to expect too much. Likewise, it should be within the realm of reason to expect graduate students to learn to apply *automatically* the following rubrics to all their preaching, teaching, and pastoral care. (While these rubrics are more easily applied negatively than positively, they should in the end have a positive thrust and result in preaching or teaching.)

1. Catholic
   Is the sermon catholic (Christian)? (Exegesis, teaching, pastoral care may be substituted for sermon.)
   a. The Nicene Creed. God is defined by Jesus Christ.
   b. Trinitarian Theology.
   c. Chalcedon Definition.
   Rules of faith differed in many details but with unanimity specified (1) God as Father, Son, and Holy Spirit and (2) the life, death, and resurrection of Jesus Christ.
2. Protestant
   Is the sermon Protestant?
   a. Final authority of Holy Spirit speaking through scripture. Scripture understood as a coherent whole.
   b. Justification by grace, not works.
   c. Priesthood of believers.

    d. Sanctity of the common life.

    e. Emphasis on the integrity of the personal, the historical. No sacrament apart from faith.

3. Reformed Perspectives

    Is the sermon Reformed?

    a. The Lordship of God, the immediacy, the activity of God, and the initiative of grace.

    b. A way of relating creator and creature, transcendence and immanence, which neither confuses them nor separates them. Antiochene rather than Alexandrian.

    c. A particular way of putting together justification and sanctification.

    See Larger Catechism question 77.

    d. A transformationist understanding of relation of Christ and culture under power of the Holy Spirit.

    Does this sermon edify, enhance love for God and love for man?

    e. An awareness of the importance of "order" in church or society.

4. Does this sermon place the hearer, the community, *Coram Deo?*

This perspective is so decisive for Calvin that it is part of the Reformed perspective. Yet its importance for classic Reformed theology and ecclesiology as well as its general Christian character justifies a fourth heading.

Subordinate to the "presence of God" but essential to it is the question "Does the sermon illuminate the 'hard facts' of human experience?"

(Heinrich Bullinger's sermon on the exposition of scripture is closely related to what is attempted here. Bullinger insisted that scripture must be explicated (1) according to the proportion (analogy) of faith, (2) according to its historical setting, (3) in the context of scripture as a whole, (4) in a way that enhances love for God and man, and (5) by a heart that loves God and his glory and that prays that the spirit which inspired scripture will expound it.) The occasion of this paper has justified the omission of one question that is indispensable to the tasks of preaching, teaching, and pastoral care: How does this sermon (et al.) relate to other responsible Christian groups and to religions?

"The Significance of Historical Theology in the Education of Ministers"
April 20, 1960

Inaugural Address on Installation as Professor at Union Theological Seminary

The only appropriate word with which to begin an address on the occasion of one's installation as a professor in Union Theological Seminary is a word of gratitude.

It is a privilege to share in the life of an institution that has played so significant a role in the history of our church.

It is a privilege to have the comradeship of those who teach in and guide the affairs of this institution.

It is especially a privilege to share in the education of those who study here and who will go out to be ministers of Jesus Christ in churches throughout the South.

For these privileges I am deeply grateful today.

An inaugural address offers at least two options as to topic. One is a study of some theological problem in its historical ramifications. The other option is the prior question, Why historical theology at all? Why should courses in historical theology be injected into an already over-crowded curriculum? This question is personal as well as academic. Why should one devote his life to the teaching of historical theology? Every Christian should be able to give some better justification for his daily work than the fact that it happens to be a pleasant way to make a living.

I have therefore chosen as our theme the following question: What is the significance of historical theology in the training of a minister? The emphasis is on the word *minister*, the minister of a local congregation. Our primary concern as an institution of our church is the training of pastors of congregations. What does historical theology have to contribute to the making of good ministers of Jesus Christ in the Reformed tradition?

The foundation for all Christian theology is the revelation of God culminating in Jesus Christ and the witness to the resurrection of Jesus as attested in scripture. The Bible provides the interpretative framework—creation, fall, redemption, consummation—within which Christian theology explicates the faith. The Bible also provides language not only of theology but also of the believing, confessing community. All Christian theology acknowledges the Bible as the final authority.

Christian theology takes place in the church—the worshiping, believing, confessing congregation. Faith cannot be sustained apart from the work of the Holy Spirit in the fellowship of the believing, worshiping, witness community. The believing community sustains and is enriched by the individual believer.

Christian theology has been written historically in the active life of the church. In the ancient church, theology was written largely by bishops; in the medieval church by monks; in the Reformation by preachers; in the post-Reformation church by preacher-professors in universities committed to Christian faith. Theology since the Enlightenment has been written more and more in increasingly secular universities, by professors who are more and more oriented by the professional guild. The goal of theology is less and less to edify, as Calvin insisted, and to equip the pastor of a local congregation to preach and nurture a congregation as a believing and worshiping community. The aim of theology is increasingly to impress the academic community by its intellectual sophistication.

Christian theology that is under the authority of scripture and that takes place in the church has many other dimensions of less crucial importance. It is in dialogue with Christian experience, with culture, with living religions, with language, and with the claims of logic and the warrants that justify any assertion. Its end is edification and explanation of the affirmations of Christian faith in intelligible words and sentences. In theology, faith seeks intelligibility.

The central thesis of this presentation is that a thorough knowledge of the history of doctrine is essential not only for the work of the theologian, but also for the Reformed pastor. Christian doctrine is the church's reflection upon the Christian revelation and the church's understanding of that revelation, less official than dogma and less general than Christian thought. Doctrine reflects Christian experience as well as intellectual activity. It finally must be confirmed in the experience of the Christian community. The history of doctrine does not replace revelation, but it does embody the depth and breadth of the Christian community's reflection on revelation. Every Christian theologian should ideally recapitulate in his or her life the whole history of doctrine. Human limitations set the parameters for this recapitulation. No theologian is ever truly catholic or ecumenical. But every theologian can hope that his or her exposition of a particular tradition contributes to a truly catholic theology.

The study of the history of doctrine is crucial for the theologian and for the well-being of the church for at least four reasons.

1. Historical theology is significant for the education of ministers because it is an aid to the recovery of a Christian memory.

The uprootedness of human existence is one of the tragedies of our time. People are bereft of roots in the past and become the victims of the tyranny of the present. In the words of Reisman's study, they are other-directed because they have no inner direction and no tradition to give strength to their lives. Christians have rootage in the past because they belong to the great tradition of the people of God.

Yet it cannot be said that all who call themselves Christian have a real Christian memory, have a sense of belonging to a community whose roots go back through the centuries. This is a special temptation of American Protestants. Many are in a bad sense of the word twentieth-century Christians. Yet, as Professor Albert Outler has well expressed it,

> It was in some sort of historical community that each of us heard the Gospel preached and at a time when we could not judge whether it was preached well or ill. Then, as we discovered the past of our own communion, and the past of other and disparate communions, we began to have some fuller measure of the common meaning of the Gospel we have heard and believed and the Gospel as believed and practiced by others.
>
> In this respect, the discovery of our total Christian past is the means to a fuller initiation into the whole Christian family. Man is a creature capable of inheriting acquired characteristics—not through his genes but through his traditions. Children are knit into family life by hearing the reminiscences of the family. It is the sense of this particular family tradition that makes its members truly kin, since the blood relation in itself is not sufficient to produce the feeling of truly belonging. (*The Christian Tradition and the Unity We Seek* [1957], 41).

A Christian memory is the recollection of the story of one's life as it reaches back through the ages. It is a thrilling fact this morning to recall that between each one of us and the events of the New Testament, indeed between us and Abraham and Adam, there is an unbroken succession of believing men and women who have heard the voice of the living God and in faith and love have obeyed. It is not without significance that early

Protestant histories of the church, as well as such confessions as the Scots Confession of 1560, trace the history of the church back to Adam.

Historical theology is *church* history, not the history of Christianity nor the history of theological texts. Professor Trinterud in his presidential address before the American Church History Society rightly said, "The most crucial of these assumptions for the church historian is the assumption that the church is a community of people redeemed by God in history through Jesus Christ. Apart from this assumption there would be no church history, but rather the history of the Christian religion." Historical theology is nothing more and nothing less than the recollection of the reflection of Christians through the centuries concerning their creation and redemption by God.

H. E. W. Turner in his excellent book, *Patterns of Christian Truth,* has well written, "All the major doctrines of orthodoxy were lived devotionally as part of the corporate experience of the Church before their theological development became a matter of urgent necessity." Historical theology does not deal with beliefs in the abstract, but with belief as it has been lived and confessed by the Christian community. The *Lex Orandi* is the *Lex Credendi,* which are in turn the source of Christian action, the *Lex Agendi* (*Patterns of Christian Truth*).

The life of the Christian community that historical theology seeks to recover is the life of the ecumenical church. It is also the life of the particular tradition and in our case the Reformed tradition. The two are not in conflict. We can serve our own particular tradition best when we see and understand it within the ecumenical church, and we can serve the ecumenical church when we bring to it the treasures of our particular heritage. The recovery of catholicity in the theological enterprise is one of the pressing needs and bright hopes of the contemporary situation. In no small measure the theological achievements of the fourth and fifth centuries were due to the catholicity of theological endeavor, a catholicity which from that point on was increasingly lost and that is only now being recovered.

Historical theology is the effort to take seriously the life of the church, the covenant community, through the centuries. It is hardly possible to take seriously the covenant community without taking seriously the covenant community's history. *The recovery of a Christian memory is nothing more than an awareness of the history of the church as the story of one's life.*

The question may be raised whether the scripture alone of the Protestant does not make the living memory of the church a dispensable possession. The answer must imagine what our situation would be if we were bereft of this living memory. Let us suppose that some holocaust in the third century had not only destroyed the Christian community from living memory but had also destroyed every known Bible. Then let us suppose that a Bible were found in some Dead Sea cavern. Now let us think through the possibilities and difficulties that would be involved in this newly discovered Bible becoming the center of a community of faith, worship, and action such as we know the Christian community to be today.

The historical fact is that the Bible was never alone in the theological work of Luther or Calvin. Recent studies have pointed out Luther's very great indebtedness to the traditions of medieval Catholicism. Calvin, fascinated as he was by the radical reformers, never succumbed to their antihistorical outlook. He could not bring himself to the point of saying that any whole segment of history of the church had been nothing but a great mistake, though he was certain that the church fell about the time of Gregory the Great. Yet he does not try to leap over the thousand years that intervened between the Reformation and Augustine, though he first tarries for long with Augustine. He claims fellowship with such theologians as Aquinas and Bernard of Clairveaux. His mastery of the fathers and his appreciation of the ancient church are well-established facts. He deliberately worked as a theologian and as a worshipper in the tradition of the church.

Some radical sectarians have believed that they can get along without Christian history. In fact, they have insisted that salvation is to be found in the incredible gymnastic leap over fifteen centuries of church history to the New Testament. Even Protestants have sometimes fancied they could jump from the present to the New Testament with only brief refueling stops in the sixteenth, fifth, and fourth centuries.

The plain fact, however, is that all Christians depend more upon tradition than many have admitted. The discrepancies in interpretation—the idiom of theology—betray the tradition that is unconfessed. A theologian who succeeds in freeing himself from a Christian tradition takes his stance in an alien tradition. The Bible may be interpreted in terms *of* and *from* the viewpoint of the particular spirit of the age in which the interpreter lives, a spirit of the age that is bereft of the wisdom of what Christians through the centuries have discovered the Bible to mean. The secular traditions of society may be substituted for the traditions of the Christian church, but no person can sit down traditionless to interpret the Bible.

Actually the church found very early in its history that the historical theology of the church as enshrined in the rule of faith was indispensable to the interpretation of scripture. Irenaeus, Tertullian, and Athanasius all discovered that heretics could quote scripture. Therefore, they insisted that the Bible must be understood in the light of the church's rule of faith, and the church—with the exception of certain sectarian groups ever since—has insisted that the theology of the church as summarized in some rule of faith must be the guide to Biblical interpretation.

A fundamental Protestant conviction is that the living memory of the church, which is the concretion of the church's apostolic memory, stands under the authority of the Bible. Another fundamental Protestant conviction is that the Bible is not alone. Hence the question is not the rejection or acceptance of one or the other, but the proper relation that must exist between them. The problem of the tradition and the traditions—or the Bible and tradition, which is now becoming one of the liveliest issues in theology—is a relevant concern for the person who wishes to speak the Christian message to people in our time.

2. Historical theology is significant for the education of ministers because history judges dogma and thus lays bare its real significance and meaning.

We never know the full meaning of any exegesis of scripture or any theological reflection until we see it submitted to the test of time. A statement from the Old Testament declares that the man who puts on his armor ought not to boast as does the man who takes it off. (I suppose this means that any inaugural address is a very tenuous enterprise.) Surely this is true of the theological enterprise. Any cavalier treatment of older theologies that have stood the test of history is an amazing presumption. Professor James Orr of the old United Free Church of Scotland in a remarkably fine book, *The Progress of Dogma,* has put it this way: "The history of dogma criticizes dogma; corrects mistakes, eliminates temporary elements, supplements defects; incorporates the gains of the past at the same time that it opens up wider horizons for the future." Of course, as Professor Orr well understood, history is no infallible judge of dogma. In Protestantism there is no infallible judge, but the historic wisdom of the Christian community as it has reflected upon the Bible is the best judge we have.

History judges dogma intellectually. In history an individual theologian's reflections upon the meaning of Christian redemption or a council's decree is subjected to the evaluation and judgment of many Christians in many different places and in many different situations.

History also judges doctrine morally and socially. James Orr speaks of the correlation of doctrine with vital Christian experience and with its practical effects. John Calvin, who wrote his *Institutes* not only as a guide to the study of the scriptures but also as an aid to piety, declared that a doctrine that did not edify was theologically unsound. Moreover, edification was one of the guiding principles of Calvin's worship. A preliminary principle that our Presbyterian forefathers attached to the form of government declared, "Truth is in order to goodness; and the great touchstone of truth is its tendency to promote holiness."[2] The final expression and decisive test of a minister's scholarship is written in the life of the congregation.

We never know the full meaning of a Christian doctrine or an interpretation of scripture until we see it embodied in the life of the Christian people and in the life of the Christian community. As John Mackay has put it,

> "The Christian revelation shall continue to have its crowning significance not in great systems of thought or in masterpieces of art, but in the renewed lives of plain people. Not in scholars and connoisseurs, not in poets and artists, persons who were enthralled and transfigured by the grandeur of the revelation, but in a community of believers, saints in the New Testament sense, men and women who heard and obeyed the Gospel of God, and were recreated in Christ Jesus, did the revelation of God reach the end which was also the beginning."[3]

History judges theology and exposes something of its meaning that can be found nowhere else, by laying bare its embodiment in the life of the Christian believer and in the life of the Christian community. For example, the real meaning of Arianism and the Nicene faith can be more clearly seen in their embodiment in the culture and in the imperial politics of the fourth century than in the theological tomes.

History judges dogma in still a third way, by what H. E. W. Turner has called the instinctive judgment of the Christian community. Orthodoxy is established not simply by theologians, but also by ordinary Christians who are in no sense professional theologians. As Turner writes, "Behind the instinctive rejection of heresy there lay a kind of Christian common sense exercised at all its levels within the Christian Church, which is merely another name for the guidance of the Holy Spirit leading the Church into all truth and dividing to every man severally as he wills."

Again this is no infallible judgment. But in the long run, as I think history indicates, the common-sense judgment of the Christian community

---

[2]Presbyterian Church (U.S.A.), *Book of Order* (Louisville, Ky.: The Office of the General Assembly, 1960–1961), G1.0304.

[3]John Mackay, *Christianity on the Frontier* (New York: Macmillan, 1950), 200.

is more reliable than the judgment of theological faculties or church councils. In any case, most Christian doctrines—including that most crucial of all doctrines, the Nicene faith—have been established through the common-sense judgment of the Christian community rather than through the action of church councils.

> 3. Historical theology is of significance in the education of ministers because it contributes to theological competence.

Historical theology develops theological competence by bringing to us the accumulative insights, methods, and conclusions of the Christian community as it has reflected upon the creation and redemption of God. We do not have to start from the beginning in the interpretation of the Bible or in reflection upon the significance of the Christian message.

Few if any theological problems or difficulties for faith that Christian people face today have not been faced in essential substance before. Few if any heresies that threaten Christian faith from within today do not bear a remarkable resemblance to gnosticism, Arianism, Manichaeism, Pelagianism, or deism and the various heresies of the centuries. Many of the issues that the church faces today and that many seek to evade are precisely the issues that the church found at Nicea or at Orange or at Worms and could not ignore. The Christian minister who speaks to intelligent Americans is greatly helped in his task if, through his knowledge of the Christian past, he can detect the incipient gnosticism, Arianism, Pelagianism, or deism of the present, and if he knows the questions and issues that language or the climate of opinion frequently obscure in contemporary theology.

Historical theology contributes to theological competence by providing perspective for contemporary theologizing. History teaches few things as clearly as the blindness of particular cultures to truths that are obvious and clear in other situations. Errors can be so endemic in a particular culture that truths which are very obvious in other cultures cannot be recognized. Evil can be so pervasive in a society that good men are unaware of its existence.

Herbert Butterfield, in his book *The Origins of Modern Science,* has pointed out how a climate of opinion prevented some of the greatest minds in the history of the human race from seeing certain things that are now obvious to any schoolchild.

> "The supreme paradox of the scientific revolution is the fact that things which we find it easy to instill into boys at school, because we see that they

start off on the right foot—things which would strike us as the ordinary way of looking at the universe, the obvious way of regarding the behavior of falling bodies, for example—defeated the greatest intellects for centuries, defeated Leonardo da Vinci and at the marginal point even Galileo, when their minds were wrestling on the very frontiers of human thought with these problems. . . . It required their combined efforts to clear up certain simple things which we should not regard as obvious to any unprejudiced mind, and even easy for a child."[4]

The history of theology indicates that the same problem exists for a theologian. The intellectual and social climate in which he works makes it easy for him to see certain truths and difficult to see others. We wonder today how the liberal theologians of the nineteenth and early twentieth centuries could have been so indifferent to certain theological and biblical truths. We wonder, and are somewhat ashamed, that some of the ablest theologians and ministers—some of the most brilliant minds that Southern Presbyterianism has ever produced—used Christian theology and the Bible to tolerate slavery or even to justify it. In our amazement at the blindness of some of our predecessors, we ought not to forget that if anything is clear from history, it is certain that some of our successors will think of us as incredibly obtuse in certain theological and ethical concerns and blind to certain truths that should be obvious to any Christian.

No one can fully extricate himself from the social situation. But if we are aware of the way the prevailing climate of opinion penetrates our thinking, we will be less likely to fall victim to all its snares. The history of the theological reflection of the Christian community in every age is a protection against blind spots and the overemphasis of particular ages.

Historical theology contributes to theological competence in a third way by providing training in theological conversation. Someone has said that whatever may be the religion of the average American, he is unable to talk intelligently about it. Unfortunately the same can be said about many ministers. We can talk more intelligently about the operation of the church than about its faith. We can, to be sure, make assertions about the faith, but this is not conversation, even if we abuse a great word and call our assertions "proclamations." Conversation is the interchange of thoughts, the testing of opinions, the working out of implications.

Historical theology ought to enable us to enter into conversation with great Christian minds of the past and thus should prepare us to engage our own age in conversation concerning the meaning of the redemption of God in history through Jesus Christ.

[4]Herbert Butterfield, *The Origins of Modern Science* (New York: Macmillan, 1957), 2.

4. Historical theology contributes to the training of ministers by telling the story of the Christian community's engagement with culture, in particular with the intellectual life of culture. This engagement is a twofold affair.

As Kenneth Latourette in his monumental study of the *Expansion of Christianity* has pointed out, the Christian community influences the environment and is influenced by the environment. We neglect either aspect of the engagement at serious risk not only to our Christian life but to the soundness of our theology.

Culture always leaves its imprint upon theology. For, as Paul Tillich has written, the form of theology is always cultural, if for no other reason than that theology has to use language, which is a product of culture. The history of theology teaches the intrinsic datability of theological works. The accents and the idiom betray the cultural context. For this reason, European theology written in a European culture—which experienced an idealism, a romanticism, and a historicism more radical than anything in the intellectual history of America and in the context of a political and economic history vastly different from that of America—cannot be simply repeated in America without either misunderstanding or irrelevance. It is a notorious fact that amateur Barthians are mistaken for fundamentalists, and sometimes not without reason.

Historical theology makes one aware of the cultural conditioning and the cultural idiom of all theology and of the necessity of translating every theology into the cultural idiom of one's own society.

Christian theology has not simply been influenced by culture; it has influenced and shaped culture. It has engaged culture for the sake of converting culture. In the past, intellectual revolutions have not defeated Christian faith but have become the occasion for new statements of the faith in terms of the intellectual climate. This was the great work of Thomas Aquinas and of Calvin. Today we need to learn from the past how the Christian community has dealt with cultural and intellectual revolutions, for we live in a day of cultural and intellectual revolution. At least three great cultural crises will increasingly be the cutting edges of theology during the ministries of those who now come to our seminaries.

The first is the scientific revolution, which has wrought more drastic changes in our manner of thinking than anything else in human history. It has radically affected our way of looking at the world and human existence, and it raises a host of theoretical as well as practical questions for the Christian community to answer.

The second situation that challenges the Christian community is the increased contact with historic formal religions such as Mohammedanism and Buddhism and with new religions such as communism. Increasingly the Christian community shall have to say a word about their significance in the providence of God and the responsibility of the Christian community over against them.

The third cultural situation that challenges the Christian community is the revolution taking place in the breakup of patterns of life and in the shaping of new patterns. Christian people have a right to expect from ministers and professors guidance and help in the theological understanding of the radical changes that are taking place and guidance and help in obedience to Jesus Christ in the midst of the changes. The really critical test of theological teaching will not be found in classrooms, but in the embodiment of this teaching in the life of the church, especially in the life of the local congregation.

Adolph Harnack, quoting Troeltsch, once declared, "One must overcome history by history, i.e., one must accept his destiny, love it and transform it into something better." We study history in order to intervene in the course of history. Historical knowledge becomes an instrument of actions in the present. Harnack no doubt overemphasized the fact that man is "in the world to act in it, not to contemplate it."[5] And yet he said something that is profoundly true. Historical theology, and for that matter all theological learning, will in the end be a vain thing unless it comes to embodiment in human life. As John Mackay has put it, "The finality of Christian doctrine can never be purely speculative. Reformed thinkers are not interested in prying open the secrets of the universe in order to indulge a speculative bent. They theologize in order that divine truth may be more perfectly known, so that in turn the divine will may be more perfectly obeyed."[6]

Historical theology, by reminding us of the way in which Christians have dealt with the crises of the past, throws light upon the role of Christians in the intellectual and cultural crises of the present.

I have tried to give four reasons that historical theology is significant for the education of a minister. It aids in the recovery of a Christian memory that is indispensable to an understanding of the Christian faith. It is the record of the judgment of Christian dogma by history, which lays bare the meaning of dogma. It develops theological competence by making avail-

[5]G. Wayne Glick, *The Reality of Christianity* (New York: Harper and Row, 1967).
[6]*Christianity on the Frontier.*

able the methods and conclusions of nineteen centuries of theological reflection by opening up the perspective of the centuries and by training in theological conversation. It tells of Christianity's engagement with culture during the past nineteen centuries and gives us some insight into our role as Christians amid the cultural crises of the twentieth century.

Historical theology records the way the Christian community has understood the Christian faith and life and how the community has proclaimed and witnessed to that faith and life. As such, historical theology is a guide and source of strength as we think through the meaning of Christianity and life today and proclaim it to the time in which we live. For this reason the history of Christian doctrine is of crucial importance for those of us in seminaries whose primary task is to educate students to become effective preachers and pastors in local congregations.

PART SIX
ISSUES BEFORE
THE CHURCH

"Gambling—What's Wrong with It?"
1956

Written for the Board of Christian Education, Presbyterian Church U.S.

Why Christians Oppose Gambling

Gambling is today a serious problem in the life of the American people. More than 50 million Americans engage in some form of gambling, and no one knows how much money is involved. In 1950 the estimates ran from $6.8 billion to $12.5 billion. In that same year we spent $5.8 billion for public education. Gambling is a prevalent and expensive fact in our national life.

It is not likely that any large number of Christians are engaged in the more sinister forms of gambling. This does not mean, however, that Christians are not involved in gambling or that it is a matter of little concern for the Christian community. Christians are responsible members of their community; more than this they have the responsibility of bearing Christian witness. There are a sufficient number of Christians in almost every American community to put an end to gambling if Christians really believe that it is wrong. Yet the plain fact is that honest Christians have aided and supported commercial gambling by condoning its existence and by using petty gambling as a means of raising money for worthy causes. For this reason Christians who themselves do not gamble must examine it in the light of Christian faith. Is gambling wrong?

Responsible Protestant Christians oppose gambling for two reasons. First, they believe that gambling is condemned by what it does to human personality and to community life. Second, they believe that gambling is condemned by the Christian understanding of the significance and responsibility of human existence.

Gambling is against the law

Every state except Nevada has laws restricting gambling. These laws do not have their origin in Puritanism, but in the hard fact that gambling has undermined community life. They are not arbitrary impositions on a community, but a means of protecting community life. Yet these laws are poorly enforced. Why? In many cases the gambling interests are politically and financially powerful. There is, however, another reason. A dangerous law-breaking tradition has developed in American life. This has been true at different times and places of such diverse crimes as murder, dueling, robbery, illegal liquor traffic, black markets, prostitution, and violation of civil rights. Individual citizens have reserved the right to decide which laws they will obey. In some instances they have resorted to violence in defiance of the law.[1]

When Christians engage in illegal forms of gambling, they are undermining respect for law and order. There may be a real connection between the illegal participation of parents in bingo and other games and the delinquency of young people. Gambling is wrong when it undermines respect for the law.

Gambling preys on the desire to get something for nothing

Gambling encourages the belief that a man can enjoy the advantages of a prosperous society without making a significant contribution to that society. Gambling arouses false hopes and gives little in return.

Statisticians tell us that "the mathematical odds or probabilities in all gambling games are so determined that only the operator or proprietor or bet-taker can win during the continued conduct of the game. This mathematical advantage runs from a minimum of 1.5 percent to a maximum of about 90 or 95 percent. Expressed in layman's language, the operator or proprietor or bet-taker devours from 1.5 to 95 percent of all the money wagered by the players."[2] The operator does not take a chance. He is certain to get his money. The gambler always loses in the end.

Gambling is an economic parasite

"Gambling is parasitic by nature. It creates no new wealth and performs no useful service. At best, it merely redistributes wealth from the possession

---

[1] *The Annals of the American Academy of Political and Social Science* 269 (May 1950): 9 ff.
[2] Ibid., 77.

of the many into the hands of the few. And those few who do benefit from the transfer tend to be members of the underworld who corrupt business and government."[3]

It is sometimes claimed that every business enterprise is a gamble, that life itself is a gamble. The difference between the legitimate risk in business and the risk in gambling is that business enterprise offers the possibility of achieving something worthwhile and of making a real contribution to human welfare. It is a risk worth taking. The risks involved in gambling are attempts to escape responsible work, and they offer no possibility of worthwhile service to the community.

Gambling is closely associated and allied with many other evils

The recent congressional investigation of organized crime revealed an intimate connection between gambling and crime of every kind. It was associated with political corruption and bribery and with vice of the most sordid kind, and it frequently led to violence and murder.[4]

Gambling contributes to dishonesty. Virgil Peterson, director of the Chicago Crime Commission, in a study of over twenty of the largest surety companies declares that the principal factors contributing to employee dishonesty are gambling and extravagant living standards. Some companies blamed gambling for 30 percent of the losses of the company, but others held it responsible for as much as 75 percent of their total losses.[5]

The Massachusetts Citizens' Committee found that merchants in the vicinity of race tracks note an increase in unpaid debts and a decrease in business during the racing season.[6]

Gambling has corrupted sports. It led to scandals in baseball in the 1870s and in 1919. More recently it played havoc with college basketball.

Gambling is symptomatic of personality disorders

Psychologists speak of a gambling neurosis. They have found that gambling is a symptom of personality illness just as alcoholism frequently indicates deep-seated personality problems. Gambling, like drinking, may be an effort to escape from the demands of life. Normal people who are

---

[3]Virgil W. Peterson, "Legalized Gambling?" *The Rotarian* (May 1951): 27.
    [4]Interim Report on Investigations in Florida and Preliminary General Conclusions of the Special Committee to Investigate Organized Crime in Interstate Commerce.
    [5]*Information Service*, Department of Research and Education, Federal Council of Churches of Christ in America. Dec. 2, 1950.
    [6]Ibid.

stable and strong do not exhibit a passion to risk their possessions under a compulsion that goes beyond all reason.[7] It is not enough to condemn gambling. It is important to go behind the actual fact, asking, Why does this man gamble?

Some have contended that petty gambling may be a good thing for a lot of people, because it enables them to cast off the harsh realities of modern society.[8] Even if this is true, it must be weighed against the fact that gambling may become an addiction and that it does aggravate human weaknesses. There are better ways of relaxing than gambling.

A man's convictions about gambling are in large measure determined by his convictions about life, about the world in which he lives, and about God. The Protestant Christian believes that gambling is condemned by certain basic beliefs about the meaning of human existence.

A man's life is a sacred trust from God

No man is self-made. Life and that which sustains life are gifts from God. Moreover, no man lives without the help of his fellow man. The boast that a man's life and his money are his own is a falsehood. By himself he could have neither. This is a plain fact of life.

The Christian is convinced that his life is a gift from God. He believes that his life is not simply the result of the accidents of nature and society. He believes that he is because God willed for him to be. He believes that the purpose of God lies behind his life and that the meaning of his life is to fulfill this purpose. Gambling does not help a man fulfill God's purpose in his life.

Men are brothers

God made men for life in community. A solitary individual, for example, would never learn to talk or develop many of the other capacities of personality that we take for granted. It is simply impossible to be a person except in community with other people. Yet community life is possible only as each person makes his contribution to the general welfare. Gambling is always a defiance of the community, as it seeks to take from the community while refusing to give anything in return.

---

[7] *The Annals of the American Academy of Political and Social Science*, op. cit., 93 ff.
[8] Herbert L. Marx Jr., ed., *Gambling in America* (New York: H. W. Wilson Company), 10.

It is a fundamental Christian conviction that every man is his brother's keeper. He is responsible for his spiritual as well as his physical welfare. As Paul once wrote, "If food is a cause of my brother's falling, I will never eat meat, lest I cause my brother to fall" (1 Cor. 8:13). It is an indisputable fact that gambling causes many men and women to fall, and for the Christian the inference is plain.

The really great purpose of life is to grow into the image of Christ

Human conduct is largely determined by a man's goal and purpose. For some the chief purpose of life may be wealth or fame or status of one kind or another. The Christian believes that the chief purpose in life is to grow into the image of Christ. All that contributes to this growth is wholesome and good.

Gambling does not help men become more Christlike. It aggravates human weaknesses. It stimulates greed and breeds covetousness. It encourages men to believe that they can get something for nothing. It has a great attraction for vice and crime. It keeps men from achieving the one purpose in life without which nothing else really matters.

In the early church an unknown Christian wrote, "Do not be a dice-thrower but a Christian: cast your money on the table of the Lord at which Christ presides and the spectators are angels and the martyrs are present; and the patrimony which you are about to squander with that ruinous passion divide instead among the poor: lose your wealth to Christ."[9]

Gambling stands condemned on the one hand by what it does to human personality and society and on the other by the basic convictions by which a Christian lives.

> And sitting down they watched Him there,
> The Soldiers did.
> There, while they played with dice,
> He made His sacrifice,
> And died upon the Cross to rid
> God's world of sin.
>
> He was a gambler too,
> My Christ,
> he took His life and threw

---

[9]Quoted in Igino Giordani, *The Social Message of the Early Church Fathers* (St. Anthony Guild Press), 67.

It for a world redeemed.
And e'er His agony was done
Before the westering sun went down,

Crowning that day with its crimson crown
He knew
That He had won.
                              (G.A. Studdert-Kennedy)[10]

---

[10]G. A. Studdert-Kennedy, *The Best of G. A. Studdert-Kennedy* (New York: Harper & Brothers), 82.

"Church Union: A Practical Necessity
but Not the Critical Issue Confronting Presbyterians"
December 20–27, 1982

Presbyterian Outlook

The vote on the proposal to unite the Presbyterian Church in the United States and the United Presbyterian Church in the U.S.A. is a solemn decision and calls for responsible reflection and decision by all Presbyterians. The proposed union, in my judgment—based on more than forty years of observation of, participation in, and reflection upon the cause of union—is a practical necessity; but it is not now, even if it once was, the critical issue confronting Presbyterians.

A Different Situation

The striking characteristic of this decision for many who advocated the plan of union in 1954 is the very different situation we face today. Union in 1954 promised much, or so it seemed to many, in theology, in ecclesiastical depth, and in breadth of outlook. Union would achieve freedom for the faith against fundamentalism and overcome the "burden" of Southern history. Today, few if any of these reasons for the union still hold. The problems that many thought union would resolve have now been handled in other ways. Likewise, the reasons that some so passionately opposed union in 1954 are no longer convincing.

For some of us for whom union was a cause and crusade in 1954, union today is much more a matter-of-fact aspect of church affairs and a pragmatic necessity. The practical considerations that make union a necessity include the following:

1. The increasing overlap of the constituencies resulting from the United Presbyterian mission into the South and from the mobility of people

2. The emergence of union presbyteries
3. The union that now exists in programs through board and court actions
4. The advantages of a national church

The union also will open up new possibilities for church renewal in the two denominations in which, by most quantifiable measures, things are not going well. One may argue that neither denomination has recovered from recent reorganization and that the emergence of the new organization will be very expensive in financial resources and human energy. Yet the breakup of established patterns at least offers the possibilities of a church in which there is a new commitment to a church life and program that is theologically responsible to scripture and the tradition, that is ecclesiastically responsive to the actual Presbyterian community, and that is effective in doing the work of the church.

In 1954 much was said about the Presbyterian heritage. The past still figures in the rhetoric of union, but there is little to indicate now that union will be the occasion of either a recovery of the past in memory or a significant appropriation of it in meeting the challenges of today.

The failure to unite likely will cause severe problems, particularly for the Presbyterian Church in the U.S., which has not yet fully acknowledged the long-range consequences to the Presbyterian witness in the South of the PCA pullout. It is doubtful if the continuing pullouts will be stopped by the refusal to unite under the present plan. There is no convincing evidence that the PCUS can handle any better the problems it faces (I do not believe it can handle them as well) by voting down the union.

No one ought to underestimate the cost of the union in money, time, and human energy, or the new problems it will create. Yet many of us are convinced that union offers the best hope of a strong Presbyterian community twenty-five years from now. Insofar as the union recovers a sense of the great Presbyterian and Reformed tradition in this country, this will be an added virtue, but as of now little evidence indicates that this will happen.

Humility and Modesty

The union more likely will serve us well if we approach it with a great deal of humility and modesty.

A. *Humility in assessing praise or blame for what we perceive to be division or unity.* The Presbyterians in the North and South whose actions divided the church in 1861 were every bit, if not more so, as bright and committed as any of us. The perspective of a hundred years or more allows us to see things differently, but we cannot boast that we shall fare better or even as well from the perspective of a hundred years. We have to offer what we do to God with the prayer that he will bless what is good and forgive what is ill-conceived, time bound, and wrong.

Robert L. Calhoun, as brilliant a theologian as the twentieth century has known, put this whole matter very well.

> A first fundamental insight, shared by all of us, is that both our unity and diversity—even our division—arise out of God's working with men in history. To try to separate divine initiative and human response in the life of the Church is to obscure the real nature of our problem. To assign diversity and division, for example, solely to human obliquity gives a false impression of the depth and subtlety of the task of seeing the unity that is vital to the Church's being. It is necessary to recognize that the unity we seek cannot exist at all without diversity, in which are disclosed the bounty of God and the manifold gifts of his Spirit, not less truly than the weaknesses of men. Even our divisions and dissensions, which we are in duty bound to overcome, bear witness—sometimes in tortured ways—to God's demand for devotion to truth, as well as to man's frequent confusion as to what is true. It may well be that more vivid realization of other dimensions of our problem than those we are accustomed to see and to stress can bring us an important step closer to the unity we need. (*The Nature of the Unity We Seek* [1958], 52)

B. *Humility in identifying the historical forms of church unity.* The unity as well as the reality of the church inheres in hearing the word of God. Yet, when we move to the embodiment of this unity in human forms and procedures, we need to be modest in our claims. A very great deal of cruelty has been perpetrated and harm done to the church by those who were too sure they knew the embodiments of the church's unity.

C. *Modesty in estimating our contribution.* Each denomination contributes, and together we shall be richer and more catholic, or we ought to be. But none of us can boast. In 1954 many in the PCUS who passionately advocated union hurt their cause and also the possibility of a good union by their guilt over the burden of Southern history. The increasing and disproportionate number of ministers nurtured and trained in the North and West who energetically seek pastorates in the South is sufficient evidence that the contributions will flow both ways.

D. *Humility in predicting the consequences of the union.* It is a sobering fact that the new church at the best estimate will have fewer members than the United Presbyterian Church had in 1969 when union discussions started. There are reasons to believe that the union in the long run may serve to renew the life of the church, but this is not likely in the immediate future. Unless present trends are reversed, the new church may have fewer members in 1993 than the UPCUSA does now. The record of actual union of denominations during this century in North America and Great Britain is sufficient warning that church union does not bring this kind of church renewal.

For some the final decision on the plan of union must be something like this: the union is a pragmatic necessity. It opens up possibilities for church renewal. It may serve to recover something of the greatness of the Presbyterian and Reformed tradition in this country, but this is not certain. We need to take this step with great solemnity, *coram deo*, and with humility and modesty.

Other Commitments Needed

The plan of union when enacted will not resolve the problems that confront the church now as well as after the union. For this reason the plan of union will be the occasion for renewal only if it is accompanied by other actions and commitments. Three commitments are of critical importance.

First, we need to recover the authenticity of the court or judicatory system. The strength of church courts is greatest when the reality of the courts is congruent with the reality of the church as the people of God, the priesthood of believers. In the civil order this is not so immediately important, since the civil order has an IRS and a marine corps. The church has only personal or spiritual power. In a voluntary church in a free society, organizational and bureaucratic power is an illusion. Whenever the "connectional" church becomes a code word for coercion, violence is done to the historical meaning of Presbyterianism with tragic consequences in the life of the church.

The quota system, the representative principle, management procedures, and preoccupation with processes and with the political apparatus—whatever the virtues of these policies and activities—have led to a disjuncture between the courts and the bureaucracy on the one hand and the people on the other. The new movements and emphases since the mid-1960s have not worked to guarantee that those who actually do the concrete work of the church, who have documentable records in building up the church, are adequately involved in the representation and governance of the church, at least in the PCUS. It is increasingly foolish to talk about the mandate of the church court if the church is not in fact as well as law representative of the people of God who are the church.

Second, we need to recover a true catholicity of the church, which includes diversity and which has respect for believing people and for believing, worshipping congregations. The plan says much about ethnic minorities, but it does not indicate a similar concern for "minorities" (perhaps, in some cases, majorities) who have styles, communities, institutions, or programs that grow out of a particular place and history.

There is considerable evidence that the real opposition to church union arises at this point. No real theological issues against union are present; but there may well be reason to fear that the new church will not be sufficiently catholic, will not respect institutions, traditions, programs, and communities that have come into being through the labor and devotion of Presbyterians through years, even centuries. Not much in previous Presbyterian unions in this country reassures people who have these worries.

If this union is to enhance the life of the church, the new church will have to be less coercive and more catholic than present trends encourage many to believe will be the case.

Third, the church is primarily a community of faith in God. The crisis of the church today is fundamentally a crisis of faith. The recovery of the sense of the reality of God, of the Bible as the word of God, of the church as a worshipping, believing community is the critical need. The church lives by hearing the word of God, by the interpretation and application of the word of God. The future of the church is found not in organizational processes, not in management, not in the political apparatus, and not in causes. The future of Presbyterianism in America will be determined by the recovery of the preaching and teaching of the word of God, and by pastoral care that incorporates persons into the worshipping, believing, and confessing community, more than by any other facts.

The union of the church is a practical necessity, and the union will open up new possibilities of church renewal. Yet union in and of itself will accomplish little. Apart from the recovery of the reality of the church courts, apart from the recovery of a true catholicity, and apart from a recovery of preaching, teaching, and pastoral care, the future of Presbyterianism in this country, union or not, is very bleak.

"Baptized Children in the Church and Admission to the Lord's Table"
October 26, 1978

Western Theological Seminary, Holland, Michigan

Our theme is relation of the baptized to the church and the admission of the baptized to the Lord's Supper.

I

A convenient starting point is John Calvin's understanding of the sacrament of baptism and its significance for those, in particular children, who have been baptized.

The primary context for Calvin's doctrine of the baptism of infants is the doctrine of the covenant and the promise that "the covenant which the Lord once made with Abraham is no less in force today for Christians than it was of old for the Jewish people" (*Institutes*, IV, 16, 6). The covenant is for you and for your seed. The children of Christian parents, even of one Christian parent, are considered holy. The community of birth, of nature and history, has significance for the community of faith. "The children of believers are baptized not in order that they who were previously strangers to the church may then for the first time become children of God, but rather that, because by the blessings of the promise they already belonged to the Body of Christ, they are received into the Church with this solemn sign" (IV, 15, 22). Children of a church member are members of the church by birth.

In our highly personalistic, voluntaristic, and rationalistic culture, such a strong emphasis on the community of birth immediately raises questions, as it did with Emil Brunner and Karl Barth. They were in part moved to their positions by the disparity between the baptized and any reasonable understanding of the church in Europe, and they were impelled in the direction of asserting that the church is constituted on the human

219

level by the free act of faith. Yet just as they found evidence to indicate that birth is not a simple automatic entrance into the church, there is also evidence that the significance of birth—of the natural community for faith—cannot be minimized. Most of us are in the church first of all because we were born into the church. A clear fact of life is that human existence is shaped by the nature and history into which a person is born. Students of human personality have in recent years emphasized the environment into which a person is born, but increasing attention is now being given to biochemical and genetic inheritance. The ambiguity created by the fact that the church can be neither identified with the natural community or separated from it is the source of our ambiguity concerning baptism.

Our Christian faith is that human existence has as its ultimate source the electing love of God, and the church also is rooted in his electing love. The church exists because God calls the church into being. And so our faith is that the validity of baptism does not depend upon the community or family in which it takes place, but upon the blessing of the Holy Spirit, upon the promise of God to us and to our children. Here again it is best to understand baptism as both a divine and human work, works that cannot be separated and that must not be confused. The Christian life is rooted in the natural community, the importance of which ought not to be minimized, but the ultimate origin of the Christian life is the love of God.

Having placed baptism in the context of the covenant and the promise, Calvin goes on to make at least four assertions about the effect of baptism upon the baptized.

First, baptism confirms the promise that is given to pious parents (IV, 16, 9). The sacraments certify, confirm, attest, and seal the promises of the action of God. We all know in common human experiences that outward and visible actions confirm deeply personal promises, as for example a handshake, the giving of a ring, or the signing of our name. And so it is in baptism. The practical consequences of this public confirmation of the promise of God and of our hope in that promise are as varied as our experiences. Who can estimate baptism's significance as a ground for hope in any day, and especially in our day when so many parents say that if they had it to do over again, they would not have children at all? One of the most alarming facts in our time is the increasing number of people who do not think that children are worth the price and who choose to have no children. In response to a question of Ann Landers, 70 percent of her respondents declared that if they had it to do over, they would not have children. When allowance is made for the vagaries of such a poll, the response is still disconcerting.

Second, Calvin says that children receive some benefits from their baptism (IV, 16, 9). They are engrafted into the body of the church, and they are thereby commended to the church—that is, to other church members. In baptism, the congregation obligates itself to be the child's sponsor to the end that this child shall grow up trusting God and seeking to do his will. Sometimes this responsibility has been made more specific through the use of godparents, but generally Reformed churches have placed this responsibility upon the entire congregation.

Third, Calvin says that when the baptized grow up, "They are spurred to an earnest zeal for worshipping God, by whom they are received as children through a solemn symbol of adoption, before they were old enough to recognize him as Father" (IV, 16, 9). Martin Luther, as is well known, appealed in moments of crisis to the fact that he had been baptized. Perhaps not many young people whom we know take comfort in the fact that they have been baptized. But again perhaps more than we know do take comfort in it. Perhaps more would take comfort in it, if the meaning of baptism were more frequently set before them in preaching and teaching.

The importance of baptism and of birth in a historical community that has been shaped in part by Christian faith has been excessively devalued in our concern to appreciate the good in a secular culture. Certainly until now the conversion of a person in Western culture to Christian faith has differed significantly from the conversion of a person from another culture. Ortega y Gasset has a very remarkable autobiographical statement in one of his books: "When I was a child, I was a Christian; now I am no longer. Does this mean strictly speaking, that I do not go on being a Christian? The Christian I was is dead, annihilated? Of course not; of course I am still a Christian, but in the form of having been a Christian."[1] There is a certain indelibility about baptism that Protestants can affirm. The baptized has received the mark of the Christian. Once either by birth or by free choice the baptized lived in the circle of faith.

Calvin, however, was thinking more of the baptized who are more closely associated with the worshipping life of the church. While baptism celebrates a work that is complete in the work of Christ, it also celebrates a work that is never complete in human history, namely our sanctification. Baptism looks to the future. John Baillie declared that Baptism is for all Christians the beginning of the Christian life.[2] Or as Barth says, "Baptism is the first step of the way of a human life which is shaped by looking to Jesus Christ!"[3]

---

[1]José Ortega y Gasset, *Revolt of the Masses* (New York: W. W. Norton, 1932).
[2]John Baillie, *What Is Christian Civilization?* (New York: Charles Scribner's Sons, 1945), 35ff.
[3]Karl Barth, *Church Dogmatics*, IV/4 (Edinburg: T & T Clark, 1969), 149.

The Westminster Larger Catechism speaks of improving our baptism:

> The needful but much neglected duty of improving our baptism is to be performed by us all our life long, especially in the time of temptation, and when we are present at the administration of it to others, by serious and thankful consideration of the nature of it, and of the ends for which Christ instituted it, the privileges and benefits conferred and sealed thereby, and our solemn vow made therein; by being humbled for our sinful defilement, our falling short of, and walking contrary to, the grace of baptism and our engagements; by growing up to assurance of pardon of sin, and of all other blessings sealed to us in that sacrament; by drawing strength from the death and resurrection of Christ, into whom we are baptized, for the mortifying of sin, and quickening of grace; and by endeavoring to live by faith, to have our conversation in holiness and righteousness, as those that have therein given up their names to Christ, and to walk in brotherly love, as being baptized by the same Spirit into one body. (Question 167)

Karl Barth has also related baptism to a similar theme that is increasingly common in our time. Baptism is ordination to Christian ministry. "Baptism . . . [is] a consecration or ordination to take part in the mission which is committed to the whole church" (*Church Dogmatics* IV, 4, The Christian Life, 201). Barth has an antipathy for the hierarchy and for orders given to particular individuals, however necessary for the ordering of the church. Such orders, positions, or titles are secondary to the ordination that every Christian receives in baptism. "All those baptized as Christians are *eo ipso* consecrated, ordained, and dedicated to the ministry of the church. They cannot be consecrated, ordained, and dedicated a second, third, or fourth time without devaluing their baptism" (Ibid., 201).

The fourth benefit that the baptized received from the sacrament, according to Calvin, belongs to the effective work of the spirit through the sacrament. "Infants are baptized into future repentance and faith, even though these have not yet been formed in them, the seed of both lies hidden within them by the secret working of the Spirit" (IV, 16, 20). Here is the mystery of the sacrament that is hidden from our eyes. This effective work of the spirit cannot be tied to the sacrament. Calvin vigorously opposed every attempt to fasten the indeterminate and infinite God to that which is determinate and finite, to that which is in our control. Calvin takes the sacraments seriously, but never so seriously as to bind God to them. God's spirit works in the hearts of people as he chooses and beyond our imagining. In baptism we claim the promise that the baptism with water will be the means of God's grace by the power of the Holy Spirit to work repentance and faith in a human life.

Calvin's doctrine of the sacrament is cognitive, causative, and ethical. It is cognitive, in that it confirms and certifies our election, our forgiveness. It is causative, for the sacrament is a means of grace. It is ethical, for it is an action of the people in response to God's grace. Calvin combines the effective action of God in the sacrament with the ethical action of the baptized.

II

Calvin's understanding of the sacraments has been called in question by contemporary culture, which, for better or worse, affects the life of the church. If we are to continue to practice baptism, and in particular the baptism of infants, we must do it in a way that makes sense in contemporary church life.

The context of covenant and promise is called in question by a pluralistic, secular, and mobile society, as well as by the state of our churches, which sometimes resemble aggregations of individuals with individual needs rather than a community that lives a shared life in a common hope, common faith, and a common spirit. The preeminent example of covenant making in human experience has been marriage and the family. Can we maintain a doctrine of the covenant and the promise in a society where human covenants and human promises are so frequently broken in divorce?

The confirmation of the promise to the parent is challenged by the freedom our culture offers young people to change their family traditions. Young people in our time have a greater freedom—enhanced by the news media, transportation, and a permissive society—to reject the ways of their parents than any young people in the history of the human race.

The stimulus to improve one's baptism is also lacking in our culture. The supports that an older Protestant culture or that Christendom gave to Christian lifestyles are lacking.

The church is now entering a new time and a new culture, a culture that is different in America from Europe. Hence we can learn from Europeans about baptism, but we cannot simply repeat what they have to say about their situation. In this new culture we shall have to work out new ways of relating the community of birth and history to the community of faith, of relating the sacrament as a divine mystery and work to the sacrament as a human work. We shall have to learn to relate these two dimensions of our community life and these two dimensions of the sacrament without doing injustice to either, without confusing them, and without separating them.

How then shall the church meet this new situation? Let us first accept with gratitude the reality of the Christian family and the Christian church that does exist. The ultimate judgment that all of our family life and all of our churches fall short of the glory of God must not obscure the relative judgment that the family does still embody the Christian faith in remarkable ways, and churches do maintain their integrity as Christian communities.

In any case, the Christian life cannot be abstracted from the natural community or the historical community. Therefore we have to take seriously what is happening in the family. No one knows what the consequences of the present divorce rate will be ten or fifteen years from now. No one knows the consequences of a secular and pluralistic society. We only know that the Christian life will be inextricably bound with these social realities. Hence we have to take seriously what we have and build upon it.

As we face this future and our responsibility to the baptized, we shall need, I think, to recover the concept of the church as the mother of the faithful. The church will again have to provide the support, the nurturing, and the fellowship that were formerly provided by Christian families and especially by the Christian society, that is, by Protestantdom or Christendom.

This means concretely a great increase in pastoral care. The pastor must know the children in the congregation by name, and the children must come to trust their pastor as a Christian friend. In a recent continuing education group a pastor told proudly of the PET program that he had set up in his church. One parent replied that he would rather have a pastor who knew his children by name. Pastoral care must also be provided by the elders and the adult leadership of the church. Many children grow up in situations where the extended family no longer exists, knowing no adults except their parents as friends.

Pastoral care includes a community, if not a peer group, that supports the Christian faith and the Christian way of life. This may not be easy. Community life cannot be programmed, certainly not the life of faith and worship. Yet by taking thought and by action we can provide the context in which it is more likely to take place. Once when a high school student was suffering some social ostracism because of a moral stand she had taken during the civil rights controversies, an elder called to the attention of the session that they had participated in her baptism and asked what they were now going to do on the basis of this fact. This incident is a clear expression of the kind of community of faith in which baptism makes sense.

Pastoral care involves the provision of facilities and organizational arrangements that help young people live in agreement with their baptism. Many communities do not have decent facilities for social life. Perhaps in the area of recreation and social life the churches will have to do more in the future than they did in a past when the community provided these facilities.

Pastoral care involves giving real help to real people. One church, for example, has a committee to help its young people get jobs, a continuation of a service rendered to returning Vietnam servicemen.

In addition to pastoral care, the church must provide teaching. In an older day the community traditioned the faith as well as the church. Today public schools are secular. Faith must be taught in the church. This teaching will include the memorization of scripture, practice in the use of the Bible, knowledge of biblical content, a sense of church history, and a comprehension of Christian doctrine. The old insistence that communicant members of the church should be instructed in the creed, the law, the prayer, the sacraments, and the duties of the Christian life still holds for our day.

Finally, the church must provide worship in addition to pastoral care and teaching. Of course all churches worship God. But must we not admit that worship is sometimes slovenly in a day when young people see expert performance on television? Worship is not a performance, and it is not, in my judgment, enhanced by gimmicks. The answer to the performance and gimmickry of television and of performances that now are invading the church is the authenticity of a community of faith that truly worships with heart and mind and strength. Reformed worship has always insisted on simplicity, intelligibility, and theological integrity. The rhetoric is in the content more than in the medium. This requires hard work and solid commitment. In worship we must not offer to God that which costs us nothing. In the context of this worship, baptism makes sense.

III

The practice of baptism has been further complicated in our time by problems concerning admission to the Lord's Supper.

The contemporary problem has as its long-term background the failure of the church to arrive at any standard or uniform practice. Infants as well as children have received the sacrament of the Lord's Supper as well as baptism. The doctrine of transubstantiation and the association of confession with the participation in the mass (Fourth Lateran Council, 1215) placed some restraint upon the participation of children. However, the question of the admission of children was still a matter of debate at the time of the Reformation.

John Calvin made admission to the Lord's Table the focus of discipline in the Genevan church. This meant catechetical training and examination for young people. Calvin believed that ten years of age was an appropriate time for this training. The situation in Geneva was that of a Christian society, and the admission to the Lord's Supper had a different social significance from that which it has in a free, voluntary, pluralistic, and secular society. Admission to the Lord's Table in the Christian society of Geneva had its primary significance in the ordering of the church's life.

Calvin was aware that children and even infants had been admitted to the sacrament. He also was aware that some questioned how children could be admitted to the sacrament of baptism but kept from the Lord's Supper. In reply he pointed to differences between the sacraments. Baptism is the sacrament of initiation. Children are born into the membership of the church, and the church in the sacrament affirms this fact and claims the promises of God. The Lord's Supper is a sacrament of growth and nurture. It is frequently observed. It sustains and nourishes the Christian life. It requires of the believer a responsible decision and the ability to discern the Lord's body.

Calvin was very much aware of the perils of magic. Magic when directed toward people is the effort to bypass conscious choice and decision. When directed toward God, magic is the effort to fasten the infinite and indeterminate God to that which is finite and determinate and under the control of man. The practice of admitting infants and children to communion was magic on both counts. Protestant and Reformed doctrine insisted upon this rubric: No sacraments apart from faith, that is, responsible personal decision. For Calvin, any notion of the sacrament as a medicament or as "the medicine of immortality" was a violation of basic Reformed conviction about the ways of God with his people.

The role of admission to the Lord's Supper as the disciplinary focus of church life and as the place for conscious decision for church membership has been in increasing tension with developments in church life. In some churches the age of admission to a communicants' class has been advanced to sixteen years of age or even older. The purpose has been more serious instruction, but the age requirements have left many young people in a precarious situation in regard to church membership and in particular in regard to participation in the Lord's Supper. Hence many denominations are now considering new practices that allow young people to come to communion without going through the traditional communicants' class. The traditional communicants' class is kept as a condition for other privileges and responsibilities of membership.

There is no easy answer to this problem. Probably no single answer is adequate for all situations. Yet in working out an answer, some facts are clear. First, children of worshipping parents want to participate in worship; for this reason, participation in the Lord's Supper cannot be postponed beyond a point that is hard to define without damage to the child. Second, the New Testament accounts all portray the Lord's Supper as involving responsible participation: namely the ability or the knowledge to (1) discern the Lord's body, (2) examine oneself, (3) remember Jesus Christ, and (4) know that one gathers at the table in the fellowship of the Christian community. The time at which a child comes to have faith and when a child can responsibly participate cannot be determined precisely. Faith is certainly an early fact for the child who lives in a community of faith, and faith and responsible participation are possibilities at earlier ages than we sometimes have thought.

My own solution to the problem would be to choose an early communicants' class, at ten or possibly even nine years of age, for admission to the Lord's Table in preference to other solutions. My reasons for this solution are threefold. The first is positive. The early catechetical class permits children who do believe and do wish to participate to commune. We ought not to underestimate the power of belief and sense of community at this age. Second, the early communicants' class helps to maintain the integrity of personal decision in faith. The line between magic and religion is always thin. To put it less pejoratively, it is important to emphasize the Protestant insistence that no sacrament exists apart from faith. Faith as a personal act involves the rational and the critical. The intention of some advocates of admission of children to communion to give infants the sacraments and thus to unite the baptism of infants with the Lord's Supper is sufficient evidence of the need for this Protestant emphasis. Third, the admission of children to the Lord's Supper without the communicants' class and without the public commitment will complicate church life in the future. It is, in my judgment, unrealistic to think that all children who have been admitted to the Lord's Supper are going to attend membership classes at sixteen or eighteen years of age for the added privileges and responsibilities of voting in congregational meetings and pledging to the church budget. The pressure to admit children to the Lord's Table who have not been baptized as infants further complicates the situation. We may increasingly have a constituency made up of "adherents" rather than members who have publicly committed themselves to the work of the organized church whatever their commitments to the Lord may be.

In the work of the church, respect for the past is the condition of "successful" work in the future. Practices that have worked very well in the past should be discarded only with care and with deliberation. Changes under the pressure of the moment are likely to have many unintended consequences.

"Theological Reflections on the Death Penalty"
1979

Written for the General Assembly Mission
Board of Presbyterian Church U.S.

The theological questionableness of capital punishment has been put with clarity and emphasis by Karl Barth, the most distinguished Reformed theologian of the twentieth century:

> If the command to protect life is accepted and asserted in some sense in a national community, then it is impossible to maintain capital punishment as an element in its normal and continuing order. It is an astonishing and disturbing fact that for nineteen hundred years there has been a Christian Church, and for four hundred a Protestant, which has not only failed to champion this insight but has continually opposed it. And it is one of the disconcerting blessings of the divine overruling of history that nevertheless it has been very widely accepted, being adopted far more readily and energetically by the children of the world than by the children of light. . . . It is not too late, therefore, for the Christian Church to espouse this renunciation on a worldwide scale. . . . For from the point of view of the Gospel there is nothing to be said for its institution, and everything against it. (*Church Dogmatics* III, 4, 445–46)

While not all Christians agree with Barth's conclusion, all must agree that the death penalty is in tension with basic Christian conviction and that all Christians ought to take a responsible position in regard to it.

The purpose of this paper is to bring to bear upon the practice of capital punishment some theological and practical considerations that in the writer's judgment call into question its practice as a part of the regular system of criminal justice. Many factors go into a responsible discussion of capital punishment: the rules and values to which we give credence, our theological convictions about God and the world, our dominant understanding of the nature of the Christian life, and our analysis of what is actually taking place when capital punishment is exacted. There is no one conclusion with which all Christians agree, but all Christians need to come to some conclusion about this practice and to work for a consensus not simply as citizens but as Christians.

In this paper, attention is focused upon capital punishment as a regular part of the system of criminal justice and punishment. The right of the state to take life is not at issue. The power of the state depends upon this right, and in some instances the state has no other option open to it, as may be true in cases of violence, revolution, or international conflict. The argument here is more limited. The thesis of this paper is that capital punishment is neither necessary nor justifiable as a part of the regular and ordinary system of justice. Some of the factors that led to this conclusion follow.

I. Personal Responsibility

The practice of capital punishment in our society is the responsibility of every citizen. The old Hebrew procedure by which the community pronounced sentence and then executed the sentence had the virtue of making personal responsibility for the execution clear to everyone. The common stoning of the victim made it impossible to conceal responsibility (Deut. 21:21).

Today the responsibility for an execution is so diffused that neither the police, nor the prosecutor, nor the jury, nor the judge, nor the governor has to take full responsibility. Citizens in general are far less aware of their personal responsibility for the execution. The common stoning, when each member of the community had to cast a stone, had the advantage of clarifying the issue. Personal responsibility does not prejudge the rightness or wrongness of the death penalty; it does mean that all Christians and citizens ought to hold themselves accountable for public policy on this issue.

II. Theological Considerations
Weighing Against Capital Punishment

Capital punishment is difficult to reconcile with at least four basic Christian convictions about human life and experience. These convictions form a strong bias against the death penalty, convictions that would therefore have to be overruled by convincing reasons if Christians are to support capital punishment.

First of all, capital punishment is difficult to reconcile with the preciousness, mystery, and wonder of human life, which comes to all as a gift from God. Nothing in all the created order is comparable to being alive as human beings. Neither the majesty of the mountains nor the mystery of the ocean nor the vitality of living beings compares with the emergence in the history of the universe of human beings with the power of the human mind, language, and memory, with the capacity of the human spirit to objectify its own existence and to reach out beyond every human achievement toward God. As Augustine wrote of every human being, "Thou hast made us for thyself and restless is our heart until it comes to rest in thee" (*Confessions* I, 1).

Yet the preciousness of human life, for all its wonder, inheres first of all not in itself but in its origin in the intention and purpose of God. God looks upon every human being (Psalm 139) and knows even the hairs upon our head (Matt. 10:30). God gives to each person an identity, an individuality, a name, a dignity that must not be abused.

The death penalty by its very nature does violence to the wonder and mystery of human existence. It is the deliberate, planned, rational, intentional, clinical taking of a human life. Yet in spite of the clinical trappings, executions are sometimes bungled badly, and all of them have qualities that are offensive to human sensitivities. Most executions mutilate the body. All of them do violence to the dignity and privacy of the human person. All the rituals—all the shutters, shades, and blindfolds—cannot hide the inherent indecency of the planned, rational taking of a human life. The physical contortions of the human body in the moment of execution are secondary to the violence inflicted on the human spirit. The final indignity and brutality to the human person is the cooperation of the victim with executioner. The final tribute that executions must pay to the inherent dignity and mystery of human life is the apparent impossibility of devising a clean, dignified method for the taking of a human life. Executioners are never likely to be respected members of human society. The coolly rational and deliberate taking of life has an obscene quality about it, for it desecrates what is incomparably wonderful and beyond the power of human beings to create.

In the case of war, revolution, mob violence, or human passion, persons are killed in anger or necessity. In many situations the only option is to kill or be killed. The taking of life is necessary to maintain life and order. None of this necessity or passion exists in the case of an execution. A totally helpless individual, whose existence is no present threat to life and order, is put to death in a coolly rational, deliberate, and clinical way.

Supporters of capital punishment may argue that life is taken to protect life. The question of deterrence will be addressed later. At the time of execution, however, the victim is totally helpless. This total helplessness of persons executed at the hands of the executioners, who need not be persons of courage or integrity because they have power, simply adds to the obscenity of an execution. Supporters of capital punishment, whether their arguments are its usefulness in society or its moral appropriateness, must somehow justify the obscenity of an execution that violates the basic dignity of human life.

Second, capital punishment is difficult to reconcile with the limitations of human beings as creatures, subject to time and space, to the limitations of the human mind and heart. Is any human being wise enough, even apart from being good enough, to decide deliberately to take another human life when the victim is no immediate threat to any human life? Our human limitations are such that it is difficult to master the public data that is accessible to us. We have difficulty enough in every area of public life in knowing the facts that are available, in putting them together, and in coming to a wise judgment about them. In addition, certain information is beyond the reaches of human intelligence. Karl Barth has stated well that "the worst cases of willful destruction of life are perhaps those which cannot be fathomed by a human court, so that the state can perhaps exercise its retributive justice only on those who are really murderers to a lesser degree" (*Church Dogmatics* III, 4, 442). Only the most obvious forms of murder come to our attention. The most sinister and destructive forms may be beyond our awareness.

Karl Barth has spoken of capital punishment as the "usurping of divinity." Human beings are creatures, and their judgments should be appropriate to their creaturely condition. Judgments have to be made to maintain society, but they should be made with modesty. When human beings seek to penetrate the secrets of the universe and when they pass judgments on their fellow human beings, they should exhibit the restraint that is appropriate to their condition.

The death penalty by its very nature is hard to reconcile with the modesty that is appropriate to human beings. The deliberate taking of a human life is an utterly irreversible act. The irreversibility of the act as well as the precious quality of human life underline the need for human modesty. Human beings are not God, and they cannot make God's judgment for him.

Third, capital punishment is hard to reconcile not simply with human creatureliness but with human sinfulness. The world has always been aware of the evil of "bad" people, but the Protestant Reformation exposed the sins of "good" people. Luther knew that we sin not simply in our worst deeds but also in our best deeds. Human pride is such that it has always been easy for good people to forget that they, too, are sinners. The practice of capital punishment is a temptation to self-righteousness.

Capital punishment fosters the notion that human beings can be neatly divided into good people and bad people. It obscures the pathetic, tragic, and ironic dimensions of life. The fact is that we are all flawed human beings. In addition, we are also sinners, and only God knows the measure of our sin.

The maintenance of society demands that relative judgments must be made about human beings. The ultimate judgment that in the presence of God we are all sinners must not obscure, as Reinhold Niebuhr continually pointed out, that among sinners there are very significant differences. Some persons are so selfish and so violent that they disrupt the social order and make human community impossible. Hence, the relative judgments that some people are better than other people must be made. Yet here again these judgments need to be made with the modesty of those who know that they themselves are sinners and must be forgiven. Only God is good enough as well as wise enough to make final judgments about human beings. When such judgments are forced upon us, there should always be the element of tragic necessity. Again, remember that capital punishment is the taking of the life of a person who is in "jail" and therefore helpless. It is different from those tragic situations, as in the case of war, anger, or violence, when no option is available, save to take life. The power and right of the state to take life when life itself, as well as the order of the community, is at stake can only be denied by those who, for the sake of their witness, have given up responsibility for order. In the case of the death penalty as a regular part of the system of justice, this tragic necessity does not exist.

In the fourth place, capital punishment is hard to reconcile with the indeterminate possibilities that reside in every human being and with what some Wesleyan historians have called the optimism of grace. Capital punishment passes a final, irreversible judgment upon a particular human as being worthless and unfit to live. In this pronouncement, human beings are less patient than God. When men wanted to take the life of Cain, God was patient with Cain. God gave Cain space and time that he did not deserve. This example of the patience of God should encourage us to be patient with human beings, to give them time and space that they do not deserve (Genesis 4; see also Barth, *Church Dogmatics*, II, 1, 412).

The practice of capital punishment again reveals an arrogance that assumes the right to determine that a human life has no future possibilities. It also reveals an arrogance about the possibilities of divine grace. The human situation is discouraging, and it tempts to a pessimism about the grace of God as well as human possibilities, to impatience, and to terminative and irreversible actions. The example of God's patience of which we are all beneficiaries and the Christian doctrine of God's grace warn us against impatience and pessimism. A Christian by definition understands the human situation in the light of the revelation of God, not God in the light of the human situation.

In summary, these theological reflections are basically twofold. First, capital punishment as the deliberate, planned, rational, clinical, though frequently bungled taking of a human life is most difficult to reconcile with the wonder, preciousness, and possibilities of every human life. Second, the coolly deliberate character of the judgment to execute a human being is incongruent with the modesty that is appropriate to any human being as a creature and a sinner.

These Christian convictions have a relevance to the death penalty that they do not have to the basic power and authority of the state to take life under certain moral conditions. The execution of the death penalty is not necessary to maintain life or order. Hence, the reasons for overruling these basic theological convictions are not present as they are in instances of anarchy and war.

III. Retribution and Expiation

Retribution and expiation are theological convictions that some believe support the death penalty. The crimes for which the death penalty is exacted rightly excite moral indignation. Charles Hodge, the nineteenth-century Presbyterian theologian at Princeton Theological Seminary, found it "plain that the infliction of capital punishment was not included in the prohibitions" of the sixth commandment.

> Such punishment is not inflicted to gratify revenge, but to satisfy justice and for the preservation of society. . . . It is a dictate of our moral nature that crime should be punished; that there should be a proportion between the offense and the penalty; and that death, the highest penalty, was the proper punishment for the greatest of all crimes. (*Systematic Theology*, III, 363–64)

Crimes for which the death penalty is inflicted violate the moral order. Such crimes cannot be dealt with arbitrarily by whose who believe in a moral order. To do so is to depreciate the value of human life and to violate the moral order. When wrong has been done, the debt must be paid; the evil must be expiated. The foremost Reformed theologians of the twentieth century, Emil Brunner and Karl Barth, recognized the cogency of this argument for capital punishment, yet neither of them was sufficiently convinced by it to endorse capital punishment.

In the first place, the demands of justice and of the moral order can be satisfied without resorting to capital punishment. Prison sentences that are quickly and fairly given and other special restrictions that come within the means of society can satisfy the demands of justice and the Christian sense that justice must be expiated.

Second, the appeal by Christians for expiation has limited validity because of the Christian conviction that in Jesus Christ the sins of us all have been expiated. Karl Barth has written,

> The retributive justice of God has already found full and final expression, the expiation demanded by Him for all human transgression has already been made, the death sentence imposed on human criminals has already been executed. God gave His only Son for this very purpose. . . . Who, then, is not included? Which category of particularly great sinners is exempted from the pardon effected on the basis of the death penalty carried out at Calvary? Now that Jesus Christ has been nailed to the cross for the sins of the world, how can we still use the thought of expiation to establish the death penalty? (*Church Dogmatics*, III, 4, 442–43)

Barth's position, when taken in an absolute sense, undercuts all human efforts to maintain a moral order, but in a relative sense his position warns that human beings are not God and that their efforts to maintain the moral order should be appropriate to their situation.

In the third place, as Emil Brunner points out, the desire for revenge frequently lurks in the call for expiation. Furthermore, the idea of expiation has been a

> fertile soil for the growth of the most hateful, harsh kind of Pharisaism. Certainly the guilty person ought to make expiation. But who is the guilty person? In the whole casual series of crime, for reasons of convenience, we hold only the last link in the chain guilty. . . . It is this which constitutes the intolerable falsity of this principle of expiation. (*The Divine Imperative*, 476)

Christians, conservative and liberal alike, are easily tempted to have others crucified for their sins. The secular *New Republic* (October 21, 1978), in a discussion of the World Council grant to the Front groups in the Rhodesian conflict, notes that liberal, white, American Christians have found it easy to have whites in Rhodesia sacrificed to assuage their own sense of guilt. The execution of a human being whom society has condemned can be an occasion "for an arrogant Pharisaism" and "a sadistic enjoyment of cruel punishment." Self-sacrifice cannot be a public policy, for then it becomes a sacrifice of other people. The self-righteous, above all, must beware of the subtle temptation of wanting others to be crucified for their sins.

IV. The Questionable Necessity of the Death Penalty

A moral decision concerning the death penalty also involves an analysis of what is actually happening in our society. The social sciences provide valuable information about the ordering of society and about the functioning of the death penalty. (Among numerous studies of the death penalty, see Hugo Adam Bedau, ed., *The Death Penalty in America;* Philip English Mackey, ed., *Voices Against Death;* and L. Harold Dewolf, *Crime and Justice in America*.) Much of this analysis is beyond the limits of this paper. Yet something must be said about the role of the death penalty as a deterrent to crime and about the actual infliction of the death penalty in our society.

The significance of the death penalty as deterrent to crime has played a large part in the argument about capital punishment. The debate has been inconclusive and is colored by the commitments of those engaged in the arguments. Yet many societies exist without the death penalty as a part of their regular system of criminal justice. Furthermore, if the death penalty is in some measure a deterrent to crime, this is no conclusive argument for it. The deterrence would have to be sufficiently clear and significant to overrule the theological convictions that form a bias against it. And still further, other deterrents are also effective, such as the speed and certainty of punishment as well as the actual prison sentences. Even if the death penalty is a deterrent, which has not been proved by convincing evidence, it is still neither a necessary deterrent nor one that is proven to be superior to imprisonment.

In connection with the discussion of deterrence, some indicators show that imposition of the death penalty actually incites violence. In any case, inflicting the death penalty is a highly public example of the taking of a human life in a planned and rational way. It is a demonstration of the brutality that strips every dignity from a human life. For this reason, no discussion of the death penalty can avoid coming to terms with the brutal qualities inherent in the act itself and with the influence of this example on society.

A society that can send people to the moon can devise ways of maintaining order without resorting to the death penalty as a part of the regular system of justice. Some argue that the present system is ineffective, that dangerous criminals are quickly paroled. These are serious problems, but as arguments for the death penalty, they are counterproductive. The same system and authorities that cannot handle the matter of parole are entrusted with the responsibility of executing human beings. The simple fact is that order can be maintained without resorting to the death penalty.

The ability of American society to maintain order and to protect life without resorting to the death penalty is important for the argument of this paper. No evidence has yet been produced that the death penalty as administered in American society is such a sufficient or necessary deterrent to crime as to override the theological convictions that rule against it. Furthermore, other forms of deterrence, now in practice or yet to be devised, can be equally effective in maintaining order and protecting life.

V. The Selective Character of the Death Penalty

Any responsible decision about the death penalty must take into account the way in which the death penalty is actually imposed in American society. When this writer first graduated from seminary, he was a minister in Mobile, Alabama, where he came to know a Presbyterian elder who had wide experience as a trial lawyer. On the basis of his experience as a lawyer, this elder declared his opposition to the death penalty because of the caprice, the chance happenings, and the mistakes of the legal process. No personal judgment can be decisive evidence, but this judgment of a conservative elder and lawyer made a lasting impression.

Charles R. Black of Yale University Law School has declared "that the problems of mistake and caprice are ineradicable in the administration of the death penalty" (*Capital Punishment: The Inevitability of Caprice and Mistake,* 14). Discretion also plays a significant role in the execution of any person, from the initial actions of the police and prosecuting attorneys to the final imposition of the verdict. Black does not argue that the system is corrupt. His contention is that the "death penalty cannot be imposed, given the limitations of our minds and institutions, without considerable measure both of arbitrariness and of mistake," as well as of discretionary judgment. The result is that the very few are selected out of many who might equally well have been selected for the death penalty. The persons who are finally given the death penalty are usually financially poor, powerless, sick, and confused. They are frequently not the worst criminals in our society, nor are they any more destructive of human order than thousands of others who escaped the death penalty.

One solid, pragmatic ground for opposing the death penalty is the arbitrariness, caprice, and human discretion that are always at work in its imposition. The result is a great selectivity that is standardless in the imposition of the death penalty, frequently rendering it upon the more pathetic rather than the more arrogant and powerful criminals. The contemporary practice of the death penalty, apart from more substantive arguments, is unfair and unjust.

VI. Hope for Future as Christian Realism

This paper does not argue against the necessity of the use of force in human affairs nor against the right of the state to take life. There are good theological reasons for believing that force will always be a factor in the ordering of human society. As human beings we are all creatures of instinct and impulse, and we are all without exception corrupted by self-interest. In addition, the power of the human spirit to transcend every human achievement complicates all human activities. The freedom of the human spirit means that in every human person reside indeterminate possibilities of hate, brutality, and greed, as well as indeterminate possibilities of love, loyalty, and humanenesss. The animal will to survive can be transmuted by the human spirit into the will to dominate or into the will to give oneself in sacrifice. The corruption of the human spirit by self-centeredness and the instinctual, impulsive nature of human life mean that, when unrestrained by opposing power, individuals and communities always impose on their neighbors. In some instances the state has no other option than to take life when its own existence is at stake, as in the case of revolution or war. The goal of human society cannot realistically be a community in which force is obsolete, but one in which the centers of power are sufficiently reduced and moderated that the use of force will be as minimal as possible. A Christian realism that neither underestimates the residual good in bad people nor the residual evil in good people is our best hope for the future.

The argument of this paper is that the coolly calculated, rational, clinical taking of life in capital punishment is an offense against the Christian understanding of human existence and incongruent with our human status as creatures who are not only limited by time and space, but also by our own sinfulness. The paper further argues that the death penalty is unnecessary as an ordinary means of maintaining order and as a regular part of our system of criminal justice. In its actual practice, it is highly selective and arbitrary and, therefore, unjust.

Our hope for the future is a Christian realism that is neither cynical nor utopian, that neither denies human dignity nor human sin. Such a hope will bring the best minds and hearts of Christian people to the task of working out better and more imaginative ways of maintaining order and protecting life than we now have in our society.

"Theological Perspectives on Economics"
May, 1979

Resume of an Address Delivered at a Seminar on the Church
and Economics, Hilton Head, South Carolina

An assessment of theological perspectives that bear upon the economic
activity of human beings suggests two preliminary observations. The first
is the question whether theological commitments influence economic
activity at all. Karl Marx in the middle of the nineteenth century insisted
that the way people earn their living shapes their theological and ethical
views. There is overwhelming evidence that economic situation does influence faith commitments. Marx can be criticized only in that he believed
that this influence was overwhelming. At the beginning of the twentieth
century the German sociologist Max Weber—in a notable study, *The
Protestant Ethic and the Spirit of Capitalism*—insisted that theology shaped
economic activity. The German historians Ernst Troeltsch and Karl Holl
and the English historian Tawney argued in a similar vein. The Weber thesis has been widely debated, but no one has demolished the basic argument that Reformed theology and ethics were significant factors in the
shaping of Anglo-Saxon capitalism. The fact is theology both shapes and
is shaped by economic activity.

The second preliminary observation has to do with the relation
between Christian faith and economic systems. This paper maintains that
there is no Christian economic system. Reinhold Niebuhr argued persuasively against Christian political parties and economic systems. Christian
faith has existed in communities with many diverse economic and political systems. While this coexistence has been more congenial in some
situations than in others, in no situation has there been any simple identification of any economic or political system with Christian faith. There
are no Christian economic systems. Christian people engage in political
and economic activity, but none of their political and economic activity

can be identified with the kingdom of God. All economic and political actions are complex, involving good and evil, though some involve or produce more good and evil than others. Economic or political activity should always be striving for the kingdom of God, but identifying any such action with the kingdom is always perilous.

Christian faith is, however, highly relevant to economic activity even though no economic system can be called "Christian." In some sense all Christian doctrines bear upon economic action. The following doctrines of the faith have particular relevance.

I. Creation

The universe according to Christian faith has its origin in the purpose of God. It is neither the product of irrational power nor a chance happening. The universe is wholly dependent upon the will and power of God. It is also good, for the God who redeems is the God who creates. The cultural significance of this conviction about the nature of the universe is attested in the history of Western Europe and America. On the one hand, the universe is accessible to human observation and reason. Also, the created order—including not only nature but human existence in time—is good. Salvation is to be found not in escape from nature or history but in life in the world under the dominion of God.

Lynn White in a widely quoted essay has argued that the Christian doctrine that God gave man dominion over the world has led to its exploitation. This thesis, however, underestimates the significance of the Christian insistence that human dominion is always under the dominion of God.

The doctrine of creation also roots the life of the individual, of the person, not simply in the processes of nature and history but primarily in the purposes and knowledge of God. The value and preciousness of a person inheres not in productivity and function but in the knowledge and intention of the creator.

II. Stewardship

Human existence is responsible existence. A person is accountable to God. Therefore, every person must interpret his own life in terms of responsibility. H. H. Farmer in a study of the New Testament parable of the Rich Man and Lazarus insists that only when we interpret life in terms of responsibility can we make sense out of its apparent inequities. The rich man may have been a hard worker and very intelligent. Lazarus may have been shiftless and inept. In any case he was sick. The parable does not condemn the rich man because he was rich nor does it praise Lazarus because he was poor. The problem was the rich man's interpretation of his situation in terms of privilege for himself, not in terms of responsibility; therefore, his life did not make sense in God's world. Only by interpreting one's own existence in terms of responsibility under God for the whole created order can one make sense out of life.

III. Vocation

According to the New Testament God calls us to be Christian. It was Martin Luther's great insight that this call to be Christian covers the whole range of human existence, including daily work. The medieval church had divided life into the secular and religious, into the profane and the sacred. Luther insisted that all of life ought to be sacred. Daily work is not something one does in spite of or in addition to one's Christian commitment. Daily work is one of the primary ways in which a Christian embodies Christian faith and fulfills the purposes of God. Useful work that enhances human existence is more significant, Luther argued, than the mumbling of prayers in one's cell. Luther certainly did not substitute vocation in the world for worship, but he insisted that worship cannot be a substitute for meaningful work. The Christian life is to be lived in the world.

IV. Predestination

The Reformed theologians conceived God not so much as truth or beauty but as energy, activity, intention, and moral purpose. They understood the Christian life not only as personal faith but also as the working out of the divine purposes in human history. The sharpest focus of this faith was the doctrine of predestination, which had to do not only with the eternal destinies of heaven and hell but also with life here and now. The impact of predestination upon political and economic activity is not simply the need to embody the will of God as evidence or assurance of one's election but also the incentive of knowing that one's life embodied the divine purposes and served not merely one's own needs but also the glory of God. This conception of the Christian life intensified the activity of the Christian in human history. It did not allow anyone to rest under the mulberry tree when the needs of physical comfort had been obtained.

V. The Doctrine of Man

Christian theology has defined the uniqueness of human existence in terms of freedom and the human spirit, which is able to transcend every human achievement. No act of love and no human achievement ever exhausts the possibilities of human existence. Human beings are not bound as animals are by instinct and impulse, nor are they bound by cultural patterns or even their own past. This freedom is never absolute, but it always is a characteristic of the truly human.

Langdon Gilkey, in an analysis of Reinhold Niebuhr's philosophy of history, has emphasized three themes that are rooted in the capacity of the human spirit to transcend itself and its every achievement. First, human beings are incurably creative. They can always imagine a better future than their present. Second, as a result, no society is ever final. The human spirit can never be bound by any static pattern of life. Therefore, all systems and patterns of life are subject to change. Third, human freedom means that the possibility of the "fall" lasts as long as human history lasts. There can be no guarantee of any permanent utopia.[1] Every good can be and always is corrupted through actions of human freedom. No permanent solutions to human problems are available. The human proclivity to evil, even on every new level of goodness, brings continual falls, but the grace of God offers the possibilities of continual renewals. The human prospect is proximate—no final solutions to problems; falls and renewals rather than utopia. The human prospect is more moderate than either the classical utopians or the liberation theologians imagine, but it is not pessimistic.

The Christian understanding of human existence also takes human sin seriously but not too seriously. It seeks to avoid cynicism and despair on the one hand and sentimental optimism on the other. Christian understanding takes sin seriously because the human spirit can transmute the will to survive into the will to dominate. Our best deeds as well as our worst deeds are flawed by self-interest. Self-interest is a permanent factor in human activity and is most dangerous when denied. As Reinhold Niebuhr insisted, self-interest cannot be suppressed, and no one is wise enough or sufficiently free of it to regulate it for others. Therefore, it must be used as a factor in obtaining a just society in which self-interest is recognized and moderated. Self-interest cannot be eliminated, but interests can be balanced against each other.

---

[1]Langdon Gilkey "Reinhold Niebuhr as Political Theologian" in *Reinhold Niebuhr and the Issues of Our Time*, ed. Richard Harris (Grand Rapids: William E. Eerdmans Publishing Co., 1986), 157–182.

Christian theology has been tempted to forget the residual capacity for good in all people, but in its best moments it has known that capacities for good remain even among the "totally depraved." Hence, an evaluation of an economic system must be made in the light of a Christian realism that takes seriously the sin of all people, the good and the bad, and that takes seriously the capacity for good in all people, the bad as well as the good.

VI. Simplicity as a Style of Life

No emphasis of the Reformed tradition is more pervasive than the advocacy of simplicity. The Reformed always opposed the pretentious, the ostentatious, the pompous, the contrived, the artificial, and the redundant. They believed that such activities or qualities covered up reality. The simple is close to sincerity, for it uncovers reality. Therefore, the Reformed insisted upon simplicity in writing style, in sermons, in liturgy, in dress, in living style and social activity.

VII. Eternal Life

The doctrine of eternal life is a warning against the illusion that economic achievements can give a final meaning to life. Our present society is suffering the pain of unrealistic expectations from careers, from affluence, from physical comfort. The plain fact is that economic achievements cannot satisfy the deepest needs of human beings. As Augustine put it, "Thou hast made us for thyself and restless is our heart until it comes to rest in thee." The New Testament puts the issue more sharply: "What will it profit a man, if he gains the whole world and forfeits his life?" (Matt. 16:26). "Do not fear those who kill the body but cannot kill the soul" (Matt. 10:28). "A man's life does not consist in the abundance of his possessions" (Luke 12:15).

This listing of theological perspectives that bear upon economic decision is not exhaustive. Furthermore, no one can move directly from a theological doctrine anymore than from a biblical text to a judgment about economic activity. These judgments also require careful analysis of the actual facts in the situation and ethical reflection about the way in which the Christian doctrines illuminate those facts. A Christian may come to the same conclusion about certain economic activities as a non-Christian, but the Christian's judgment will always be shaped in part by the theological perspectives that shape life for a Christian.

PART SEVEN
REFORMED-LUTHERAN DIALOGUE

"The Starting Point and Purpose of Lutheran and Reformed Conversations"
February 1962

Reformed-Lutheran conversations together are complicated by our history. Once we were engaged in conversation. Calvin himself was a "Lutheran." But for a long time there has been very little theological conversation between us. Each of us has a history that we share and a history that we do not share with the other. This background gives us on the one hand a real basis for conversation, and on the other hand it complicates what we have to say to each other today.

I. The Starting Point

Our fathers were engaged in this conversation four centuries ago. Shall we take up where they left off, or shall we begin anew? The fact is that we can do neither.

We cannot take up where our fathers left off because while we are sons and daughters of our fathers, we have been in alien countries or at least alien times. There are few, if any, "pure" Lutheran or Reformed theologians. Most theologians, even those who think of themselves as confessional, are incredibly eclectic. In most theologians, as I would assume in most of us, one finds the motifs of Lutheran, of Reformed, of Enlightenment, and of post-Enlightenment theologies. Most of us at any rate cannot begin where the old controversies left off because our theology is no longer purely confessional. The old controversies and marks of distinction have become blurred, which is on the one hand a gain, for it lessens theological acrimony and restores perspective, but which is on the other hand a loss, for it means less theological passion and acumen.

Furthermore, we live in a different time, in a world that has known Marx, Darwin, Freud, Nietzsche, and Einstein. The issues that confront us in both the church and the world are different. The theological battles of the Reformation were either settled or burned themselves out. The passion and enthusiasm that they engendered are not repeatable occurrences. Nothing would be more sterile than an artificial revival of the sixteenth century in the twentieth, no matter how sophisticated the revival. We and our times are new, unique as all times are; we cannot simply take up where our fathers left off in the theological debates of the sixteenth and seventeenth centuries.

Another possibility is to begin anew. The thrill of contemporary biblical study seems to have suggested this possibility. But this likewise is not a real option. On the one hand, we have been formed theologically by the doctrine of the Reformation. We cannot begin as though the Reformation never happened. Furthermore, if we could begin at the beginning we would have to do all over again the theology of the Reformation. We might discover after we were tired of working that we were not as far along as our fathers were centuries ago.

We cannot take up where the theological controversies left off and neither can we begin anew. A more promising option is to acknowledge frankly that we are persons of Reformed and Lutheran persuasions who have been influenced positively and negatively by Enlightenment and post-Enlightenment theologies, and who live in a world whose economic, cultural, political, and social problems would have been beyond the imaginative powers of the sixteenth-century Reformers.

Furthermore, our Protestant conviction is that our primary loyalty is not to the Reformers who speak to us through their writings and controversies, but to Jesus Christ, the Lord of the church, who speaks to us through his word amid the crises of our own time.

II. Purposes

The hope that a renewal of Lutheran and Reformed discussions will be a worthwhile undertaking has its warrant in the achievements of ecumenical conferences of our time. More specifically, the Reformed and Lutheran discussions in Europe are an encouragement. The conferences in France not only arrived at common agreements but also contributed to our understanding of the ministry and provided a moving liturgy for ordination. The Dutch theses on the Lord's Supper clarify the issues at stake and reach a measure of agreement. The Arnoldshain theses represented refined theological effort, but perhaps they are too refined. They give the impression of having been worked so thoroughly that they no longer have a theological bite, especially on the Lord's Supper. In any case we have ample warrant and promise for our undertaking in the ecumenical movement in general and in conversations that are already underway between Lutheran and Reformed churchmen.

What then are the areas in which we can hope that our work may have profitable results?

The Ecumenical Movement

One of the great facts of our time is the recovery of the catholicity of the theological enterprise. Perhaps not since the fifth century has theological endeavor been as catholic as now. We are all in some measure participants in the ecumenical movement, and the work that we have done in the ecumenical movement contributes to the work that we shall do as Reformed and Lutheran churchmen. Also what we do as Reformed and Lutheran churchmen will, we hope, contribute to the larger ecumenical movement. Until now, the special theological positions that our traditions represent have not been the focus of theological discussion. I am not competent to state the reason for this. Perhaps we have not been as bold in stating our claims of catholicity or as clear and passionate in our historic theology. In any case the theological issues that have characterized our tradition have not been discussed and debated. Yet our traditional emphases, it seems to me, can be the source of significant service to the ecumenical movement at the present time. Our classic creeds were written for the holy catholic church, and our privilege and responsibility is to offer them to the holy catholic church today.

First, our discussions may serve to shift the focus of ecumenical discussions from questions of polity and order to questions of theology. One may well suspect that all ecumenical problems would not be solved if something were agreed concerning the episcopate. In fact, the problems that remained could well be the more difficult. Our churches have never tied the unity or the existence of the church to any point of polity or of order. We have said that the church exists where the Word is rightly preached and the sacraments rightly administered. The Reformed churches sometimes added the right administration of discipline as a mark of the church, but discipline was in part a means to the Word rightly preached and the sacraments rightly administered. Perhaps our conversations can serve to call attention to our conviction that the presence of Christ in Word and sacrament, the gospel, is the basis of the church's existence and of her unity, a conviction that has been obscured by preoccupation with the episcopate.

Second, as churches that are unashamedly theological, we can serve the ecumenical movement by calling attention to new questions that must be raised and answered in the light of theological considerations. Much of the ecumenical movement's success has been achieved by the blurring or evasion of theological questions and by preoccupation with administrative and organizational concerns. The initial enthusiasm and success of the movement and the inherent rightness of the desire for the unity of the church is such that an ecumenical orthodoxy can develop that would be just as sterile and dangerous as the orthodoxies that we have known in our own histories, but that would not have behind it the careful theological work of the sixteenth and seventeenth centuries. To put the issue another way, we are now at the stage where we must beware of labeling a person ecumenical or antiecumenical in the light of some doctrinaire concept of the unity of the church, where we must bring many problems under the surveillance of careful theological study; in the early years of the ecumenical movement, these problems could be neglected in the light of more pressing demands.

Our own theological traditions indicate that we should begin to ask what does theology, in total rather than piece fashion, have to say about the church. The ecumenical movement has given attention to individual doctrines such as the church or Christology, but very little has yet been said, for example, about the significance of anthropology, justification by grace through faith, or providence for either the doctrine of or the historic life of the church. What is our task as churchmen in the light of our total theological commitments?

A host of questions are now arising that may in the end be answered on the basis of expediency or organizational efficiency, because on the surface they appear to involve simply practical concerns. Among these questions are:

1. What is the significance of organizational unity for the unity of the church?
2. Is there a danger that councils in our times, as in Luther's, may too easily assume that they are the church?
3. Is the church as visible in the committee, council, or assembly as in the worship, obedience, and faith of the local congregation?
4. Is it as possible for the large organization to be the church as it is for the smaller organization? Is there a point at which the size of

membership, council, and boards becomes a hindrance to the reality of the church?

5. Is it true historically that the large church or the national church is as effective in its witness as the multiplicity of denominations?

6. Is organizational effectiveness sufficient justification for organizational unity?

7. Can the unity of the church be realized in the context of a multiplicity of organizational structures?

These questions may be exasperating to those who have labored long in the ecumenical movement, but to dismiss the questions or those who raise them as unorthodox or outside the ecumenical movement would be a sign of immaturity. Our own churches, which have always prized theological integrity above social effectiveness, can render our best service to the ecumenical movement by insisting that such questions be answered in the light of the total theology of the church. Certainly we cannot be satisfied with considerations that would be adequate for a businessman or that would satisfy those who really belong to a cultural-Protestantism or who are indifferent to issues of theological integrity.

The Role, Function, and Purpose of Creeds

Lutheran and Reformed churches have been confessional churches from the beginning and alike require creedal subscription of ministers and church officers. The revival of creedal studies indicates that our churches are more self-consciously confessional now than twenty-five years ago. One value in our conversations would be a new understanding of the role and functions of creeds in the life of the church today.

The Theological Enterprise

One area that needs clarification is the significance of confessions in the theological enterprise. As mentioned above, pure Lutheran or Reformed theologians either do not exist at all or do not exist in very large numbers. The theologian today is eclectic. He reads Calvin and Luther. He may value the theologians of the second century as well as Augustine. He has felt the impact of the industrial and scientific revolutions and the ferment of the nineteenth century. He has gone through liberalism, not around it. His theology has many sources. What does this mean for someone who theologizes under the Reformed or Luther banner? Is such a person, who may be under ordination vows, free to pick and choose theology in the eclectic fashion to which we have become accustomed, a practice that in many cases came as a refreshing and liberating experience after the sterile bondages of orthodoxy? Have we not sufficiently liberated ourselves from creedal bondage that we must now ask what does it mean to theologize responsibly under allegiance to a confession?

Subscription

A second problem that needs exploring is the meaning of subscription. Indications are that subscription is increasingly the subject of confusion and the object of concern following the lull after the fundamentalist controversies, especially in the Presbyterian Church U.S. Among the questions that arise are, What is the relation of the creed to the Bible? What is the nature and extent of subscription? Do we subscribe to the creed because it is biblical or insofar as it is biblical, or do we subscribe in both senses? What is the meaning of such phrases: "as containing the sum and substance of the doctrine of Reformed church," "as being in all the essential and necessary articles, good forms of sound words and systems of Christian doctrine," "as containing the system of doctrine taught in the holy scripture"? Is a creed affirmed only in terms of the options that existed when it came into being or in terms of the theological options of the twentieth century?

Confessions in the Ecumenical Movement

A third role of confessions that needs clarification is the significance of confessions in the ecumenical movement. This problem has become urgent in the light of the enlarged ecumenical participation of the Orthodox, who are not likely to talk with us too much about polity but who may force theological issues. Have we not been able to avoid the confessional issue in the ecumenical movement up until now largely because it has not been raised? Will not the presence of the Orthodox in the World Council shortly force us to face basic theological issues? What shall be the significance of our confessions, for example, when we are confronted by the pneumatic ecclesiology of the Orthodox communions? Further, developments in Protestant–Roman Catholic relations may compel us to do some very hard theological work. There can be no better preparation for these encounters than the study of our confessions so as to provide us better theological self-identity and sharper awareness of the theological issues involved in our own understanding of Christian faith and order.

Confessional Witness

Another area that needs clarification is significance of the confession in the life and witness of the church. The confession is more than a theological norm. It is the confession, praise, commitment, and battle cry of the church. In this sense of witness and life, can we say that we are today confessional churches? To be sure, the issues are not so clearly drawn as at Barmen, but issues are involved in the existence of a confessional church in American culture. Does the confessional allegiance distinguish confessors and make a significant difference in the manner of a person's life? Surely the final and most significant embodiment of a confession is always in life and society. But is there such a reality as Reformed, Lutheran, or Protestant personality or society?

There is the additional problem of a confessional church in a highly mobile society and in a church situation where denominational loyalties are taken very lightly. The mobility of population is likely to increase in the years ahead, and the pluralism of our society is now an accepted fact. New patterns of economic and social life will pose additional problems for the confessional church that places emphasis upon life of the mind as the service of God. Unless we can meet these practical problems of church life, the work of committees on theology will not amount to much.

The Reconstruction and Repair of Doctrine

A third service that our conversations can render may well be in the realm of the reconstruction and repair of doctrine. As Presbyterians and Lutherans we are at one in our conviction that the theological enterprise through the centuries has been the service of God and that it has contributed to a deeper understanding of the faith. We have not regarded theology as either a mistake or a tragic necessity. Our task is not simply historical, and neither is it simply a handmaid of the ecumenical concern. It is the constructive task of theology, which carries on in the language and idiom of our time the work that was begun in earliest days of the Christian church.

Theological Renewal

A fourth service that we ought to expect from our conversations is a theological renewal in our churches. One of the most serious aspects of the current situation (and here I speak out of my limited experience) is that we are being called upon to make serious decisions in the realm of theology and polity, and we do not have the theological and ecclesiastical backgrounds and competence to make these decisions. In many cases these decisions are made on the basis of axioms drawn from our American way of life quite as much as theological and biblical sources. In our assemblies we are ready to debate matters of organization and policy and to exhort one another to greater effort, but everyone is afraid of real theological debate and discussion. I suspect this is less true of the Lutherans than of the Presbyterians. In Presbyterianism we are still, at least in many situations, in reaction against the acrimony of the fundamentalist debates. In the Deep South these debates are not yet altogether history.

How the committee's discussions can become the occasion for theological renewal is not fully clear. However, theological renewal must become part of the work of the committee if we are to achieve really significant goals. One of the great problems now in the life of the church is the abyss that separates committees, councils, assemblies, and the particular congregations.

The Unity of the Church

Our conversations ought to contribute to the acknowledgment of our unity in Jesus Christ. We have not met with any doctrinaire conception of unity, but neither can we prejudge what in the providence of God may take place. Believing that the church is one, we shall thank God for every evidence of its unity in our midst.

The unity of the church is a common Christian conviction. Our difficulty arises in our definition of unity. What is the nature of the unity of the church, and how is it made visible? How do we understand and judge the statements on unity at St. Andrews and New Delhi? Perhaps a study of these statements would help us clarify our own relations and also our relation and obligation to the ecumenical movement as a whole. Certainly we cannot take seriously our classic understanding of the church without eventually talking seriously about intercommunion and mutual recognition of the ministry. At this point, it seems to me, the scandal of denominations is most evident, not in the fact that we have separate boards of education and mission. Yet we must also face the question of the unity of the church and organizational unity, for this issue is being forced to a decision in part by sociological facts and in part by conscientious convictions of many churchmen.

We have gathered as Reformed and Lutheran churchmen who, in obedience to the example of our fathers, shall pay heed to Jesus Christ, the head of the church, who speaks to us through his word and spirit. For this reason, we have high hope for something more than we can now predict or we have otherwise any right to expect.

PART EIGHT
LIFE IN THE CHURCH

"The Message of Christian Faith on the Occasion of the Burial of the Dead"
1983

Journal for Preachers, Volume 6

The funeral is a critical moment in the life of any Christian congregation. Death breaks community and threatens faith and life with meaningless-ness. Frequently a funeral leaves a painful void in the personal existence of the bereaved. On the occasion of death, the church is challenged to con-fess the faith and to assert the reality of its communal existence.

There is no uniform Reformed practice in regard to burying the dead. The ecclesiastical Ordinances in Calvin's Geneva simply declare, "The dead are to be buried decently in the place appointed. . . . It will be good that the carriers be warned by us to discourage all superstitions contrary to the Word of God. . . ." The first *Book of Discipline* in the Church of Scotland states, "We desire that burial be so honorably handled that the hope of our resurrection may be nourished; and all kind of superstition, idolatry, and whatsoever thing proceedeth of the false opinions may be avoided" (*The Westminster Directory*).

These quotations are sufficient to indicate that the burial of the dead must be carried out with decency and soberness. They also reveal an awareness that death is the occasion for much superstition. Hence they all seek to reform the practice of burial by dependence upon the regular preaching and services of the church and by reducing the rites of burial to a bare minimum. Perhaps the Reformers reacted too violently, but the superstitious practices against which they protested are a warning that funerals are easily perverted by the imagination of the human heart.

In the course of the years, Reformed communities have sometimes wanted a precise rite of burial. Such a rite would have served very useful purposes in communities without ordained ministers. However, absence of an established pattern for the burial of the dead has certain advantages.

The uniqueness of every death demands more freedom of response and witness than the established rituals provide. The Christian community is free to confess its faith and to demonstrate the reality of its community in ways appropriate to the situation.

The following reflections are given in response to a request from the editors. They are not intended in any sense to be definitive, but are simply presented as conclusions from one minister's experience in the pastorate and in theological reflection.

1. "Good taste" is always in order in the presence of death. This admonition may appear trite, but it is nonetheless important. Death is an awesome moment, and in its presence soberness is a virtue. The occasion of death should never be exploited by the minister or by the church for controversial or eccentric purposes. Neither should it be used to teach or to exhort. At the burial of the dead the community listens to the Word of God and confesses the faith that is the common experience of the gathered company of believers.

   In my own experience, the death and the burial of the dead are times when kindness should take precedence over our own ideas or preferences. Calvin resolutely refused to subordinate truth to love. There is, of course, a point beyond which we cannot go in accommodating the desires of the bereaved. Yet I found that I could participate in funerals in which the family wanted practices that I personally found objectionable, so long as I did not have to be responsible for them.

   The basic point I want to make is that in the presence of the awesomeness of death, "good taste"—in dress, in words, and in acts—is eminently in order.

2. Death and the burial of the dead are occasions when ministers should be very much aware that they are ministers *of the church.* The minister, on the occasion of the burial of the dead, does not give a personal testimony as to his or her faith, but rather confesses the faith of the church. The eccentricities and novelties of a particular minister's faith or lack of faith are inappropriate for the funeral. The ancient prayers of the church, the theology that has stood the test and challenges of time, the language that is the common vocabulary of the faithful, the hymns that are substantive confessions and supplications of the faith are the proper material of the burial service. The burial of the dead is not an appropriate occasion for either theological or liturgical experimentation.

3. Death and the burial of the dead are occasions for the actualization of the Christian community. Church people attend funerals because the death of any member is a concern of the community, not primarily because of personal relationship with the deceased. The gathering for the burial demonstrates community. In addition, the confession of faith testifies to the reality of the church as a community composed of the living and of the dead. The host of heaven also gathers with the church on earth for the burial of this believer.

   The reality of the church as community is actualized by deeds of kindness for the bereaved, food, and useful services, as well as by supporting words. In these practical ways the church reasserts its community in the presence of the challenge of death.

4. In the burial of the dead, a word of thanksgiving for the deceased is appropriate. When I finished the seminary, I was committed to the same service of scripture and prayer for all people. These services had an occasion for the mentioning of the name of the deceased and for a brief word of thanksgiving for the life of the deceased in the prayer and for his or her relationship to the family. I had learned this from ministers who were reacting against the pretentious and inauthentic eulogies that became common for many funerals.

   I gradually moved away from this practice, because in actual experience I found that the burial of certain persons irresistibly demanded some public affirmation of their service in the life of the Christian community as well as in society. The Second Helvetic Confession, 1566, disapproves of the cynics who never say a good word about the deceased. No one ought to want to go back to the old eulogy or to saying words on the occasion of a funeral that are not authentic and that are not self-authenticating among the hearers when pronounced. Appropriate references to distinguished service in the community or to a powerful Christian witness can be made in a discreet and sober way. When done soberly, the speaking of a good word does not create a precedent requiring a eulogy when it would not be appropriate. In the case of several very distinguished public figures, I found it fitting to interweave the Christian message with a more elaborate thanksgiving for the life of the deceased.

5. The service on the occasion for the burial of the dead is an appropriate time to affirm in a fundamental way the faith of the church. As I have indicated, my first funeral sermons were compilations of great scripture passages with a few introductory remarks. Every

funeral service should contain a reading of the very great passages of scripture that have meant much to Christian believers in every age. No burial should be without readings from the Psalms, John 14, Romans 8, 1 Corinthians 15.

The hymns that are sung on the occasion of a funeral are also opportunities to bear witness to the faith. My own preference is for the great hymns that confess the faith and that center attention upon God. The hymns that I particularly like for funerals are the following: "All People That on Earth Do Dwell," "How Firm a Foundation," "A Mighty Fortress Is Our God," "Thine Is the Glory," and "Now Thank We All Our God."

I have increasingly come to the conviction that the burial of the dead is the proper occasion for the church to confess its faith using the Apostles' Creed. The Lord's Prayer also gives the people an opportunity to affirm their faith and claim God's grace.

In recent years, I have given the message on the occasion of burial a more theological structure. These burial sermons have tried to assert in the presence of death the reality of the Christian community, the meaningfulness of life, and the grace of the God and Father of our Lord Jesus Christ upon which the first two affirmations depend.

The theology that is appropriate for a funeral message should be the tried and tested theology of the church. It should be a theology that the minister has mastered and can conceptualize in his or her own words. It should be expressed in plain, simple English sentences that are distinguished by their coherence and clarity. The funeral is not the occasion for amateur theology. If the choice is between amateur theology and a service simply of prayer and scripture reading, then the latter is clearly the proper choice.

I have also found that the burial message is a proper place to assert the Christian faith over against the absurdity of many deaths. In a fundamental sense every death is absurd and a challenge to faith. Yet some deaths are an acute challenge to faith and are blatantly absurd. On the occasion of such a death, we can only honestly face the absurdity, trust God, and seek in our own actions to give some meaning to a death that otherwise is irrational. In the church the absurdity of death should be accepted, understood, and overcome.

Long ago, Augustine did not try to explain away the brutality that Christians experienced at the hands of the Goths in the sacking of Rome. The difference, Augustine said, between Christians and non-Christians was not in what happened to them in the world, but in their responses to what happened to them. Christians were distinguished by the faith, hope, and love with which they responded to the tragic events of their own lives.

On the occasion of a death that was especially poignant for me—the sudden death of a beautiful, brilliant, committed twenty-nine-year-old woman, an honor graduate of a great university, a wife and a mother, I said the following words:

A Funeral Sermon

We have gathered here this morning as those who knew and loved _____. We have also gathered here in awe before the mystery of life and in fear before a death that appears so absurd, that threatens our community and our faith. But we have gathered as the church to reaffirm the reality of the church itself in the face of death, to give thanks *for* and to pay tribute *to* the life she lived in our midst, to declare again our faith.

I. It is very fitting that we gather as the church and that in the presence of the death of _____ we reaffirm its reality.

She was born into the church, and even those closest to her by ties of flesh and blood knew her in the church as soon as they knew her in the human community. And so we have come together not only as human beings who know human sorrow, but as the church of the living God to confess our faith, to share together in the common life that has sustained us this far, and to affirm the reality of the church in the face of death.

In this life together, we knew _____ in the keenness of her mind, in the graciousness and humanness and gentleness of her person, in the quiet dignity and stability of her life, in her commitment to and love for the church.

We knew in her the wonder of human existence and the joy of human fellowship. By this fellowship we were all enriched. We find words inadequate to say precisely how we understood the wonder of her life and the wonder of our fellowship together. Yet we know that in knowing one another and in sharing in the common life of the church, we were deeply enriched and strengthened in the faith. And now we can best think of _____'s life as a means of God's grace to us. We give thanks for the special human being she was—intelligent, kind, understanding, interested, committed to something more than herself.

When she was married in this church in December 1973, she asked—somewhat unusual for a wedding service—that these words from the Sermon on the Mount should be read. And I think she would want them read now.

"Therefore I tell you, do not be anxious about your life, what you shall eat or what you shall drink, nor about your body, what you shall put on . . ." (Matt. 6:25–34).

We take assurance now in the truth of our faith that the church is a body composed of the living and the dead (some of whom are very dear to _____) and that in Christ, the head of the church, we still have communion one with another. We are glad that we knew _____; and it is our hope that we shall know her again in the fullness, beauty, and wonder of that life into which by God's grace _____ has passed and into which we shall soon go.

II. Now as the church, we confess our faith in the presence of death that the meaning of life, its significance and purpose, is revealed not in this death, which appears so irrational to us, but in the love of the God and Father of our Lord Jesus Christ. We understand death in the light of God's love, not God and life in the light of death.

Over against _____'s death we make at least three basic confessions of faith.

1. First of all, we confess our faith that _____'s life was established in the purposes of God. At the beginning of her life this faith was confessed in baptism. Her parents and the church claimed the promises of God for her. Her name was called, indicative of our faith that God thought of _____ before she was, called her into being, and gave to her her identity, her individuality, her name, her dignity. And now at death we confess again this faith that was affirmed at baptism. We establish our hope in the fact that the eternal God knows us by name, that he searches us out and sets us behind and before (Psalm 139), that he numbers the hairs upon our head, and allows not a sparrow to fall without his notice (Matt. 10:29–30).

2. We also as the church confess our faith that the eternal God who called us into being will complete and fulfill the work that he has begun in us.

"Let not your hearts be troubled; believe in God, believe also in me . . ." (John 14:1–6).

3. We come together as the church finally to confess that the last word today and every day is the grace of God. The evil in the situation, even the absurdity of this death, is not the last word. The last word is the grace of God, that enables us to take whatever comes and to use it in the building of a life of beauty and wonder and authenticity, that enables us even in the presence of this death to praise God and to enhance the meaning of human existence. God has made the world in such a way that deaths such

as this do occur, but he has also made the world so that this death is not the final word. The final word is God's grace. In the faith that _____ liked to confess, we confess now that God works with those who love him for good in all things (Rom. 8:28).

God made the world so that human life is precarious. In this world our hopes are frequently frustrated. We have to live in this dangerous world, where from the perspective of our hopes many events are irrational and absurd for those who believe in the God and Father of our Lord Jesus Christ. If God intended to make us comfortable, then clearly this is an incredible world. But God does not treat those whom he loves as his favorites. He causes his sun to shine and his rain to fall upon the just and unjust alike. Biochemical systems and the structures of the world impinge upon the good and evil with impersonal impartiality. The important differences between people are not so much in what happens to us as in our responses to what happens to us. If God's purpose was to bring many sons to glory (Heb. 2:10) or to bring us to human maturity, as Paul said (Eph. 4:13), then this is the kind of world that challenges us to grow into the maturity of faith, of trust, of human sympathy. God could not and cannot by definition create mature human beings. He could and did create persons with the possibility of human maturity. And this maturity comes only as we respond to the crises and challenges of our lives. In the words of Unamuno's great prayer, may God deny us peace but give us glory.

It is good to push back the boundary of death and to fight against death, but more important than postponing death for a few years is the receiving of a wisdom, and insight, and a grace that enables us to face death and all the challenges of life with the dignity, poise, and serenity that comes from a great faith in God. So our final word is to claim the grace of God that works with those who love him for the good in all things, and to pledge ourselves to find in the irrationality and absurdity of this death an occasion to praise God and to enhance the meaning of human life.

We cannot and we ought not deceive ourselves. This death is an absurdity in God's world. It will remain an absurd, irrational fact unless it becomes a means of God's grace by which God's purposes for his people are fulfilled. To this end we commit ourselves to work to make some sense out of _____'s death as a final tribute to her life.

"Tribute to Dr. E. T. Thompson and the
Brown Brothers and Presentation of a Portrait"
June 14, 1975

Presbyterian Outlook Dinner,
Presbyterian General Assembly, Charlotte, North Carolina

I have been asked by the board of directors of the *Presbyterian Outlook* to express our esteem for Dr. E. T. Thompson and to pay tribute for his role in the history of the *Presbyterian Outlook*. Dr. Thompson has been intimately connected with the *Presbyterian Outlook* for forty years. He kept the old *Presbyterian of the South* alive by sacrificial efforts that are certainly out of the ordinary. He brought Aubrey Brown to the *Outlook* as editor and has continued to give his advice and support.

I am going to include in this tribute Aubrey Brown and his brother James, for they have carried on in a remarkable way the Thompson tradition in the work of the *Presbyterian Outlook*.

I

The most appropriate tribute to make tonight is to note the high sense of Christian vocation and also the high sense of ministerial vocation that has informed the work of Dr. E. T. Thompson and also of the Brown brothers. No finer example of Christian vocation in our denomination exists than their work with the *Outlook*. In their fulfillment of their vocation they have set an example for all of us. Their sense of Christian vocation and their work with the *Outlook* as the fulfillment of a divine calling is critically important for the church today.

Church service is in danger of being fully secularized, scarcely distinguishable from any work in any American corporation. Increasingly, pulpit committees are noting that the difference is disappearing between calling a pastor and hiring someone to work for General Electric or for McDonald's. The sure way not to get a call from a church or to teach at a

263

seminary has been, until quite recently, to seek such a call or position. This was even more true of the position of moderator of the General Assembly. Certainly as late as the early 1960s, to have intimated that you wanted to be moderator of the General Assembly would have disqualified you for the position. Increasingly, ministers seek calls, aided and abetted by the call procedures that are developing in our presbyteries and in our General Assembly. The election of a moderator now is preceded by political activity scarcely distinguishable from that which takes place in secular society.

For Dr. Thompson and for the Browns, the work of the *Presbyterian Outlook* was not a position you sought, but was a divine calling that came to you from God through the board of directors of the *Outlook*. The pay was never a decisive factor for either Dr. Thompson or for the Browns. Dr. Thompson maintained the *Presbyterian of the South* without any compensation, working out of his office at Union Theological Seminary. Finally, the *Outlook* decided it should pay Dr. Thompson for his Sunday school lessons and other writings, and the board allotted something like twenty-five dollars per month. The record keeper reported that Dr. Thompson was contributing far more to the support of the *Outlook* than he was receiving; so to simplify the record keeping, the salary was discontinued.

Aubrey Brown and James Brown have worked as editor and business manager for the *Outlook* frequently for less than the minimum salary paid in many presbyteries. As a member of the board of directors I am embarrassed at how little we have been able to pay. The resources of the *Outlook* are very minimal. Most independent church papers are now extinct due to lack of financial support. An independent church paper can only be maintained with considerable sacrifice. The Browns as well as Dr. Thompson have not hesitated to serve the *Outlook* when they could have made more money in many other church operations. It has been said that the secret of Calvin's influence was that he never was corrupted by money or what money could buy. The same can be said of Dr. Thompson and the Brown brothers with their work with the *Outlook*.

Dr. Thompson and the Brown brothers have set before us an example of Christian vocation.

II

In paying tribute to Dr. Thompson and to the Brown brothers, we also honor the role of a free church press, a role whose importance cannot be overestimated. We who praise the role of a free and critical press in public life must also be committed to a free and critical press in the life of the church. Free church papers are now almost extinct. They have been replaced by official house organs enhanced by the budgets of churches. Official church papers can no more subject the affairs of the church to critical and responsible review or to advocate causes not on the official agenda than a White House publication would have uncovered and reported Watergate or advocated a program not on the president's agenda. The Presbyterian church today suffers because independent church papers have inadequate budgets that do not permit on-the-scene reporting of GEB meetings and investigating what is happening in the life of the church and its institution. Fortunately, the wide contacts and the intimate knowledge that Dr. Thompson and Aubrey Brown have of the church have compensated in part for this financial deficiency. The editors of the *Presbyterian Survey*, in its more prosperous day, were always amazed that the *Outlook* had information that they could not get with their far larger expense account and official resources.

III

The third quality that has characterized the work of Dr. E. T. Thompson and the Brown brothers at the *Outlook* is personal integrity. They may have been mistaken on certain occasions, but never to my knowledge did any of them ever violate his own personal integrity, character, and commitments. They were, in an impressive way, impervious to the pressures put upon them. They were in reality an independent press with a critical mind and judgment.

Some of us used to joke that if you wished to influence Aubrey Brown, it would be better to be his enemy than his friend. It is not likely that either enemy or friend influenced him much. He was very suspicious of his friends trying to use the *Outlook* for their own particular causes. As I have said, the *Outlook* may have been mistaken on occasions, but the integrity of the editors was never violated, at least to my knowledge.

The *Outlook* has never been pushed around by the various pressure groups that have arisen in the church. Everyone knew that it was an independent newspaper. Dr. Edward Grant was speaking to me about this not too long ago. He said that it was much easier to be Aubrey's friend and to speak kindly of the *Outlook* now than when he was no longer an executive. The *Outlook* uncovered and published what the executives did not want uncovered.

Conclusion

The *Presbyterian Outlook* was established by Dr. E. T. Thompson, who was always characterized by a high sense of Christian vocation, a commitment to publish and to uncover the news, and integrity. It is now appropriate to remember the very great contribution of the *Outlook* to the life of the Presbyterian church in the last forty years.

1. The *Outlook* gave leadership in the transition of the parochial church of the 1920s to a church with a global vision.
2. It has stood for freedom of scholarship from the beginning, when very little scholarship existed in our Presbyterian seminaries and colleges.
3. The *Outlook* has insisted on the application of Christian conviction to economic, social, and political issues in our society. Dr. Thompson was one of those who led the creation of the old committee on social and moral welfare. Under his leadership on that committee and then the editorship of the *Outlook,* a Christian social conscience was brought to a church that had emphasized the spirituality of the church.
4. The *Outlook* has always had an ecumenical vision. The movement toward union with the United Presbyterian Church is inconceivable apart from the work of the *Outlook.* The *Outlook* has also stood for participation in the ecumenical movements and gatherings of our time on a worldwide basis.

In sum, no group, individual, or institution has had as great an influence in shaping the changes that have occurred in the Presbyterian Church U.S. from the pre–Second World War era to 1975 as has the *Presbyterian Outlook.*

In retrospect it is increasingly clear that what we now call the *Presbyterian Outlook* would have disappeared apart from the vision, the commitment, the dedication, and the hard labor of Dr. E. T. Thompson in those late days of the late 1930s. We are grateful to him for what he did then and for his bringing Aubrey Brown to succeed him as editor.

The presentation of a portrait of Dr. E. T. Thompson to Union Theological Seminary is a highly appropriate way to express our honor of his commitment and of his labor and leadership in the Presbyterian church in general and the work of the *Presbyterian Outlook* in particular.

"Remarks on the Occasion of Affixing a Plaque
on the Wall of Watts Chapel
in Memory of James Archibald Jones"
April 28, 1982

We are engaged tonight in an act of traditioning, of handing on the faith to a new generation. Plaques on the wall are not so much honors for those whose names they bear as they are symbols and images that remind us of the rock from which we were hewn and that tell us who we are.

It is appropriate that we pause for this rite of passing in an increasingly pluralistic, secular, mobile, mass-media-dominated culture to say to all the world, at least to all who will hear, that James Archibald Jones belongs to the heritage, to the community that defines our lives, that tells us who we are. As a character in Steinbeck's *Grapes of Wrath* put it, "How do we know it is us without our past?" Today we are saying in this official way that James Jones is our past as the seminary community, and because he is our past he is also our present and our future.

Traditioning of the faith and community is never simple. It would be easy on an occasion such as this to become hagiographic, sentimental, and too personal. James Jones was a person around whom legends easily grew. He engaged in great and significant enterprises. He was very affable and personal, but also very private, authentic without public exposure of the truly personal. The stories would be entertaining, but our task is more serious, namely the traditioning of the faith, of the community which for many of us here defines our lives and tells the world who we are.

I

Let us begin with the facts. James Jones was born in Laurinburg, North Carolina, on October 3, 1911. It is of incalculable significance that he was born in a small town, in a church family, and in a culture that had been shaped by Highland Scot immigrants, by Protestantism, by Puritanism, and by the American experience of this heritage in a small, rural community. His life was formed before television or even radio brought alien traditions into our living rooms, our kitchens, our bedrooms. And he bore the marks of this heritage to the day of his death.

His life was lived in the Presbyterian church. He appeared to receive some satisfaction from the fact that he belonged to the Commonwealth Club, to the Country Club of Virginia, and to other such groups, but he also communicated the awareness that these communities were subordinate to the church, which was his home and his identity. He was in the world, and he was sensitive to what he considered irresponsible attacks upon it, but he clearly was not of it. I think he wanted very much for those whose primary identity was in the country club or this or that elitist secular group to know that while he could be there with them, he had chosen another identity about which no one was ever in doubt.

He attended Davidson College and Union Theological Seminary. He received a Thomas Cary Johnson Fellowship, and he studied at New College in Edinburgh. He married Mary Boyd, the daughter of a minister. He was pastor of the Presbyterian Church in Henderson, North Carolina, and of the Myers Park Presbyterian Church in Charlotte. He served on the boards of Queens College, Hampden-Sydney College, and Richmond Memorial Hospital. He was a member of the General Council of the Presbyterian Church from 1949 to 1956 and its chairman from 1954 to 1955. He was an influential member of the Ad Interim Committee on Study of Assembly's Agencies and a chief author of its report (1949). He served on the Board of World Missions from 1946 to 1958 and from 1960 until his death. He was chairman from 1957 to 1958 and from 1962 until his death.

He was called to be president of Union Theological in 1955. He was president of the American Association of Theological Schools from 1960 to 1962.

He literally died in his office (November 17, 1966) as he left a continuing education seminar on the state of the church, which he had opened and introduced with his accustomed dignity and poise.

II

How then shall we assess this life that we now declare to be our tradition, our family history? First of all, it must be said that any real assessment belongs only to God, but we can and we shall say what he meant to us. And we believe this witness is true.

James Jones was a great human being. He was a very secure and confident human being. Not because he had more wealth than some, not because he was clever and brighter than some, but because he knew that he was a child of God, whose life was rooted in the divine intention and whose worth was guaranteed by God.

He was afraid of no human being, and he knew that the powerful are also fragile and frail. He could be, when the occasion demanded, a feisty human being. Edward Grant once said to me that James Jones in a remarkable way used the mystique of money in the service of the kingdom. Yet the real reason he had confidence in the presence of any person or persons, no matter how powerful, was not that he thought he could stand on the same ground with them, which he surely did believe, but because he, as a child of God, spoke on behalf of the work of God. He was cautious, but he was never intimidated.

James Jones was never overwhelmed by problems. In part, he trusted his ability, but more fundamentally, it was again his faith. Those of us who were on the faculty had the security of believing that if something went wrong, James Jones could take care of it.

He was not only a secure human being; he was also an authentic person. He did not hide behind a facade.

His life had a dignity that was simple and plain but unmistakable. I suppose he was something of an aristocrat, yet he was a Presbyterian, not an Episcopal aristocrat.

He believed quality was a human virtue. "If you cannot go first class, do not go," he would say. And he had reference more to the dignity and the competence of life than to physical comfort. He knew God could forgive sin, but he doubted even God could forgive vulgarity, crudeness, or slovenliness.

He embodied the virtues of the tradition of which he was a part: courage, dignity, simplicity, and authenticity, and an abhorrence of the pretentious, the pompous, the contrived, and the artificial.

James Jones was a churchman. To be James Jones was to be the church, and in particular the Presbyterian church. The vocation to be the church manifested itself in many ways.

First of all was the honor in which he held the church of the living God. He knew that where the word of God was heard, in spite of poverty, there was the church of the living God, creator of heaven and earth. No minister, however celebrated, has a right to refuse a call because of its humble character.

Second was the priority that he gave to preaching, teaching, and pastoral care. In comparison with these tasks, everything else was secondary.

Third was a profound sense of call. He disliked self-seeking, especially in the church. You do not seek church office; this was his conviction. His sense of call was so great he never understood those who needed help in getting a call, or how much his own abilities and identity helped the Holy Spirit. Only God knows how he would have been revolted by the adoption of secular personnel practices by the church today. Can anyone who knew him imagine James Jones applying for a job or filling out a modern dossier? James Jones always believed that teaching at Union Theological Seminary was first a calling from God, a service to the church, and only secondarily a way of making a living. He had a deeply felt aversion for those who were self-righteous because of their "sacrifices" for the kingdom or the ministry or the church.

Fourth was a passion for missions. He embodied the great thrust of the missionary movement that began with William Carey: "Expect great things from God. Attempt great things for God." When he was president of Union Theological Seminary, no one could doubt that the missionary in the traditional sense of one who preaches the gospel, makes converts for Christ, and establishes the Christian community around this planet had a place of honor on this campus.

James Jones was also a statesman in theological education. He came to Union Theological Seminary with a sense of vocation. One suspects that he would rather have been doing other things. Yet he knew there is no more responsible task than the training of persons for the ministry. This was his vocation.

He gave himself with great devotion to the task. He spent inordinate amounts of time preparing for very simple responsibilities in which he represented Union Theological Seminary. He had a lofty sense of what it means to represent the seminary. Does anyone remember any introduction, however simple the occasion, that was not assiduously prepared?

And his work paid great dividends.

In eleven years he raised more money for Union Theological Seminary than any other person ever has, perhaps as much as all the other presidents combined. He established the relationships between the seminary and its constituency that still undergird the seminary today.

He was elected president of the American Association of Theological Schools and gained for Union Theological Seminary a respect that still abides.

In sum, James Jones was a great human being, a great churchman, a great theological statesman. Yet we best remember him as a man with a vocation from God to be the church, the people of God, and who embodied in his life in a remarkable way the Christian tradition in its Protestant, Puritan, and Presbyterian form. He did not have a job at Union Seminary; it is not enough to say he was loyal to Union Theological Seminary; he *was* Union Theological Seminary. So in our day when so many forces conspire to undermine this identity of person and community, we tonight affirm that James Jones embodied and handed on to us the tradition in which we live and do our work. And we do this by fixing to the wall the tablet enshrining his name.

"The Theology of Call and Ordination"
February 1972

Consultation on the Church's Use of Ordained Ministers
Montreat, North Carolina

The purposes of this paper are to (1) state briefly the theology of call and ordination as understood in the Reformed tradition, (2) relate this theology to the present crisis and malaise of the ministry, and (3) make certain proposals to alleviate the present crisis of the ministry.

I. Calling

The theological concept of call is firmly rooted in the New Testament. The Gospels present Jesus as the one who calls sinners to repentance and the weary and heavy-burdened to come to him for rest. The example of Jesus gathering his disciples and calling them from fishing boats and tax tables is forever the vivid memory of the church. Paul speaks of God as the One who calls men to be the church. In fact, calling appears so frequently in Paul's writings that it acquires a technical character. The Christian life is itself described as a calling. Christians are the called and the congregation is God's elect. The emphasis is on God, who in Jesus Christ does the calling to which man's faith and obedience is correlative.[1] Calling in the New Testament and in Christian theology has its primary and basic reference not to life work, but to Christian existence and to the church as the people of God.

Several important truths flow from the New Testament doctrine of calling. *The first is that all Christians are equally called.* The distinction between clergy and laymen is a fiction of church history. Martin Luther wrote,

---

[1]Cf. articles on *Kaleo* and related words in Kittle's *Theological Dictionary of the New Testament.*

Let everyone, therefore, who knows himself to be a Christian be assured of this, that we are all equally priests, that is to say, we have the same power in respect to the Word and the sacraments. However, no one may make use of this power except by the consent of the community or by the call of a superior. . . . And therefore this 'sacrament' of ordination, if it is anything at all, is nothing else than a certain rite whereby one is called to the ministry of the church.[2]

Calvin likewise emphasized the same truth: "In him we are all priests, to offer praises and thanksgiving, in short to offer ourselves and ours to God."[3] This priesthood of all believers is predicated upon the priesthood of Jesus Christ through whom all men have access to God. It means on the one hand that each Christian is accountable for himself and on the other hand accountable for his neighbor. There is no higher calling than the call to be the church, and in this call all the people of God share alike. Christians are equally Christian, and there is no higher order of existence.

This leads us a step further. *All Christians are called to ministry.* "All this is from God, who through Christ reconciled us to himself and gave us the ministry of reconciliation; that is, in Christ God was reconciling the world to himself, not counting their trespasses against them, and entrusting to us the message of reconciliation. So we are ambassadors for Christ, God making his appeal through us" (2 Cor. 5:18–20a). These words were addressed to the Corinthians as individuals and as the church. Every Christian has his ministry, but this ministry is not isolated from the ministry of the church. As the people of God, the church has the responsibility for the ministry of preaching, teaching, and pastoral care.

The rediscovery in our time of the old Protestant doctrine of the priesthood of all believers—of the universal responsibility of the people of God for ministry—has been an occasion for renewal in the life of the church. It has helped keep the church a community of participants and not simply a gathering of spectators, of proclaimers and not simply listeners. It has enabled Christians to unify their lives and to understand their daily work and their avocations as ways in which they express and embody their faith. It has been the occasion of innumerable deeds of kindness and proclamations of the gospel.

The priesthood of all believers and ministry of every Christian on the one hand must be clearly distinguished from the responsibility of the minister of the word on the other. Any confusion of the ministry that belongs

---

[2] *Luther's Works,* ed. A. R. Wentz and H. T. Lehmann, vol. 36 (Muhlenberg Press), 116.
[3] John Calvin, *Institutes of the Christian Religion,* LCC Edition IV, xix, 28.

to the Christian by virtue of his baptism and the ministry of the word that is authorized by ordination only serves to impoverish both ministries. Professor Robert Johnson quotes John Calvin on the "ministry of the laity" and then gives his own analysis.

> Must they go out into the streets to preach the truth of God? Must they mount pulpits and call meetings? No. Rather, inasmuch as the Lord calls to the ministry of his word Apostles or Prophets, or messengers, or whatever other name he is pleased to give to those whose voices he chooses to employ in public, it is not necessary that all men should everywhere attempt to do the same thing. It is not expedient. In fact, it is even unbecoming.
>
> What is required rather is that each should consider for himself what befits his own vocation and order. By pursuing the activity that is called for here, each will best discharge his duty. On those whom the Lord destines for the ministry of his Word he bestows, as it were, a kind of public character, in order that their voice may be heard in the light and rise trumpet-tongued above the house tops! Others, abstaining from the public office of Apostles, must prove themselves Christians by performing the duties of private life. (*Tracts and Treatises* 3, 366–67)

Elsewhere, Johnson writes,

> This would appear to be the point that is frequently needed in quarters where this emphasis is threatening to be more confusing than clarifying. The present (widely different) conceptions of "the ministry of the laity," "lay participation," and "church work," that are floating about freely in the American church almost invariably (even if unconsciously) tend to take the "public" or "special" ministry as the pattern—so that the image of the ideal layman, male or female, is simply a thinly disguised diminution of the prevailing image of the "ideal" pastor. (The consecrated layman is a clergyman writ small.) There are real possibilities here of finally outdoing the Anabaptists and introducing untold confusion.
>
> The ingredient most often missing is the doctrine of vocation. The "lay servant" (or minister), who has not been called by the church to participate in the "public ministry," *is* called by God through the church to serve Jesus Christ. This is not, however, a call to serve in addition to, but *in* his own vocation and order, by integrity and obedience in "the duties of private life."[4]

In Protestant and Reformed theology, calling also has reference to the minister of the word. This usage has justification in scripture, though it is subordinate to the calling that is the foundation of Christian existence and of the church. Beginning with Moses there have always been persons who

---

[4]Robert C. Johnson, "What Is the Christian Ministry" (mimeographed), 5–6.

were called to special functions in the life of the people of God. In the Old Testament there were the judges and the prophets, and in the New Testament Jesus calls out his disciples and sends them out on special missions. Paul was called to be an apostle, and Acts and the epistles tell of a variety of ministries that had their origin in a divine call. With significant unanimity the persons who performed special functions in the life of the church stood over against the community as well as the world in the name of God. For this reason Calvin describes the ministry not simply as a function, but as the gift of God to the church and spoke of the minister, in words that should fill every minister with awe, as the "mouth of God." Any rejection of this description, out of a commendable sense of fallibility, cannot, however, provide an escape from the awesome responsibility of the minister of the word, even if expressed in less bold language.

The calling that constitutes the ministry of the word is internal and external. The internal call "is the good witness of our heart that we receive the proffered office not with ambition or avarice, not with any other selfish desire, but with a sincere fear of God and desire to build up the church."[5] This internal call is essential, but Calvin does not deal with it at length, possibly because only God can finally stand in judgment here. Therefore, Calvin—as is his emphasis on the organized church—must allow for the "extraordinary" ministry.

The external call is, however, within the judgment of the church, and Calvin places great emphasis upon it. It is not enough for a person to believe that his call is authentic; his judgment must be approved and confirmed by the church. The outward and solemn call that has to do with the public order of the church is divided by Calvin into three parts. The first is the examination by which the church seeks to determine the candidate's knowledge of scripture and his capacity to communicate that knowledge in an edifying way, the integrity of his faith and his ability as a theologian, and finally whether his habits and conduct are appropriate to the faith. In the minister's life, learning must be joined with piety.

The second part of the call is election by the people in a context of awe and solemnity. The importance of the call of the people became so important a part of the outward call of the minister in the Reformed tradition that the *Book of Church Order* speaks of it as an inalienable right. The important point in this paper, however, is that something is lacking in the call of a minister until he has received the approbation of the people of God.

The third part of the call is ordination by which one is admitted to the

[5]Calvin, op. cit., IV, III, ii.

responsibilities of the ministry. Ordination will be discussed in a subsequent section of the paper. These three parts of the outward call have been preserved in the Reformed tradition and in our *Book of Church Order*.

II. Calling to Ministry

When God in Jesus Christ calls a man, he calls him to service and to ministry. This has become axiomatic in contemporary discussion of the church, but the purpose of the divine call in ministry therefore is not clear. For "ministry" and "service" are very general words, and while they usually denote and connote worthwhile activities, they do not necessarily in common speech convey a definitive Christian meaning. "Service" and "ministry," when applied to the Christian in general and especially to the minister of the word, must be defined by Jesus Christ. In particular they must be defined by ministry to any human need, but in the church we are especially concerned with human needs and service to human needs as defined by the New Testament witness to Jesus Christ.

The minister of the word is not the minister of any word, but of a particular word that was embodied in Jesus of Nazareth. The minister's preeminent task is the proclamation of this word in the three primary duties of preaching, teaching, and pastoral care. Professor Johnson has cogently argued that the verbal proclamation of the word will always have first importance in the ministry of the word.[6] There is no encounter with God in Jesus Christ apart from verbal communication, from testimony to what God has done in human history and the interpretation of the meaning of that event for human life today. By the word of preaching the church lives, and for the proclaiming of this word the church calls and ordains ministers. The administration of the sacraments has been limited to ministers simply because the church has believed they should be observed only in the context of competent teaching and preaching. The only quality that should usually distinguish ministers from other Christians is greater competence in preaching and teaching the Word of God, and by this competence—not by the possession of any magical powers—along with a life that is appropriate to the faith, humanly speaking a ministry is validated. The ministry of the word must not be confused with the ministry that belongs to every Christian, nor with some secular notion of ministry.

Competence in theology does not guarantee that one will be a good minister, but without competence in theology there is no responsible min-

[6]Johnson, op. cit., 19.

istry. No skill with techniques, no competence in the sciences and culture can compensate for theological incompetence. Indeed the minister's skill in fields other than theology will be duplicated and likely exceeded in the larger community. If a minister depends upon these skills, he will find that he is dispensable even in the life of the church. The one skill for which he is uniquely responsible and on which the church counts so much is his skill in interpreting the Word of God. The minister is the minister of the word, the Word incarnate in Jesus of Nazareth.

III. Ordination

(Due to limitation of space, ordination is discussed here only in relation to minister of the word.)

Ordination is the solemn act by which men are set apart for the Christian ministry. Various sections of the church have understood it in a variety of ways. Roman Catholicism and Greek Orthodoxy have regarded it as one of the seven sacraments, but the Society of Friends does not have any rite of ordination. This diversity in church practice is rooted in the New Testament itself. "In the New Testament there were large sections of the church where no special action was performed to assign a particular ministry, but it is equally certain that there are within the period covered by the New Testament other sections of the church that are familiar with such action."[7] Paul and Barnabas were sent out on their missionary journey with the laying on of hands (Acts 13:1–3). The appointment of the seven was likewise by laying on hands (Acts 6). Paul admonishes Timothy not to neglect the "gift you have, which was given you by prophetic utterance when the council of elders laid their hands upon you" (1 Tim. 4:14). Again Paul warns Timothy not to be hasty in the laying on of hands (1 Tim. 5:22).

In the Reformed tradition Calvin did not regard rites of installation or ordination as indispensable. In defense of Poullain, the minister of the Church of Frankfort, he asked if "the inhabitants of the place assembling themselves with him and listening to his doctrine do not in point of fact elect him, though the customary formalities may have been neglected."[8] But Calvin could also write, "The laying on of hands, by which ministers are consecrated to their office, I do not quarrel with them for calling a sacrament."[9] In the Ordinnances of Geneva ordination is a ceremony and

[7]Eduard Schweizer, *Church Order in the New Testament* (S.C.M. Press), 25b.
[8]John Calvin, *Letters,* vol. 3, 242.
[9]———, "True Method of Giving Peace and of Reforming the Church," *Tracts,* vol. 3, 291.

in his primary discussion of ordination in the *Institutes* it is a rite.[10] Charles Hodge defined ordination as "the public, solemn attestation of the judgment of the church that the candidate is called of God to the ministry of reconciliation; which attestation authorizes his entrance on the public discharge of his duties."[11]

The *Book of Church Order* defines ordination as "the authoritative admission of one duly called to an office in the church of God, accompanied with prayer and the laying on of hands, to which it is proper to add the giving of the right hand of Christian fellowship."[12]

Two questions must be raised concerning ordination. Is ordination necessary? Does ordination confer an indelible character? In answer to the first question Martin Luther declared with great emphasis that the Word of God is alone essential to the existence of the church. While the Reformed tradition, certainly from Calvin on, placed great emphasis upon church order, there is no confusion as to the fact that the church exists where the word is heard, believed, and obeyed. God is not limited to any order of the ministry, and in a particular situation God will "raise men in an extraordinary manner to restore the church."[13] In the Poullain case the reality of ministry took precedence over order. The church does not depend upon its ministry but upon the Word of God alone.

Ordination is not therefore insignificant. It confers no peculiar status, and it grants no "power" that does not belong to any Christian. Yet it is the church's way of ordering its life so that the Word of God will be preached and taught with competence, the sacraments responsibly administered, and pastoral care exercised with integrity. The emphasis placed upon ordination and the ministry in this sense by Calvin, by the Westminster Assembly, and by the Reformed tradition generally leads to the conclusion that on the human level nothing is so critical in the life of the church as a competent and dedicated ministry. This ministry is not in competition with the ministry that belongs to every Christian by baptism. Indeed, the ministry of the word is crucial for the coming into being of the ministry of Christians generally. The ministry may have assumed a relatively greater emphasis in Presbyterianism than in other traditions because of the Reformed emphasis on preaching, teaching, and the life of the mind in the service of God.

[10]Cf. Calvin, *Institutes* IV, xix, 28.
[11]Charles Hodge, *Discussions in Church Polity,* 144; Cf. J. H. Thornwell, *Collected Writings,* vol. 4, 92ff.
[12]*Book of Church Order* (Presbyterian Church [US]: 1970), 23–4.
[13]*The French Confession of Faith,* 1559, XXXI.

The Reformed answer to the question"Is Ordination necessary?" must be that it is not essential but is highly useful and not to be denigrated.

Does ordination confer an indelible character? If one is once ordained, is he always ordained? Martin Luther answered the question with a decisive "No." "That fiction of an 'indelible character' (is) a laughingstock. I admit that the pope imparts this 'character,' but Christ knows nothing of it; and a priest who is consecrated with it becomes the life-long servant and captive, not of Christ, but of the pope, as in the case nowadays." . . . "So I cannot understand at all why one who has been made a priest cannot become a layman. . . ."[14]

There is in principle no reason that ordination may not be laid aside, at least in Reformed theology. God who calls a man to the ministry of the word may call him to a different ministry. In practice, however, there was from the beginning a strong conviction that the ministry was a lifetime vocation, that those who entered it did so with this understanding, and that the laying aside of ordination was desertion.[15] This understanding of the ministry became part of the ethos of the church.

The lifetime character of the vocation of the minister was rooted in solid facts of psychology and experience. The experience is indelible, as is the case with all experiences. Once a man is a minister, he is eternally the man who was once a minister. Furthermore, there is some question whether a person can make the kind of commitment the ministry usually requires if he does not intend for it to be a lifetime commitment. Moreover, the culture of the sixteenth, seventeenth, and eighteenth centuries when this ethos developed was relatively static. Until the twentieth century, change was unexpected; life was expected to go on being as it always had been. The writings of Robert J. Lifton and Alvin Toffler have sufficiently documented that our culture is radically different. The notion that laying aside ordination is always culpable, always desertion, is simply unwarranted by the facts of experience. The general expectation in the church that the ministry is a lifelong vocation may imprison men today, just as Luther said Roman doctrine imprisoned them in the sixteenth century.

IV. The Crisis

The crisis of the ministry is preeminently a crisis of faith and meaning. This is a crisis of our culture, but it is preeminently the problem of the minister.

---

[14] *Luther's Works,* op. cit., 117.

[15] James L. Ainslie, *The Doctrines of Ministerial Order in the Reformed Churches of the 16th and 17th Centuries,* (Edinburgh: T. & T. Clark), 191ff.

For the work of the minister is difficult, indeed impossible, when faith in God erodes. The death-of-God theologies as well as sociological studies point to the seriousness of this crisis. All ministers must pray, "Lord, I believe; help thou my unbelief," and all ministers are saved by grace through faith. This ultimate judgment under which all ministers stand with all other human beings must not, however, obscure the responsibility of the office of the minister of the word. The ultimate judgment that no man's faith is perfect must not eclipse the proximate judgment that the measure or the level of faith is significant in the ordering of the church's life. A wavering faith in the life of a church member should be accepted, understood, and hopefully overcome in the church that lives by grace and not by the merit of its belief. But the wavering of faith in the minister may incapacitate him for the function to which he has been called and for which he is supported by the church. Hence the erosion of faith in the life of the minister is always more serious for church order than the erosion of faith in the life of a Christian as such.

Note, however, that the minister does not simply proclaim his own faith. He proclaims the faith of the church, which is not subject to the vagaries of his own life. And he continually tests his own proclamation by the Word of God embodied in Jesus of Nazareth, as attested in scripture. Nevertheless, unless this faith of the church is in significant measure the living faith of the minister, the tasks of the ministry become impossible.

The temptation when faith erodes is to seek meaning in places other than the gospel. The organization, the liturgy, even social action may become escapes from the crisis of faith. A Christian faith that does not express itself in the struggle for justice is fraudulent, but a faith that is primarily social action is dead. The questions of war, race, and poverty, as important as they are, are all subordinate to the question "Did the Lord God, creator of heaven and earth, if there is such a god, become incarnate in Jesus of Nazareth?" The answer to this question gives meaning to the organization, the liturgy, and social action. Therefore, the basic crisis in the church is always, and particularly in our day, the crisis of faith.

The church must take with utmost seriousness and never as a perfunctory performance the question put to candidates, "Do you, as far as you know your own heart, believe yourself to be called of God to the office of the ministry of the word?" and to candidates for ordination, "Have you been induced, as far as you know your own heart, to seek the office of the holy ministry from love of God and a sincere desire to promote his glory in the gospel of his son?" Martin Luther put this very well in that remarkable thesis sixty-two of October 31, 1517: "The true treasure of the church is the most holy gospel of the glory and grace of God."

The crisis of the ministry is also a crisis of life. Again it cannot be said too clearly that ministers are men who are saved by grace through faith. The contemporary minister has known this, and many of the artificial and false claims on the minister have been removed. Yet it is very interesting that precisely when ministers have been claiming the right to life like other men, the counterculture has raised its protests against experts who do not embody their expertise.[16] The counterculture's revolt is not directed primarily against the ministry, but certainly the ministry must take the protest seriously. It is not likely that experts will be taken seriously unless they in some significant measure embody their expertise. One sign of the crisis in the church and in the ministry is the reluctance of presbyteries to deal seriously with crises of faith in the form of heresy and the crises of life in the form of immorality and broken obligation. In part this reluctance grows out of a revulsion against self-righteousness, which is commendable. But in part, must we not admit, it grows out of a loss of certainty about the revelation of God and his will for human life.

The crisis of the ministry is a crisis of purpose. Is the mission of the church to comfort or to challenge, to cope with reality or to change society? Is the gospel gift or demand?[17] Unfortunately the mission of the church has sometimes been defined in practice either to comfort or to challenge, though in theory most would insist that it is always both. In practice a faith that expresses itself in the struggle for justice and peace and in the relief of human suffering is difficult to realize. Yet whenever a ministry exhausts the gospel in giving comfort or whenever it exhausts the gospel in changing society, the consequences for the minister's well-being are disastrous.

The crisis of the ministry is a crisis of competence. A fundamental justification for a professional ministry is competence in preaching, teaching, and pastoral care. The minister today is better trained than ever in the history of the church, but not better trained in relation to the general competence level of the congregation. A century ago it could be assumed that the Presbyterian minister was generally the best trained person in his community. This is no longer true.

[16]Theodore Roszak, *The Making of a Counter Culture.*
[17]Jeffrey K. Hadden, *The Gathering Storm in the Churches* (Doubleday) 6ff.

The one competence that the minister has that is not duplicated anywhere else in society is that of interpreter of scripture and theologian. This competence determines how well he or she does the three indispensable tasks of the pastoral ministry: preaching, teaching, and pastoral care which is more inclusive than counseling. The minister's competence as an organizer, promoter, fund raiser, counselor, and social action leader are duplicated and many times exceeded elsewhere in the community. The one competence that the minister must have to maintain his own respect and the respect of society, to say nothing of performing his specific task, is that of theologian. Yet it is precisely this competence that erodes amid the general pressures of the ministry. Presbytery examinations make it abundantly plain that many ministers go for years without reading any really serious books in theology and perhaps lose the capacity to do so. A conference on the ministry must take seriously the polls that indicate a decline in the public respect for the ministry.

The general malaise of the ministry is complicated by the crisis of the system. The overwhelming demands of a pastorate that keep the minister from his primary responsibility, the experience of isolation and loneliness, the mismatches of pastor and congregation, and the difficulty in changing pastorates all conspire to break the minister's spirit and to rob his life of a sense of direction and purpose. Yet persons in many occupations face these same problems. The minister should not exaggerate his problems in relation to other persons in our society.

V. Proposals

The assignment for this paper called specifically for concrete proposals for the ordering of the ministry. The first two proposals have to do with the life of the church and minister and cannot be legislated, but we can at least hope for their realization. The remaining proposals can become part of the church's ordering of its life.

A Reordering of Priorities

Joseph Sittler has written of the maceration of the minister.[18] The minister today is literally chopped to bits by the multiple demands upon his

---

[18] *The Church and Its Changing Ministry,* ed. Robert Clyde Johnson. The General Assembly of the United Presbyterian Church in the United States of America, 79ff.

time and life, demands that keep him from his primary tasks of preaching, teaching, and pastoral care. The priority of the gospel and the proclaiming of the gospel in preaching, teaching, and pastoral care—the subordination of everything in the life of the church to this gospel—requires discipline on the part of the minister and on the part of the congregation. Yet effective Christian action in society and meaningful organizational life are only possible if rooted in a community life of faith, love, and hope. The renewal of the church must begin with a resolution on the part of the congregation as well as the minister to reorder the priorities so that the work of the minister and the life of the church are subordinate to the gospel.

A Ministry That Lives by Grace

Ministry is a gift of grace. The minister also lives by grace. Indeed the ministry is possible only if the minister knows that his ministry is finally saved by grace through faith. Unless the minister balances the command to be perfect as his Father in heaven is perfect with the promise of forgiveness, he shall become either a fanatic in his self-righteousness or a despondent soul in the awareness of his failures. On the other hand, if he does not balance the promise of forgiveness with the command to be perfect in his ministry, he shall become a freeloader on the generosity of his congregation without the respect of God or man. The minister is not saved by his success, but by the grace of God even in his ministry. Indeed the ministry is possible only in this faith.

The Provision of a Probationary Status Before Ordination, Similar to the Provisions for Licensure Previously Provided by the *Book of Church Order*

Traditionally the probationary period offered the candidate for the ministry an opportunity to test his gifts and skills and the church an opportunity to register its approval or disapproval. Today the problems of vocational decision provide an additional reason for such a probation. Probation would provide the candidate further time to make his vocational commitment, and it would confront him with the realities of the ministry in a degree that is not possible in seminary internships. The probationary period should not extend for more than three years with a renewal for one year. Provision for careful supervision by presbyteries will be essential for the usefulness of a probationary period.

Provision for the Temporary Laying Aside of the Active Exercise of the Privileges and Responsibilities of Ordination

This provision should allow a minister to engage in a nonchurch vocation without the responsibilities of ordination. Such a withdrawal would be for a limited period of time, probably one year, subject to review and renewal by the presbytery. It would include withdrawal from membership in presbytery, from the right to administer the sacraments and to officiate at weddings, and provide for membership in a local church designated by the presbytery at the request of the person whose ordination is temporarily laid aside.

Provision of Clear Guidelines for Active Membership in Presbytery and for the Minister of the Word

While the determination of the privilege of continuing as a minister of the word must finally be the judgment of presbytery, useful guidelines can be formulated. These may include such tests as the following:

• Is the minister's work subject to supervision of a church court? It may be necessary for presbyteries to create committees to exercise some supervision over certain types of work that are outside the boundaries of church courts, somewhat after the example of the committee on chaplain in the military. There does not appear to be adequate reasons for a minister to retain the active privileges and responsibilities of ordination, at least over a period of time, unless he is accountable in some way to church courts for his work.

• Is proclaiming the gospel integral to his work? Good and useful work that is the responsibility of every Christian does not in itself qualify one for the responsibility of minister of the word. Furthermore, the ministry is not defined by lifestyle or status, but by function, though the church requires a lifestyle appropriate to Christian faith. Ordination is given for functions that are important for the church's life. Ordination has no relation to work outside the organized church. The minister of the word in Presbyterian polity makes sense only in the context of the church's ordering of its life so that certain functions are performed with competence, decency, and order. When this responsibility is not exercised, the ministry can only be interpreted as a lifestyle or status and not as a function.

Provision for Laying Aside Ordination

The provisions of the present *Book of Church Order* are only partially adequate. Even if the church does not wish to minimize the lifetime dimensions of the commitment at ordination, there must be recognition that men make vocational mistakes with no culpability, that changing situations—some physical, some social and psychological—make it desirable for a man to lay aside the responsibilities of ordination. The church should provide opportunity for this to be done with dignity and with an appropriate ceremony. The decision to lay aside ordination should never be done lightly and only after a period of waiting and of consultation with the presbytery. The church should also provide, perhaps only on the assembly or synod level, help in making the transition and finding a new vocation. Reinstatement of ordination would require meeting the standards of ordination, including examinations.

Provision for Continuing Education

Unquestionably a feeling of incompetence contributes to the malaise of the ministry. Many of the pastoral activities that pay immediate dividends do not contribute to the growth of the minister. Hence special provision must be made for growth as a churchman and as a theologian. A plan that would require churches to pay to the treasurer of presbytery a sum of $150 to $200 annually and accumulative for a period of three years to finance the continuing education of the minister in some program approved both by the session of the church and presbytery would provide a foundation for a solid program of continuing education. Any viable program must provide financial aid and some guarantee that serious study will be done.

Increased Attention to Nurture of Candidates for the Ministry

Many problems in the ministry arise because persons in responsible positions have been kind rather than honest in the nurturing of candidates for the ministry. Other problems have arisen out of a mystical and romantic view of the ministry that has minimized questions of competence. Problems in the ministry may be prevented by such provisions as these:

• A denominational program to provide for the careful testing and examination of candidates for the ministry. This program may be supplemented at presbytery level, but it would provide a minimal base.

• Support for a high level of competence in theological education. A call to the ministry is not a call to be Christian. That is presupposed. It is a call to perform a function that requires a high level of personal and intellectual competence. Piety, as indispensable as it is, is not a substitute for competence. Theological seminaries must be encouraged by church courts to insist on levels of competence appropriate to the responsibilities of the ministry.

• Serious attention to presbytery examinations for ordination or licensure. It is a well-known fact that presbytery examinations for ordination for the ministry of the word are not taken with the same seriousness as medical or legal examinations in most states. This fact seriously reflects on the minister's image of himself and on the church's awareness of the responsibility of the minister. Consideration should be given to establishing a set of examinations for ordination on the denominational level. The denominational examination should not relieve presbytery of its responsibility. Ordained ministers transferring to the Presbyterian Church U.S. should be required to take the denominational examination, unless at their ordination they had passed a similar examination.

• The vows for candidacy, probation, and ordination should only be taken in the context of solemnity and seriousness. The busy rush of the average presbytery meeting is hardly the proper context.

Establishment of Presbytery
Committees on Ministerial Development

This committee should have responsibility for continuing education, ministerial morale, spiritual enrichment, sustenance, and career counseling. This committee could also include responsibility for candidates.

Consideration of the Usefulness
of "Tent-Making" or Part-time Ministries

The evidence for and against the usefulness of "tent-making" ministries is ambiguous. There is no clear evidence as to the extent of their usefulness in solving the problem of pastorless churches. There is also some evidence of dangers and problems in "tent-making" ministries. A formal proposal could institutionalize the practice of having two "jobs," both providing financial remuneration without solving any problems. The ministry as a "part-time job" has serious limitations. An authentic *non-stipendiary* ministry of one who has met the educational standards of the ministry has possibilities. Hence the proposal here is simply to keep the possibility of some form of "tent-making" ministry open. "Tent-making" ministries must be honest and not a cover for two salaries. Paul earned his living and preached without stipend (Acts 18:3).

"Reformed Theology and the Style of Evangelism"
1973

Presbyterian General Assembly Mission Board

The responsibility to bear witness to the gracious presence of God in Jesus Christ "in Jerusalem and in all Judea and Samaria and to the end of the earth" has been the perennial task of the Christian community from the beginning. But the style and form of evangelism has varied according to time and place. There is no one way of evangelism, as the history of Christians witnessing and confessing their faith makes very clear. The life of the Christian community has been and is enriched by a variety of evangelistic styles and by multiple theological confessions.

There is, however, a limit to possible Christian theologies, and the pre-eminent theological task of the church is to test its proclamation by the word of God in Jesus Christ, as attested in scripture, to see that it is within the boundary. There is also a limit to the legitimate styles of evangelism. Some styles of evangelism corrupt and others strengthen the witness, but more significantly, style always betrays the real content. "There is an intimate but seldom seen connection between a person's thought and his style, which Alfred North Whitehead defined precisely as the 'ultimate morality of mind.'"[1]

The purpose of this paper is to relate Reformed theology to the form and style of evangelism. The paper presupposes that evangelism as shaped by Reformed theology is a valid and effective form of evangelism, but it does not presuppose that such form of evangelism is the only form that has validity or effectiveness. It is hoped that this proposal will be the occasion for self-criticism in the work of evangelism and for renewal of theological and ecclesiastical life in the Reformed tradition.

---

[1]Roger Hazelton, *New Accents in Contemporary Theology* (New York: Harper & Brothers, 1960), 20.

I

Reformed theology has never been precisely defined, and its boundaries are uncertain. There is no one normative Reformed theology. Here the term is taken in a general sense to indicate the theological perspective that had its origin with Zwingli, Bullinger, and Calvin in sixteenth-century Switzerland and that has been maintained by such theologians as William Ames and Turretin in the seventeenth century, by Edwards in the eighteenth, by Hodge in the nineteenth, and by Karl Barth and Emil Brunner in the twentieth. In order to sharpen its focus, this paper is based specifically on the theological works of Calvin. The most distinguishing characteristics and emphases of classic Reformed theology as embodied in the theology of Calvin were

1. The lordship and sovereignty of God
2. History as the working out of the purposes of God
3. Simplicity in style
4. The importance of theological knowledge and understanding
5. The Christian life as the embodiment of the purposes of God and conformity to his will
6. The importance of church organization

Each of these emphases influences the form and shape of evangelism.

The Lordship of God. For Calvin the most important fact is God, and the most important task is the honor and the service of God. This is the important truth that older churchmen tried to convey in that strange question alleged to have been put to candidates for the ministry. Are you willing to be damned for the glory of God? However one may judge the merits of the question, it clearly indicated that something is more important than the salvation of one's soul. The question exposed the self-centeredness of those whose own righteousness is too precious and who are excessively concerned with the salvation of their souls. The question also suggests there is something good about the cautious piety of those who seek to do God's will and leave the salvation of their souls to him.

Karl Barth, the great Reformed theologian of the twentieth century, comments that in the theology of Tholuck, a German revival theologian of the nineteenth century, "the religious individual cannot be more important, all the rest cannot be more shapeless, biography cannot replace theology more emphatically, the Christian cause cannot be more thoroughly taken up into the person of the Christian man."[2] For this reason, Barth goes on to say, revival theology can never be great theology. It is too absorbed with the state of the human soul and too little involved with the great reality of God. Revival theology is too eager to report the anatomy of feeling—or the state of the soul—to be able to proclaim adequately the mighty act of God.

The New Testament scholar, E. C. Colwell, recently observed that in the New Testament,

> We have too little from Jesus about Jesus. He lost Himself in devotion to God. Long before his execution on the cross, he lost his life. Thus he became—to our bafflement—an incarnation of the saying "He who would save his life must lose it."
>
> He talked about our obligation to God, not about God's love for us. The First Commandment is the central focus of his teaching. And because he had integrity, he talked about that and the second, derivative commandment and not about himself. Love of God came first: love of neighbor followed.
>
> Because of the consistency of this priority in his message, it is difficult to cast his mantle over the current exhortation to find yourself first. The pagan Greeks had a word for it (*Gnothi seauton*), but the good news of Jesus Christ does not. The Gnostics rejoiced in finding themselves, but the majority of Christians would have none of it as the prime quest. For them, as for their Lord, the primal quest was to find God."[3]

Evangelism can never be primarily a means of personal identity or even of personal salvation. It is first of all the acknowledgment of God's gracious presence and loyalty to his cause.

Calvinism also has been characterized by a passionate conviction that purposes of God are being worked out in history. Predestination, writes Eustace Percy in his biography of John Knox, refers not so much to the ultimate destinies of heaven and hell, but to human life in history.[4] The elect person has been called to fulfill the purposes of God in time and space. For this reason the Calvinists became the great converters of culture and transformers of civilization. Christopher Dawson, the Roman Catholic historian of culture, declares that no Christian community has ever exceeded

---

[2]Karl Barth, *Protestant Theology in the Nineteenth Century, Its Background and History* (Valley Forge, Pa.: Judson Press, 1973), 511.

[3]From *New or Old?* by Ernest C. Colwell, (Philadelphia: Westminster Press, 1970). Used by permission.

[4]Lord Eustace Percy, *John Knox* (London: Hodder and Stoughton, 1937) 108ff.

the Calvinists in their understanding of the cultural and historical role of the Christian.[5] Wherever they went they carried with them the vision of holy community, and they sought to transform society into the Christian community.

The holy community was never fully realized in Geneva or Scotland or seventeenth-century Massachusetts. The result was despair. In the context of disappointed hopes, Calvinists were tempted to think of the Christian life as a lonely pilgrimage through this vale of tears and to replace vision of the Christian commonwealth with personal evangelism, conceived as snatching lost souls from the burning.

Another temptation was to define the Christian life exclusively in terms of personal piety instead of responsibility for society. Reformed theology has always been concerned with personal piety, with evangelism as the salvation of the individual soul, and with eternal life as the fulfillment of human existence. But Reformed theology can never be satisfied with the definition of the Christian life simply in these terms. In fact, the abstraction of these dimensions of the Christian life from the fully orbed understanding of salvation that Reformed theology once knew makes their integration back into Reformed theology difficult. Once we define the Christian life as personal piety—as personal evangelism and the salvation of the individual soul—understanding that this is not classical Reformed theology is very difficult. By the same token, the more recent definition of the Christian life simply in terms of social responsibility, of evangelism as social action, and of Christian life as authentic existence in the world also makes it difficult to recover the full dimensions of Christian existence as Reformed theology has understood it.

A third characteristic of Reformed theology is simplicity. Over and over again in liturgy, in lifestyle, in theological writing, Calvin insisted on simplicity. Calvin's intention was never to use two words when one word would do. He did not gild the lily. He disliked embellishment and ornateness. A sermon, a person, a building should be able to communicate who and what they are without ostentation. Simplicity for Calvin was a synonym for integrity. Reality must not be obscured by words, clothing, craftiness, or pompousness of any sort.

Closely related to this emphasis on integrity and simplicity is Calvin's rejection of magic in religion. Magic is on the one hand man's effort to master and control God by fastening the infinite and indeterminate to the

[5]Christopher Dawson, *The Judgment of the Nations* (New York: Sheed and Ward, 1942), 44ff.

finite and determinate. If God, who is creator of heaven and earth, can in some way be tied to what man can control in sacrament, liturgy, or evangelistic procedure, then God himself can be controlled and manipulated. The control of God was the province of the ancient medicine man with his strange ways. This was also the temptation of medieval Catholicism in development of the sacramental system. And it is the peril of some contemporary forms of evangelism as the movie *Marjoe* illustrates.

The human counterpoint of magic as the attempt to manipulate and control God is magic as the endeavor to manipulate human beings and to bypass conscious, responsible decision. Modern psychology has made us aware of the significance of nonverbal communication and of the influence of many forces on personal life that are outside the range of personal awareness. Yet before the days of modern psychology, Luther and Calvin insisted that faith—a responsible, personal decision—was essential to participation in the sacraments. Today the possibility of bypassing conscious personal decision through personal charisma, oratory, or sacraments has been greatly enhanced by the skills of modern psychology and the techniques of modern communication, including mass media. The old Protestant slogan, "No sacrament without faith," must be enlarged to include no evangelism without responsible, conscious, personal decision.

Evangelism in the Reformed tradition can only be conceived in simple, direct, and unadorned fashion. The baroque, or any attempt to overwhelm, is off-limits. The rhetoric of Reformed evangelism will be primarily its content, not the medium of its expression. The medium will express, not obscure, the content. It will seek to convince, not to beguile. Above all, it will be honest and authentic. Reformed evangelism will always be self-critical, subjecting its content and method to continual examination. Only in this way can the evangelist guard against becoming the charlatan. All who have seen the movie *Marjoe* know how effective charlatanry can be and how imperative self-criticism is for those who in any sense speak for God.

A fourth characteristic of the Reformed theology has been an emphasis on knowledge and understanding. Catechetical instruction was one of the primary means of evangelism in Geneva, and admission to the Lord's Table was based on a commitment of life and knowledge of the faith. While Calvin insisted that the knowledge of faith is existential—more of the heart than of the head—he never trusted emotion or feeling when not subjected to critical reflection and rational understanding. While he rejected curiosity and speculation in theology, he clearly stands in the tradition of those who insist that faith seeks understanding. He knew that any religion that requires the sacrifice of the integrity of the human mind with its critical functions is bad religion, for God is the creator of the human mind.

Calvin was an intellectual, believing that all truth comes from God and that the life of the mind may be an important service to God. As a humanist, he did not disdain rational procedure and disciplined study. He did not reject intuition or the significance of direct experience as avenues to truth, but he insisted that disciplined intelligence and direct experience should never be separated. For that reason, he emphasized that Christians should know intellectually as well as personally what they believed.

One of the primary forms that evangelism took in Calvin's Geneva was teaching. The catechetical class was the condition for admission to the Lord's Table. The sacraments were to be administered only in the context of teaching. Preaching in Geneva was instruction in scripture, theology, and Christian living. Indeed, the *Institutes of the Christian Religion* were written as a guide for Bible study and for an intellectual grasp of Christian faith. Calvin regarded the founding of an educational system in Geneva as one of his greatest accomplishments. For Calvin, learning and piety were always joined together.

Evangelism that is rooted in the Reformed tradition must be in large measure teaching. This does not mean that all teaching even in the church is evangelism. Teaching may be and sometimes is heretical in that it does not build up the life of the Christian community. Certainly Calvin knew this. He also knew and believed that there is no evangelism that is not also teaching.

A fifth characteristic of Reformed theology is a strong emphasis on the Christian life. The human focus of the Christian life was not self-understanding or the state of the soul or even the vision of God, but a life that embodied the purposes of God. Christian faith was a way of living, deciding, and acting in the world. The Christian person was the responsible person.

Martin Luther had said that the primary use of the law is to convince people that they are sinners and thus to turn them to Christ. In fact, Luther so emphasized the spontaneity of the Christian life that on occasion he could say that Christians no more need the law to tell them how to obey God than a husband needs a law to tell him how to love his wife. Calvin, however, insisted that the primary purpose of the law is to guide and stimulate the Christian in living the good life. He refused to separate law and gospel, as Luther had done. Even in the liturgy of the church he

294 John H. Leith

included the Ten Commandments after the prayer of Confession and the comfortable words promising forgiveness.

Calvin's emphasis on the law and on ethics led to unfortunate excesses of legalism when the Christian life was defined too exclusively in terms of law, to self-righteousness when Calvinists prematurely convinced themselves that they obeyed the law, and to obscurantism when they uncritically identified the law with a particular pattern of life. The failures of Reformed theology and the consequent caricatures of it should not obscure the real greatness of Calvin's vision of the Christian and the Christian society as embodiments of the purpose of God and of the achievements of that vision in history. No Christians have ever exceeded the Calvinists as shapers of culture and transformers of society.

Evangelism in the Reformed tradition must be concerned with sanctification and must never forget that the gospel includes the law. The call of the evangelist is not simply to an ultimate destiny, but to a way of life here and now in time and space.

II

The sixth distinctive characteristic of Reformed theology is its concern with the organized life of the church. Calvin devoted more than one-fourth of the *Institutes of the Christian Religion* to the "external means of grace." One of his most influential books, probably most influential next to the *Institutes*, was his Ecclesiastical Ordinances for the Genevan church. Private Christianity was no more a possibility for Calvin than it was for the New Testament. To be a Christian is to be the church. Baptism is incorporation into the life of the church. Evangelism is the means by which human beings are related vertically to the God and Father of our Lord Jesus Christ and by which they are horizontally integrated into the one holy, catholic, and apostolic church.

Evangelism in Reformed theology is always an activity of the church, though not necessarily of the church bureaucracy. It is never the work of a lone-star ranger snatching solitary individuals from the pit and turning them to heaven. Evangelism on the horizontal level is the work of people who are the church, inviting other people to share in the common life of the body of Christ.

Evangelism is incorporation into the community where the word of God is preached and heard and where the sacraments are offered and received. The simplest definition of the church is the community that hears the word of God in faith and obeys in love, for the sacraments are the gospel acted out.

There are many different kinds of communities, but the church differs from other communities in that its members share in a common life that is rooted in the word of God. The church is not an aggregation of believers but a communion that shares in common hopes, commitments, and lifestyles, common loves, and common actions.

The common life that is the church is no simple achievement. It cannot be programmed, summoned, or coerced. It is not always evident to human experience. In part, the Christian life is believing that the church exists, as the Apostles' Creed declares, when the reality is not so apparent. Yet the reality does exist, and to this common life, evangelism calls a person on the horizontal level. The dilemma of the evangelists is that they cannot guarantee the church, for the church, like salvation itself, is always the gracious gift of God. As Calvin put it, the church is the elect. The church is the work of the Holy Spirit and the work of Christian people, but it first of all is the work of God's free and sovereign Spirit.

Evangelism is incorporation into a community in which the members are members one of another and share with each other their gifts. One of the signs of the church is the common meal in which bread is shared. The importance of sharing bread cannot be minimized in a world that has such great extremes of wealth. But neither can other signs of the church as the communion of saints be minimized, as for example when the congregation gathers in the face of death to affirm faith that is greater than death, to affirm the reality of the church as a community against a threat to community, and to give real help to fellow members who have been bereaved of the physical presence of a loved one. In our new secular, pluralistic society, in which many of the traditional props that have supported people in crisis situations are gone, the church is the community that gives support to people as they share in the common life of the body of Christ.

Evangelism is incorporation into a community of theological discourse. Every person is a theologian by the sheer fact of humanity. Human existence is existence filled with decisions. Animals so far as we know do not make decisions. They simply follow their instincts and impulses. But before any person has been up three hours, he or she is compelled by the nature of existence to make decisions about life, about neighbors, about values. Christians are distinguished not by the fact that they live by faith but by the fact that they live by the faith that Jesus Christ is the revelation of God. In his light they seek to understand the common experiences of their lives. The church is the community in which people talk about life, its origin and its destiny, its meaning and its values, in the light of their common Christian conviction and under the norm of the Christian revelation.

Theology that is critical reflection upon the meaning of life and Christian theology that is reflection upon the meaning of existence in the light of God's presence in Jesus Christ is not undisciplined speech. It is not sharing personal opinions or making unsupported assertions. Theology is disciplined speech in a disciplined community. It is rooted in and loyal to the scriptures, which are the record of God's revelation. Theology is guided by the way in which Christians in all ages have understood that revelation. Theological discourse is, humanly speaking, the lifeblood of the church. Only as Christians engage in a common theological discourse can they embody the fullness of the church. Only in this way can the Christian community be distinguished from other communities, and only in this way can the Christian life be enriched, broadened, and deepened.

Evangelism is incorporation into a community of moral discourse. The Christian life is not following a party line; nor is it withdrawal from the political, social, or economic decisions of life. It is serious engagement with those issues in the light of faith commitments. The church is the place where the issues of the day can be analyzed, thought through, and acted upon in the light of the disclosure of God in Jesus Christ. The church is the community in which actual people are given real help in thinking through the real issues of their lives. It therefore has to be a community of moral discourse, as James Gustafson has said.[6] Again moral discourse is not undisciplined speech. It is not the sharing of personal opinions or unexamined convictions. It is disciplined discourse that is rooted in the Bible and the Christian tradition, and it takes place in the disciplined life of the Christian community.

Evangelism is incorporation into a community of worship. The one indispensable factor in the life of the church is the Word of God, and the high and central event in the life of the church is worship when the community gathers to hear the Word of God and to receive the sacraments, to adore, and to give thanks. Worship is the personal center of the community of theological discourse, of moral discourse, of mutual assistance and support. In worship, common life in a shared community is expressed in common prayer, hymns, and faith commitments.

Evangelism is incorporation into a community of being and action that embodies, however fragmentarily, the purposes of God for individuals and for the world. Karl Rahner, the Roman Catholic theologian, and Vatican Council II have rightly spoken of the church as the sacrament of the world.[7] It is the outward and visible sign, however broken, of the true reality of the

---

[6]James Gustafson, *The Church as Moral Decision Maker* (Philadelphia: Pilgrim Press, 1970), 84.
[7]Karl Rahner, *The Church and the Sacraments* (New York: Herder and Herder, 1963), 18–19.

world, and it exists to serve the world. The very existence of the church, as the sacrament of the world's true destiny, is a means of God's grace for the transformation of the world and for the healing of its wounds.

III

The great disparity between Calvin's Geneva and the last third of the twentieth century must be noted in any effort to relate evangelism and the Reformed faith. Between Calvin and twentieth-century Christians stands the greatest break in all of humanity's intellectual and cultural history: the scientific revolution and the Enlightenment. There is a far greater difference between the way modern people think about the world and the way Calvin thought about the world than between Calvin and the disciples of Jesus. Furthermore, the relation of the church to society is radically different now from what it was in Calvin's Geneva or from what it was just a few years ago in our own history. We have passed from the parish church in Christendom (or in our own immediate past from the Protestant church in Protestantdom) to the voluntary church in a free, pluralistic, secular, mobile, urban, industrial society that is mass-media-dominated— or as Martin Marty summarizes, from a society in which all the props of society support the church to a society in which few props support the church.

These two great changes are interrelated, and together they make the task of evangelism increasingly difficult. Less and less will society support specifically Christian styles of life. The church will have to become more and more responsible for its own life and for nurturing its own people, especially its young people and its married couples in the faith. In Calvin's words, "The church is the common mother of all the godly, which bears, nourishes, and brings up children to God, kings and peasants alike, and this is done by the ministry."[8]

Evangelism can no longer assume that the masses know the meaning of the great Christian words or that society will support Christian faith commitments. For this reason evangelism is humanly dependent upon the renewal of the reality of the church.

IV

In classical Reformed theology, evangelism was not an identifiable, discrete activity of the church. It was the total life of the church. Today certain

[8]John Calvin, *Commentary on Ephesians* 4:13.

particular activities may be called evangelism for the sake of convenience, but for Reformed theology and ecclesiology any such activity must be integral to the whole life of the church. Evangelism is the church reaching out and incorporating those on the outside into its life.

The renewal of the church, humanly speaking—and by the same token, the renewal of evangelism—depends upon the theological competence and dedication of its ministers more than it does upon any other single factor. There is no possibility of any evangelism congruent with classical Reformed theology that is not supported by and informed by a theologically competent minister and a theologically literate congregation. For this reason a great deal of the energy expended in seeking some new theology of evangelism or some modern technique of evangelism could more profitably have been used in basic Biblical and theological study. The same point must be made concerning studies of church management and the dynamics of groups. The church welcomes and uses all knowledge and techniques that are effective and agreeable to its convictions about God and man. But no mastery of group dynamics and process will ever make an evangelist out of a person who has not mastered the biblical material and who cannot or does not read serious theology.

Someone will protest that theology alone will not itself relate people to God or incorporate them into the church. This is true. Theology as an academic exercise or a parlor sport will not. But Calvin understood theology as a practical science, and he insisted that it must be understood and expressed in such a way as to illuminate life and to give meaning to common experience. Theology must speak of the grace of God in Jesus Christ in words that are intelligible. There is not as yet, nor is there ever likely to be, any substitute for the Christian, and particularly the minister, being a theologian.

Theology alone will not evangelize, for people must be engaged. Theology will evangelize only when it is confessed to actual people. In part this confession takes place through the life of the Christian community and its impact on the larger community. The early church made converts when those on the outside beheld in the church a life in which they wanted to share. Evangelism in this form continues to take place. Yet the church has always reached out through its members and invited those outside the life of the church to share in its common life. An old professor of pastoral theology used to say that a house-going preacher made a church-going people. The same is true in the wider context of evangelism. Calvin never faced this problem, for almost everyone in sixteenth-century Geneva was officially Christian. But it is likely to be increasingly our problem. For never in fifteen hundred years has there been so much freedom as now to be or not to be the church. As yet, no substitute has been found for individual Christians telling others about life and the grace they share in the church. Various forms of mass evangelism are supplements to, not substitutes for, personal evangelism in the context of the church.

V

Evangelism is the church's witness to the grace of God in Jesus Christ. No one has ever become a Christian apart from a witness who tells the story of God's love for that person in creation and redemption. Evangelism is the witness and the context in which a person comes to a knowledge of God in Jesus Christ—a knowledge that saves and transforms life. This knowledge of God's presence in Jesus Christ may come through years of gradual maturation in the church. It may come in a dramatic crisis that radically shifts the whole orientation of life. The work of evangelism is done when a person comes to confess that Jesus Christ is Savior and Lord.

God alone is the Savior. Neither the Christian community nor the witness saves except in an instrumental sense. No Christian tradition has emphasized this more than the Reformed. Yet this does not mean that human works are unimportant. Evangelism is the human works that have their warrant in the New Testament and that provide the ordinary occasion for human salvation.

Changes in our society make it critically important that the people who are the church must be very busy in the works of evangelism and Christian witness. For on the human level, the whole existence of the church is increasingly at risk in our society. Evangelism is telling a story. The stories that have shaped American life are now being challenged. On the secular level, chants on university campuses declare that Western civilization has got to go. The underlying assumption is that all cultures are equally good. In ecclesiastical and theological circles, pluralism is a new orthodoxy. The underlying assumption is not only that all forms of Christian faith are equally good, but that all religious stories have equal validity. The triumph of the Enlightenment is the notion that many roads lead to God.

Evangelism grows out of the conviction that in the providence of God, Jesus Christ is the Savior of the world, that on the cross he bore the sins of all people and that God raised him to be the Lord, not simply of the Christian community but of all human history. Evangelism is not just a church program or a technique but the passionate conviction that Jesus Christ is the Word made flesh for our salvation.

The church in recent years has had difficulty in saying that faith in Jesus Christ is *crucially* significant, not only for life on this planet but for human destiny. On the level of the church as the people of God, that is, the congregation, the issue is much clearer. *Apart from the passionate conviction that the story of the Bible culminating in Jesus Christ is my story and that God, in Christ, is my Savior, there is no convincing reason that a person should worship God in Christian churches or be the church at all.* Evangelism finally will become alive not through Assembly actions or bureaucratic pronouncements, but through the recovery of a passionate conviction.

<h1 style="text-align:center">VI</h1>

Evangelism, as shaped by the classical Reformed theology, is not a program nor a technique but the life of the church in its outreach and impact upon the world. Evangelism, understood in this way, should not be mistaken for the "old" evangelism, for the minister who is the preacher-teacher-church theologian, even in a broken way, has been a rarity. Congregations that have been communities of theological and moral discourse and that have understood their existence as the embodiment of the purposes of God have been equally rare. Yet they do exist. Whenever such congregations have come into being, they have been the result of years of responsible churchmanship. *This churchmanship is the real program of evangelism.*

Evangelism, as the work and the life of the church in the world, does not mean that programs, techniques, or group skills are unimportant. Theology is certainly no substitute for visitation, for one person telling another person about the grace of God. Neither is theology a substitute for such mundane matters as records or prospect lists or systems for discovering the new people in a community. But all of these are subordinate to the theological and ethical life of the community, which on the human level validates everything else.

It must be said again, as the conclusion for this paper, that evangelism is the work of the spirit of God who speaks when and where he chooses and whose work can be neither programmed nor guaranteed. There is, however, the promise of God; and if we in the church do certain things, then it is more likely that the Church, which is the gift of God's grace, shall grow in our midst.

"Address to the Bicentennial Meeting of the Synod of the Associate Reformed Presbyterian Church"

June 15, 1982

Address Delivered as Representative of the Presbyterian Church U.S. and of the World Alliance of Reformed Churches

You were gracious through your moderator to invite me here as the guest of the Bicentennial Synod. Hence, I would like first to express my personal gratitude to the synod for what it has meant to me through the years, and in particular to Erskine College. Dostoyevsky once said that one good memory is perhaps the best education. This very room (Lesesne Hall) holds many good memories for me. Here as a boy I listened to oratorical contests. Here, at a YMCA reception, I spent my first evening with the person who became my wife. On this platform I received my college diploma. In this building I had my first theological courses with Dr. R. L. Robinson. Many of Dr. Robinson's contemporaries in Due West would have been surprised at the breadth of his reading and with the ideas he entertained. In this building I had my first classes in Greek under Dr. Harold Raltson. And across the street, as a junior and a senior at Erskine College, I took every course that Dr. G. G. Parkinson taught in theology at the seminary. My, what a clear, sharp analytical mind he had! I hope I can make this further comment without being misunderstood. I have often wondered what impact he might have had if he had been teaching in the context of a wider audience. It is well to remember the early pioneers—Dr. Clark, for example—but also the Associate Reformed Presbyterian Church, which I remember was embodied in persons such as Dr. R. L. Robinson, Dr. G. G. Parkinson, and Dr. James P. Pressly, together with laypersons Edgar Long and Robert Galloway, among many others—all persons who in different ways were great human beings and great churchmen. And there are so many more to whom I am indebted as teachers and as friends.

But you are gathered here as a church court. And in addition to being invited as the guest of the synod, I have been asked to represent the

Presbyterian Church in the United States and the World Alliance of Reformed Churches. Hence it is incumbent upon us to talk quite specifically about the community and the tradition that have made us what we are and their fate in the modern world. As Presbyterians, each of us has at least four basic Christian identities.

1. Each of us is a Christian, sharing with all Christians the convictions of the ancient catholic church as embodied in the Apostles' Creed, the Nicene Creed, and the Chalcedonian Definition. We worship the triune God, whom we acknowledge as the unfathomable ground of our existence, our Creator, our Redeemer, and our Sanctifier. We share with all Christians that basic declaration of our faith, the Nicene Creed.

2. We are also here as Protestants, sharing and shaped by the convictions of Martin Luther's great writing of 1520: (a) the supreme authority of the Holy Spirit when speaking through scripture, (b) justification by grace through faith, (c) the priesthood of all believers, (d) the sanctity of the common life, and (e) the emphasis upon personal responsibility and decision, or the rejection of all magical attempts to get control of God or to bypass human decision.

3. We are also Reformed Protestants, in contrast to Lutherans, to Anglicans, and the left wing of the Reformation. This Reformed tradition has provided us the peculiar ethos and quality of our way of being Christian.

4. We are Reformed, Protestant Christians in the American context. Having been shaped by the American experience of the frontier and in a pragmatic, egalitarian society, we are Christians in somewhat different ways from persons anywhere else in all the world.

We would be different personalities, and we would be a different society if we were not heirs of the Christian, Protestant, Reformed traditions. We may add to that such experiences as the Puritan Revolution and the American frontier, with its revivalism and its camp meetings. Even in reacting against the revivals, we were shaped by them.

Possibly as many as seventy million Christians are Christian in the Reformed way, close to the number of Lutherans and certainly larger than the number of Methodists or Baptists or Anglicans. The value of the tradition, however, is not in its numerical strength, but in its theological and social commitments that have shaped us and made us the people we are. As a character in Steinbeck's *Grapes of Wrath* exclaims, "How do we know that it is us without our past?"

In the brief time allotted to me, I would like to make four comments concerning our tradition and our community.

First, we need to recover the importance of tradition. Thirty years ago, tradition could be taken for granted. Traditions were given to you by birth and by history. One could escape from traditions only through very courageous, very clever, very momentous actions, usually called revolutions. Today the situation is different. We have experienced in our time the end of the parish church in Christendom, and we now live in a free, secular, pluralistic, mobile, mass-media-dominated, urban society. The church has become a highly voluntary community, more voluntary than it has been in some sections of the Western world for fifteen hundred years. In fact, our society forces young people to choose the tradition in which and by which they will live. No society in the history of the human race has ever placed so much responsibility on the choosing of a tradition as does ours. Hence the question that we all face today is, How does the church transmit its traditions in so voluntary, so secular, so pluralistic, so mass-media-dominated a society?

Second, the greatest contribution we can make to society in our time and to the ecumenical church is to bring to it the treasures of our Reformed tradition. If we do not do this, no one else will. Lionel Trilling, the great teacher of English literature at Columbia University, once declared that his first responsibility as a teacher was to represent with integrity the tradition of English literature. If he did not do this, no one else would. Similarly, our society today shall be bereft of a great treasure if we do not represent to it the treasures of our peculiar way of being Christian.

Furthermore, we can do this better than we can do anything else. We cannot do better what the Baptists and Billy Graham do best. We cannot do better what the Orthodox or the Roman Catholics do best. Let us therefore be alert to the beguilements of the popular ideologies, of the shortcuts and the gimmicks that are always used by free operators, loose from any tradition, who flit around on the surface of history exploiting every emotional, social, or political crisis for ecclesiastical position and advancement. Let us beware of those who would rob us of our heritage while exploiting the resources that heritage has built. Let us not in the critical time in which we live sell our heritage for a mess of porridge that will turn to bitterness in our mouths.

Third, it is appropriate in a bicentennial celebration such as this to give thanks for the Scotch-Irish. We have a tendency to bypass Ireland on the way to getting back to Scotland. In actual fact, almost all Presbyterians in this area of the country came to America through the Protestant community in northern Ireland that had been established from the migration of the lowland Scots, the English Puritans, and the French Huguenots. The achievements of the Protestant community in northern Ireland as well as of the Scotch-Irish in America were notable. An Episcopalian from Charleston visited the back country of South Carolina in the late 1760s. He declared that the Scotch-Irish must be the most wretched of all the earth, desperately poor, dirty, uncouth, immoral, without religion, seditious, and with no respect for the king. He was right in part. They were surely seditious; they were without respect for the king; they were no doubt poor and dirty. But they were not immoral, nor were they without religion and a concern for learning. In the midst of their poverty, without government help of any kind, they carved out communities in the foothills of the Appalachians, and they built churches and educational institutions which still stand today from the Piedmont of Georgia to the Delaware River basin and westward into Ohio. Amid the traumas and difficulties of northern Ireland today, we ought to acknowledge our indebtedness to a great tradition that was bequeathed to us from the experience of Protestants in Ulster.

Fourth, a bicentennial celebration such as this, an emphasis upon the importance of tradition, calls attention to the significance of a learned and dedicated ministry. Without a learned and dedicated ministry, the preservation of a great tradition in the church is almost impossible. Humanly speaking, the well-being of the church depends more upon the competence and the dedication of its ministry than it does upon any other one factor. Presbyterians mightily shaped the history and the culture of this area of the country because one hundred years ago one could take for granted that the Presbyterian minister would usually be the best-trained person in the community. This can no longer be taken for granted. The education for ministers may have improved, but it has not improved as rapidly as has education and professional competence generally.

The training of ministers is not simply a matter for theological schools. There is an old saying that it takes two generations to produce a good shoe cobbler. Those of us who are first-generation ministers hope this is not necessarily true. And yet there is some truth in the fact that it does take two generations, generally, to produce a good minister. Students who come to theological seminaries having been nurtured in great church families bring with them a depth of understanding and wisdom that cannot be acquired in theological education, no matter how efficient it may be. Hence the provision of an adequate ministry is the concern not simply of theological schools, but of the homes of church people. I cannot document it, but I have a disconcerting notion that old established Presbyterian homes are sending fewer of their *ablest* sons and daughters into the Christian ministry.

All of us have been ordained by our baptism to the Christian ministry, which is embodied in our homes, in our activities in society, in our daily work. This ministry is of crucial significance. We have rightly emphasized it. Yet there is, practically speaking, no way for a great church to come into existence or to continue in existence without ministers of great technical, professional competence and a matching dedication to their calling. If we are to maintain our traditions in our kind of society, we shall have to give attention to calling our ablest young persons into the ministry of the word and to the nurture of them in our traditional church families and local congregations.

It is great to be alive in these awesome but wonderful days. But it is great to be alive because in the church we sing and confess, as I hope Associate Reformed Presbyterians always shall:

> . . . the Lord is God indeed;
> Without our aid He did us make;
> We are his folk, He doth us feed,
> And for his sheep He doth us take.
> . . . the Lord our God is good,
> His mercy is forever sure;
> His truth at all times firmly stood,
> And shall from age to age endure.
>   (*The Psalter,* Psalm 100)

PART NINE
BRIEF EDITORIALS,
PRESBYTERIAN OUTLOOK

"If Not by Grace, Then by Law"
November 18, 1963

It is a sad and tragic commentary on the performance of countless people of obvious Christian motivation that in all too many instances delay in adjusting to inevitable new patterns in race relations is so prolonged that the possibility of honor is lost.

One instance of this is seen in the recently reported resolution of Mecklenberg Presbytery where in an almost unanimous action the body pleaded with the trustees of the Presbyterian Hospital in Charlotte to open its facilities on a basis of need rather than on race (*Outlook*, Nov. 4).

The trustees met and discussed the request, but took no action.

Only a few days later the U.S. Fourth Circuit Court of Appeals made it clear that the trustees of the Presbyterian Hospital, like many others, no longer have any choice in the matter. In a Greensboro, N.C., case, it was declared that hospitals receiving federal funds under the Hill-Burton Act become "integral parts of a comprehensive joint or intermeshing state/federal plan." Such restrictions as are required in segregated hospitals were declared to violate the Fourteenth Amendment guaranteeing equal protection of the laws.

In many a situation it would be far better to do what generous and humanitarian principles require rather than to wait for what the law compels.

For the Church's Integrity

Presbyterians have always insisted that Jesus Christ is the sole lawgiver in Zion, and they have sometimes been willing to sacrifice every earthly good for the "Crown Rights" of the Redeemer in his church. They have insisted that the church is where the Word is rightly preached and the sacraments rightly administered. In short they have taken seriously the integrity of the church of Jesus Christ.

Today this integrity is endangered by the racial crisis. Ministers who have stood for the integrity of the ministry and the church, who have insisted that Jesus Christ is sole Lord of his church, have all too frequently found, when they have met difficulty, that they were without support of their brethren and of the courts and agencies of the church.

"Successful" ministers and "successful" church executives are always embarrassed by the minister who is asked to resign over problems arising from the race issue. Instead of providing help they explain such a minister away as a personality problem or a poor pastor. A well-liked minister always has difficulty with the fact that a minister who speaks the truth, even in love, on the issues of the day, is not likely to fit the image of the well-liked minister. But after all, Paul and Jesus do not fit this image either.

Seminaries have not distinguished themselves in providing support for their graduates who have been in difficult situations. Neither have the various agencies of the church. Too frequently presbyteries and commissions have acted on the premise that the man must be sacrificed but the institution must be saved, though there is no New Testament basis for the premise.

While many ministers have been forced out of churches, no congregations have been dissolved or significantly disciplined for refusing to acknowledge the Lordship of Jesus Christ or abide by the constitution of the church (i.e., for refusal to obey Jesus Christ in the issues involving race).

The plain fact is that in some instances ministers who have been in difficulty over their faithful witness in the race issue have received more real help from outside the denomination than from within. The time has therefore come when it is imperative that those who are concerned for the integrity of the Presbyterian Church in the South must come to the aid of ministers who are hard pressed.

This means that the seminaries and courts and agencies of the church must assume more responsibility for supporting all faithful ministers.

This means that a fund must be provided for the support of ministers and their families when they have been forced out of pastorates. If some agency or court of the church does not take this step in the immediate future, then this work must be done by ministers and laymen who are genuinely concerned about the right preaching of the Word and right administration of the sacraments, in short, about the integrity of the church. This is the issue that is at stake.

"Presbyterians and the Fair"
New York, 1964

The New York World's Fair is both evangelistic and theological; the language, content, and methods are secular, but the theological fact is nonetheless real. Amid much that is phony, banal, and crudely materialistic, there is much that is good.

The theology and the evangelism of the churches is there. The tower of Billy Graham's pavilion stands out over the fair grounds, and inside, a movie narrated by Billy Graham and adapted to the scientific, technological tone of the fair ends with an "altar" call. The Roman Catholics have as their prize exhibit La Pieta, displayed with Madison Avenue flair, and at the entrance they have written those remarkable words of Paul IV expressing appreciation of the world and avowing the intention of the church to be a servant, not a ruler. The roles of the less traditional churches are impressive. The Church of Christ has as large a place in the Protestant pavilion as any other church, if not larger. The Seventh-Day Adventists, the Swedish Evangelical Covenant Church, the Salvation Army, the Assemblies of God, likewise have sizable rooms in the Protestant pavilion. The Mormons have a large pavilion of their own in which disciplined young people proclaim the gospel as Mormons understand it. The Christian Scientists have their own attractive building. And there are others.

The Protestant Pavilion, designed by Edward Stone, is impressive. It houses not only the Protestants, but also the Orthodox. The most impressive activity in the pavilion is the controversial movie *The Parable*. For those who are willing to think, it is meaningful, indeed. There is nothing in the movie that compels the identification of the clown with Jesus Christ. He may be any Christian. In a simple but purposeful way he involves himself in the lives of the heavily burdened and the abused. The circus theme and setting is a warning against any literalism and a call to Christian imagination. *Newsweek* with justification called it the best film at the fair.

For many who have been disenchanted with traditional words and symbols, *The Parable* speaks the only language they will likely hear, even though it is an ambiguous language. For many it may be too sophisticated. For this reason at least one visitor to the fair is also glad for the Billy Graham film *Life in the Fifth Dimension,* which speaks a language that anyone who was reared in and still lives in Protestant America can understand.

The Protestant Pavilion does not effectively present the history or the teaching of Protestantism. A visitor to the fair may come to know the heroes of technology and its meaning for life today. He is not likely to discover the heroes of Protestantism or its message for today. The boothlike rooms in the pavilion, manned mostly by denominations and confessional groups, as well as the lack of unity and focus, suggest the weakness of Protestantism. (One of these booths is sponsored by the Reformed Church in America and the United Presbyterian Church.) Nowhere is there a clear statement of what Protestant Christianity is or has to say to the world today.

One fears that the theology most people hear at the fair is not dispensed in the pavilions that bear churchly names. In the United States Pavilion a well-modulated voice speaks out of the darkness and declares that man is God manifest. In General Motors one hears the optimistic eschatology of man's unlimited possibilities. Bell Telephone, as well as Martin Buber, can tell us that life is communication. The Free Enterprise Pavilion proclaims the gospel of the greatest good for the greatest number. Johnson Wax's film *To Be Alive* is the Christian doctrine of creation—at least, many important elements in it—in secular language. The Illinois Building presents Abraham Lincoln, who, some would argue, was America's greatest theologian of the nineteenth century. Walt Disney almost raises him from the dead as he stands and speaks to the assembled gathering, leaving one uncertain whether the phoniness or the showmanship is the more impressive.

Everywhere the final thrust called for is decision, to buy, if not for life commitment.

Where in all of this was the Presbyterian Church in the United States? The answer is, hardly anywhere. The Board of Christian Education did underwrite a tower to John Knox in the courtyard of the pioneers at the Protestant Pavilion. Otherwise, Presbyterians, U.S., are not there as a denomination. Why? Is it because we do not believe that we have a message for the nation? Is it because we have no strategy for the strange, new, industrial, urban society that is so clearly evident at the fair? Is it that we do not believe that Thornwell and his colleagues deserve a place in the courtyard of the pioneers? Is it that we cannot break the traditional grooves and that we are content to be a sectional church? In any case we, as Presbyterians, U.S., are not at the fair. And we should be.

"Frankfurt, 1964"
September 21, 1964

The recent meeting of the Alliance of the Reformed Churches in Frank-furt, Germany, was the largest in the history of the Alliance, but its real significance lies in the new forces that were operative in its proceedings rather than in its size.

First of all, the Younger Churches, especially African churches, had a large representation. Members of this delegation were uninhibited and not infrequently spoke from a background of obvious faith and piety. Those responsible for the Alliance saw to it that they were accorded recognition and honor. Perhaps no greater task confronts Christendom than the nur-turing of these churches in new roles of leadership. This responsibility has its rewards, for these churches have something to contribute to the rest of Christendom as well as to receive.

Nevertheless, the Younger Churches, in Africa, for example, may not have the same relation as we have to the Reformed tradition as it has devel-oped in Europe and America. They ought not to have the same relation, for their task is to translate the gospel into the idiom of their own language and culture. For this reason there may well be, perhaps there should be, a tension between the service the Alliance renders Presbyterians in America and member churches in Africa. In this matter of spiritual ancestry, we need also to remember that when Augustine, our father in the faith, was writing theology in northern Africa, our fathers according to flesh were barbarians in northern Europe.

A second new force was the influence of united churches that included members from other traditions than those that have been prominent in the Alliance. For some the name Presbyterian is a bad, sectarian word. An effort was made to eliminate the word Presbyterian from the official title, but this move was defeated with the passage of a resolution to encourage the use of the title "World Alliance of Reformed Churches." Some said they did not feel the need to quote Calvin so much as do some from churches more directly in his line of influence.

A third force is the influence of churches living under economic and political systems different from our own. Theology is in part culturally determined, and any international meeting makes this fact abundantly clear. In America we need to know this about ourselves as well as recognize it in others.

A fourth influence at work was an affirmative theological attitude toward the world as the creation of God. While an ardent proponent of the theology of Barmen, Wilhelm Niesel, was elected president, it was clear that the Alliance as a whole was unwilling to be so exclusively Christocentric. It affirmed that the Holy Spirit is at work in the whole world and that it is important for the church to know what the Holy Spirit is doing in the world as well as in the church.

These new forces may cause fears for those who would like for the Alliance to be more cozily Calvinistic and Presbyterian. A point surely exists beyond which the Alliance cannot go without calling in question its own need to exist. In fact, some do call in question the need for confessional organizations. But for those of us who do believe that the ecumenical movement is safer and more catholic because of confessional organizations, there is still reason to welcome the new forces. Surely in our time our heritage is wholesome only as it is alive to and in dialogue with new movements—theological, ecclesiastical, social—within as well as without our fellowship.

No reference to the Alliance should end without some word of appreciation for its austerity in all bureaucratic operations.

"The Liberalism of the Reformed Tradition"

Presbyterian Educational Association
of the South
June 1952
October 1952

For the past two decades it has been almost a fad among theologians, both amateur and professional, to write obituaries for the liberal theology that is now on the wane. Yet no man can seriously contend that liberal theology did not make a genuine contribution to the church or that the church in its theologizing can ever ignore this period in its history. Certainly it challenges us among whom liberalism was seldom known except in anathema to search for the true liberalism of the Reformed faith.

The Enlightenment and the nineteenth century happened whether we like it or not. We ought to be grateful for the liberals who insisted that we as theologians and preachers must take seriously this new knowledge of science, society, and history. My mother knows about the nineteenth century on the top of her mind, but she continues to say her prayers as though this were 1600. For us who are preachers and teachers this is not an option. For us, theological time and chronological time must engage each other.

The very fact that we are a Reformed church means that we are a liberal church. It is our conviction that no human institution, no outlook upon life, no creedal statement is ever absolute and irreformable. The whole of life, within the church as well as without the church, must be continually reformed in the light of the Christian community's apprehension of what God has said in Jesus Christ. This Word of God in Jesus Christ alone is absolute, but our understanding of it is never absolute or final. Jesus Christ, not some creed, not some polity, not some particular institution, is the living Lord of the church and of the conscience.

Calvin Saw Man's Frailty

It is a well-known fact that John Calvin emphasized the solidarity of all men in sin. In theory at any rate he made no exceptions. If we take this

315

doctrine seriously, then we must insist that the whole life of the Christian community—its theology, its polity, its social conscience—be one of repentance and endeavor after new obedience.

Calvin was not always true to his doctrine. So far as I know, he never intimates that his own reason was not fully competent to manipulate the infallible Biblical materials into a theological system that came very near to being infallible. Once Calvin was confronted with the fact that heretics were burned in Geneva as well as by Rome. What was the difference? The difference, Calvin said (and here I quote his exact words), is that we "possess the infallible truth." This suggests that the theologian is exempt from the limitations of the creature before the Creator and from the perils of sin.

Many of Calvin's disciples have likewise been convinced that they too possessed the infallible truth. Whenever they have been thus convinced, they have, figuratively and sometimes not so figuratively, burned heretics.

Necessity for Continual Reform

It is time for us who call ourselves disciples of Calvin to rediscover another aspect of his theology that emphasized the necessity for continual reform of life under the word of God. We do not and we cannot possess, manipulate, and control the living word of God. Rather this word must possess and control us. We cannot lock the living word in a neat, tidy formula. Sometimes we must confess that we stand nearer the word of God amid the tension of opposing views than in the presence of dogmatic pronouncements. The truth manifest in the person of Jesus Christ can never be adequately expressed in abstract propositions. Theology must always remain symbolic.

The question that confronts us is, "Do we have the courage and the energy to be truly liberal in the Reformed tradition?" Do we have the courage to admit that Presbyterianism may not be the last word in polity, that we must continually listen to what God has to say to us in Jesus Christ? Do we have the courage to recognize that the Westminster Confession and Catechisms are not infallible and must be continually reformed?

Do we have the courage to reform our attitudes on race, on economics, on politics, according to God's word to us?

Do we have the courage to carry on in the life of the church the reformation that we praise so highly in the sixteenth century? If we had lived then, would we have been found with the men who were satisfied with the polity, creed, and practice of the church, or would we have ventured and dared with those who brought under the judgment the life of the church?

It is a well-known fact that societies organized to honor revolutions are seldom revolutionary. Is there not a danger that in honoring the Reformers of the sixteenth century when we have denied them in the twentieth century?

God Spoke—He Speaks

We are under the conviction that God demands of us that we see the daily tasks in which we are engaged under the light of the Word that he spoke to us in Jesus Christ. In this particular Man the mind of the Lord God, creator of heaven and earth, is acted out in human life so that all men can see and understand. But our hearts are never pure enough, nor our minds great enough, to understand completely. So from day to day, indeed from generation to generation, it is our specifically Christian task to listen to the living voice of God.

As heirs of the Reformation we must keep alive the task of reformation. No creed, no polity, no institution, no social conscience is ever final, absolute, or irreformable.

In practice as well as in theory our whole life must be continually reformed in the light of the Christian—not simply the Presbyterian—community's apprehension of what God says to us today in Jesus Christ, our Lord.

This is the liberalism of the Reformed tradition.

"The Church, a Voluntary Organization: Organizational Crisis and the Withholding of Money"
October 3, 1994

All Presbyterians are grateful to our moderator, Robert W. Bohl, for the leadership he gave at the General Assembly and for the possibilities his leadership opens up for the future.

However, the statement that withholding money is an ecclesiastical sin needs serious qualification. I do not know of anything in Presbyterian or Reformed history that would justify labeling the withholding of money as an ecclesiastical sin. It may be a bureaucratic sin, but even in that case, it is a very recent invention. In the history of the church withholding money has sometimes not simply been good stewardship but a Christian responsibility. Furthermore, those who withhold money from the support of particular actions of church governing bodies are frequently the most generous givers in the church.

Presbyterianism existed in this country for 150 years with virtually no bureaucratic structure whatsoever. Most of the work of the church was done through voluntary boards and agencies. The need for bureaucratic structure was even debated in the late nineteenth century. The modern bureaucratic structure of the church is largely the work of the last 50 years.

Members of the former Presbyterian Church U.S. were free to give their money to various causes in the church until the mid-1960s. At that time a policy of equalization was established through a central treasurer. The attempt to coerce contributions by organizational activity is very recent.

The church is a voluntary organization. It has no marine corps or IRS, and it lives by moral suasion. It is interesting that as the leadership of the church loses the capacity to persuade people on the congregational level, it increasingly resorts to coercive action. Such a policy is always self-defeating.

The really serious problem is that church governing bodies and bureaucratic staffs no longer adequately represent the people who sit in the pews on Sunday morning and give the money. In the work of the church no practices are more fraught with danger than the running of a congregation or the denomination with other people's money or with members others have brought into the church or with endowments others have raised. Until the people who attend church and who give their money are more adequately represented, the problems in the Presbyterian Church will not go away.

A word of caution must be said also about the use of unity as a rhetorical device. Unity is not necessarily good; it may be very destructive. Robert Calhoun, arguably the most brilliant American theologian of the twentieth century, once noted that disunity may contribute more to the catholicity of the church than unity.

The appeal to unity calls for a definition of the grounds of this unity. Traditionally the unity of the church consisted in hearing the word of God and in the passionate conviction that Jesus Christ was God incarnate and therefore the revelation in the light of which all other revelation is understood, including human experience; that in Jesus Christ, God has wrought the salvation of all people; and that the primary task of the church is to bring human beings to a saving knowledge of Jesus Christ as Lord and Savior. Recent events have made it very clear that there is no consensus that the unity of the church consists in the classical, Christian affirmations about Jesus Christ and about scripture as the word of God.

The appeal to church mission and especially to missionaries as a rallying point in the church must also be qualified. It is now clear that work does not unite, while theology divides. In recent years work has divided the church more than theology. In a former time missionary activity united the church because there was a consensus that God has wrought the salvation of all people in Jesus Christ, and the great missionary task was to proclaim the gospel in order to bring people to a saving knowledge of God in Jesus Christ and to build churches. When all this was done, the church would engage in medical, educational, and humanitarian work. This consensus has also broken down and in recent decades many have conceived the missionary work of the church in terms of political and social agendas.

The way out of the present crisis in the church cannot be achieved by rhetoric or by superficial compromises. The issues in the church today involve the very foundation of the church and of the church's mission. Some are now suggesting that we are in a Barmen situation, a time when ministers and church members must boldly say that the unity of the church is founded upon what God has done in Jesus Christ in revealing himself and saving us from sin.

The Christian church is not a political party, not an advocate of social, political, and economic causes. It is a worshipping, believing community that, in the light of what God has done in Jesus Christ, commits life and brings all of life under God's judgment. The time has come when the membership of the Presbyterian Church will have to declare that the Presbyterian Church is either an authentic manifestation of the one holy catholic and apostolic church or simply another advocacy group with its own agendas.

None of us is good enough or wise enough to say what ought now to be done. With this qualification and as one who has no confidence in rhetoric, public relations activities, or conferences to improve the situation, I make two suggestions.

First, let us devote one year to recovering the foundations of church life, specifically:

1. Renewed emphasis on the worship and preaching service on the Lord's Day.

   Documentable records of participation in the worship of a congregation, stewardship of money, and effectiveness in bringing members into the church should be a precondition for staff being given leadership positions in the denomination.

2. Reading, study, and memorization of the scriptures as the word of God and as they are written. The application of scripture can wait until we know scripture.

   Reading, study, and memorization of scripture will give us the language spoken in the Christian community and the data of the faith.

3. Study of the creed and the confessions so that we shall know the faith of the church that has called congregations into being, that has sustained them, and that has received the approbation of the people of God over a period of time.

   A recent study of the decline of the Presbyterian Church has emphasized the significance of the emergence of church leaders and officers who know neither the Bible nor the theology of the church (*First Things*, March 1993, 13–18).

Second, the structures of the churches must be brought back into the tradition of Protestantism and Presbyterianism, specifically:

1. The quota system must be modified so that those who worship God on the Lord's Day and who support the church with their money are better represented.

2. The General Assembly Council and staff must be broken up into separate boards and staffs.

   The highly centralized board and staff are very open to political activists and caucuses. It is relatively simple for a small group of people to control the whole operation of the church. We would not tolerate this centralization in the civil order.

   We must always remember that the leaders of the Presbyterian Church are never voted on by the people as mayors, governors, congressmen, and presidents are. This allows persons who have never paid their dues in building up congregations, much less organizing them, to be leaders in the church.

   It is good for the General Assembly to make declarations, but little is likely to change the direction of the denomination until structures are changed and until staff changes bring into the leadership of the church more persons who have a record for bringing persons into the membership of the church and who give priority in their public work to proclaiming basic Christian doctrines and maintaining the theological integrity of the church.

3. Give congregations more freedom in developing their own programs, in electing officers, and especially in calling of pastors.

4. Reform seminaries to prepare students more effectively to be pastors and to gather and to build up congregations.

"On Keeping a Proper Perspective:
The Sexuality Debate"
May 13, 1991

No issue in recent decades has aroused the Presbyterian Church and elicited so vocal a response as has the Majority Report of the Special Committee to Study Human Sexuality—not even the union of the churches. This vigorous response is based on sound reasons, and for it we can be grateful. Apart from any position the paper takes on human sexuality, its theological commitments and methods repudiate four centuries of Protestant Reformed theology as well as the theology of the ancient catholic church. The use of such words as *expertise, Reformed tradition and theology, biblical mandate* seem to this reader to be tendentious. The paper, if adopted, would represent an almost 180-degree turn in the theological nature and commitment of the Presbyterian Church.

This report also seems to me to violate the canons of privacy and good taste. Public discussion of the deeply personal dimensions of human life destroys the mystery of the self and does violence to the image of God. Human beings are persons, not animals. The intimate concerns of life must be discussed in relative privacy and with awe and wonder. Public exposure of personal and physical life is always very dangerous and is likely to become obscene and destructive of personal existence.

For these reasons we can be grateful that so many have spoken out.

Disquieting Signs

Yet there are disquieting signs that must be taken seriously. One is the "bandwagon psychology." Very little theological insight, much less courage, is required to oppose a theological document when more than 80 percent of the church membership are obviously on your side and the cause is popular. The enthusiasm of the response reminds us of the church's great need for persons who have the theological courage and the commitment to speak up when it is obvious that not even a majority of the church are aware of the issues involved.

The tremendous protest against this particular report raises the disquieting question of where the protesters were back ten, fifteen, twenty years ago when decisions were being made in the life of the church that culminate now in this particular report. Where were they at the Assembly of 1987 during the election of a moderator and the discussion of the overture that led to the special committee? The final document could have been and indeed was predicted from the appointment of the committee.

This report, however, has its origins not simply in the Assembly of 1987 but in the long history of theological malaise and indecisiveness that has characterized the Presbyterian Church in the last few decades.

This document has its origin also in the changed political character of the church whereby relatively small groups, highly organized but with little basis in local congregations, have been able through the processes and procedures of the church's governing bodies to gain control of the political apparatus and bureaucracy of the church.

The appointment of the committee itself raises many questions. The church has in its membership many of the ablest historians, scientists, physicians, lawyers, and people knowledgeable in business and public life to be found in the world, who are also committed church people; but their names seldom appear on church committees, including this one. Theologians and pastors who have demonstrated the ability to gather congregations and to build them up as the communion of saints also seldom appear on committees.

In Protestantism, validity for church service is given not through ordination and the endorsement of special-interest groups, but through Christian dedication, through the ability to interpret and to apply the scriptures, and through the approbation of the people of God, which is most authentically done not by a governing body or by staff and advocacy groups, but by the local congregation. The Special Committee to Study Human Sexuality did not have the confidence of the people of God. This lack of approbation is most apparent in the reception of the report. Such a committee would have been unthinkable in the church as few as twenty-five years ago.

A second disquieting factor about the tremendous protest against the report is pragmatic. The high level of emotional involvement and the arousal of persons who are not familiar with all the ramifications of theology and ethical issues, to say nothing of church politics, could lead not simply to the rejection of this report but also to decisions that will have a subversive influence upon the life of our denomination. The very fact that this report has elicited such a tremendous opposition may mean that the wisest policy for the Assembly is to dismiss the committee, to decline to receive the report, and to declare a moratorium, at least for a year or two, on official discussion on matters of human sexuality.

The church needs time for quiet reflection and for the biblical and theological study, Catholic, Protestant, and Reformed, that is necessary for a discussion of human sexuality. The time may come when a statement can be written in the light of the best knowledge we have, under the authority of scripture as God's word written, and in the context of the church's theology, which for centuries has received the approbation of the people of God.

All of us need to remember that our apprehension of God's will is flawed by our own limitations and that the complexity of many human situations as well as the freedom of the human spirit defy precise prescriptions for human behavior, especially when made in the name of the transcendent God.

(Some of the material in the minority report, it should be noted, is balanced, competent, and pastorally as well as theologically sensitive.)

The third disquieting sign in the tremendous protest arises from the fact that human sexuality is not the most important issue before the Presbyterian Church at the present time. The most serious issue confronting the church today and the most serious responsibility of the church in every day is its witness to the work of God in Jesus Christ, our Lord and Savior.

The most important task of the church is to bear witness to the fact that the eternal God, creator of heaven and earth, was incarnate in Jesus Christ, that in Jesus Christ God wrought our salvation, and that God raised Jesus Christ in actual fact from the dead. This witness by which the church lives is very much at risk in our world and in the Presbyterian Church.

Why is it that such an emotional protest was aroused by the report on human sexuality while so much indifference abounds about the witness to the Christian gospel in our seminaries, in our churches, and in our denomination? It is quite obvious that the focus of the church's energy is not so much on preaching the Christian gospel as it is with issues that are at best derivative from this gospel.

The whole issue is vividly illustrated at the recent meeting of the World

Council of Churches, if newspaper reports are true. The presentation identifying the Holy Spirit with many spirits that abound in our world is far more destructive of the integrity of the church's life than this particular report on sexuality. Political and social orthodoxies of the church unfortunately arouse more passion than the faith by which the church lives.

The report on human sexuality is in no small measure the consequence of our lack of concern about the role of "political correctness," about the influence of "post-Christian theologies" that undermine such fundamental Christian doctrines as Jesus Christ, the Word made flesh, and the Christian conviction that God did in fact raise Jesus Christ from the dead.

There is enthusiasm in church and seminaries for "bashing" "fundamentalists" who no longer exist in the Presbyterian Church, but a strange and ominous silence about secular humanism and "post-Christian theologies" that are undermining the church's life.

The real root of the church's problems is not in the report on human sexuality—as important as a theologically and biblically sound statement on sexuality for the church today may be. This report is a *consequence* of the crucial problem. The fundamental malaise of the church's roots is a loss of passion for the integrity of the Christian witness in a pluralistic society.

The fundamental question is the question Jesus put to his disciples, "Who do you say that I am?"

"A Confused and Destructive Debate"
(The Homosexuality Debate)
January 3, 1995

The debate concerning the ordination of homosexuals appears to me to be very confused and likely in the end to be destructive. It is important to focus the issue, noting what the issue is not and what the issue really is.

In my judgment:

1. The issue is not right to ordination. There is no ecclesiastical right to ordination, much less a civil right.
2. The issue is not justice. Justice has very little to do with ordination. The language of ordination is more that of the Sermon on the Mount and the language of sacrifice. Ordination in the classical sense of the word has nothing to do with entitlements, benefits, contracting, or in contemporary language "perks." Ordination is a calling to do a job for which there may be no remuneration whatsoever as was the case with many of the pastors who established Presbyterianism in this country.
3. The issue is not simply behavior. The church has always ordained homosexuals, some of whom have served with remarkable effectiveness. Moreover, every person who is ordained is a sinner saved by grace. No one is good enough to be ordained. The church, however, has never allowed sinners who come to ordination to witness to their sins and to ask the church to approve their sins and/or eccentricities.

The critical issue in the debate is, in my judgment, twofold:

1. The first is the use of ordination as an occasion to confess, to witness to, and to demand that the church approve sin or eccentricity.

Ordination thus becomes the occasion when the church certifies a way of life that is in contradiction to the biblical and confessional doctrine that God created human beings male and female and that the nuclear family is the primary form of human society. The issue is on the bottom line biblical and confessional. Under the terms in which the debate has been shaped, the ordination of homosexuals means the repudiation of the witness of scripture and the testimony of the confessions.

2. The second issue is social, the certification of human relationships as equivalent alternatives to the nuclear family, that is, this man and this woman and this child who are bound together by irrevocable and unique physical, psychological, communal, and in the Christian community covenantal relationships.

It is indeed unfortunate that the Presbyterian Church (U.S.A.) should be engaged in a process that would certify that other human relationships deserve the blessing of God and that various relationships are equivalent alternatives to the nuclear family in which by the providence of God and by the order of creation every human life is set. This is especially so when the breakdown of the nuclear family is one of the primary sources of violence in our time and the deterioration of the educational system.

The issue is not sexuality as such or homosexuality as such, but the political use of ordination to undermine the normative character of what the church has taught as God's will for human life.

The critical issue is the use of ordination to legitimize a style or styles of life that have no basis in scripture or confessions.

"The Protestant Principle and a Free Press"
January 1, 1996

Paul Tillich popularized the notion of the Protestant Principle. He meant by this that no individual, no group, and quite specifically no church organization can claim divine dignity for its power, its decisions, and its various activities. The prophetic spirit begins not with the criticism of society but with self-criticism. To be a Protestant is to be critically self-critical.

The human tendency to claim sanctity for one's self and for one's own organization is so great that Tillich went on to argue that Protestantism requires a secular reality over against it to puncture its pretensions and correct its errors. Protestantism cannot desire a monopoly or totalitarian control. Human nature being what it is, Protestantism requires external criticism for its own health.

Thus the very nature of Protestantism requires a free press. The church, as an organization, is not safer than the nation would be if Americans were dependent simply on the news releases of the White House, of Congress, and of the various government bureaucracies. The health of the nation depends upon a free press to uncover news and to provide critical comment. The United States of America would be impossible without the *New York Times, The Washington Post,* and many other newspapers, as well as commentators.

The importance of a free press for society is generally recognized in democratic countries. Yet ironically, church leaders who rejoice most in a free press are reluctant to encourage a free press in the church.

The importance of a free press in the church becomes evident when we reflect on the current situation. Members of congregations, for the most part, are dependent on the official news releases of presbyteries, synods,

328

and General Assemblies and their various bureaucratic offices. In addition, the only information that members of the church have about church institutions, colleges, and seminaries are the public-relations handouts of these institutions. Church conferences are not subject to the public scrutiny that all conferences and conventions are in the public order. Citizens of the state, for example, are more aware of the policies and actions of the boards of secular colleges that are covered by the secular press than church members are of the actions and policies of their seminaries as well as church colleges.

The paucity of a free press in the contemporary church is due, on the one hand, to the tremendous expense and sacrificial devotion a free press requires and to the reluctance of church leaders to support a truly free press.

The paucity of a free press can be very well illustrated in the history of *The Presbyterian Outlook*, which would not exist apart from the sacrificial devotion of E. T. Thompson, who for many years kept it alive. He received no financial remuneration for his work for *The Outlook*. It is also illustrated in Thompson's successor, Aubrey Brown, as editor, and in the work of his brother, James Brown, as business manager (later publisher and general manager). For many years they kept *The Outlook* going on very minimal salaries and a very small office staff.

A free church press also has to resist the pressure of advertisers and contributors. In the relatively small community of a denomination, the editors of a free press are also under continual pressure of friends and acquaintances, a pressure that is not so acute in the large civil society. A free press is no easy achievement.

The glory and the difficulty of a free church press were dramatically presented at a dinner honoring Aubrey Brown during the Shreveport General Assembly of the Presbyterian Church U.S. in 1978. Edward Grant, formerly the secretary of the Board of Christian Education of the Presbyterian Church U.S., one of the great church leaders of the South during his generation, was the speaker. After Grant retired from the board, he had a notable career in the state government in Louisiana and also a notable business career as president of Grant Chemical. He was happy to speak in honor of Aubrey Brown, but he stated at the beginning of his speech that he would have been very reluctant to have commended Aubrey Brown when he was the executive of the Board of Christian Education. *The Outlook* kept the Board of Christian Education, located across the street from *The Outlook*'s office, under surveillance. Now, in retrospect, he was willing to testify to Aubrey Brown's importance for the health of the Board of

Christian Education. This illustrates, I think, the problem and the glory of a free press in the church.

The problem and necessity of a free press is an illustration of the human problem. No human being and no human organization is good enough or wise enough to be exempt from accountability to another and from criticism of a power that stands over against it.

PART TEN
CLASSROOM

Questions and Suggestions for the Study of John Calvin's *Institutes of the Christian Religion*

Institutes I, 1–10

I. Knowledge of God, the Creator
   A. From creation
      1. Human existence
         (a) *Sensus divinitatis*
         (b) *Conscientia*
      2. Creation generally
         (a) Wonders of creation
         (b) More recondite proofs
      3. History and providence
      4. Value of this knowledge from creation
         (a) Not adequate for salvation
         (b) Exposes our sin
         (c) Positive role: cf. comments on sermons of Paul in Acts 14 and 17; cf. "Calvin's use of Cicero in the *Institutes I, 1–5*" in *Archive for Reformation History 1971, No. 1.*
   B. From scripture
II. Knowledge of God, the Redeemer
   From scripture *alone*
III. The scripture
      1. Illustration: spectacles
      2. Authority of scripture: God is the author
      3. Testimony of the Holy Spirit
      4. Arguments: Style
                      Prophecy
                      Miracles
                      Preservation of books
                      Harmony of the Gospels

Power of simple men to speak profound truth
Consent of the church
Martyrs
5. Relation between word and spirit

Doctrine of God

Institutes 1:1–10

Chapter 10: Scripture, to Correct All Superstition, Has Set the True God Alone over Against All the Gods of the Heathen.

1. The Scriptural Doctrine of God the Creator
   a. Is the knowledge of God set forth in the created universe consonant with that expressed in the word?
      (1) This question is too long for a thorough discussion here.
      (2) Present purpose merely to provide an index of what to look for in scripture and how to seek it out.
   b. Limits of the present discussion
      (1) The covenant with Israel eventuating in the coming of Redeemer will not at present be considered.
      (2) Rather, those scriptural passages that describe how God, the Maker of heaven and earth, governs the world—his goodness, his righteous vengeance, and his forbearance—will be pointed out.
2. The Attributes of God according to Scripture Agree with Those Known in his Creatures
   a. Scriptural passages show us not as God is in himself, but as he is toward us: kindness, goodness, mercy, justice, judgment, and truth.
      (1) Ex. 34:6–7
      (2) Ps. 145
      (3) Jer. 9:24 (1 Cor. 1:31)
   b. The purpose of this scriptural knowledge of God: fear—trust—true worship—full dependence upon him.
3. Even Worshipers of Idols Knew the Unity of God
   a. Scripture rejects all gods of the heathen
   b. Polytheists never completely lost the awareness that there was really only one God.
      (1) Thus, their persistence in polytheism is evidence of their own vanity and of Satan's deceptions and is inexcusable.
      (2) All, from the rude multitude to the sophisticated philosophers, have corrupted the truth of God.

(From F. L. Battle's *Analysis*)

The Trinity

Institutes 1:13

Calvin expounds the doctrine of the trinity in a more or less traditional way, i.e., as the doctrine had been expounded by Augustine.

Calvin emphasized the full deity of each "person" and the *unity* of God in three persons. How does Calvin define "person"?

Relate Calvin's teaching to the teaching of the Cappadocians and Augustine.

Note carefully what Calvin writes about theology in I, 13, 3–5.

Institutes I, 10–15

  I. Read with special care chapters 10, 11, 14, 15.
 II. Paul Tillich writes that Calvin's polemic against idolatry is basic to his theology. Hence it is important to grasp what he means by *idolatry*. I have written what I know about the subject in "Calvin's Polemic Against Idolatry" in *Soli Deo Gloria*, edited by J. M. Richards.
III. What does Calvin believe about art? What is the role of art in teaching the faith? Read carefully I, 11, 8. Read carefully I, II, 12–13.
 IV. Central themes: Creation
    1. Creation
    2. Creation is good.
    3. The Devil: A created and fallen good
    4. Spiritual World
       a. Created
       b. Good
       c. Messengers of God
    5. Creation for man
    6. Thanksgiving: Proper response to creation
  V. In chapter 15 try to decipher Calvin's understanding of the following concepts:
    1. Body
    2. Soul
    3. Image of God
    4. Understanding
    5. Will

Providence

  I. Calvin's views on chance and fate.
 II. Notice distinctions Calvin makes in doctrine of Providence.
    1. General and special providence

2. Willing and permitting
3. Unity and manifoldness of will of God
4. Note definitions and distinctions in more popular expositions of Providence in tract against the Libertines Ch. XIV and "Eternal Predestination of God" Ch. X.

III. Providence and Second Causes
IV. Providence and the Use of Means
V. Providence and Sin
VI. Meaning of Providence for Christian Life
VII. Note in general Calvin's emphasis on the immediacy of God's action; on his comparative indifferences to structures, natures, and causes; and on the doxological character of his theology.
VIII. Is Calvin's view of providence tenable today?
Is it proper to pray for rain?
Having read Calvin, comment on the following revision of the *Book of Common Prayer*:

> Almighty and most merciful Father, we humbly beseech thee of thy great goodness, to restrain these immoderate rains wherewith thou has afflicted us. And we pray thee to send us such seasonable weather, that the earth may, in due time, yield her increase for our use and benefit, through Jesus Christ our Lord.

A proposed alternative is:

> O God who in thy loving relation to all things sharest with us the unfinished struggle and the accidents of natural processes, sustain us in our search for a more humane and fruitful life in our natural environment; encourage our search for new resources for the control of floods and drought, lead us always to acknowledge that we belong in the one great society of being, and give us grace to share our goods and our hopes with all thy creation, through Jesus Christ our Lord.

Institutes II, 1–13

I. Original Sin
   (a) Nature of Adam's sin
   (b) Definition of original sin
   (c) Original sin as guilt
   (d) Original sin as corruption
   (e) "Total depravity" (total in what sense?)
II. Calvin on Freedom
   (a) Necessity of will
   (b) Compulsion of will
   (c) Freedom as spontaneity (voluntary will) and freedom as power of contrary choice

III. Grace
   (a) Operating grace
   (b) Cooperating grace
   (c) Grace and the will
IV. Effects of Fall
   (a) On reason
   (b) On will

Institutes II, 4–5

I. How does God work in the human person?
   (a) Note illustrations
   (b) Note significance of difference between person and stone
   (c) Note answer to this question in II, 5, 2 (p. 322)
   (d) Note integrity of the human will (cf. II, 3, 14)
II. In what sense are good works man's own work?

Institutes II, 6–8

I. Note carefully the significance of chapter 6 for organization of the *Institutes*, for the problem of "Gospel and Law."
II. The object of faith in II, 6, 4.
III. What are the three functions of the law? What is principal function?
IV. Relation of Ten Commandments to law engraved in the hearts of men. What is Calvin's understanding of natural law?
V. Principles for interpreting the Ten Commandments: II, 8, 6–12.
VI. Study in particular Calvin on Commandments 1, 2, 4, and 8.
VII. Read with care II, 8, 51–59. Paragraph topics are a good guide.

Institutes II, 9–11

I. The relation of gospel and law
II. Similarities between the Testaments
III. Differences between Testaments
IV. Covenant theology
V. Note emphasis on unity of the Testaments

Institutes II, 12–17

I. Why did Christ become man?
II. Incarnation as fulfillment of creation and/or Incarnation as means of redemption. Calvin's view. Your view.
III. Supralapsarian? II, 12, 5
IV. Osiander's error.
V. What is Calvin's doctrine of person of Christ? Especially as found in chapters 13 and 14. Note Calvin's emphasis on humanity in II, 16, 12 and in II, 16, 5.

VI. Calvin's views on the following:
    (a) The Virgin Birth
    (b) The sinlessness of Christ
    (c) Love of God and the atonement: II, 16, 3–4
    (d) Dead and buried
    (e) Descended into hell
    (f) Ascended into heaven and benefits of ascension
    (g) *Extra Calvinisticum:* II, 13, 4
VII. Work of Christ
    (a) Prophet
    (b) Priest
    (c) King
    (d) Role of obedience in atonement: II, 16, 5
    (e) Summarize Calvin's doctrine of the atonement

Institutes III, 1–2

I. Definition of faith: III, 2, 7
II. Calvin on the following items:
    (a) Implicit faith
    (b) Formed and unformed faith
    (c) Faith as knowledge
    (d) Faith as matter of the heart
    (e) Object of faith
    (f) Certainty of faith
    (g) The word of God and faith
    (h) Revealed in our hearts by Holy Spirit: III, 2, 33ff
    (i) Faith and doubt
    (j) Faith and assurance
    (k) Faith and perseverance
    (l) Faith and love
    (m) Faith and hope
III. Work of Holy Spirit as bond of our union with Christ

Institutes III, 3, 6–9

I. Repentance (sanctification or renewal)
    (a) Mortification and vivification
    (b) Persistence of sin in life of the redeemed
    (c) Interior nature of repentance
    (d) Repentance and forgiveness
    (e) The unpardonable sin
    (f) What is Calvin's doctrine of sin on the basis of III, 3, 10–12?
    (g) What does Calvin teach about fasting, about "exercises" of piety?
II. What does Calvin teach about confession? III, 3–15
III. What does Calvin teach about absolution?
IV. What does Calvin teach about prayers for the dead?

    V. Christian life as self-denial
       (Read chapter to grasp general meaning of self-denial)
   VI. Christian life as cross bearing
  VII. Christian life as meditation on the future life

Institutes III, 10

    I. What was Calvin's basic attitude toward "earthly benefits"?
   II. Note in detail the basic and subordinate principles that guide Christians in the "right use of earthly benefits."

Institutes III, 11–19

    I. Note double grace we receive in Jesus Christ: III, 11, 1.
   II. Calvin's definition of justification.
  III. Error of Osiander.
  IV. Role of faith in justification.
   V. Two types of righteousness.
  VI. Relation of justification to God's honor and to confidence of the believer: III, 13.
 VII. Good works:
     (a) Good works of the pagans
     (b) Good works of believers. Note Calvin's emphasis on persistence of sin in life of believers in Chapters III, 14–18.
VIII. How does Calvin relate Gospel and Law? (III, 17). Relate to earlier discussions of theme.

    I. Definition of Christian freedom (three parts)
   II. Christian freedom and the weak (Note difference between offense given and offense taken.)
  III. Christian freedom and the purity of the faith
  IV. Christian freedom and discipline
   V. Christian freedom and the state

Institutes III, 20

This chapter is important for an adequate understanding of Calvin's life and works.

    I. Why is prayer necessary?
   II. What are the rules of right prayer?
  III. What is the relation of forgiveness to prayer?
  IV. Why is prayer made in the name of Jesus?
   V. What does Calvin say about intercession of the saints?

VI. What does Calvin teach about private prayer?

VII. What does Calvin teach about public prayer, about "windy" prayers?

VIII. What does Calvin say about church buildings?

IX. What does Calvin teach in this chapter about public worship, about singing, about worship in language of the people?

X. What are uses of the Lord's Prayer? 34–35, 48–49.

XI. How does Calvin divide the Lord's Prayer? Note carefully his comments on each division.

XII. Calvin's teaching on discipline of prayer. 50–52.

Institutes III, 21–24

I. Note reasons Calvin is interested in predestination in III, 21, 1.

II. Note Calvin's comments on curiosity and "learned ignorance."

III. Note definition of predestination and the distinction from foreknowledge in III, 21, 5. Note also summary statement in conclusion of III, 21, 7.

IV. In III, 22, 1, note mystery of existence in relation to predestination. Why men and not oxen? Note also Christ as "mirror of election" (cf. also III, 24, 5–6).

V. Note what Calvin says about reprobation in III, 22, 11; III, 23. List objections and brief summary of Calvin's answers.

VI. How does Calvin deal with objections to predestination in III, 23? List objections and brief summary of Calvin's answers.

VII. What is relation of election to calling, to faith, to certainty of election, to perseverance in III, 24, 109?

VIII. What is cause of "hardness of heart"?

IX. What is significance of Calvin's doctrine of predestination? See especially his estimate of impact of preaching in III, 24, 12–13. Also relate predestination to his comments on preaching in III, 23, 12–14; IV, 3; IV, 8, 9.

Institutes III, 25

1. What did Calvin teach about resurrection of the body, the immortality of the soul, "honoring the body"? Compare Calvin with Augustine on death and the body.

Institutes IV, 1–13

1. What does Calvin say about need for organized church in IV, 1, 1; IV, 1, 5?

2. How does Calvin interpret article on church in The Apostles' Creed?

3. Communion of Saints?

4. Visible—invisible church?

5. What are criteria of membership in church?

6. How does Calvin define the existence of the church in IV, 1, 9–12?

7. How is the church holy?

8. How is forgiveness related to existence of the church?

9. What does Calvin say about schism and unity in IV, 2, 5–6?

10. What is Calvin's judgment of the Roman Catholic Church? IV, 2, 11–12.
11. Why are ministers necessary?
12. What officers does the church have? What are the duties of each?
13. What does Calvin say about the "call"? About ordination?
14. What does Calvin say about church possessions? IV, 4, 6–8.
15. What are the powers of the church in doctrine?
16. What is the authority of a church council?
17. What is the power of the church in making laws? IV, 10. What does Calvin mean by bondage of conscience?
18. What does Calvin teach about Church constitutions? IV, 10, 27–32.
19. What is the power of the church in jurisdiction?
20. What are the purposes of church discipline?
21. What are the limits of church discipline?
22. What are the purposes of fasting?
23. How is discipline of clergy related to discipline of people? IV, 12, 22.
24. What does Calvin teach about clerical celibacy?
25. What rules does Calvin establish concerning vows? IV, 13, 2–4

Institutes IV, 14–20

1. What is Calvin's definition of a sacrament? cf. IV, 14, 18–19.
2. What is the relation of Word and sacrament? cf. also IV, 14, 14; IV, 14, 17.
3. What is the relation of faith to the sacrament?
4. What is the relation of Holy Spirit to the sacrament?
5. What is the relation of sacraments of the Old Testament and the New Testament?
6. What is Calvin's definition of baptism?
7. Baptism is a token of what?
8. Relation of baptism to
    (1) original sin
    (2) faith
    (3) merit of the administrator
9. Is rebaptism permissible?
10. What is proper form of baptism?
11. Is baptism necessary to salvation? cf. also IV, 16, 26.
12. Does Calvin teach concerning the baptism of infants? If so, why?
13. What is the relation of baptism and the Lord's Supper? cf. also IV, 17, 1.
14. What does Calvin say about appropriateness of signs of bread and wine? Attitude toward signs? IV, 17, 5.
15. What is the chief function of the Lord's Supper? IV, 17, 4.
16. What is the relation of faith to the Lord's Supper? What does Calvin say about "to eat is to believe"?
17. What does Calvin say about signification? IV, 17, 11.
18. What does Calvin say about spatial presence of the body of Christ? cf. also IV, 17, 16–31.
19. How are we to think of presence of Christ in the Supper? IV, 17, 19.
20. How does Calvin interpret words of institution?

21. What does Calvin say about adoration of the elements?
22. Note uses of sacrament:
    (2) confession IV, 17, 37.
    (3) quicken love IV, 17, 38.
23. Relation of Lord's Supper to the Word?
24. What does Calvin say about unworthy partaking?
25. Are faith and love required?
26. How should the sacrament be celebrated? IV, 17, 43–50.
27. What does Calvin say about private masses? IV, 18, 8.
28. What does Calvin say about the sacrament as sacrifice? IV, 18, 13.
29. Read carefully Calvin's summary statement in IV, 18, 10–19.
30. Calvin on ordination. IV, 19, 28.
31. What is relation between civil government and spiritual government?
32. What is Calvin's doctrine of civil government, i.e., duties and authority under God?
33. What does Calvin say about (1) form of government, (2) right to wage war?
34. What is Calvin's teaching about judicial functions and the Christian's involvement in them?
35. What does Calvin teach about resistance to the magistrate? Note addition in 1559 to IV, 20, 32.

Syllabus for the Course: History of Christian Doctrine
1984

Union Theological Seminary in Virginia

A

The course has a threefold purpose: (1) to enable the student to relate Reformed theology to the broader theological context of the one, holy, catholic, and apostolic church; (2) to introduce the student to the study of such issues as the relation of faith and reason, and of scripture and tradition, God's grace and man's responsibility, person and work of Jesus Christ, the sacraments, and the nature of the theological enterprise; (3) to help the student attain a thorough knowledge of the classic creeds and some representative theologians.

I. Motives for the study of historical theology (taken, with some additions, from a syllabus prepared by Professor Albert C. Outler).

1. The objective survey and analysis of the theological enterprise within the Christian community.

2. The development of a productive understanding of the role and function of theology in the church's life.

3. The acquisition of criteria for the critical evaluation of historical generalizations concerning the identity, continuity, and variety of Christian interpretations of the gospel and the Christian life.

4. A clearer view of the interaction between Christian thought and thinkers and the cultural and intellectual milieu of the successive epochs of European and American history.

5. A means toward the recovery of a Christian memory.

6. Significant stimulus toward the repair and reconstruction of contemporary Christian thought about the gospel and the Christian life.

It has been said that those who do not study history are doomed to repeat it. Those who do not study historical theology are likewise doomed to repeat it.

II. Methods of study in the history of Christian Doctrine (taken, with some additions, from a syllabus prepared by Professor Albert C. Outler).

   1. The history of Christian doctrine is a historical discipline, which acknowledges the same rightful demand for objectivity, firsthand acquaintance with primary data, comprehensiveness, and scholarly scruple as any other historical discipline. Its first and basic aim is to *understand* rather than to exploit; its proper concern is to be *descriptive* and *empathetic*, rather than partisan and dogmatic.

   2. As far as the data allow for it, the organization of the study of historical theology ought to follow the actual historical sequence of theological development and evolution in the history of the church; it should avoid schematism based on abstract or systematic pattern.

   3. Historical theology is one branch of the history of ideas; hence, the development and alterations of secular intellectual patterns and the impact of cultural change (as these are felt in the Christian community) are of constant interest to the historian of Christian doctrine.

   4. The most important methodological concern of the historical theologian is the discriminating use of the data of his field.

      a. Primary theological data: Formal theological treatises; texts of creeds and other symbols; canons of ecclesiastical councils and other collective formulations of common faith and order; fragmentary remains or "fugitive" religious writing from periods otherwise devoid of significant theological literature.

      b. Primary parallel data: Major works in philosophy, literature, and science that can be seen to have affected the milieu of Christian thinkers.

      c. Secondary data: Histories of Christian dogma, doctrine, and thought; monographs on particular theological periods or problems; church histories; biographies and memoirs.

      d. Tertiary data: The so-called "history of religions"; social and cultural history (of the Graeco-Roman world, Europe, and America); history of philosophy; history of fine arts; the history of science.

   5. The historical theologian ought to be particularly interested in the successive major crises that he discovers in the church's unfolding historical existence; he will inquire into the theological impulses that went into the making of the crisis and the theological outcome of the church's reaction to the crisis.

III. Various conceptions of the scope and function of historical theology (taken, with some additions, from a syllabus prepared by Professor Albert C. Outler).

   1. F. C. Baur: the application of Hegelian dialectic to the history of Christian thought.

   2. D. Thomasius: the distinction between "central" and "peripheral" doctrines—J. R. Hagenback: the distinction between "general" and "special" doctrines.

   3. Adolf Harnack, A. C. McGiffert: the history of doctrine in the light of the Ritschlian rejection of metaphysics and philosophical theology.

4. J. Tixeront: the "official" Roman Catholic version of the history of dogma.

5. G. P. Fisher, Reinhold Seeberg, R. L. Calhoun: the historical unfolding of the theological enterprise, surveyed by "periods," "stages," and "leading figures."

6. M. Werner: Theology as the de-eschatologizing of primitive Christianity.

7. John Henry Newman: *An Essay on the Development of Christian Doctrine*. Theology as development.

8. Jaroslav Pelikan: *Luther the Expositor*, Chapter 1. History of theology as the interpretation of scripture.

9. G. Ebeling: "History as the Exposition of Scripture." *The Word of God and Tradition*.

10. Karl Rahner, "The Development of Dogma" in *Theological Investigations*, Vol. I.

11. Leslie Dewart: *The Future of Belief*.

12. Alfred Adam: *Lehrbuch der Dogmengeschichte. Die Zeit der Alten Kirche* (1958). Dogma as developing understanding of the New Testament message.

13. Jaroslav Pelikan: *Historical Theology, Continuity and Change in Christian Doctrine*. Jaroslav Pelikan: *The Christian Tradition*; Vol. I (1971), *The Emergence of the Catholic Tradition* (100–600); Vol. II, *The Spirit of Eastern Christendom*, 600–1700; Vol. III, *The Growth of Medieval Theology*, 600–1300.

IV. **Basic Texts:**

Jaroslav Pelikan: *The Christian Tradition*

Reinhold Seeberg: *Textbook of the History of Christian Doctrines*
The most reliable text in English.

A. C. McGiffert: *History of Christian Thought*
Readable and helpful, but written with Ritschlian bias.

J. N. D. Kelly: *Early Christian Doctrines*

J. N. D. Kelly: *Early Christian Creeds* (3rd edition) (indispensable)

E. Gilson: *The History of Christian Philosophy in the Middle Ages*

James Orr: *Progress of Dogma*

F. L. Cross: *Early Christian Fathers*

Bernhard Lohse: *A Short History of Christian Doctrine*

Justo L. Gonzalez: *A History of Christian Thought* (recent)

Pelican Guide to Modern Theology, Vol. II, *Historical Theology*
Good review of Patristic scholarship

Cunliffe-Jones: *A History of Christian Doctrine* (1978)

Carl A. Volz: *Faith and Practice in the Early Church* (1983)

Other Surveys:

A. Harnack: *History of Dogma* (a classic)

Bethune Baker: *Introduction to the Early History of Christian Doctrine*
Excellent for word studies

G. P. Fisher: *History of Christian Doctrine*
Brief summary

Neve: *History of Christian Thought*
P. Tillich: *History of Christian Thought*
   Excellent for Tillich's insights
J. Tixeront: *A Handbook of Patrology*
J. Tixeront: *History of Dogma*
Congar: *A History of Theology*
L. C. Patterson: *God and History in Early Christian Thought*
Richard Norris: *God and World in Early Christian Thought*
B. Hagglund: *History of Theology*
A. Nygren: *Eros and Agape*
Hefele: *History of the Councils*
J. Quasten: *Patrology*
Prestige: *God in the Patristic Thought*
   Excellent
Prestige: *Fathers and Heretics*
J. K. S. Reid: *Christian Apologetics*
Turner: *Redemption in Patristic Thought*
Cochrane: *Christianity and Classical Culture*
   Excellent
Campenhausen: *The Fathers of the Latin Church*
J. Danielou: *A History of Christian Doctrine Before the Council of Nicea*, Vol. I–III
Sources of Early Christian Thought
J. Patout Burns: *Theological Anthropology*
William G. Rusch: *The Trinitarian Controversy*
Richard A. Norris: *The Christological Controversy*
V. **Source Materials:**
P. Schaff: *Creeds of Christendom*
   Excellent
Library of Christian Classics
   We shall depend upon this in class.
Ayer: *Source Book for Ancient Church History*
Ancient Christian Writers
The Fathers of the Church
J. Stevenson, ed.: *A New Eusebius*
Bettenson: *Documents of the Christian Church*
Bettenson: *The Early Christian Fathers*
Leith: *Creeds of the Churches*

Every student is asked to spend one hour in the library browsing through such collections as Migne, Ante-Nicene Fathers, Nicene and Post-Nicene Fathers. Berlin Corpus: *Die griechischen christlichen Schriftsteller der ersten drei Jahrhunderte.* Vienna Corpus: *Corpus scriptorum ecclesiasticorum latinorum: Ancient Christian Writers,* ed. J. Quasten and J. Plumpe, 1946 ff; *The Fathers of the Church,* ed. L. Schopp, 1947 ff; *Sources chretiennes,* ed. H. de Lubac and J. Danielou. 1941ff.

B

I. Introduction
   1. Significance of history of doctrine and its place in the theological curriculum.
   2. Definitions
   3. Problems of methodology
   4. The unevadable theological task in history
      M. Wiles: *The Making of Christian Doctrine*
      Harnack: *History of Dogma*, Vol. I
      Werner: *The Formation of Christian Dogma*
      Turner: *The Pattern of Christian Truth*
      Robert L. Calhoun: "The Role of Historical Theology," *Journal of Religion*, 1941
      J. Pelikan: *Development of Christian Doctrine, Some Historical Prolegomena*
      J. Pelikan: *Historical Theology*
      Peter Toon: *The Development of Doctrine in the Church* (1979)
      Owen Chadwick: *From Bousset to Newman* (1957)
      R. P. C. Hanson; *The Continuity of Christian Doctrine* (1981)
II. The Apostolic Fathers: The Problem of Christianity in a New Culture
   Clement, Ignatius, Polycarp, Didache, Hermas, Barnabas, Papias
   C. C. Richardson: *The Christianity of Ignatius of Antioch*
   T. F. Torrance: *Doctrine of Grace in the Apostolic Fathers*
   Virginia Corwin: *Ignatius and Christianity at Antioch*
   John Lawson: *An Historical and Theological Introduction to the Apostolic Fathers*
   R. M. Grant, ed.: *The Apostolic Fathers*
   L. W. Barnard: *Studies in the Apostolic Fathers and Their Background*
   Leonhard Goppelt: *Apostolic and Post-Apostolic Times*
III. Gnosticism and Other Irregular Versions of the Gospel: The Problem of Heresy and the Language of Faith
   Robert Grant: *Gnosticism and Early Christianity*
   Hans Jonas: *The Gnostic Religion*
   E. C. Blackman: *Marcion and His Influence*
   R. Wilson: *Gnosis and the New Testament*
   F. C. Burkitt: *The Church and Gnosis*
   F. L. Cross: *The Jung Codex*
   Albert Outler: *Christian Tradition and Unity We Seek*
   H. E. W. Turner: *Thomas the Evangelist*
   H. E. W. Turner: *The Pattern of Christian Truth*
   S. L. Greenslade: *Schism in the Early Church*
   Jeremy Taylor: *The Liberty of Prophesying*
   Van Unnik: *Newly Discovered Gnostic Writings*
      Best short summary
   Robert Wilson: *The Gnostic Problem*
      Best general survey

Beitil Gartner: *The Theology of the Gospel According to Thomas*
W. Bauer: *Orthodoxy and Heresy in Earliest Christianity*
IV. The Apologists: Problem of Christianity and Truth
Justin Martyr, Quadratus, Aristides, Justin Athenagoras, Tertullian, Minu-cius, Felix, Tatian, Theophilius, Bardesanes, Origen, Cyprian, Arnobius, Lactantius, Athanasius
Henry Chadwick: *Early Christian Thought and the Classical Tradition*
L. W. Bernard: *Justin Martyr*
E. R. Goodenough: *The Theology of Justin Martyr*
E. F. Osborn: *Justin Martyr* (1973)
L. W. Bernard: *Athenagoras* (1972)
V. Irenaeus: Problem of the Catholic Synthesis of Theology
John Lawson: *The Biblical Theology of St. Irenaeus*
Wingren: *Man and the Incarnation*
VI. Tertullian and Cyprian: Problem of Theological and Ecclesiastical Orthodoxy
Evans's introduction to his translations are excellent studies of Tertullian.
Warfield: *Studies in Tertullian and Augustine*
Tertullian's Treatise Against Praxeas, Treatise on the Incarnation, Prescrip-tions Against the Heretics
VII. Alexandrian Theology: Problem of Christianity and Culture
Cadious: *Origen*
J. Danielou: *Origen*
Hanson: *Allegory and Event*
Hanson: *Origen's Doctrine of Tradition*
Charles Bigg: *The Christian Platonists of Alexandria*
G. W. Butterworth: *Origen on First Principles*
E. F. Osborn: *Philosophy of Clement of Alexandria*
Jaeger: *Christian Paideia*
VIII. Rules of Faith, Especially the Apostles' Creed
J. N. D. Kelly: *Early Christian Creeds*
H. Lietzmann: *The Founding of the Church Universal*, chapter 4
A. C. McGiffert: *The Apostles' Creed*
Oscar Oullman: *The Earliest Christian Confessions*
E. Stauffer: *Theology of the New Testament*, Part III
D. L. Holland: "The Earliest Text of the Old Roman Symbol: A Debate with Hans Lietzmann and J. N. D. Kelly." *Church History*, Sept. 1965
IX. The Canon
Souter: *The Text and Canon of the New Testament*
Filson: *Which Books Belong in the Bible?*
Westcott: *A General Survey of the History of the Canon of the New Testament*
Reus: *History of the Canon of the Scripture*
Daniel Theron: *Evidence of Tradition*
Hans von Campenhausen: *The Formation of the Christian Bible*
Albert C. Sundberg: "The Making of the N.T. Canon" in *Interpreter's One Volume Commentary*
Kümmel: *Introduction to the New Testament*, Part II

XII. The Image Controversy, Council of Nicea 787
      G. Florovsky: *Origen, Eusebius and the Inconoclastic Controversy, Church
      History Since 1950*
      E. J. Martin: *A History of the Iconoclastic Controversy*
      L. W. Bernard: *The Graeco-Roman and Oriental Background of the Icono-
      clastic Controversy* (1974)
XIII. Augustine and the Doctrine of Man
      1. Augustine's Intellectual Development
      2. Problem of Knowledge
      3. The Being of God: Time and Eternity
      4. The Created World and the Fall
      5. Results of the Fall
      6. Original Sin
      7. Controversy with Pelagius
      8. Redemptive Grace: The Renewal of the Believer
      9. Predestination
      10. Christology and Doctrine of the Trinity
      11. Church and Sacraments
      12. Theology of History
      13. Augustine Summary: A Christian Worldview
      14. The Semi-Pelagian Controversy
      15. The Second Council of Orange
            G. Bonner: *Augustine and Modern Research on Pelagianism* (1972)
            Teselle: *Augustine, The Theologian*
            R. Battenhouse: *A Companion to the Study of Augustine*
            T. Burke: *Augustine's Quest for Wisdom*
            G. G. Willis: *Augustine and the Donatist Controversy*
            J. N. Gigis: *Political Aspects of Augustine's City of God*
            J. Richaby: *St. Augustine's City of God*
            N. P. Williams: *The Ideas of the Fall and Original Sin*
            J. Ferguson: *Pelagius*
            R. F. Evans: *Pelagius Inquiries and Appraisals*
            C. N. Cochrane: *Christianity and Classical Culture*
            E. Gilson: *The Christian Philosophy of Saint Augustine*
            Burleigh: *The City of God*
            G. Bonner: *Augustine of Hippo*
            P. Brown: *Augustine of Hippo*
            John A. Mourant: *Introduction to the Philosophy of Saint Augustine*
            Portalie: *A Guide to the Thought of St. Augustine*
            R. Markus: *Saeculum: History and Society in the Theology of St. Augustine*
            (1970)
XIV. Doctrine of the Church and Sacraments from Augustine to Luther: The
      Problem of Scripture and Tradition
      Vincent of Lerins: *Commonitory*
      F. F. Rogers: *Peter Lombard*
      J. Jeremias: *Infant Baptism in the First Four Centuries*
      H. T. Lehmann: *Meaning and Practice of the Lord's Supper*

Dugmore: *The Mass and the English Reformers*
Francis Clark, S. J.: *Eucharistic Sacrifice and the Reformation*
Aulen: *Eucharist and Sacrifice*
See especially LCC: *Early Medieval Theology*
O. D. Watkin: *History of Penance*
Aland: *Did the Early Church Baptize Infants?*
Jeremias: *The Origins of Infant Baptism*
Robert Grant: *A Short History of the Interpretation of the Bible*
J. S. Preus: *From Shadow to Promise: Old Testament Interpretation from Augustine to the Young Luther*
Campenhausen: *Ecclesiastical Authority and Spiritual Power*
Richard Hanson: *The Christian Priesthood Reexamined*

XV. Abelard and Anselm
Sikes: *Abailard*
J. Ramsay McCallum: *Abailard's Christian Theology*
A. V. Murray: *Abelard and St. Bernard*
Leif Grane: *Peter Abelard*
Jasper Hopkins: *A Companion to the Study of Anselm* (1972)
G. R. Evans: *Anselm and a New Generation* (1980)
G. R. Evans: *Anselm and Talking About God* (1978)

XVI. Thomas Aquinas
D'Arcy: *Thomas Aquinas*
Copleston: *Thomas Aquinas*
Thomas Aquinas, *Summa Theologica*, Vol. I (Blackfriars)

XVII. The Dissolution of Scholastic Theology
Leff: *Bradwardine and Pelagians*
Carre: *Realists and Nominalists*
N. Micklem: *Reason and Revelation*
C. R. S. Harris: *Duns Scotus*
Henry Bett: *Nicholas Cusas*
A. C. Flick: *The Decline of the Medieval Church*
Nicholas Cusanus: *Of Learned Ignorance*
E. Bettoni: *Duns Scotus: The Basic Principles of His Philosophy*
Dolan: *Unity and Reformed, Selected Writings of Nicolas Cusas*
Obermann: *Forerunners of the Reformation and The Harvest of Medieval Thought*
Weinberg: *Short History of Medieval Philosophy*
P. Vignaus: *Philosophy in the Middle Ages*
D. Knowles: *The Evolution of Medieval Thought*
S. Ozment: *The Age of Reform*
Obermann: *Masters of Reformation*
Gordon Leff: *The Dissolution of the Medieval Outlook* (1976)
Gordon Leff: *Medieval Thought*

PART ELEVEN
BIBLIOGRAPHY
1942–2000
JOHN HADDON LEITH

Books

1963 (as editor) *Creeds of the Church: A Reader in Christian Doctrine, from the Bible to the Present* (New York: Doubleday; Rev. ed., Richmond, Va.: John Knox Press, 1973; 3d ed., Atlanta: John Knox Press, 1982).

1965 *The Church: A Believing Fellowship* (Richmond, Va.: CEC Press; Rev. ed., Atlanta: John Knox Press, 1981).

1973 *Assembly at Westminster: Reformed Theology in the Making* (Richmond, Va.: John Knox Press).
Greenville Presbyterian Church: The Story of a People, 1765–1973 (Greenwood County, S.C.: Greenville Presbyterian Church).

1977 *Introduction to the Reformed Tradition: A Way of Being the Christian Community* (Atlanta: John Knox Press; Edinburgh: Saint Andrew Press, 1978; Rev. ed., Atlanta: John Knox Press, 1981).

1984 (as editor) *John Calvin—The Christian Life* (San Francisco: Harper & Row).

1988 *Reformed Imperative: What the Church Has to Say That No One Else Can Say* (Philadelphia: Westminster Press).

1989 *John Calvin's Doctrine of the Christian Life* (Ph.D. diss., Yale University, 1949; Philadelphia: Westminster Press).

1990 (as editor) *Calvin Studies V: Papers Presented at the Colloquium on Calvin Studies, 1990.*
From Generation to Generation: The Renewal of the Church According to Its Own Faith and Practice (Louisville, Ky.: Westminster/John Knox Press).

1992 (as editor) *Calvin Studies VI: Papers Presented at the Colloquium on Calvin Studies, 1992.*

1993 *Basic Christian Doctrine* (Louisville, Ky.: Westminster/John Knox Press).
(as editor, with Stacy Johnson) *Reformed Reader: A Sourcebook for Christian Theology* (Louisville, Ky.: Westminster/John Knox Press), 2 vols. (Volume 2, edited by George Stroup).

1994 (as editor) *Calvin Studies VII: Papers Presented at the Colloquium on Calvin Studies, 1994.*

1996 (as editor) *Calvin Studies VIII: Papers Presented at the Colloquium on Calvin Studies, 1996.*

1997 *Crisis in the Church: The Plight of Theological Education* (Louisville, Ky.: Westminster/John Knox Press).
Greenville Presbyterian Church: The Story of a People, 1765–1997 (Greenwood County, S.C.: Greenville Presbyterian Church).

1998 (as editor with Robert Johnson) *Calvin Studies IX: Papers Presented at the Colloquium on Calvin Studies, 1998.*
"Calvins theologischer Realismus und der bleibende Einfluss seiner." In *Zur Zukunft der Reformierten Theologie,* Michael Welker und David Willis (hg.) (Neukirchener, 1998).

Articles in Volumes of Collected Essays

1962 "Calvin's Theological Method and the Ambiguity in His Theology." In *Reformation Studies: Essays in Honor of Roland H. Bainton,* edited by Franklin H. Littell, 107–14. Richmond, Va.: John Knox Press.

1964 "Ernest Trice Thompson and the Theological Outlook and Ethical Concern of The Presbyterian Church in the United States." In *Ernest Trice Thompson: An Appreciation,* 30–48. Richmond, Va.: Union Theological Seminary in Virginia.

1966 "Creation and Redemption: Law and Gospel in the Theology of John Calvin." In *Marburg Revisited: A Reexamination of Lutheran and Reformed Traditions,* edited by Paul C. Empie and James I. McCord. 141–51. Minneapolis, Minn.: Augsburg Publishing House.

1968 "John Calvin's Polemic against Idolatry." In *Soli Deo Gloria: New Testament Studies in Honor of William Childs Robinson,* edited by J. McDowell Richards. 111–24. Richmond, Va.: John Knox Press.

1969 "Reconciliation and Ecumenism." In *Reconciliation in Today's World,* edited by Allen O. Miller. 50–67. Grand Rapids, Mich.: Wm. B. Eerdmans Publishing Co. Six study papers presented in anticipation of the meeting of the World Alliance of Reformed and Presbyterian Churches and the International Congregational Council to be held in Nairobi, Kenya, August 20–30, 1970.

1981 "The Doctrine of the Will in the *Institutes of the Christian Religion.*" In *Reformatio Perennis: Essays on Calvin and the Reformation in Honor of Ford Lewis Battles,* edited by B.A. Gerrish in collaboration with Robert Benedetto. 49–66. Pittsburgh Theological Monograph Series, vol. 32. Pittsburgh: Pickwick Press, 1981.

1982 "The Westminster Confession in American Presbyterianism." In *The Westminster Confession in the Church Today: Papers Prepared for the Church of Scotland Panel on Doctrine,* edited by Alasdair I. C. Heron. 95–100. Edinburgh: Saint Andrew Press.

1986 "James Luther Mays." In *The Hermeneutical Quest: Essays in Honor of James Luther Mays on His Sixty-fifth Birthday,* edited by Donald G. Miller. 1–10. Princeton Theological Monographs Series, vol. 4. Allison Park, Pa.: Pickwick Publications.

1987 "Calvin's Awareness of the Holy and the Enigma of His Theology." In *In Honor of John Calvin, 1509–64,* edited by Edward J. Furcha. 204–32. ARC Supplement, no. 3. Papers from the 1986 International Calvin Symposium, McGill University. Montreal: Faculty of Religious Studies, McGill University.

1989 "James Henley Thornwell and the Shaping of the Reformed Tradition in the South." In *Probing the Reformed Tradition: Historical Studies in Honor of Edward A. Dowey Jr.,* edited by Elsie Anne McKee and Brian G. Armstrong. Louisville, Ky.: Westminster/John Knox Press.

1992 "Foreword." In *Later Calvinism: International Perspectives,* edited by W. Fred Graham. *Sixteenth Century Essays & Studies* vol. 22. Kirksville, Mo.: Sixteenth Century Journal Publishers.

2000 "The Significance of History of Doctrine in Theological Study." In *Theology in the Service of the Church: Essays in Honor of Thomas W. Gillespie,* edited by Wallace Alston. 128–39. Grand Rapids, Mich.: Wm. B. Eerdmans Publishing Co.

Periodical Articles

1942 "Life in the Shadow of Death." *The Presbyterian of the South* 117 (30 December 1942): 1–5.

1944 "Watch Thy Foot When Thou Goest into the House of God." *Associate Reformed Presbyterian* 84 (30 August 1944): 7–9.

1948 "Life Everlasting." *The Pastor* 11 (January 1948): 7.
      "John Calvin and Social Responsibility." *Associate Reformed Presbyterian* 88 (22 September): 1, 6.

1949 "God In Nature." *Adult Teacher* (Methodist) (June 1949)

1951 "Our Fallen Towers of Babel" (Sermon of the Month). *Presbyterian Outlook* 133 (15 January): 5.
      "They Said Something! The Church and Scholarship." *Presbyterian Outlook* 133 (15 January): 7.
      "Europe Today (1)." *Presbyterian Outlook* 133 (8 October): 5–6.
      "Europe Today (2)." *Presbyterian Outlook* 133 (15 October): 6–7.

1952 "They Said Something! Such a Church Crumbles." *Presbyterian Outlook* 134 (14 January): 7.
      "They Said Something! Lesson for Us." *Presbyterian Outlook* 134 (17 March): 6.
      "What American Students Can Learn from Europe." *Presbyterian Survey* 42 (March): 40–41, 46.
      "Success." *Presbyterian Outlook* 134 (25 August): 7
      "The Liberalism of the Reformed Tradition." *Presbyterian Outlook* 134 (20 October): 7

1957 "Fruits of the Reformation." *Day by Day* 19 (20–26 October): 21–27.

1958 "Some Distinctive Features of Our Presbyterian-Reformed Heritage." *Earnest Worker* 59.
      "Our Heritage in Church Government." (January): 1–5.
      "The Significance of the Bible." (February): 1–5.
      "The Liturgy for Corporate Worship." (March): 1–4.
      "A Class Church Develops." (April): 1–4.
      "Education Is the Service of God." (June), 1–3, 79.
      "The Relation of Church and State." (July): 1–4.

1960 "What the Bible Says about Man." *Day by Day* 22 (17–23 January): 21–27.

1961 "Challenging Spirit for a Changing Culture." *Presbyterian Survey* 51 (January): 37–38, 56–57.
      "Our Biblical Heritage." *Day by Day* 23 (1, 3–8 April): 5, 7–12.

1962 "Christians in a Disintegrating Society." *Presbyterian Outlook* 144 (1 October): 5–6.

1963 "Heroes of the Reformation." *Day by Day* 25 (21–26 October): 22–27.
"If Not by Grace, Then by Law." *Presbyterian Outlook* 145 (18 November): 8.
1964 "The Church and Race." *Presbyterian Outlook* 146 (27 July): 6.
"Frankfurt, 1964." *Presbyterian Outlook* 146 (21 September): 4.
"Presbyterians and the Fair." *Presbyterian Outlook* 146 (12 October): 4.
1965 "To Guide Us in Christian Action." *Presbyterian Survey* 55 (January): 12–14.
"A Question of Priorities." *Presbyterian Outlook* 147 (15 March): 4.
"Calvin, the Politician." *Presbyterian Survey* 55 (July): 16–17.
1966 "Professor Probes Church-Related Questions." *Florida Presbyterian College Bulletin* (March).
1968 "Critical Juncture" (letter to the editor cosigned with four other professors of Union Theological Seminary in Virginia). *Presbyterian Outlook* 150 (11 November): 2.
"Union with the RCA Debate: No." *Presbyterian Survey* 58 (December):19, 21–23.
1970 "Crisis in the Church: Its Meaning for Us." *As I See It Today* 1 (November).
"The History of Christian Thought." *The Christian Ministry* 1 (November): 33–35.
1971 "John Calvin: Theologian of the Bible." *Interpretation* 25 (July): 329–44.
1972 "The Crucifixion and the Mystery of Freedom." *Presbyterian Outlook* 154 (27 March): 5–6.
1974 "Can the Ministry Reform Itself?" *Presbyterian Outlook* 156 (21 October): 5–6.
1975 "The Declaration and Theological Decision" (in two parts). *Presbyterian Outlook* 157 (7, 14 April): 5–6; 5–6.
"Some Recollections" (letter to the editor on the death of Robert McNeill). *Presbyterian Outlook* 157 (25 August): 2.
"Speaking the Truth." *As I See It Today* 6 (December).
1976 "The Bible and Theology." *Interpretation* 30 (July): 227–41.
"The Declaration and Theological Decision." *Presbyterian Outlook* 158 (8 November): 5–7.
1977 "Calvin Study for Today." *Interpretation* 31 (January): 3–7.
"Becoming a Christian Community." *Presbyterian Outlook* 159 (28 February): 5–7.
"The Crisis in the Theology and Practice of Baptism." *Reformed Review* 31 (Fall): 4–14.
1978 "Teaching Theology in the Local Congregation." *Journal for Preachers* 1 (Pentecost): 76–82.
"Taking the Theological Task Seriously." *Presbyterian Outlook* 160 (18 September): 6.
"A Perspective on Presbyterian Reunion." *Presbyterian Outlook* 160 (25 September): 5–6.
1979 "Response (to Professor Klooster on Reformed Theology)." *Theological Forum* (Reformed Ecumenical Synod) 6 (April): 31–33.
"A Christian View of Economics." *Presbyterian Survey* 69 (May): 23–24.
1980 "Preparation for Ministry." *Adult Bible Studies* (Methodist) 13 (7–28 December): 8–36.
"The Nicene Creed." *Adult Leader* (Methodist) 13 (December–February 1980–81): 4–6.

1981 "The Book of Hebrews." *Adult Bible Studies* (Methodist) 13 (3–31 May): 65–95.

"The Church's Doctrine of Jesus Christ." *Adult Leader* (Methodist) 14 (December–February 1981–82): 15–18.

"Magnificent Mystery." *Presbyterian Survey* 71 (December): 28–31.

1982 "Felix Gear (1899–1982)." *Presbyterian Outlook* 164 (9 August): 24.

"The City of God and the Nations of Earth: Isaiah 40:6–17, Romans 8:28–39, 13:1–7." *Presbyterian Outlook* 164 (29 November): D-J.

"Church Union: A Practical Necessity but Not the Critical Issue Confronting Presbyterians." *Presbyterian Outlook* 164 (20–27 December): 5–6.

1983 "William Childs Robinson: 1897–1982." *Presbyterian Outlook* 165 (10 January): 15.

"The Message of Christian Faith on the Occasion of the Burial of the Dead." *Journal for Preachers* 6 (Lent): 20–25.

"What Is the Gospel? A Sermon Appropriate to the Luther Anniversary." *Presbyterian Outlook* 165 (14 November): 7–8.

1985 "Vocation to Learning and Piety." *Presbyterian Outlook* 167 (15 April): 6–9.

"John Calvin and Stewardship." *Journal for Preachers* 9 (Advent): 2–7.

1986 "The Writing of a Reformed Confession Today." *The Reformed World* 39: 501–17.

1988 "Our Protestant Vocation." *Presbyterian Outlook* 170 (10 October): 5–7, 11.

1989 "Calvin's Doctrine of the Proclamation of the Word and Its Significance for Today in the Light of Recent Research." *Review and Expositor* 86 (Winter).

"Review Essay of Philip Schaff's *Bibliotheca Symbolica Ecclesiae Universalis: The Creeds of Christendom, with a History and Critical Notes.*" *American Presbyterians: Journal of Presbyterian History* 67.

1991 "On Keeping a Proper Perspective." *Presbyterian Outlook* 173/18 (May 13): 6.

"Remembering the Protestant Reformation." *The Presbyterian Record* 115/10 (October): 26–28.

1992 "A Tribute to Vernon Broyles Jr." *Presbyterian Outlook* 174/12 (March 30): 2.

Commentary on "Presbyterians: Where Have All the People Gone?" by Richard John Neuhaus. *First Things* (28 December), 66–68.

1994 "A Confused and Destructive Debate." *Presbyterian Outlook* 176/1 (January 3–10): 9.

"Disappointed by GAC Action." *Presbyterian Outlook* 176/10 (March 14): 2.

"The Church as a Voluntary Organization." *Presbyterian Outlook* 176/34 (October 3).

1995 "On Choosing a Seminary Professor." *Presbyterian Outlook* 177/8 (February 27): 6.

1996 "The Protestant Principle and a Free Press." *Presbyterian Outlook* 178/1 (Jan. 1): 8–9.

"Reflections on Being at Peachtree." *Presbyterian Outlook* 178/16 (May 6): 6.

"Reflections on Being at the First Presbyterian Church of Charlotte, North Carolina." *Presbyterian Outlook* 178/33 (May 6): 5–6.

"Tribute to Donald G. Miller." *Presbyterian Outlook* 1.

Encyclopedia and Dictionary Articles

1981 *Abingdon Dictionary of Living Religion,* edited by Keith Crim (Nashville, Tn.: Abingdon Press), s.v. "Apostles' Creed," "Arminius, Jacobus," "Athanasian

Creed," "Augsburg Confession," "Calvin, John," "Catechism," "Chalcedonian Definition," "Covenantus," "Edict of Nantes," "Helvetic Confession," "Hugenot," "Knox, John," "Nicaea, Council of," "Reformed Churches," "Theology, Contemporary Christian," "Thirty-nine Articles," "Westminster Confession."

1983 *New Dictionary of Christian Theology,* edited by Alan Richardson and John Bowden (London: SCM Press). s.v. "Creeds."

1984 *Encyclopedia of Religion in the South,* edited by Samuel S. Hill (Macon, Ga.: Mercer University Press), s.v. "Spirituality of the Church," "Westminster Confession of Faith."

1987 *The Encyclopedia Americana: International Edition.* 30 vols. (Danbury, Conn.: Grolier), s.v. "Reformed Churches."

The Encyclopedia of Religion, edited by Mircea Eliade, 18 vols. (New York: Macmillan Publishing Company), s.v. "Farel, Guillaume," "Knox, John," "Presbyterianism, Reformed."

1989 *Theologische Realenzykloplidie,* edited by Gerhard Müller (Berlin: de Gruyter), s.v. "Kirchenzucht."

The Encyclopedia of Southern Culture, edited by Charles Reagan Wilson and William Ferris (Chapel Hill, N.C.: University of North Carolina Press), s.v. "Calvinism."

Anchor Bible Dictionary (Ann Arbor, Mich.: University of Michigan Press), s.v. "Creeds, Early Christian."

1992 *Encyclopedia of the Reformed Faith,* edited by Donald McKim (Louisville, Ky.: Westminster/John Knox Press), s.v. "Schaff, Philip," "Theology, Reformed," "Westminster Confession of Faith."

A New Handbook of Christian Theology, edited by Donald W. Musser and Joseph L. Price (Nashville: Abingdon Press), s.v. "Ecclesiology."

The Anchor Bible Dictionary, edited by David Noel Friedman. 6 Vols. (New York: Doubleday), s.v. "Early Christian Creeds."

1995 *Concise Encyclopedia of Preaching,* edited by William H. Willimon and Richard Lischer (Louisville, Ky.: Westminster/John Knox Press), s.v. "John Calvin."

Dictionary of the Presbyterian and Reformed Tradition in America, edited by D. G. Hart (Downers Grove, Ill.: InterVarsity Press), s.v. "American Presbyterians and the Sacraments."

Book Reviews and Notes

1945 Review of *Pastoral Work: A Source Book for Ministers,* by Andrew W. Blackwood. *Presbyterian Outlook* 127 (9 July): 15.

Review of *Greater Good Neighbor Policy,* by Wade Crawford Barclay. *Presbyterian Outlook* 127 (24 September): 15.

Review of *Event in Eternity,* by Paul Scherer. *Presbyterian Outlook* 127 (24 December): 15.

1946 Review of *The Holy Spirit,* by L.T. Wilds. *Presbyterian Outlook* 128 (25 March): 15.

Review of *God in Us,* by A. Campbell Garnett. *Presbyterian Outlook* 128 (6 May): 21.

Review of *The Living Bible,* by William Clayton Bower. *Presbyterian Outlook* 128 (20 May): 21.

Review of *Whose Leaf Shall Not Wither,* by James Lichliter. *Presbyterian Outlook* 128 (28 October): 15.

1947 Review of *Skeptic's Search for God,* by Barbara Spoffoul Morgan. *The Pastor* 11 (October): 34, 36.

1950 Review of *The Gospel and Our World,* by Georgia Harkness. *The Pastor* 13 (January): 37–38.

1951 Review of *About the Gospels,* by C.H. Dodd. *The Pastor* 14 (April): 37, 39.

1952 Review of *The Church Militant,* by Harold Bosley. *Presbyterian Outlook* 134 (17 March): 15.

1959 Review of *Segregation and Desegregation: A Christian Approach,* by T.B. Maston. *Christian Advocate* 3 (10 December): 17.

1962 Review of *Reason and God,* by John E. Smith: *Presbyterian Outlook* 144 (10 December): 15.

1963 Review of *Word and Spirit: Calvin's Doctrine of Biblical Authority,* by H. Jackson Forstman. *Interpretation* 17 (January): 89–91.
Review of *Constantine and Religious Liberty,* by Hermann Dörries, translated by Roland Bainton. *Presbyterian Outlook* 145 (18 March): 15.
Review of *Zwingli: A Reformed Theologian,* by Jaques Courvoisier. *Theology Today* 20 (October): 436–37.

1965 Review of *The Minister in the Reformed Tradition,* by Harry G. Goodykoontz. *Theology Today* 21 (January): 531–32.

1966 Review of *England's Earliest Protestants 1520–1535,* by William A. Clebsch. *Archiv für Reformationsgeschichte* 57 (June): 281–82.
Review of *The Palatinate in European History, 1559–1660,* by Claus-Peter Clasen. *Archiv für Reformationsgeschichte* 57 (June): 284–85.
Review of *White Protestantism and the Negro,* by David M. Reimers. *Christian Century* 83 (5 January): 15.

1969 Review of *Development of Christian Doctrine: Some Historical Prolegomena,* by Jaroslav Pelikan, and *Interpreters of Luther: Essays in Honor of Wilhelm Pauck,* edited by Jaroslav Pelikan. *Christian Century* 86 (16 July): 959–60.
Review of *A Commentary on the Confession of 1967 and An Introduction to "The Book of Confessions,"* by Edward A. Dowey Jr. *Princeton Seminary Bulletin* 62 (Autumn): 88–89.

1970 Review of *Calvin and the Amyraut Heresy: Protestant Scholasticism and Humanism in 17th Century France,* by Brian G. Armstrong. *Presbyterian Outlook* 152 (14 September): 15.
Review of *On Religion,* by Friedrich Schleiermacher. *Presbyterian Outlook* 152 (12 October): 15.
Review of *Luther: An Introduction to His Thought,* by Gerhard Ebeling. *Christian Century* 87 (21 October): 1264, 1266.

1971 Review of *A History of Christian Thought,* vol. 1, *From the Beginnings to the Council of Chalcedon,* by Justo L. Gonzalez. *Presbyterian Outlook* 153 (4 January): 15.
Review of *The Pelican Guide to Modern Theology,* vol. 2, *Historical Theology,* by J. Danielou, A.H. Couratin, and John Kent. *Presbyterian Outlook* 153 (4 January): 15.
Review of *Pulpit in Parliament: Puritanism During the English Civil Wars, 1640–1648,* by John F. Wilson. *Christian Century* 88 (17 March): 355–56.

Review of *Elizabethan Puritanism*, edited by Leonard J. Trinterud. *Presbyterian Outlook* 153 (24 May): 15.

Review of *Luther, His Life and Times*, by Richard Friedenthal. *Journal of Church and State* 13 (Autumn): 531–32.

Review of *Calvin's Doctrine of the Church*, by Benjamin Charles Milner Jr. *Church History* 40 (September): 324.

Review of *The Constructive Revolutionary: John Calvin and His Socio-Economic Impact*, by W. Fred Graham. *Presbyterian Outlook* 153 (6 September): 15.

Review of *Calvin's New Testament Commentaries*, by T.H.L. Parke. *Presbyterian Outlook* 153 (1 November): 15.

1972 Review of *Arminius: A Study in the Dutch Reformation*, by Cail Bangs. *Presbyterian Outlook* 154 (20 March): 15.

Review of *The Humanness of John Calvin*, by Richard Stauffer, translated by George Shriver. *Presbyterian Outlook* 154 (3 April): 15.

Review of *John Calvin: Selections from His Writings*, edited by John Dillenberger. *Church History* 41 (June): 261–62.

Review of *Calvin*, by Wilhelm Neuser. *Church History* 41 (June): 262.

Review of *Reinhold Niebuhr: Prophet to Politicians*, by Ronald H. Stone. *Presbyterian Outlook 154* (6 November): 15.

1973 Review of *The Absoluteness of Christianity and the History of Religions*, by Ernst Troeltsch, translated by David Reid. *Presbyterian Outlook* 155 (8 January): 15.

1974 Review of *Contemporary American Protestant Thought: 1900–1970*, edited by William R. Miller. *Presbyterian Outlook* 156 (14 January): 15.

Review of *Essays on Nature and Grace*, by Joseph Sittler. *Interpretation* 28 (April): 242–43.

Review of *Protestant Theology in the Nineteenth Century: Its Background and History*, by Karl Barth. *Christian Century* 91 (10 April): 401–2.

Review of *The Psychology of Religion*, by Wayne E. Oates. *Presbyterian Outlook* 156 (22 April): 15.

1975 Review of *Whatever Became of Sin?* by Karl Menninger. *Interpretation* 29 (October): 435–37.

1976 Review of *The Spirituality of John Calvin*, by Luden J. Richard. *Church History* 45 (March): 109.

1977 Review of *Profiles in Belief*, vol. 1, by Arthur C. Piepkorn. *Christian Century* 94 (August 31–September 6): 762.

Review of *The Unity We Seek: A Statement by the Roman Catholic/Presbyterian/Reform Consultation*, edited by Ernest L. Unterkoefler and Andrew Harsanyi. *National Catholic Reporter* 14 (28 October): 12.

1978 Review of *Eugene Carson Blake: Prophet with Portfolio*, by R. Douglas Breckenridge. *Christian Century* 95 (25 October): 1019.

1979 Review of *Milton's Imagery and the Visual Arts: Iconographic Tradition in the Epic Poems*, by Roland Mushat Frye. *Theology Today* 36 (July): 284–86.

1981 Review of *The Authority and Interpretation of the Bible*, by Jack B. Rogers and Donald K. McKim. *Interpretation* 35 (January): 75–78.

Review of *Catholicism*, by Richard P. McBrien. *Christian Century* 98 (25 February): 207–8.

Review of *Does God Exist? An Answer for Today*, by Hans Küng. *Presbyterian Survey* 71 (May): 47.

1983 Review of *Luther: Witness to Jesus Christ*, by Marc Lienhard. *Christian Century*
      100 (19 October): 942, 944.
      Review of *The Nature and Function of Faith in the Theology of John Calvin*, by
      Victor A. Shepherd. *Presbyterian Outlook* 165 (31 October): 13.
1984 Review of *The Faith of the Church*, by M. Eugene Osterhaven. *Theology Today*
      40 (January): 506–7.
      Review of *The Christian Polity of John Calvin*, by Harro Höpfl. *Church History*
      53 (March): 95–96.
1985 Review of *The Assembly of the Lord: Politics and Religion in the Westminster
      Assembly and the "Grand Debate,"* by Robert S. Paul. *Presbyterian Outlook* 167
      (16 September): 11.
1986 Review of *John Calvin: On the Diaconate and Liturgical Almsgiving*, by Elsie
      Anne McKee. *Theology Today* 43 (April): 119–20.
1987 Review of *Reformed Theology in America: A History of Its Modern Development*,
      edited by David F. Wells. *Presbyterian Outlook* 169 (28 September): 6–7.
      Review of *The Metaphysical Confederacy: James Henry Thornwell and the Syn-
      thesis of Southern Values*, by James Oscar Farmer Jr. *Presbyterian Outlook* 169 (2
      November): 7.
1988 Review of *Leaders of the Reformation*, edited by Richard L. DeMolen. *Church
      History* 57 (March): 89–90.
      Review of *Hersschaft Tugend' Vorsehung: Hermeneutische Deutung und Veröffent-
      lichung handschriftlicher Annotationen Calvins zu sieben Senecatragödien und der
      Pharsalia Lucans*, by Alexandre Ganoczy and Stefan Scheld. *Church History* 57
      (September): 417–18.
1993 Review of *Luther and Calvin on Secular Authority*, edited and translated by
      Harro Höpfl. *Sixteenth Century Journal* XXIV/4 (1993): 1004–5.
1995 Review of *The Yoke of Christ: Martin Bucer and Christian Discipline*, by Amy
      Nelson Burnett. *Sixteenth Century Journal* XXVI/4 (1995).
1997 Review of *Christian Confessions: A Historical Introduction*, by Ted A. Campbell.
      Theology Today 54/1 (April): 140.
1998 Review of *Interpreting John Calvin*, by Ford Lewis Battles. *Theology Today* 55/1
      (April): 108–11.
      Review of *The Outrageous Idea of Christian Scholarship*, by George M. Marsden.
      Theology Today 55/2 (July): 108–11.

Miscellaneous

1992 "Foreword" in *Instruction in Faith* (1537), by John Calvin, edited and trans-
      lated by Paul T. Fuhrmann (Philadelphia: Westminster Press, 1949; Louisville,
      Ky.: Westminster/John Knox Press, new edition, 1992).

Church Court, Agency, and Board Reports

1956 "Gambling . . . What's Wrong with It?" Presbyterian Church in the United
      States, Board of Christian Education.
      "The Presbyterian Church and Education." President's Address. In *Minutes of
      the Forty-Second Annual Meeting of the Presbyterian Educational Association of
      the South, Montreat, N.C., June 26-30, 1956*, 40–43.

1961 "Report of the Ad Interim Committee on Possible Revision of Chapter III of the Confession of Faith to the General Assembly of 1961, Presbyterian Church in the United States" (except for Section IV). In *Minutes of the One-Hundred-First General Assembly of the Presbyterian Church in the United States, Dallas, Texas, April 27–May 2, 1961,* 132–39.

"Teaching Christian Beliefs through the Educational Work of the Church." Foundation Paper VIII, Presbyterian Church in the United States, Board of Christian Education.

1963 "Historical Preface for the Form of Government and the Rules of Discipline" and "Historical Preface for the Directory for the Worship and Work of the Church." *The Book of Church Order of the Presbyterian Church in the United States.* Rev. ed. (Richmond, Va.: Presbyterian Church in the United States: Board of Christian Education).

1972 "The Theology of Call and Ordination in the Reformed Tradition." Resource Paper for the General Assembly Conference on the Minister (Presbyterian Church in the United States), Montreat, N.C., March 2–4.

1973 *Reformed Theology and the Style of Evangelism.* Presbyterian Church in the United States, Office of Evangelism and Church Development.

1979 *Theological Reflections on the Death Penalty.* Presbyterian Church in the United States, General Assembly Mission Board, Division of Church and Society.

1986 "Proposal Toward a Confession of Faith." Paper presented to the Special Committee on a Brief Statement of Reformed Faith, Presbyterian Church in the United States. May. (Mimeographed)

1987 "Statement to the Governor's Seasonal and Migrant Farm Workers' Board." Governor, Commonwealth of Virginia. March 11. (Mimeographed)

Consultations and Colloquia

Reformed and Lutheran Theological Consultations. Papers.
1962 "The Starting Point and Purpose of Lutheran and Reformed Conversations." February. (Mimeographed)

1972 "The Lutheran-Reformed Conversations in Historical Perspective." April. (Mimeographed)

Calvin Studies: Papers Presented at Colloquia on Calvin Studies at Davidson College Presbyterian Church, Davidson, North Carolina; and Davidson College, Davidson, North Carolina.
1982 *Calvin Studies I* (as editor, with Charles Raynal).

1984 *Calvin Studies II* (as editor, with Charles Raynal).

"Calvin's Doctrine of the Proclamation of the Word and Its Significance for Today in the Light of Recent Research."

1986 *Calvin Studies III* (as editor).

1988 *Calvin Studies IV* (as editor with W. Stacy Johnson).

Tape Recordings

Held in the Library, Union Theological Seminary in Virginia
1959 *The Christian Meaning of Thanksgiving.* Thanksgiving Service Sermon, Union Theological Seminary in Virginia, November 26. Richmond, Va.: Union Theological Seminary. Sound cassette.

1960 *The Significance of Historical Theology in the Education of Ministers.* Inaugural Address, Union Theological Seminary in Virginia, April 20. Richmond, Va.: Union Theological Seminary. Sound cassette.
Contemporary Theology, no. 1–3. Lectures delivered at Montreat, N.C., August 14-15. Atlanta, Ga.: Sermons & Pictures. Sound cassette.

1961 *Distinctions of Presbyterian Heritage.* Lecture delivered at Montreat, N.C., July 9. Atlanta, Ga.: Sermons & Pictures. Sound cassette.
Our Presbyterian Heritage in America. Lecture delivered at Montreat, N.C., July 10. Atlanta, Ga.: Sermons & Pictures. Sound cassette.

1962 *The Salt of the Earth and the Light of the World.* Lecture delivered at Montreat, N.C. Richmond, Va.: Union Theological Seminary. Sound cassette.

1965 *Discerning the Signs of the Times.* Lecture delivered at Christian Education Covenant Life Conference, Montreat, N.C. Richmond, Va.: Union Theological Seminary. Sound cassette.
The Scandal of Christmas. Sermon, Union Theological Seminary in Virginia, December 16. Richmond, Va.: Union Theological Seminary. Sound cassette.

1966 *The Living God.* Sermon on Isaiah 40:9–31, Montreat, N.C., July 3. Atlanta, Ga.: Sermons & Pictures.

1967 *Perseverance of the Saints.* Sermon delivered at Montreat, N.C., July 16. Richmond, Va.: Union Theological Seminary. Sound cassette.

1968 *Doctrinal Preaching.* Pastors Institute, Richmond, Virginia, February 20. Richmond, Va.: Union Theological Seminary. Sound cassette.
The Theology of Teilhard de Chardin and Karl Rahner. School of Theology, Union Theological Seminary in Virginia, July. Richmond, Va.: Union Theological Seminary. Sound cassettes:
   Teilhard de Chardin: The Phenomenon of Man. July 23.
   Teilhard de Chardin: The Divine Milieu. July 24.
   Teilhard de Chardin: Conclusion. July 25.
   Karl Rahner: The Prospect for Dogmatic Theology. July 26.
   Karl Rahner: The Development of Dogma. July 27.

1969 *The Gospel for Today.* Sermon on Mark 2:5, Romans 8:31, Montreat, N.C., June 29. Atlanta, Ga.: Sermons & Pictures. Sound cassette.

1971 *What Is the Gospel?* Sermon, Second Presbyterian Church, Richmond, Virginia, July 25. Richmond, Va.: Union Theological Seminary. Sound cassette.

1977 *An Awareness of Destiny.* Protestant Hour, Pilgrimage of a People, March 13. Atlanta, Ga.: Protestant Radio and TV Center. Sound cassette.

1978 *Theology in the Practice of Teaching in the Pastorate:* Columbia Forum Alumni Lectures, Columbia Theological Seminary, Decatur, Georgia. Richmond, Va.: Union Theological Seminary. Sound cassettes:
   The Reformed Perspective: The Catholicity and Holiness of the Church. February 1.
   The Freedom of the Word and Spirit: A Theology of Power in Church Life. February 2.
   The Teaching of Theology in the Local Congregation: A Way It Can Be Done. February 3.

1982 *New Testament Theology (Christian Theology).* Conference on Interpreting the Faith, Union Theological Seminary in Virginia, July. Richmond, Va.: Union Theological Seminary. Sound cassettes:

The Person and Work of Jesus Christ. July 6.
Holy Spirit and the Means of Grace. July 7.
Justification and Sanctification. July 8.
Visions of the Christian Life. July 9.
The Christian Hope. July 10.
Are You the First Man That Was Born? Sunday Morning Worship, Presbyterian Heritage Conference Honoring Dr. E. T. Thompson, Montreat, N.C., August 13–15. Montreat, N.C.: Montreat Tapes. Sound cassette.

1985　*A Theologian's Perspective on the Church and Politics.* From the Church in the Public Square series. Union Theological Seminary in Virginia, March 30. Richmond, Va.: Union Theological Seminary. Sound cassette.

1986　*Sermon on Acts 2:22–24.* Union Theological Seminary in Virginia, March 25. Richmond, Va.: Union Theological Seminary. Sound cassette.
Sermon on Luke 24:1-11. Union Theological Seminary in Virginia, March 26. Richmond, Va.: Union Theological Seminary. Sound cassette.
The Reformation and History: How It Has Been Understood, How It Has Shaped History. Union Theological Seminary in Virginia, October 21. Richmond, Va.: Union Theological Seminary. Sound cassette.

1987　*Christian Witness Today: What the Church Has to Say That No One Else Can Say.* Thomas White Currie Lectures, Austin Presbyterian Theological Seminary, Austin, Texas, Feb. 2–5. Austin, Texas: Austin Presbyterian Theological Seminary. Sound cassettes:
The Preacher as Witness: Mystery and Revelation.
The Power of God for Salvation.
God's Providing, Ordering, and Caring.
Destined in Love to Be His Sons: God's Power and Presence.
Teaching and Proclaiming the Reformed Faith at Union Theological Seminary. 175th Anniversary of Union Theological Seminary in Virginia, October 13. Richmond, Va.: Union Theological Seminary. Sound cassette.

Compiled by Martha B. Aycock, Associate Librarian, Union Theological Seminary in Virginia.